Anthropological Papers
Museum of Anthropology, University of Michigan
No. 87

Wari Imperialism in Middle Horizon Peru

Katharina J. Schreiber

with a foreword by Jeffrey R. Parsons

Ann Arbor
1992

© 1992 by the Regents of the University of Michigan
The Museum of Anthropology
All rights reserved

ISBN 978-0-915703-26-5 (paper)
ISBN 978-1-949098-85-3 (ebook)

Cover design by Katherine Clahassey

Library of Congress Cataloging-in-Publication Data

Schreiber, Katharina Jeanne.
　Wari imperialism in Middle Horizon Peru / by Katharina J.
Schreiber ; with a foreword by Jeffrey R. Parsons.
　　p. cm. — (Anthropological papers / Museum of Anthropology,
University of Michigan ; no. 87)
　Includes bibliographical references.
　ISBN 0-915703-24-6 : $18.00
　1. Huari Indians—Politics and government. 2. Huari Indians-
-Antiquities. 3. Incas—Politics and government. 4. Jincamocco
Site (Peru) 5. Huari Site (Peru) 6. Imperialism. I. title.
II. Series: Anthropological papers (University of Michigan . Museum
of Anthropology) ; no. 87.
GN2.M5　no. 87
[F3429.1.H828]
306 s—dc20　　　　　　　　　　　　　　　　　　　　　91-44776
[985'.01]　　　　　　　　　　　　　　　　　　　　　　　　CIP

Contents

List of Tables	*vii*
List of Figures	*viii*
Acknowledgments	*xi*
Foreword	*xiii*

CHAPTER 1. PREHISTORIC EMPIRES	1
Imperial States	3
From Sargon to Exxon: Variations on a Theme	3
The Foundations of Empire	6
The Mechanics of Conquest	9
The Sequence of Expansion	10
Archaeological Correlates	11
Imperialism Viewed from the Provinces	13
Consolidation of Control	14
Collaboration/Mediation	15
Strategies of Consolidation and Collaboration	17
Residual Local Authority and Strategies Available to Local Elites	27
Economic Reorganization	28
Imperial Infrastructure	29
Temporal Dynamics	31
Imperialism in the Provinces: Some Archaeological Correlates	32
Decline and Fall	34
The Legacy of Empire	36
Conclusion: Archaeological Approaches to the Study of Imperialism	37
CHAPTER 2. THE INKA EMPIRE: IMPERIALISM IN ANDEAN FORM	41
Ecological Complementarity	42
Coastal Desert	44
Sierra	45
Montaña	48
The Relation between Andean Environment and Cultural Developments	49

The Inka Empire	50
The Foundations of Empire	50
The Expansion	51
The Inka Occupation of the Provinces	53
The Inka Mosaic of Control	62
Economic Control under the Inka	64
Inka Ideological Control	67
Summary	68
CHAPTER 3. THE PROBLEM OF THE MIDDLE HORIZON	71
Tiwanaku and the Definition of the Middle Horizon	72
The Wari Heartland	79
The Site of Wari	79
The Regional Context of Wari	83
Wari in Spatial and Temporal Context	93
The Wari Horizon Outside the Heartland	94
Highland Sites	96
Coastal Sites	105
Site Summary	107
The Offering Deposits	108
Offering Summary	111
Explanations of the Wari Expansion	113
CHAPTER 4. THE CARHUARAZO VALLEY: THE NATURAL SETTING AND HUMAN ADAPTATION	115
The Geographic Setting	116
Environment and Ecology	119
Geomorphology	119
Natural Environment	120
Modern Cultural Adaptation	121
Prehistoric Cultural Adaptation	128
Plants and Animals Exploited	128
Climatic Differences	129
Terraces and Irrigation	131
Summary: Environment and Ecology during the Middle Horizon	132
CHAPTER 5. ANALYSIS ON A REGIONAL LEVEL: SETTLEMENT PATTERNS IN THE CARHUARAZO VALLEY	133
Field Strategies	134
Settlement Patterns of the Kancha Phase	138
Ceramic Definition of the Kancha Phase	138

Sites of the Kancha Phase	139
Kancha Phase Settlement Pattern and Political Organization	143
Settlement Patterns of the Willka Phase	144
Material Definition of the Willka Phase	144
Local Sites and Settlement Patterns	146
Changes in Local Settlement Patterns during the Willka Phase	149
Terrace Construction	149
Nonlocal Sites	151
The Middle Horizon in the Carhuarazo Valley	160
CHAPTER 6. JINCAMOCCO: ANALYSIS AT THE LEVEL OF THE SITE	**165**
The Site of Jincamocco	166
The Excavation of Jincamocco	168
Research Design	168
The Sampling Strategy	171
Wall Trenching and Site Plan	172
Excavation Strategy, Techniques, Areas Excavated	175
General Stratigraphy	176
The Architecture of the Enclosure	177
Results of Excavation of Individual Units	179
Archaeological Formation Processes	179
Excavation Summary	181
Summary of Deposits	192
Absolute Dating of the Willka Phase Occupation of Jincamocco	192
Relative Dating of the Occupations at Jincamocco	194
The Architecture of Jincamocco	196
Overall Plan	196
Spatial Patterning	197
Temporal Variation	199
Comparison of Jincamocco with Other Wari Sites	200
Conclusion	202
CHAPTER 7. THE EVIDENCE OF THE ARTIFACTS FROM JINCAMOCCO	**205**
Ceramic Vessels	206
Attribute Recording System	207
Ceramic Classes	209
Plainware	209
Local Decorated Styles	215
Red-Slipped Ware	226

v

Slip-Painted Ceramics	227
A Primary Association of 12 Exotic Vessels	234
Nonceramic Artifacts	246
Lithics	246
Ground Stone	248
Animal Bone	249
Human Remains	249
Ceramic Disks and Spindle Whorls	250
Special Objects	250
Temporal Patterning of the Artifacts	251
Spatial Patterning in the Willka Phase Deposits	252
The Function of Jincamocco	256
CHAPTER 8. THE MIDDLE HORIZON AND ANDEAN IMPERIALISM	259
The Wari Occupation of the Carhuarazo Valley	259
The Wari Strategy	263
Implications for Archaeological Investigation of Imperialism	263
Evidence of Wari Imperialism	266
The Wari Expansion	268
Evidence for the Wari Mosaic of Control	269
The Wari Empire	275
Wari Ideology	277
What We Don't Know About Wari	278
Wari and Tiwanaku	279
Wari and the Inka	281
BIBLIOGRAPHY	285
APPENDIX A. SURVEY DATA	301
Table A.1 Counts of ceramic categories, village sites	302
Table A.2 Counts of ceramic categories, small Wari sites	304
APPENDIX B. JINCAMOCCO DATA	305
Table B.1 Summary counts of ceramic diagnostic vessels from all excavated proveniences	305
Table B.2 Lithics from all excavated proveniences, by raw material and artifact type	312
Table B.3 Summary counts of artifact types, and artifact densities, from all excavated proveniences	318
APPENDIX C. CERAMIC DIAGNOSTIC CODING SYSTEM FOR JINCAMOCCO	327

Tables

3.1.	The Middle Horizon relative chronologies of Menzel and MacNeish, with pottery styles pertaining to each epoch or phase in Ayacucho	77
5.1.	The master sequence of Andean chronology, and temporal phases in the Carhuarazo Valley	135
5.2.	Presence/absence of temporally diagnostic ceramics on village sites	140
6.1.	Possible functions of Jincamocco and archaeological implications	170
6.2.	Temporal designations of provenience units	194
7.1.	Frequencies and percentages of ceramic classes during the Kancha and Willka phases	210
7.2.	Frequencies of plainware vessel shapes during the Kancha and Willka phases	211
7.3.	Frequencies of incised bowl shapes during the Kancha and Willka phases	217
7.4.	Frequencies of general incised bowl designs during the Kancha and Willka phases	219
7.5.	Frequencies of specific incised bowl designs during the Kancha and Willka phases	220
7.6.	Frequencies and percentages of lithic raw materials in the Kancha and Willka phases	247
7.7.	Composition of twelve discrete Willka phase deposits	253

Figures

1.1.	A society organized at the level of a complex chiefdom	18
1.2.	Leaving the local hierarchy of a complex chiefdom intact	19
1.3.	Creating a local puppet ruler, with direct imperial supervision, in a complex chiefdom	20
1.4.	Removing the local ruler, and establishing direct imperial control of a complex chiefdom	21
1.5.	A society organized at the level of a state	21
1.6.	Leaving the state hierarchy intact, and leaving the local ruler intact	22
1.7.	Leaving the state hierarchy intact, but replacing the uppermost level with direct imperial control	22
1.8.	Leaving the state hierarchy intact, but replacing the top two levels with direct imperial control	23
1.9.	Eliminating the top level of state control and dividing the state into its component parts	23
1.10.	A society with a tribal level of organization	24
1.11.	A society organized at the level of a simple chiefdom	24
1.12.	Elevating one local chief to a higher level, increasing the complexity of the local system	25
1.13.	Subsuming the simple chiefdom under another province	25
1.14.	Creating a new administrative level to impose direct imperial rule over a simple chiefdom	26
2.1.	Distribution of Inka roads at the beginning of the sixteenth century A.D.	42
2.2.	Map of Peru showing the major environmental zones	43
2.3.	Map of Inka occupation discussed in the text	54
3.1.	Map showing locations of Wari, Tiwanaku, and places named in the text	73
3.2.	The Cachi hydrographic unit	85
3.3.	Ayacucho Basin map showing Huarpa phase occupation	88
3.4.	Ayacucho Basin map showing Ocros phase occupation	89

3.5.	Ayacucho Basin map showing Wari phase occupation	90
3.6.	Ayacucho Basin map showing occupation in the Huamanga phase, after the Wari collapse	92
3.7.	Map of the central Andes showing sites named in the text	97
4.1.	Location of the Carhuarazo Valley within the Department of Ayacucho	117
4.2.	The greater Carhuarazo Valley, showing modern towns and villages within areas of cultivation	118
4.3.	Ecological map of the core of the Carhuarazo Valley	122
4.4.	Two cross-sections of the Carhuarazo Valley	123
5.1.	Topographic map of the Carhuarazo Valley	136
5.2.	Settlements of the Kancha phase	141
5.3.	Settlements of the Willka phase	147
5.4.	Areas of probable Willka phase terracing	152
5.5.	Photograph of the Carhuarazo Valley as seen from the major prehistoric road entering from the southwest	159
5.6.	Settlements of the Marke phase, the period following the collapse of Wari control	162
6.1.	Photograph of Jincamocco	167
6.2.	Map of the total extent of Jincamocco	169
6.3.	Plan of the enclosure at Jincamocco	173
6.4.	Results of wall trenching in northern third of enclosure	174
6.5.	Plan of Patio 1 and Corridor 1	182
6.6.	Plan of the skull offering in the north bench of Patio 1	184
6.7.	Photograph of the skull offering in the north bench of Patio 1	184
6.8.	Detail of the southwest corner of Patio 1, west bench	185
6.9.	Plan of Patio 2	186
6.10.	Plan of Patio 3	188
6.11.	Photograph of filled-in doorway near the southwest corner of Patio 3, with niche	189
6.12.	Plan of T2/3, and division into two excavation units	191

6.13. Schematic outline plans of Pikillaqta, Viracochapampa, Azángaro, Jincamocco, and Jargampata	*201*
7.1. Profiles of four intact plainware vessels	*213*
7.2. Incised bowls from Kancha phase levels	*216*
7.3. Designs and codes for incised bowls	*219*
7.4. Jars with serpentine designs	*223*
7.5. Red slipped ware bowls and color key	*225*
7.6. Black decorated vessels	*230*
7.7. Viñaque sherds	*231*
7.8. Lyre cup fragments	*233*
7.9. Chakipampa B lyre cup from Patio 3	*234*
7.10. Lyre cup 1	*235*
7.11. Lyre cup 2	*236*
7.12. Lyre cup 3	*237*
7.13. Straight-sided open bowl 1	*237*
7.14. Straight-sided open bowl 2	*238*
7.15. Straight-sided open bowl 3	*239*
7.16. Small bowl 1	*240*
7.17. Small bowl 2	*240*
7.18. Small bowl 3	*241*
7.19. Red-slipped closed vessel	*242*
7.20. Profile of oversize face-neck jar	*243*
7.21. Front view of oversize face-neck jar	*244*

Acknowledgments

I extend my sincere appreciation to those colleagues who read and commented on earlier versions of the manuscript, including William H. Isbell, Keith W. Kintigh, Patricia J. Lyon, Jeffrey R. Parsons, Barbara Stark, Mary Van Buren, Norman Yoffee, and two anonymous reviewers. I wish to single out two individuals to whom I am especially indebted. First, John Howland Rowe provided many pages of invaluable notes, sharing with me his extensive knowledge of the Inka empire and the archaeology of southern Peru. The second is Henry T. Wright, who shared his insights and perspectives on archaeological approaches to complex societies, both in conversations, and in many useful comments on the manuscript.

I am indebted to my colleagues who looked over my drawings and photographs of ceramic artifacts, offering their greater expertise in the identification of particular styles from extremely fragmented remains. These include, especially, Patricia J. Knobloch, Lawrence E. Dawson, and Patricia J. Lyon. The ceramic drawings were prepared by Kirsten Olson and Dennis Ogburn. Figure 6.3, the plan of the enclosure at Jincamocco, was prepared by Henry T. Wright.

The research on which this study was based was funded by two grants from the National Science Foundation, SOC75-16865 and BNS80-06121. Permission to carry out the research in Peru was granted by the Instituto Nacional de Cultura, credentials 039-76-DCIRBM and 011-DCIRBM-81. I wish to thank the people and village authorities of Cabana Sur, Aucará, Sondondo, Queca, Ishua and Huaycahuacho, Ayacucho, for their cooperation. I especially thank Máximo Oscco Alarcón and Juan Montoya Valenzuela for facilitating the fieldwork in the Carhuarazo Valley. Friends, colleagues and former students who participated in the survey and excavations include Christine Brewster-Wray, Pamela Chester, Sue Grosboll, Thomas W. Killion, Keith W. Kintigh, Robert May, Anne Pyburn, and Michael Shott. And I thank William H. Isbell who first introduced me to the region.

Foreword

Jeffrey R. Parsons

At least as long ago as the early nineteenth century, scholars had begun to ponder the impressive material remains of ancient Andean society and to link them with descriptions of sixteenth- and seventeenth-century writers. This long-standing interest in the origins and development of the Inka empire that the Spanish *conquistadores* encountered in A.D. 1532 is one of the guiding forces of Andean archaeology. Contemporary Andeanists, both archaeologists and ethnohistorians, have followed the lead of these pioneers, and in so doing have taken their place among the leaders in the study of ancient imperialism. It is within this general intellectual context that Katharina Schreiber's monograph takes its place.

Schreiber sets out to comprehend the relationship between the great Middle Horizon capital of Wari and the modest provincial center of Jincamocco. Her work offers an important and almost unique perspective on what Wari was doing outside of its immediate heartland region in the Ayacucho region more than 600 years before the Inka had established their capital at Cuzco. It is important to realize that until about twenty years ago, most of our understanding of Middle Horizon polity was based on architectural, ceramic, and iconographic evidence from Wari and Tiwanaku (Bolivia) and a handful of rather poorly understood smaller sites scattered throughout the Central Andes. This evidence had been collected over a long period of time in the course of archaeological studies heavily biased toward major sites, public architecture, and funerary pottery. This imbalance began to be corrected after the mid-1960s by energetic new investigations at and around Wari (e.g., Isbell 1977; Benavides 1984; Anders 1986; Isbell and McEwan 1991).

Schreiber's work at Jincamocco is part of this pioneering renewal of Wari-related studies, but departs from most of it by virtue of its shift of focus away from the immediate Wari heartland and into a somewhat more distant region where Wari influence must necessarily have been indirect. Schreiber's work is additionally unusual in that it focuses on a modest regional center, thus opening one of the very few currently available archaeological windows onto the second or third tier of a larger organizational hierarchy. This window allows us to glimpse a wealth of architectural, artifactual, and regional settlement system components of a previously very obscure world.

Schreiber's monograph appears at a time when other publications, based on systematically collected regional data sets, have also begun to contribute to a new level of understanding of Middle Horizon society throughout the Central Andes: examples would include investigations at Tiwanaku and its environs in highland Bolivia (Kolata 1986, 1991); at Pikillaqta, a probable Wari high-level administrative center in southern highland Peru (McEwan 1987); in the Moquegua Valley on the far south Peruvian coast where there are suggestions of close interaction between Wari and Tiwanaku (Rice et al. 1989); in the Santa Valley on Peru's north coast where the impact of Wari is still very uncertain, but where large-scale sociopolitical organization is clearly indicated for the Middle Horizon (Wilson 1988); and in the Cajamarca region of north highland Peru, where earlier studies at Viracochapampa had suggested a close link (of still uncertain character) with Wari (Topic and Topic 1984). Schreiber's work is thus an important addition to this new database which also serves to reveal how much more we still have to learn about this key period of time when the first Andean supraregional states were becoming established.

One of the very important contributions of Schreiber's study is the clarity with which, explicitly or implicitly, it raises or better defines important general questions about the development of indigenous Andean imperialism. What, for example, are the implications of her study for the dynamics of Inka state-building during the century or two preceding A.D. 1440? How much of the Wari imperial experience was appropriated by the Inka, and how was this appropriation actually accomplished? Did Cuzco acquire a developmental "head start" of sorts because of the location nearby at Pikillaqta of an especially important Wari provincial center? To what degree is Inka provincial organization founded upon the remnants of an antecedent Wari regional structure? To what extent was Inka emphasis on vertical sociopolitical linkages, and regional economic autonomy based on the close integration of complementary vertical ecologies anticipated by Wari imperialism?

How were relationships between herders and cultivators changed as the result of Wari imperialism, and to what extent did changing herder-cultivator relationships figure in changing Middle Horizon geo-politics (cf. Browman 1974, 1976)? To what extent was Wari imperialism more hegemonic and less territorial than that of the Inka (cf. D'Altroy 1987)? To what extent were the long-term stages of Wari imperial development replicated by the Inka, and to what degree and in what manner and for what reasons did Inka imperial structure supercede that of Wari in terms of organizational complexity? At a more specific level in this regard, does Schreiber's finding that modeled spindle whorls occur only in the Willka phase at Jincamocco suggest that there was a qualitative shift in the larger sociopolitical significance of cloth during this florescent stage of Wari development, analogous to the well-known role of cloth as a political symbol in Incaic times (cf. Murra 1962)?

To what extent is Jincamocco typical of Wari provincial organization throughout the Central Andes during the Middle Horizon? What imperial significance might be attached, for example, to the Wari Willka site in the middle Mantaro Valley in central highland Peru (Matos 1968), which appears to be a Wari-related religious center (perhaps analagous to Pachacamac at the mouth of the Lurin Valley on the central Peruvian coast) in an area which apparently lacks a Jincamocco-like or Pikillaqta-like administrative center? Are Wari Willka and Pachacamac examples of alternative forms of Wari imperial provincial administration?; if so, how did such administration actually work, and why did the variability exist in the first place? Why, apparently, are there no Middle Horizon provincial centers like Jincamocco, Pikillaqta, or Viracochapampa in the Andean coastal valleys?

Why are the two largest Wari-related "provincial centers", Pikillaqta and Viracochapampa, situated at the frontiers of what appears to be a Wari-influenced region? This reminds me of the relationship in Classic-period Mesoamerica between Teotihuacan, in central Mexico, and Kaminaljuyu, in distant Guatemala, and there now seems little reason to believe that Kaminaljuyu was an imperial outpost of Teotihuacan. There are other parallels between Teotihuacan and Wari in terms of how the "influence" of each is differentially manifested archaeologically over space, and these parallels make me wonder about the organizational and developmental parallels which might have existed between Mesoamerican and Andean states during the first millenium A.D. Are we imputing too much centrality to Wari imperialism, just as we once did to Teotihuacan's, on the basis of architectural and ceramic affinities? Do we need to think more systematically and creatively about how local elites sought to appropriate exotic symbols of distant centers in order to enhance their own local power and prestige, particularly after a century or two of Wari "expansion" had made such symbols more available? Schreiber indicates quite convincingly that there was little organizational complexity in the Carhuarazo Valley prior to the Middle Horizon, but this need not have been the case everywhere in the Andean highlands.

Finally, why and how did Wari imperialism collapse, and how and why were different parts of its former empire differentially affected by this collapse? How, specifically, did the Wari collapse—at its center, in its provinces, and on its frontiers—provide the foundations for Inka proto-imperial development during the Late Intermediate period?

Schreiber's study makes no claim to provide complete answers to these questions. Nevertheless, by directly attacking some of them and by demonstrating the specific potential and necessity of looking outside the main centers and heartland zones of imperial systems, her work has done a great deal to alert us to the new archaeological research on state and imperial development in precolumbian Andean civilization. It is my hope and expectation that this pathbreaking study will help provide a model for future investigations directed toward the finer resolution of these and other issues.

REFERENCES

Anders, M.
1986 Wari experiments in statecraft: a view from Azángaro. In: Andean Archaeology: Papers in Memory of Clifford Evans, edited by R. Matos, S. Turpin and H. Eling, pp. 201-24. UCLA.

Benavides, M.
1984 Carácter del Estado Wari. Ayacucho, Peru: Univ. Nacional de San Cristobal de Huamanga.

Browman, D.
1974 Pastoral nomadism in the Andes. Current Anthropology 15(2):188-96.
1976 Demographic correlations of the Wari conquest of Junin. American Antiquity 41(4):465-77.

D'Altroy, T.
1987 Introduction. Ethnohistory 34(1).

Isbell, W.H.
1977 The Rural Foundation for Urbanism: Economic and Stylistic Interaction between Rural and Urban Communities in Eighth-Century Peru. Urbana: University of Illinois Press.

Isbell, W.H., and G. McEwan (eds.)
1991 Huari Administrative Structure: Prehistoric Monumental Architecture and State Government. Dumbarton Oaks, Washington, D.C.

Kolata, A.
1986 The agricultural foundation of the Tiwanaku state: a view from the heartland. American Antiquity 51(4):748-62.
1991 The technology and organization of agricultural production in the Tiwanaku state. Latin American Antiquity 2(2):99-125.

Matos, R.
1968 Wari-Willka, Santuario Wanka en el mantaro. Cantuta 2:116-28. Universidad Nacional de Educacion, Lima.

McEwan, G.
1987 The Middle Horizon in the Valley of Cuzco, Peru: The Impact of Wari Occupation of Pikillaqta in the Lucre Basin. BAR International Series S-372.

Murra, J.
1962 Cloth and its functions in the Inca state. American Anthropologist 64(4):710-28.

Rice, D., C. Stanish, and P. Scarr (eds.)
1989 Ecology, Settlement and History in the Osmore Valley. BAR International Series S-545.

Topic, T., and J. Topic
1984 Huamachuco Archaeological Project: Preliminary Report on the Third Season, June-August 1983. Trent University Occasional Papers in Anthropology, no. 1. Peterborough, Ontario.

Wilson, D.
1988 Prehispanic Settlement Patterns in the Lower Santa Valley, Peru. Washington, D.C.: Smithsonian Institution Press.

1

Prehistoric Empires

The Andean region of South America saw the rise and expansion of one of the most extensive political empires in the prehistoric world: the empire of the Inka. In less than a century the Inka had expanded from their capital at Cuzco to establish sovereign control over a domain that stretched north to Quito, Ecuador, and south to Santiago, Chile. The Inka empire is one of the best known prehistoric empires, well documented by the Spanish, who saw to its destruction in the sixteenth century.

But the Inka was just one, the last, of a series of complex societies that arose in the Andes during the three or four millennia prior to the Spanish Conquest. Inka culture, and perhaps aspects of Inka imperialism, had antecedents in earlier prehistoric times. The focus of the present study is the period called the Middle Horizon, which dates roughly to the period between A.D. 600 and 1000. At that time there were two particularly influential centers in the Andes, each of which may have been the capital of a political empire.

Because we have no native written records in the prehistoric Andes, and because we have no eyewitness accounts to guide us in the Middle Horizon, we must rely on archaeological data to document and understand the events that took place. During this time, distinctive images of a particular anthropomorphic being were found widely distributed in the Andes. This being wore an elaborate headdress with rayed appendages and a belted tunic; in each of his outstretched arms he held a vertical staff.

At one site this Staff Deity was carved on a great panel of stone, at others it was painted on huge ceramic urns. This image did not occur alone, but was often depicted with other beings: winged humans, birds with human bodies, plants and animals. Even in abbreviated form, this constellation of images was clearly recognizable at many different sites throughout the Andes. And there were apparently two substyles within this artistic tradition, one in the central Andes of Peru, the other in the southern Andes of Bolivia, Chile and Argentina. But after a few centuries, at most, the tradition disappeared in both areas, and the images were no longer depicted.

Interpretations of events of the Middle Horizon differ. What is clear is that a distinctive set of images was widely distributed throughout the Andean region; what is not clear is how this set of images came to be so distributed. Were these religious symbols, spread by proselytizing missionaries and pilgrims? Or was their distribution the result of commerce between different regions? Or were these symbols associated with the expansion of prehistoric empires?

This study focuses on the central Andes of Peru and considers the spread of Middle Horizon iconography to be the result of imperialism. Before taking up the issue of the Middle Horizon, and the Wari culture in particular, it is useful to begin with a general consideration of imperialism, and its possible manifestations in the archaeological record. Of particular interest are the provincial aspects of imperialism: the various strategies used by an empire to consolidate its political and economic control over a conquered region.

The Inka empire is treated as an Andean example of an imperial society. The Inka expansion and evidence of Inka strategies of provincial control provide a backdrop against which to view the events of the Middle Horizon. The general problem of the Middle Horizon is discussed in the following chapter, including the separation of the respective Tiwanaku and Wari cultures, and the distribution of Wari sites and artifacts throughout the central Andes of Peru.

The next four chapters are devoted to the consideration of a single valley, the Carhuarazo Valley, in which archaeological research has been carried out between 1974 and 1987. These projects have included both survey and excavations, and have been aimed at trying to document the events of the Middle Horizon. The presence of a major Wari installation, and changes in local culture at the time of the Wari occupation, argue very strongly that the Middle Horizon was a period during which Wari established sovereign political and economic control over the region.

Finally, the Middle Horizon is reconsidered, given the evidence from the Carhuarazo Valley.

IMPERIAL STATES

Empires are a particular class of states, states that come to exercise extensive political and economic control over other polities. *Imperialism* is the process through which empires are created and maintained; an *empire* is the society that results from this process. Certain polities expand beyond their core and come to control regions and peoples far beyond their boundaries; they regard these peoples as foreign, and they in turn are regarded as foreigners. Empires are polities that take over other polities, manipulating the political structure of those other societies in such a way as to exercise sovereign control over them.

Political empires have existed since at least the third millennium B.C. when Sargon of Akkad forged the first political empire in Mesopotamia. Since that time empires have increased in regional scope, and economic factors have become increasingly important in the expansion of control. Some empires expanded from well-consolidated cores characterized by a sedentary agricultural subsistence base and high population densities. Others had no such urban cores, yet still came to control a plurality of societies within a well-developed administrative system.

Before turning to the Andes, and to the Middle Horizon in particular, it will be useful to enumerate some of the salient features of empires, and how aspects of imperialism might be documented in the archaeological record.

From Sargon to Exxon: Variations on a Theme

There are many kinds of empires. From Sargon's conquest of Sumer to the emergence of the modern capitalist world system, a variety of polities and organizations have emerged that have employed various aspects of imperialism. The term "empire" includes a good deal of variability, and empires take a variety of forms. While modern multinational corporations exhibit many aspects of imperialism, our discussions here will focus on more archaic forms of empires, polities that established extensive political control over a plurality of societies. Sometimes called *patrimonial empires* (Eisenstadt 1969:22-23), examples include the Sumerian and Babylonian empires of the Near East, the ancient Egyptian empire, the Achaemenid empire of the Middle East, the empire forged by Alexander, and the early stages of the Roman empire. In the New World, examples might include the Inka and the México, and perhaps some earlier societies as well. These empires have several attributes in common. First, they expanded quickly, often making use of military conquest. Second, they did not impose direct rule in all regions, but rather manipulated local political systems to serve imperial needs; for this reason they are sometimes referred to as hegemonic states (Doyle 1986:70-75). Third, these polities turned their attention very quickly to economic interests, and controlling the production and distribution of all necessary resources. Finally, many of these empires persisted only a few generations; they did not make the transition to more permanent, institutionalized rule that many of the later historic bureaucratic empires did (see, for example, Eisenstadt 1969:117).

These empires fall into the category of states, as that term is employed by anthropologists (Service 1975), but can be differentiated from other states on the basis of several relative criteria. States have been defined in terms amenable to archaeological investigation by Henry T. Wright and Gregory A. Johnson:

> A state is defined as a society with specialized administrative activities. By "administrative" we mean "control," thus including what is commonly termed "politics" under administration. In states..., decision-making activities are differentiated or specialized in two ways. First, there is a hierarchy of control in which the highest level involves making decisions about other, lower-order decisions rather than about any particular condition or movement of material goods or people. Any society with three or more levels of decision-making hierarchy must necessarily involve such specialization.... Second, the effectiveness of such a hierarchy of control is facilitated by the complementary specialization of information processing activities into observing, summarizing, message-carrying, data-storing and actual decision-making. This both enables the efficient handling of the masses of information and decisions moving through a control hierarchy with three or more levels, and undercuts the independence of subordinates. [Wright and Johnson 1975:267]

Empires, too, have specialized administrative activities, elaborate hierarchies of control, and specialized information-processing activities; in short, they are states. Much of the difference between states and empires is simply a matter of scale. But there are some qualitative differences as well that might be considered.

Criteria that differentiate states and empires are the related notions of size of polity and manner of expansion. Empires are larger than states in relative terms, but it is difficult to specify in absolute terms any quantitative limits that differentiate one from the other. Both states and empires expand their domains, and establish political and economic control over other groups. But while states set about subsuming their immediate neighbors, empires not only do this, but they jump far beyond those neighbors and establish sovereign control over far distant regions, and diverse social groups. They may pass over whole regions and move directly to more important ones. While a state is often one of several competing polities, as in the case of what have been termed "peer polities" (Renfrew 1986), empires typically eliminate all the competition; empires go out and take over the entire "civilized world."

This manner of expansion produces several other characteristics that differentiate states and empires. While states include mostly blocks of contiguous territory—the core and the immediate periphery, empires may be territorially discontinuous. Hence, imperial political and economic control is also discontinuous. However, even within controlled regions, some areas may be directly ruled while other regions may be ruled indirectly through alliance with local elites. In the case of empires, the resulting system may be better thought of as a mosaic of different levels of control. States, being more contiguous (and smaller), tend to establish more direct forms of control throughout all controlled territory.

States and empires differ in terms of cultural diversity. Empires are multiethnic, multilinguistic and multinational entities to a greater degree than are states, which may be multiethnic but not actually multinational. The establishment of a *lingua franca* is characteristic of empires, where distant unrelated groups may be incorporated into the same administrative system; the spread of such languages as Akkadian, Latin, Mandarin Chinese, Spanish, English, and Quechua was the direct result of imperial expansions.

The territory controlled by states and empires is sometimes distinguished in terms of ecological diversity as well. States are more likely to be restricted to a consistent set of ecological parameters, while empires move beyond their own set of zones and into new and different areas, resulting in a more ecologically diverse domain. (Empires also change the new and different ecological systems so that they bear more resemblance to the core territory. Crosby [1986] has made the interesting point that empires not only move people and systems of governance into conquered lands, they also bring with them the familiar plants and animals on which their own subsistence is based, thus gradually transforming the ecological system of the foreign territory.)

Both states and empires employ military force in their expansion, and probably are not clearly distinguished on this basis, although great military campaigns are often stressed more in descriptions of imperial systems. However, it is likely that diplomacy and nonmilitary coercion were equally utilized as mechanisms of expansion. One of the great values of an imperial army is its role in public relations, where the threat of force might be equally as persuasive as its application.

And one interesting aspect of these archaic empires is that they are often associated with the names of single great individuals, particularly military leaders: Sargon, Darius, Alexander, Caesar. It may be that the major explosive expansions of empires are more directly the result of action by individuals, individuals who had both a vision of empire and sense of purpose, coupled with a political system that could support their endeavors. Alternatively, these rapid imperial expansions—usually taking place within one or two generations—are more likely to be undertaken under only one or two leaders, hence the association of a single name with the expansion.

The Foundations of Empire

In general, empires begin as polities that consolidate their control over a core region, with the result that the entire core participates in a regional economic-political system, perhaps shares a common language and ethnic identity, and shares other aspects of culture including ideology, religion, art, and basic styles of architecture and artifacts. Typically, the core polity is based on an agricultural subsistence, population density within the core is relatively high, and urbanism is generally present.

The process of core consolidation can take a variety of forms. In some cases a single state might emerge. In other cases several peer polities may exist closely spaced within the core. These might range from warring chiefdoms to small states, but in either case one polity comes to control the core. During this process of core consolidation military confrontations are probably common. The consolidated core polity then forms the basis for the ensuing imperial expansion.

There are many reasons that may account for particular cases of state origins. What is important is that, for whatever reason, there emerged a society that was both internally specialized and politically centralized.

> [T]he state appears as a very complex system, one whose complexity can be measured in terms of its *segregation* (the amount of internal differentiation and specialization of subsystems) and *centralization* (the degree of linkage between the various subsystems and the highest-order controls in society...). An explanation of the rise of the state then centers on the ways in which the processes of increasing segregation and centralization take place. [Flannery 1972:409]

That is, a hierarchically organized political apparatus emerges that integrates and coordinates the specialized parts of a complex society. Social stratification and the emergence of a ruling class are characteristics of early states. Typically, empires begin as core polities already organized at the level of a state. Without the key element of state organization, resulting in an ability to mobilize people and resources, imperial expansion is unlikely.

Imperial expansion commences when the core polity physically moves out of its home territory, and takes control of outlying regions. Why do empires expand? There are probably more answers to this question than there are empires. Imperial expansions often begin in times of instability: after an extended period of warfare between various polities, or a period of disruption of the agricultural system (Henry Wright, pers. comm.). These and other external factors may set the stage for the expansion of one polity. But it useful also to consider the motivations of the agents of expansion in the core polity, both the rulers, and the masses.

Some motivations are economic in nature. Economic control involves control over resources, and the fruits of human labor; it results in changes in patterns of both production and consumption. A frequent motivation behind imperial expansion is the desire to control directly all resources that are needed by the core polity. Economic motivation may be the single most important factor in prehistoric imperial expansion. In many ways, imperial expansion is the enlargement of an economic system for the direct economic support of the ruling core.

Some motivations may be political in nature, in the sense that the ruling elite in the core polity wishes to expand its control over people and their actions. Jonathan Haas (1982) has argued that a key factor in the rise of state level societies is the acquisition of power: power to control people. In turn this power is used to control human labor to accomplish the works of state. As he defines it,

[P]ower [is] the ability of an actor, A, to get another actor(s), B, to do something B would not otherwise do, through the application, threat, or promise of sanctions. [Haas 1982:157]

In these terms, what an empire does is to establish a power relationship over other societies. In Haas's terms, the empire is actor A, and the subjugated society is actor B.

Certainly much of this power is exercised over economic aspects of society, and used to acquire material goods for the state. But it might also be argued that there is a tendency for humans to strive to acquire power over other people, simply for its own sake. Based on his analysis of Burmese political systems, Sir Edmund Leach pointed out that to seek power is a paramount stimulus for an individual to acquire political control, and that this is a natural human motivation.

...I am always dissatisfied with functionalist arguments concerning "needs" and "goals"..., but I consider it necessary and justifiable to assume that a conscious or unconscious wish to gain power is a very general motive in human affairs. Accordingly I assume that individuals faced with a choice of action will commonly use such choice so as to gain power... [Leach 1954:10]

In addition to economic and political motivations, we might also consider ideological ones, although they are difficult to separate from political and economic motivations. Empires develop ideologies that serve to legitimize and maintain the political and economic hierarchies. Imperial societies convince themselves that they are bringing civilization and all its benefits to the barbarous and less enlightened foreign societies. Religious symbols embody concepts of power, and religious pantheons often parallel political hierarchies. Imperial rulers may find that claiming divine descent may enhance their ability to wield political power. Symbols of political power and religious icons may be indistinguishable.

Recently Conrad and Demarest (1984) have addressed the role of ideology as an explicit explanation for imperial expansions in the New World. They argue that in the cases of both the México and the Inka, the primary factors that led to political expansion were neither political nor economic, but rather ideological. In the case of the Méxica, there was a great and continuous need for sacrificial victims to feed the gods. This partially explains why the Méxica rarely consolidated their control over defeated regions: they needed to fight the same battles again and again in order to collect new offerings. In the case of the Inka, they argue that the rules of split inheritance of the Inka dynasty caused each new emperor to undertake new conquests. When an Inka ruler died, his royal lineage, his *panaca*, inherited all his material wealth to maintain his cult. His successor inherited the right to rule, but none of the material resources. Therefore, the new ruler was forced to conquer new territory, and quickly consolidate control over that territory, in order to acquire new sources of tribute to provide the financial backing for his administration, and the future cult of his mummy.

Conrad and Demarest also agree that economics motivated these expansions, but argue that they did not determine them (1984:174). While one might argue that economic concerns were the ultimate cause of these expansions (see, for example, Hassig 1985), they have made the important point that there is more to imperial expansion than purely economics, and that nonmaterialist approaches have a good deal to contribute to the study of prehistoric imperialism (Conrad 1981). Certainly the economic motivation for conquest is often emphasized to the near exclusion of other explanations, including both political and ideological causes. All three forms of control, ideological, political and economic, resulted from imperial expansions, although to differing degrees both within and between empires. Likewise, the motivations for imperial expansion involve ideological, political and economic factors, but to differing degrees in different cases.

The desire to acquire various kinds of control serves to describe the motivations of the ruling class of the core polity. Yet conquest and expansion also require great numbers of individuals who are not directly involved in the decision to expand, nor rewarded so lavishly as those in control. What motivates these individuals to participate in the expansion, to fight in the armies, to serve as bureaucrats in foreign lands?

Certainly there are economic rewards. Lower status members of the imperial society (i.e., of the core polity) could improve their economic standing as a result of new resources flowing into the core. In addition, serving in the imperial forces, military or otherwise, is a way in which to acquire economic support. Political motivations also play a role. The chance to occupy positions of political power over foreign populations might provide motivation to individuals so inclined, those without the possibility of attaining such positions within the core polity. A distant relative of the emperor might have access to limited political power within the core, but might be governor of an entire province outside the core.

And perhaps one should not overlook sex as a motivation. For soldiers, the spoils of war include access to the women of defeated groups. As Hyam points out in his discussion of the British expansion, "the rank-and-file empire builder...had many openings for the export of his sexual tensions...." (1976:137). He also goes on to add that, in contrast, "the administrative elite was, by and large, driven along by frustration" (1976:137). But some administrators found that the existence in a foreign post allowed them sexual freedom such as would be impossible at home (Hyam 1976:137-48).

Thus, there are numerous motivations that may operate singly or in concert to produce an imperial expansion. Whatever the initial motivations for expansion, the first actions taken by the expanding polity are frequently political in nature: reorganizing and establishing control over people and political systems in conquered regions. But economic matters quickly become of primary interest: controlling all necessary resources, and reorganizing the production and distribution of those resources.

The Mechanics of Conquest

It is useful here to distinguish between conquest and consolidation, both of which are elements of imperial expansion. Conquest is the action taken by the imperial society to initiate its sovereignty over another society. It is a more or less finite event, one that precedes the longer process of consolidation. Consolidation refers to the process of restructuring local political and economic organization, and integrating the conquered society into imperial political and economic networks. While conquest generally has the connotation of direct military intervention, there are a variety of strategies that an empire may use to establish its sovereignty over another society. Since imperial takeovers typically involve some degree of coercion, the term conquest is used here to describe this action. However, as I use the term here, it does not necessarily connote the use of military force.

The two general strategies of conquest are military intervention and diplomatic arrangement. The use of one or the other strategy depends on a number of factors, but, in general, military confrontations can be both costly and destructive, and therefore are to be avoided when possible. As Sun Tzu wrote, in the fifth century B.C.,

> To fight and conquer in all your battles is not supreme excellence; supreme excellence consists in breaking the enemy's resistance without fighting. In the practical art of war, the best thing of all is to take the enemy's country whole and intact; to shatter and destroy it is not so good. [Sun Tzu 1983:15]

Luttwak writes of the Roman expansion,

> In the imperial period at least, military force was clearly recognized for what it is, an essentially limited instrument of power, costly and brittle. [Luttwak 1976:2]

One factor mitigating against the use of military force is its cost, in both economic and human terms. Military battles are expensive, diplomatic missions much less so. To conquer a region by force requires the ability to move and provision large numbers of soldiers, as well as the existence of an organized and capable leadership. The loss of human life is also expensive; new soldiers must be recruited, trained, and integrated into the armies. Furthermore, when the fighting is over, much rebuilding must be accomplished, in both physical and social terms. On the other hand, diplomacy incurs much lower expense, and fewer people are involved. If a small group of imperial emissaries can persuade the rulers of a local polity to enlist in the imperial cause, then the expense of battle and rebuilding is avoided. Maximum benefit derives both to the empire and to the local polity.

However, when the group to be conquered is powerful, well organized, and a potential threat to the empire, military engagements may be more likely. In such cases the empire needs not only to demonstrate its superior abilities, but also to disrupt the local organization, and prevent future repercussions.

Marching armies also have great potential as public displays of imperial might. It may not be necessary to actually engage in major battles to persuade local groups to suborn their authority to the empire. Rather, the sheer image of imperial power, coupled with the obvious threat of invasion, impresses upon local rulers the advisability of capitulation. Military and diplomatic strategies are not entirely mutually exclusive, and may often be combined. A diplomat may be especially persuasive in recruiting support of local rulers if the imperial army just happens to be waiting over the next hill. In the event of a breakdown in diplomatic talks, the military alternative can be invoked.

The Sequence of Expansion

The geographic sequence of conquest does not necessarily follow a linear progression. The strategy of conquest may be first to eliminate the competition and acquire the important resources. Thus, the first targets are those polities that either control resources perceived as desirable to the empire, or that compete with the empire for control of those resources. Other targets for more immediate conquest, beyond economic competitors, are those polities organized at relatively more complex hierarchical levels, such as other states. Such polities can present a threat to the empire, with their greater capabilities for organization of armed resistance.

The similarity of political organization also makes such polities in some ways easier to conquer, as they are more like the imperial polity than other simpler groups. Once these major conquests have been completed the empire turns to the conquest of intervening territory and groups that present less of a threat, and are less competitive with the empire.

Some groups may require subduing more than just once. As the empire turns its attentions (and armies) elsewhere, the local polity sees its chance to eliminate imperial control, although not always successfully. Other areas may require conquering more than once simply because the empire, for whatever reason, did not consolidate its control over the region.

Empires, while perhaps motivated by the desire to control particular resources in a given territory, are conquering the people of that territory. Once conquest is successful, and those people (or their rulers, in particular) have been persuaded to acknowledge the sovereign authority of the empire, the territory must be integrated into an empire-wide system of political and economic control. Typically this involves, first, subsuming the local political hierarchy under the imperial political system. Then, when the people have been brought under control, the economic system can be manipulated in such a way as to provide the empire with those resources that it needs and desires.

Archaeological Correlates

Let us turn to a brief consideration of the archaeological data that might provide evidence of the development of an imperial society within a core polity, as well as evidence of aspects of its conquest of regions outside the core territory.

The development of the preexpansion core society can be seen archaeologically in several ways, both from site-specific and regional perspectives. The growth of an urban capital, and the construction of public architecture can signal the development of political and economic control. The development of styles of artifacts and housing, and the development of patterns of consumption that indicate elites versus commoners may signal the growth of social stratification.

From a regional perspective, the distribution of artifact styles prior to expansion may indicate the boundaries of the core polity. In the early stages these may include shared styles of domestic artifacts, while in the later stages elite styles and state iconography may become widespread throughout the region. Architecture can also indicate cultural affiliations between villages, as well as areas of public and ceremonial activities.

In terms of regional settlement patterns, the development of a state administrative hierarchy may be seen through the development of a multi-tiered hierarchy of site types and sizes. The number of levels in this site hierarchy, along with evidence of administration and information flow between the sites, may indicate the level of political complexity of the society (Wright and Johnson 1975).

As we turn to regional data within the core area in order to understand the rise of the state, and the preexpansion political organization, so we turn to macroregional data in order to reconstruct the cultural context in which the core existed. Evidence of interaction between the core and the outside world, prior to expansion, is sought. Regional surveys in surrounding, and distant, regions can reveal levels of political organization in those regions. As in the case of the core, settlement hierarchies allow reconstruction of levels of political integration, and the definition of complexity. Trade networks are indicated by the presence of objects of known origin in other regions. Isolated objects may indicate only limited exchange, perhaps organized on a reciprocal basis, but lacking higher levels of control. On the other hand, higher quantities of materials in specific contexts may indicate more elaborate trade relations, and the possible control of trade from a core area by an organized polity.

The motivations behind expansion may leave little evidence in the archaeological record. However, by looking at what an empire actually accomplished, where it put its effort, it may be possible to reconstruct some of the possible motivations for expansion. In other words, we infer the stimulus from the response. For example, if we see extensive evidence for economic manipulation of provincial groups, we might assume an economic motivation for expansion. Economic manipulation may be documented in the development of new modes of production at the provincial level, evidence of new and revised exchange systems, and evidence of increased levels of raw materials and labor being brought to the imperial core.

Mechanism of expansion, as well, may not be directly documented in the archaeological record. Evidence for militarism in the archaeological record may be seen in the existence of fortified sites, both local and imperial, as well as actual weapons. Evidence of physical trauma in human remains may also indicate direct conflict. However, evidence of military action may or may not pertain to the imperial takeover; it may equally well pertain to the local situation immediately prior to the advent of the empire. And evidence of a military presence does not tell us whether or not military confrontation actually took place. Diplomatic missions leave little direct evidence.

The temporal sequence of expansion is visible in principle to the archaeologist through the relative and absolute dating of imperial remains. This is seldom attainable, however. Accurate and detailed chronological sequences based on temporal changes in material remains, such as ceramic styles, probably provide the most reliable evidence of the relative sequence of events. However, imperial expansions may have taken place very rapidly, and changes in artifact style may have occurred much more slowly. In such a case artifact style will be of little use in discerning the sequence of conquest. On the other hand, the presence of such imperial artifact styles in far-flung regions may be one line of evidence used to define the maximum possible extent of imperial influence.

Absolute dating is especially problematic. Standard techniques, such as radiocarbon dating, lack the precision necessary to distinguish events that took place closely spaced in time. For example, in the case of radiocarbon dating, given two assays with standard errors of 100 years each, using a t-test where the critical value of $t = 1.96$, and where $p = 0.05$, the means of two dates must differ by at least 277 years in order to represent significantly different dates. For two assays with standard errors of 50 years each, the means must differ by at least 139 years. Given the rapid expansion of most empires, occurring in the space of a few generations, radiocarbon dating is not likely to be sufficiently precise enough to document the temporal sequence of expansion.

IMPERIALISM VIEWED FROM THE PROVINCES

When dealing with empires we find ourselves confronted with a rather complex set of core/periphery relations. First, there are relations between the imperial core and its consolidated territories. These might be termed the inner periphery of the empire, or the client states. Second, there are relations between the imperial core and groups outside its control, an outer periphery, the independent groups not consolidated into the empire. A third set of relationships might include those between the inner and outer peripheries, between the client states inside the empire and the independent groups outside the imperial boundaries.

There is also a dynamic element to imperial expansions that results in a constant shifting of relations between the various groups. Groups that once lay in the outer periphery become client states as the empire expands and consolidates new territory. And as the imperial boundary changes, core/periphery relations are also in a state of flux.

Consolidation of Control

Typically, most territory within the inner periphery is consolidated under imperial control, but imperial strategies of consolidation can vary widely from region to region. And some areas may be left unconsolidated. Such areas generally lack the resources and population density that make them worth incorporating into the empire.

Empires are sometimes divided into two types, based on strategies of provincial control (Doyle 1986). On the one hand are what have been called territorial empires, or imperial states. These are contrasted with patrimonial empires or hegemonies. In the case of the former, control is seen to be direct, and exercised directly by imperial administrators. The latter are characterized as indirect, where control is established through collaboration with local elites. In fact, most empires employ a combination of strategies that include varying degrees of direct and indirect control.

At one extreme, in the case of direct territorial control, local control is totally subsumed under imperial control. Whatever the form of political organization that existed prior to conquest, an imperial system is substituted, complete with rulers and administrators who pay direct allegiance to the imperial core. Direct territorial control is similar to direct military confrontation in the sense that it is costly, and ideally is to be avoided when possible. To remove local systems of control and completely replace them with an imperial hierarchy, or to build an imperial system where political organization lacks, is very costly in terms of both physical facilities and human investment. Direct territorial control is therefore less desirable than more indirect forms of control in many instances.

Indirect hegemonic control, at the other extreme, leaves local ruling elites in control. The local administrative hierarchy is left intact, as long as it fulfills imperial needs. In other words, if local leaders can be coerced into providing and maintaining adequate levels of control, and seeing that required tribute is paid to the empire, then the local system can stand on its own with little cost to the empire. The establishment of such indirect or hegemonic control depends on the existence of an adequate extant political system, and the availability of local collaborators. If these prerequisites are not present, then the more costly direct rule may be the only alternative.

In contrast with regions that are consolidated into the empire (provinces or client states), there are also regions that are not consolidated. These may be greatly influenced by the empire and interact with the empire, but they are not under control of the empire in any direct or hegemonic form.

In the case of the archaic forms of imperialism considered here, we expect to find a combination of both direct and indirect forms of provincial control, rather than one or the other.

Collaboration/Mediation

A key to understanding imperial strategies of consolidation lies in the area of collaboration and mediation. In those regions where the empire seeks to consolidate its control, there are two general factors that determine the process through which the local system is integrated into the imperial administrative system. First, the political complexity of the extant local system needs to be at a level sufficient for imperial needs. Those societies with an already existing bureaucratic hierarchy of control are most easily integrated into a wider hierarchy. Areas lacking such organization may require the creation of an administrative hierarchy, while at the other extreme, areas with too much organization (thus presenting a threat to the empire) may need reorganizing. And second, where the local system can be modified to fit into the imperial system, leaving local organization roughly intact, there must be available willing collaborators through which imperial control can be exercised.

It is apparent from studies of various empires, both historic and prehistoric, that empires tailor their strategies of control to local political and economic circumstances (Eisenstadt 1969; Lattimore 1962; Hodge 1984; Schreiber 1987a).

A particularly interesting article in this regard is one written by the British historian Ronald Robinson (1972), who calls for the development of a theory of collaboration. Although his discussion refers to the study of modern capitalist empires, his analysis is equally applicable to more archaic empires. He argues that traditional notions about European imperialism tended to explain the expansion of empires in terms of the circumstances in Europe. Thus, they tend to be ideas about European society rather than theories of imperial process. It is further assumed that all the active components must be European ones, and therefore non-European ones are excluded. Any new theory ought to recognize that an equally important factor was the collaboration of the conquered peoples: "The expansive forces generated in industrial Europe had to combine with elements within the agrarian societies of the outer world to make empire at all practicable" (Robinson 1972:118).

He describes modern European imperialism as a political reflex action between one non-European, and two European components. The European components include (1) the economic drive to integrate regions into the industrial economy, and (2) the strategic imperative to secure regions against their rivals in world power politics. But the third element, the non-European element, indigenous collaboration and resistance is often missing (Robinson 1972:119). Whatever the empire sought to do, it could not have done so without local collaborators. To paraphrase his words, in regard to all forms of imperialism, not just modern European economic expansion: from beginning to end imperialism was a product of interaction between imperial and provincial politics (vis. ibid: 119).

In making the decision to collaborate with local elites, an empire would need to consider three factors: availability of administrative personnel, cost of establishing direct rule, and resulting efficiency of the system.

In the first place, in the case of a large empire with many provinces, there simply may not be enough members of the imperial ruling class or trained bureaucrats to go around. The solution to the lack of sufficient numbers of conquerors is to use local collaborators whenever possible. In this way, the imperialists can be around to keep an eye on things, but the rank and file administrators come from the local system.

The second factor is cost. Direct rule can be expensive in terms of both physical and human resources. Foreign administrators must be supported by the empire, or at least their upkeep comes out of local tribute that otherwise would go directly into the imperial coffers. Local rulers have an existing base of support that costs the empire less. Certainly local collaborators receive gifts, privileges, and trappings of authority from the empire, but most of their support is internally generated. In most cases, when direct rule is established, rather than using existing local governing facilities, new facilities must be built; a whole new imperial infrastructure needs construction. Again, use of the local system avoids incurring most of these costs.

And third, the overall efficiency of the system may suffer, especially in the early stages of imperial occupation. Leaving a local system intact, and integrating it under the imperial umbrella, leaves an existing system operational. Establishing a new system, especially if different from the one that existed there before, not only results in a less efficient operation as the players are adapting themselves to new rules, but also may meet with local resistance.

Under certain circumstances, however, it may not be in the best interests of the empire to collaborate with the local system, despite the costs. Direct rule, or at least major revision of local systems, is to be expected if the local system is a threat to the empire, as well as in some other special cases.

Groups that exhibit overt hostility toward the empire, and resist cooperating with it, may be candidates for direct rule. By removing local rulers and undermining their power base, the empire may decrease or eliminate the threat of counterattack, or disruption of local affairs. Societies that are organized at the state level may present a threat to the empire by virtue of their ability to mobilize forces against the empire. In such cases, the political hierarchy may be dismantled, brought down to a slightly simpler level, and imperial rulers put in place of local rulers.

Direct rule rather than collaboration may also be more common in provinces lying close to the imperial core. In the first place, these provinces are in a position to damage the heart of the empire if left under local rule. And in the second place, their proximity to the core reduces somewhat the administrative costs of establishing direct rule. And as population increases in the imperial core, largely the result of an influx of people from the inner periphery, direct control of surrounding provinces may become necessary to increase the subsistence base of the core.

Strategies of Consolidation and Collaboration

In each conquered province, an empire needs an administrative bureaucracy of a complexity sufficient to organize and carry out tasks needed by the empire, and to ensure that tribute is paid to the empire. At times a more direct strategy may be preferable to a less direct one. Many regions will require extra investment on the part of the empire, due to strategic location, or the presence of particularly needed resources, or perhaps great hostility on the part of the local polity toward the empire. In this section I would like to consider those situations in which consolidation is desired and in which there are no extenuating circumstances calling for a greater than normal imperial presence.

I start with two simple premises. The first is the obvious point that empires tailor their strategies of control to local conditions, particularly the level of extant political organization in the particular region. When the local system is adequate for imperial purposes, it may be left intact. If the local system is inadequate for imperial purposes, it must be reorganized.

Second, in each province an empire needs a political system that is hierarchically organized and centralized, at a level adequate for imperial administration. Such polities include what have been called simple chiefdoms, complex chiefdoms, and states, based on the degree of centralization and number of levels of administrative hierarchy. That is, simple chiefdoms have only a small degree of centralization, while at the other extreme, states are highly centralized. The difference between each of these systems is in some ways quantitative, and it is useful to distinguish between them in terms of the number of levels in the control hierarchy.

A simple chiefdom is a small, multivillage polity, and has a single level of control over the minimal settlement. A complex chiefdom is larger, in terms of both territory and population, and is more centralized, having some sort of paramount chief in control of the various local multivillage polities (Earle 1978). In other words, a complex chiefdom has two levels of control above the minimal settlement. And a state is larger, more centralized, and more specialized, than a chiefdom; as Wright and Johnson (1975) have written, states have three levels of control above the minimal settlement. This heuristic is useful in archaeological situations where settlement hierarchies can be identified, and where they seem to parallel these levels of control.

In each consolidated province an empire ideally needs some sort of centralized control, but control that extends over a large territory and population. A society organized as a complex chiefdom (Fig. 1.1) may be able to carry out all the wishes of the empire, left entirely intact. It comprises a large territory and population, and has perhaps two levels of political hierarchy above the minimal settlement. When subsumed under the imperial administrative system, this modular unit acquires an additional level of control, that of the imperial state.

Certainly, there are many factors that complicate this scenario, cases in which higher or lower levels of hierarchy are needed. But let us consider this two-level hierarchy as the ideal modular unit that can be directly integrated into the empire. Assuming that empires try to reduce their costs by using local systems where possible, and assuming that local systems vary in terms of hierarchical organization, a number of different imperial strategies of consolidation are readily apparent.

Local System Sufficiently Complex

In the first instance we consider the integration into the empire of societies that already have two levels of administration above the minimum settlement (Fig. 1.1). That is, the local system comprises individual villages, which are then grouped into small multivillage polities headed by something on the order of a district chief. These in turn are organized into a larger group along with other such simple chiefdoms under the rule of the paramount chief (see, for example, Earle 1978). If the conditions are

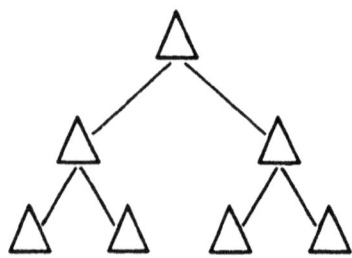

Figure 1.1. Schematic diagram of a society organized at the level of a complex chiefdom.

right to leave the system intact—it presents no threat, and there are no other conditions that argue for direct rule—then consolidation into the imperial hierarchy can take one of several forms.

In the first case, the system may be left intact and the paramount chief left in complete control (Fig. 1.2). He collaborates directly with imperial administrators at the next level up, perhaps located at an imperial administrative center located some distance away. There are no permanent imperial administrators or supervisors actually stationed in the province. In some ways, this is one of the more complex imperial arrangements. The empire must be confident of the loyalty of the paramount chief, and have faith in his abilities as an imperial collaborator. In actual fact, it is likely that such local rulers were never really autonomous, and we might perhaps better term them puppets, but ones without direct imperial supervision.

To ensure that the local collaborator remains loyal to the empire and carries out its wishes, there must be the threat of sanctions against him if he does not conform to the expectations of the empire. This might be accomplished in a most persuasive fashion by taking the sons of the ruler and sending them to the imperial capital, to be educated in the ways of the empire. In effect, the sons are held captive, despite the trappings of great prestige that are associated with going to live in the capital.

On the other hand, the empire must be generous with its collaborators, and lavish them with gifts and other perquisites of imperial office. These may include gifts of precious material items, a portion of the imperial tribute, women, and other items to reinforce the status position of the collaborator.

In the second case, the system is left intact and the paramount chief left in control, but an imperial supervisor is added to the system to keep an eye on things (Fig. 1.3). The local chief is left with his local power base, but he collaborates directly with the imperial supervisor at the same level. We might term him also a puppet, but one with direct imperial supervision.

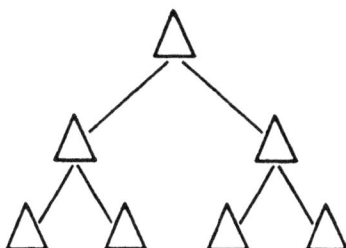

Figure 1.2. A strategy for consolidating control over a paramount chiefdom: leave the local hierarchy intact.

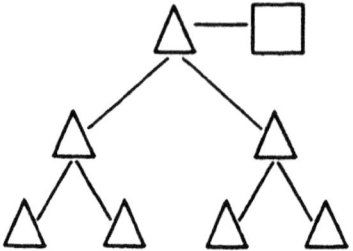

Figure 1.3. A strategy for consolidating control over a paramount chiefdom: create a local puppet ruler, with direct imperial supervision.

And in the third case, the system is left intact, but the paramount chief, the uppermost level of the hierarchy, is replaced by an imperial ruler (Fig. 1.4). This may be considered direct rule, but the local system has been left largely intact. The system has been decapitated, and a new head attached. The new head deals with collaborators in the lower level of the hierarchy, the local chiefs, and the system operates much as before.

Local System Too Complex

In the second instance, the empire may need to consolidate its control over groups that have an administrative hierarchy organized with more than two levels above the minimum settlement. For example, in this case we might envision the conquest of another state, one that is organized with three levels of administrative hierarchy (Fig. 1.5). Again, there are several possible strategies for integrating a more complex society into the empire.

In the first place, the system may be left intact (Fig. 1.6). Like the case of the complex chiefdom, the local ruler becomes a puppet, and he may or may not be directly supervised by the empire. But given that such a system presents a threat to the empire by its ability to organize resistance, it is unlikely that the uppermost level or levels of the system go unchanged. Thus, another strategy is to leave the system entirely intact, but replace the local state ruler with an imperial one (Fig. 1.7). In this case the imperial ruler collaborates with second level bureaucrats who remain in place. Alternatively, the system may be left intact, but both the state ruler and the second level bureaucrats may be removed and replaced with imperial ones (Fig. 1.8). In this case the empire controls the top two levels of the system, and collaborates with the first level bureaucrats.

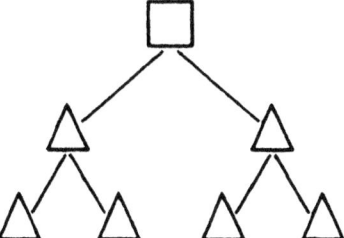

Figure 1.4. A strategy for consolidating control over a paramount chiefdom: remove the local ruler, and establish direct imperial control.

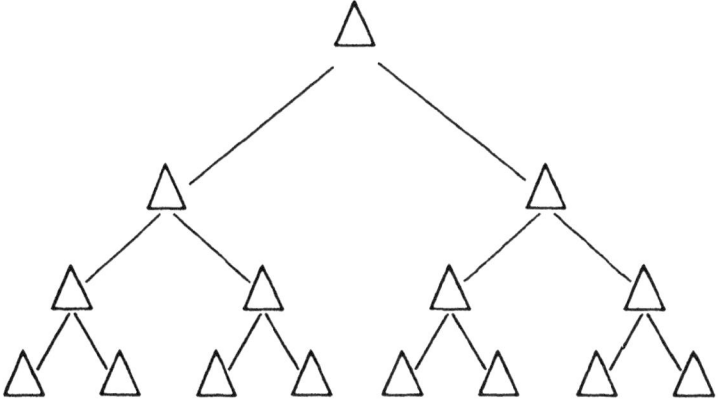

Figure 1.5. Schematic diagram of a society organized at the level of a state.

In other cases, however, the state-level society may not be left intact, but rather divided into its component parts (Fig. 1.9). In other words, the third level of the hierarchy (i.e., the over-arching state organization) is removed altogether, and the first and second levels are left intact (i.e., the constituent units, organized much like paramount chiefdoms).

At this point, the strategy of consolidation of each of the constituent units can proceed as in the case of polities with sufficient organization—the paramount chiefdoms. Thus, the three general strategies involve (1) replacing the local ruler with an imperial one, (2) leaving the local ruler in place, but adding an imperial overseer, or (3) leaving the local ruler autonomous.

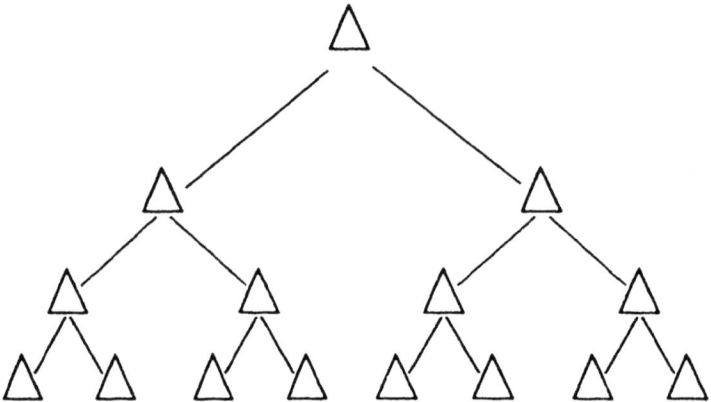

Figure 1.6. A strategy for consolidating control over a state: leave the hierarchy intact, and leave the local ruler in place.

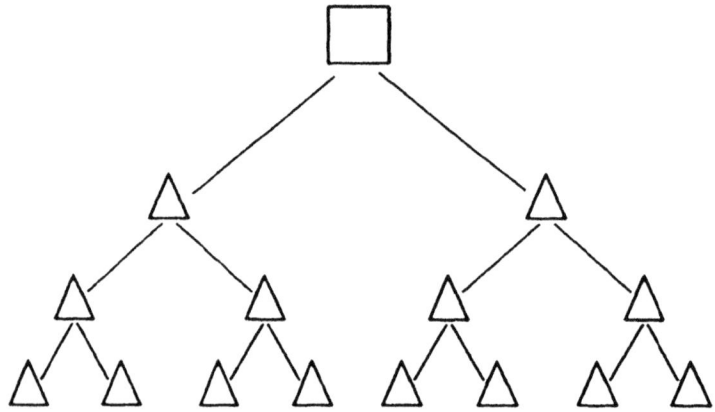

Figure 1.7. A strategy for consolidating control over a state: leave the hierarchy intact, but replace the uppermost level with direct imperial control.

Local System Insufficiently Complex

And in the third instance, we consider the situation in which the empire is dealing with societies that are not complex enough to be directly integrated into the imperial administrative hierarchy. That is, they have only one, or no, level of ruling hierarchy.

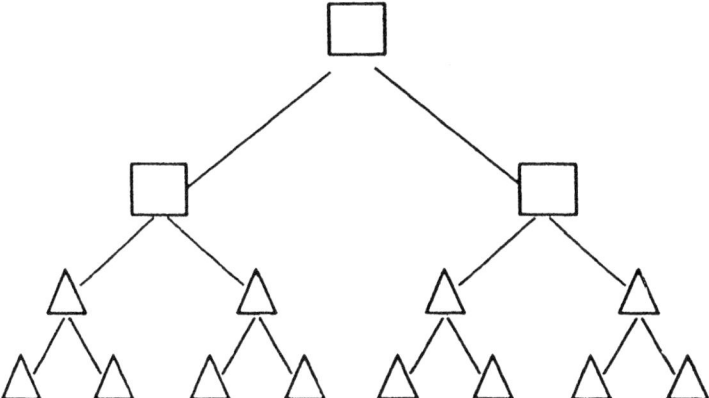

Figure 1.8. A strategy for consolidating control over a state: leave the hierarchy intact, but replace the top two levels with direct imperial control.

Figure 1.9. A strategy for consolidating control over a state: eliminate the top level of control and divide the state into its component parts; proceed as for paramount chiefdoms.

Those areas that have little or no local centralized control, areas that have few people or few resources of interest to the empire, and that present no threat to the empire, may be passed over by the empire. These areas, although lying within the overall boundaries of the empire, and perhaps adjacent to regions that are under imperial control, are just not consolidated into the imperial system. This is most likely in regions of small segmentary societies or bands that are not united together under local chiefs (Fig. 1.10).

Figure 1.10. Diagram of a society with a tribal level of organization.

Figure 1.11. Diagram of a society organized at the level of a simple chiefdom.

If consolidation is desirable, then there are two strategies of indirect control that make use of existing forms of control. First, in the situation of simple chiefdoms (Fig. 1.11), where groups of villages are grouped together into small polities under the direction of a local district chief, one local chief may be elevated to the position of paramount chief (Fig. 1.12). This then creates a local two-level hierarchy that may be consolidated into the imperial system. In this situation, more so than in the case of extant paramount chiefdoms, there may be a need for imperial overseers, as the newly appointed paramount chief does not have prior experience in this higher position. Further, the other local chiefs must be persuaded to submit to this new higher order of control.

Second, it may be possible to extend the jurisdiction of a nearby group, one that is more complex in political organization, over the underdeveloped region (Fig. 1.13). In this case, the simpler society becomes part of an existing chiefdom, and extant provincial organization suffices to integrate the region into the empire. This may be more likely in regions where the adjacent complex society is characterized by more direct imperial rule. With more direct imperial sanctions available, the more likely it is that a formerly independent group of people will submit to outside rule. But such a situation might also obtain wherein the new rulers are provincial elites.

The other strategy open to the empire, other than skipping over an underdeveloped region or subsuming it under extant authority, is to impose direct imperial rule (Fig. 1.14). This option is costly; it involves creating a centralized authority, and all the necessary infrastructure. Therefore, it is likely exercised only in those cases where there is something special about the region that makes it particularly interesting to the empire. It might lie

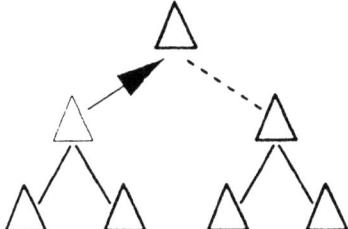

Figure 1.12. A strategy for consolidating control over a simple chiefdom society: elevate one local chief to a higher level, increase the complexity of the local system.

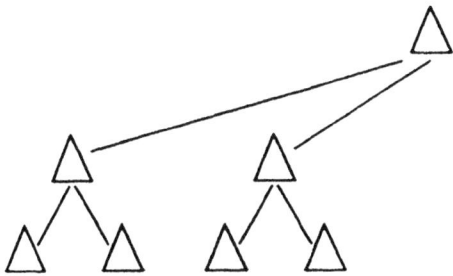

Figure 1.13. A strategy for consolidating control over a simple chiefdom society: subsume the region under another province.

close to the imperial heartland, or it might lie near a strategic border zone. It might contain some resource that the empire wishes to exploit. It might be in a strategic location, along a major transportation route.

Thus, it is in these situations, in places that were lacking in political centralization prior to conquest, where we sometimes see the greatest evidence of imperial control. In these settings, the local system was simply inadequate for imperial needs, and the imperial needs were high. We may see the construction of major imperial administrative centers, as well as an infrastructure of small imperial centers if they are needed.

In the case of simple chiefdoms, with a single level of hierarchy, we may see the addition of a second level of direct imperial control. In this case the empire creates an administrative center in the region, and directly rules the smaller, simpler, extant societies. In cases where no administrative hierarchy existed at all, we may find not only a major imperial center, but also secondary facilities, thus creating two levels of hierarchy above the extant local villages.

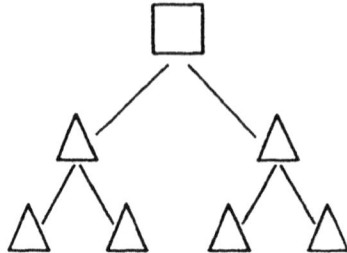

Figure 1.14. A strategy for consolidating control over a simple chiefdom society: create a new administrative level, impose direct imperial rule.

Discussion

I have begun this discussion of imperial strategies with two basic assumptions: (1) that an empire will require a centralized bureaucracy with two levels of control over the minimal settlement, essentially a paramount chiefdom, in each province, and (2) that it will make use of local political organization where possible. The strategies of control actually employed will depend in part on the extant political organization in a region, and whether this is equal to, more than, or less than that needed by the empire. It can be seen from this simplified view of imperial consolidation, that the variety in imperial strategies is immense. With only these two parameters we can generate more than a dozen different strategies for consolidating imperial control over a region, without considering all the logical permutations for each situation. With variation in the degree of centralization necessary for optimal imperial takeover, or with different interpretations of the number of levels of control extant in small polities, such as complex chiefdoms, the situation can only become more complex. But it is the *relative difference* between local levels of control and imperial needs that in many ways determines the set of options open to the empire.

It is also apparent that there are many forms of consolidation that fall between the extremes of direct and indirect control, and a single empire will make use of many different kinds of strategies.

The variations in these strategies have implications for the archaeological study of provincial control. First of all, archaeological evidence is likely to be more visible in areas of relatively direct control, areas in which the empire had to build its own infrastructure. Areas of indirect control may have little obvious evidence of imperial control, even though such regions were entirely consolidated under imperial control. Second, and related to this first point, archaeological remains are likely to be manifest to a greater degree in areas that lacked the necessary levels of control prior to conquest. That is, in areas of lesser political complexity direct control was more likely, hence the presence of imperial facilities is more likely. In more complex regions the local infrastructure may have served imperial needs with little alteration. It is in the areas of the most complex pre-empire political organization that we may find the least evidence of imperial control.

Residual Local Authority and Strategies Available to Local Elites

Returning to the theory of collaboration, we have seen that in many cases it is in the best interest of the empire to rule through local collaborators. It is a good idea to leave the local ruler with enough control, but not too much. That is, he must be able to organize the region to carry out imperial wishes—pay tribute, complete labor projects, and so forth—and also maintain enough power to keep himself in control. On the other hand, with too much power he can become a threat to the empire. Without enough, he is ineffective.

Another advantage to leaving a local ruler in place, with enough power to control the region, is the avoidance of xenophobic reactions by the conquered populace. They perceive that they are still operating within the same basic system that they know, with their own rulers. When a group of foreigners takes over, local reaction may be negative, and there may be greater resistance to conforming to the new order.

Yet, the local rulers must not retain so much power that they can turn around and become a threat to the empire. Therefore, imperial surveillance may be required at regular intervals, or imperial supervisors may be stationed on a more permanent basis—not enough to interfere with the operation of the local system, but enough to see that it meets imperial needs and does not threaten the empire.

There are several strategies that may be employed by local rulers as well. In the first place, local elites may choose to cooperate with the empire. There is of course a great advantage to this: they get to stay in control. There is a certain loss of independence, as the empire co-opts their ultimate sovereignty, but there are also certain advantages. They have access to new status goods through their connection into the imperial system of distribution; the empire offers a variety of gifts and trappings of power to reinforce the status of the local ruler, and to ensure his continued cooperation and collaboration.

On the other hand, local elites may choose to resist imperial control, and not cooperate with the empire. This entails what Haas has called refusal costs: "what will happen if demands are made of a respondent and the person refuses to comply" (Haas 1982:168-69). At the least this may involve sanctions against the local elites by the empire, and may also result in the destruction of the local elites. On the other hand, if one group of local elites chooses to resist, other elites may see their chance to move into positions of power. So local political intrigue may play into the hands of the empire in the sense that there may be found someone else who is willing to do what the empire wants, in exchange for position.

Regardless of whether or not the local elites cooperate, ultimately the empire may get what it wants. In the end, the costs of compliance, which "measure how much and when the labor, money, or agricultural products are contributed" (Haas 1982:168), will be the same. So, from the viewpoint of the local elites, resistance is a more expensive option, involving both costs of refusal and compliance—unless they are successful in defeating the empire.

Economic Reorganization

Once a region has been conquered, and the local political systems adapted to imperial political control, the focus of imperial concerns is turned toward economic matters. As empires manipulate political hierarchies to serve their own needs, so too are economic systems manipulated as the empire establishes economic control over conquered territory. Conquered populations carry out major construction projects, produce goods for the empire, pay tribute/taxes, and serve as specialists in the service of the empire.

The local domestic economy includes the direct subsistence support of the people in a region, as well as the production and distribution of craft goods, and the support of the local elite. When a new political regime is established, additional requirements are placed on producers. Imperial systems require support, including both staple and wealth items, from each conquered region (D'Altroy and Earle 1985). Hence, additional surplus must be created to support the state bureaucracy. This support may take the form of tribute payments in wealth items, or as direct subsistence support of imperial rulers in the region.

Within a conquered region, there may have existed a local level prestige economy prior to conquest. In other words, local rulers were in some ways supported by and had control over the production of subsistence and material goods. Upon incorporation into a broader imperial system, a new level of control is imposed, and the local system finds itself a component in a much larger system. Just as the political hierarchy is modified to fit into the imperial administrative, so is the local prestige economy, and to a degree the domestic economy, restructured to provide the economic support required by the empire.

Imperial Infrastructure

As control is established and new provinces are consolidated into the imperial system, there develops an infrastructure of imperial control. This infrastructure includes a bureaucracy of public officials, means of keeping records, the maintenance of a military force, systems of roads, and physical facilities including everything from storehouses to major administrative centers. An empire-wide administrative hierarchy emerges, integrating the various provinces, and centering on the imperial capital.

The imperial capital is the highest level in the administrative hierarchy. In the capital are not only the ruling elite, and migrants from various provinces, but also a cadre of bureaucrats and record-keepers. Below the level of the imperial capital, an empire may be divided into major sectors, each comprising a series of provinces. Public officials in charge of these major sectors are likely to be elites from the imperial capital, along with a support network of lesser administrators.

One of the most important tasks for officials at every level is the keeping of records: population, production, tribute requirements, tribute paid, tribute owed, contents of imperial storehouses, distribution of goods from storehouses, and many others. Empires have systems of writing, or some other mnemonic devices, for keeping such records, along with people skilled in their use. In addition to means of keeping records, a common bureaucratic language is needed. As many provinces likely speak languages other than that of the imperial society, a single lingua franca may be established as an official language—the language of the ruling elite and the administrative officials.

The physical, visible aspects of the imperial infrastructure include roads, storehouses, military garrisons, minor administrative structures, and major administrative centers. They may also include such things as religious shrines and other small features. And many of these facilities can be documented in the archaeological record.

If every conquered province comprised a group of simple chiefdoms, and the empire established direct rule over each province, then we would expect to find a small administrative center in every province. However, as shown above, the situation is much more complex than this, and imperial expansion and consolidation results in a mosaic of different levels of control in different conquered provinces. The distribution of imperial facilities is a direct reflection of this mosaic of control.

In general, we expect to find major imperial facilities where the empire established direct rule over areas of inadequate extant political organization. And likewise, we expect only minor facilities in areas that were sufficiently complex, and could be ruled indirectly. However, there are other factors that also enter into the establishment of imperial administrative centers. Larger centers may also be expected under other circumstances. For example, if an empire is divided into major units, such as halves or quarters, we might expect a major center in each one—of a greater magnitude than expected just on the basis of local vs. imperial hierarchies. Likewise, strategic locations along major transportation routes, such as at intersections of major roads, might also receive centers greater than otherwise predicted. Border zones being particularly sensitive, and perhaps requiring greater military presence, may also receive special attention. And areas in which certain important resources are located, resources that the empire has great need for, may also increase levels of administrative control above what would be expected. As well, certain sacred places, or places with some important symbolic meaning to the empire, may also receive special attention.

Thus, although a major factor in determining the magnitude of imperial administration is the local level of political complexity, the location of a province and the presence of particularly important resources may call for larger centers. The result is a distribution of imperial administrative centers and other facilities that parallels the mosaic of control, but also results from other factors critical to imperial organization.

Storage plays an important role in imperial administration. Often, extensive storage facilities are needed for agricultural produce, craft items, and other goods paid in tribute. The storehouses then serve as points of collection for items to be shipped to other centers. Storehouses can provide food for imperial administrators, feed other people working for the empire, supply the military, and in some cases food may be distributed back to the producers in the event of famine.

Another part of the imperial infrastructure involves the maintenance of military forces. This requires not only the recruitment of soldiers, but their direct support. Since the army must be mobile at all times, facilities—garrisons—are kept ready and stocked in the event they are needed.

Associated with many great empires are major networks of official roads. The Roman road system is perhaps the best known example of imperial roads, but such systems are typical of other empires as well. Roads are critical in a number of areas. First, given their spatial extent, empires need means to communicate as quickly as possible with distant regions. Before the development of such things as the telegraph or radio, such communications had to be carried by hand. A well-maintained system of official roads could greatly facilitate such communication. Second, roads are necessary for the rapid deployment of military forces to the far-reaching provinces of the empire. Third, as tribute and taxes are paid at the local level to the empire, a certain amount of this material moves to imperial centers, and on to the capital. Roads provide the means by which goods can be transported over large distances. Fourth, roads connect important places—administrative centers, lesser imperial facilities, and local population centers. This facilitates the movement of people, especially imperial administrators, through the different provinces of the empire. And finally, roads are a visible symbol of imperial power, both to the people who use them, and to the people in the provinces who see roads physically connecting them to imperial centers of political control.

The result of imperial consolidation of conquered territories is an empire that is characterized by a mosaic of different levels of control. In some areas the imperial presence is greatly felt, and very visible in terms of imperial facilities and personnel. In other areas, the evidence of imperial control is very indirect, and there may be no visible imperial facilities, and no permanent imperial personnel. Yet in both cases the regions are absolutely consolidated under the imperial administrative system. As will be discussed in later chapters, the relative lack of evidence of imperial control in some regions can be problematic.

Temporal Dynamics

Rather than being static, imperial strategies may change through time for a variety of reasons. First, there may be a gradual shift from indirect rule to direct rule within regions. In such cases, it may have been to the advantage of the empire initially to reduce costs by relying on local collaboration. But as the empire grows larger, more powerful, and richer, there may be a tendency to gradually shift to more direct forms of rule, as Luttwak (1976) has suggested in the case of the Roman empire. There may also be increasing hostility over time by conquered peoples, tired of operating under an oppressive imperial yoke. As regions suffer under imperial control, and local elites tire of being told what to do by the imperial authorities, local collaboration may become less reliable. This is a significant factor in the evolution of imperial control, because increasing levels of direct control are more costly. And the empire may need to bring in increasing quantities of tribute in order to maintain the provinces it already controls. This, in turn, results in even more local resistance as taxes and tribute requirements increase.

It is also the case that as an empire expands, so does the population of the imperial core. This is partly a result of increased reproductive success on the part of the ruling imperial elite (see, for example, Betzig 1986; Boone 1986, 1987), but mostly due to the influx of people from other areas of the empire. Elite families from various parts of the empire live temporarily or permanently in the imperial capital. There is also an increase in population due to an influx of other specialists and laborers, brought to the capital to serve the elite. And many non-elites and supporting groups find themselves in the center of political and economic control. But one result of this increase in core population is the need for greater subsistence support of the core. What may have begun as a large market town may now be a great city.

Control of the heartland may have to be extended directly to surrounding regions in order to ensure direct subsistence support of the capital. So in regions near the imperial core we may expect to see increasing levels of imperial control, as these regions become more critical to the support of the core population.

As the empire continues to grow, conditions change through time, and the infrastructure also changes. For example, a major center might be established near a sensitive border, but as the empire expands this is no longer a border region. The site might then be abandoned, or more likely (and to amortize the imperial investment in establishing the site) it may continue to serve as a major regional administrative center, controlling one or more provinces. In another case the empire may need to build a center to take direct control of a hostile region, but if the hostility is dissipated the center may not be needed, and indirect rule established. Alternatively, what began as only a small center may increase in importance as the region takes on greater importance to the empire. In this case the center may be enlarged, or additional centers created.

So in sum, the structure of control can be expected to change over time as the various conditions change, and as the empire continues to expand.

Imperialism in the Provinces: Some Archaeological Correlates

The distribution of imperial remains throughout its domain can indicate the continuity of control, and the variety of strategies of consolidation taken by the empire. Imperial control that was relatively direct is likely to leave direct evidence in the archaeological record. Imperial administrative centers will be distinct from local settlements in terms of both architecture and artifact assemblages. Architecture is likely to be of a style typical of the empire, but foreign and unlike local styles. It is therefore useful not only to have defined imperial architectural cannons, but also to have defined local architecture as well, both domestic and public.

Artifact assemblages in imperial administrative centers should provide evidence of both the foreign occupants and a constellation of activities distinct from those at local domestic sites. Higher proportions of imported, imperial styles of artifacts are to be expected in imperial centers.

On the other hand, in areas where imperial rule was indirect, the archaeological evidence of imperial control may be minimal. In such cases it is useful to reconstruct local political organization prior to incorporation into the empire. The most effective data for these purposes are the reconstruction of settlement patterns. Site size hierarchies may directly or indirectly indicate levels of bureaucratic control, and indicate the level of political organization. We also need to seek evidence of information flow between the various sites, as well as evidence of administration. These may be evident through shared styles of elite artifacts, the presence of public buildings, and the presence of artifacts indicative of administrative activities.

After pre-conquest organization is defined, the next step is to look at changes in that system during the period of imperial occupation. I have hypothesized that major imperial administrative systems are more likely to occur in areas of insufficient local development, where there is a need for higher levels of imperial control. Conversely, I have proposed above that, in a system left largely intact, but with imperial supervision, we might expect some minimal imperial facilities, but nothing suggesting a major imperial occupation. And in the case of a system left intact, complete with local rulers, the only evidence of the imperial presence may be artifactual remains in the house or tomb of the local ruler—the gifts he received from the empire, and other trappings of power.

In sum, imperial administrative centers and obvious evidence of direct control are not expected in every region within an empire. As the empire has many strategies open to it to control a region, and these strategies depend on local conditions, so too does the archaeologist look to both local conditions prior to conquest as well as evidence of the imperial occupation to more fully understand the process of imperial takeover.

Reconstructing local patterns of production and exchange can also be particularly valuable in drawing a contrast with the period of imperial domination. Changes in economic organization occurring at this time can be interpreted as being a result of imperial reorganization. Changes may include a change in subsistence focus, to supply the empire with the subsistence products it needs, and the exploitation of new or different resources, indicating the interest of the empire in those resources. Wealth and prestige items, while still consumed by local elites, may now have more complex distribution patterns, and may change in style and content, as a result of the imposition of new levels of power and prestige. Excavation data from both local and imperial sites are especially useful in reconstructing aspects of economic organization and their changes under imperial domination.

At an empire-wide level, the imperial administrative hierarchy may be difficult to discern on the basis of archaeological data. While settlement hierarchies often parallel administrative hierarchies, in the case of empires, the distribution of sites of different sizes is not likely to be a reliable indication of position in a control hierarchy. While the capital of the empire may be fairly easy to identify on the basis of great size, and location within the empire, secondary and tertiary nodes of control outside the imperial core may not be so obvious. As discussed above, the imperial investment in a conquered region, and the resulting elaboration of administrative facilities in the region, depends to a great degree on the preexisting local political system. Larger imperial centers are found in strategic regions, and regions lacking adequate political structures. The size of imperial centers does not very directly indicate position in a control hierarchy, but rather is determined by other factors. Perhaps one avenue of investigation that might provide some success is to attempt to determine in which regions the imperial investment is greater than expected, given the various factors discussed above. A site that is an important administrative node, over and above its role in local administration, might be expected to be larger or more elaborate than otherwise expected. I suspect, however, that this will be difficult to demonstrate with any degree of certainty.

DECLINE AND FALL

Viewing imperialism as a dynamic process, and the resulting empire as an ever-changing entity, we can see also that there is a great deal of potential for the development of stress within the system. And these stresses may be exacerbated as the system grows larger and more complex. Eventually internally and externally generated stresses may lead to the collapse of the imperial system altogether.

Expansion and consolidation are costly. As the empire grows there is a concomitant need for ever-increasing revenues. New territories provide new revenues, as does increasing the tribute requirements from already consolidated provinces. Over time administrative requirements may increase in some provinces, again requiring increased revenues to cover this cost. In other words, the continued growth of administrative systems requires a continued acquisition of new revenues. Without new revenues, the empire quickly finds itself in the throes of deficit spending. But at the same time, increasing tribute requirements can result in overexploitation of resource zones, and environmental degradation, thus producing new stresses.

There is great potential within an imperial system for a variety of internal political stresses to develop. At the beginning of expansion, the political elite may have consisted of a royal family and a class of nobles. As the empire expands and the need for loyal administrators increases, more and more people are drawn into the administrative bureaucracy. As the potential for acquiring power increases, so do the opportunities for abusing that power. As the power base moves beyond the limits of a single royal lineage, so too does the family altruism and loyalty to the cause become more diffuse.

As administrative needs increase, and as the administrative bureaucracy increases, this bureaucracy may become top-heavy. Increasing numbers of administrators are supported by state coffers. This puts added economic stress on producers, and takes away from the liquid reserves of the empire. And as the hierarchy increases in complexity and range, and as loyalties to the ruler become more diffuse and complicated, the result may be power struggles—even within the ruling elite. Disputes over succession, and resultant civil wars, may irreparably damage the political system.

Within the provinces, outside the core, civil unrest and internal revolts may develop. In areas of more direct rule, local rulers may come to want more control. In areas of more indirect rule, competing groups may vie for provincial control, leading to small civil wars at the local level. Or after years or generations of imperial control local people and their leaders may simply wish to throw off the oppressive yoke of imperial control, and the concomitant tribute requirements.

Other factors that threaten imperial control, and hence the whole system, are threats from the outside. Invasion by a foreign power, or continued border attacks by smaller groups, can cause the collapse of empire. Likewise, in the case of a multipolar world, competition for new territory may lead to the collapse of one system. Where new territory is needed to generate new revenues to support the administrative system, and where a competing polity takes control of those territories, the first empire may not be able to support itself.

And other causes of collapse include various natural causes such as disease or climatic deterioration. In other words, in some cases an empire may have collapsed for reasons not directly cultural—neither internal to the empire, nor the result of relations with external groups.

As an empire is directly dependent on local production, and as agricultural production is dependent upon climatic factors, climatic change can have an indirect effect on the empire. For example, in the case of the Moche IV collapse at around A.D. 500 on the north coast of Peru, Moseley (1983) has argued that agrarian collapse, occasioned by a combination of climatic and tectonic factors, had major political repercussions. I have argued in the case of the south coast, that climatic deterioration hastened the decline of the Nasca polity at about the same time (Schreiber and Lancho 1988:62).

Disease might also be suggested as a possible cause of political collapse, at least in cases of major devastating epidemics. It could be convincingly argued that disease was a major contributor to the collapse of the Inka empire in the sixteenth century. Although the proximate cause of Inka demise was takeover by another polity at a time of internal political strife, the Inka response to the Spanish was greatly weakened by the effects of newly introduced exotic diseases.

Depending on the causes, the sequence of imperial collapse may follow one of several possible trajectories. First, the empire may collapse from the top down. That is, the proximate cause of collapse is something that disrupts imperial rule in the heartland, among the imperial ruling elite. Political intrigue, civil war dividing the ruling class, or economic collapse may affect the heartland first, and cause the rupture of political control. Without control from the political center, the empire is effectively decapitated, and collapse occurs nearly instantaneously throughout the empire.

Alternatively, if collapse results from internal revolts in the provinces, or invasion from the outside, the collapse may proceed from the bottom up, or from the outside in. In this case collapse may be delayed or prevented by a swift and effective response from the imperial core. However, as time goes by and internal stresses increase, local revolts may gradually erode away at imperial control. Collapse in this case begins more slowly, but may pick up speed as one province after another is released from the bonds of imperial control.

In the aftermath of imperial collapse we need to consider what becomes of both the imperial system, and the local systems, given the conditions causing the collapse. In the case in which external factors are causal, and another group takes over imperial control, the result may be that the empire stays roughly intact but with a new ruling elite. Control shifts to a new cultural group, but the umbrella of control remains, either over the entire empire, a smaller territory, or perhaps just over the original imperial core.

However, considering collapse to be the reduction of imperial control over some or all territories, we can suggest several possible outcomes. First, the empire may simply shrink in size, but maintain control over a sizeable area, larger than the imperial core. Second, the empire may shrink right back down to the original core polity. And third, not only may the empire disappear from all provincial areas, but the original core polity may also collapse. In some cases, depending on the proximate causes of collapse, it may be intentionally destroyed by formerly subjugated groups. Or, in most cases, the collapse of the imperial system is in effect also the collapse of the local core system—they are one in the same.

The Legacy of Empire

Long after the demise of an imperial system, what effects does this have on other cultural or political developments? Once empires develop in a region, other empires follow. It appears in the case of state origins, that regions with states continue to maintain complex political organization even after the early polities fall. New forms of organization have become entrenched, and cultural systems geared to participation in a state system, such that, although a particular ruling elite may fall from power, or a particular city may no longer rule a region, some group arises to fill the vacuum. In much the same way, empires seem to occur again and again in the same general region.

Succeeding empires build on the foundations of empires that existed before. In one sense this involves re-use of earlier imperial infrastructures, much as Napoleon repaired the Roman roads to aid in his European conquests. However, in another sense, later empires learn basic lessons in strategies of control from earlier empires, use those strategies and develop new ones. From their own history, later empires are familiar with the various strategies of conquest and consolidation.

CONCLUSION: ARCHAEOLOGICAL APPROACHES TO THE STUDY OF IMPERIALISM

Empires and imperialism are extremely complex entities for archaeological study. This chapter has presented, albeit briefly and in simplified form, some of the static and dynamic aspects of archaic empires.

There are aspects of imperialism that simply leave no evidence in the archaeological record, such as individual motivations in imperial expansion. However, some aspects of imperialism do leave direct evidence in the archaeological record, and an attempt has been made to summarize some productive lines of archaeological inquiry.

Archaeological approaches to empires may be summarized into several categories, based on the kinds of remains studied, and the means of study. We may distinguish between site-specific studies, and regional studies; we may distinguish between excavation data and survey data. And in the case of empires we may usefully distinguish between research aimed at the imperial core, and research undertaken in provincial settings.

A common approach to the study of empires—or any complex political organization, for that matter—is to undertake excavations in the imperial capital. Such excavations yield useful data regarding social organization of the capital, and definitions of imperial styles of architecture and artifacts. Indirectly one can infer the influx of people, produce, raw materials, and labor from conquered provinces into the capital. Yet the picture is far from complete, both in the imperial core and even more so in the empire as a whole. Excavation of the imperial capital yields little information about processes of imperialism, the motivations for expansion, or the various strategies of consolidation.

A second approach is a regional study of the imperial core. Settlement patterns may document the rise of state and imperial-level hierarchies of control, and the consolidation of the core prior to expansion. Excavation data (and sometimes surface remains) indicate styles of architecture and artifacts that indicate pre-imperial "interaction spheres," and the evolution of complex social and political organization. Regional surveys have produced especially useful data in such regions as Mesopotamia (e.g., Adams 1965, 1981; Adams and Nissen 1972), and the Basin of Mexico (Sanders, Parsons and Santley 1979).

While studies of imperial cores yield data useful in documenting the rise of the core polity, other important data come from the provinces; yet this is an area sometimes neglected. It is only in the provinces that one can study the process of imperial takeover, and the different strategies employed by an empire in consolidating its control over conquered territories. Provincial studies may usefully include three complementary avenues of investigation: regional settlement patterns, the study of imperial sites, and the study of local sites. Each of these three areas provides a part of the evidence, yet it is rare that all three approaches have been employed in a single region.

Regional settlement patterns enable the reconstruction of local political organization prior to conquest, and changes in the system under imperial rule. Definition of local versus imperial sites provides a basis for understanding strategies of imperial consolidation. The presence or absence of imperial facilities, and the type of facilities present, in concert with evidence documenting extant local political organization, allows the definition of aspects of the imperial strategy of consolidation.

Site-specific studies of imperial sites, especially where major administrative centers are encountered, likewise provide useful evidence of imperial occupations. By looking at activities carried out within imperial sites, one can understand some of what the empire was doing in that region. In addition, architecture and artifacts may combine both local and imperial styles, documenting aspects of local-imperial interaction.

And site-specific studies of local sites, occupied before and during the period of empire, round out the picture by indicating the effect of the imperial occupation on the local culture, especially on patterns of production and consumption. Changes in the local domestic economy and prestige economy during the imperial occupation may shed light on the economic structure of the empire. Some of the most detailed studies of this type have been done with regard to the Inka Empire, and will be discussed in more detail in the following chapter. In addition, the identification of pre-empire local styles of architecture and artifacts are not only useful in distinguishing imperial facilities and artifacts, but also in documenting changes in local styles resulting from the effects of imperial domination.

And finally, it is useful to look beyond just the imperial core, and the individual provinces, and take a longer view of imperialism. First, the world political system prior to expansion may indicate a good deal about the motivations behind the expansion. Second, the macro-regional picture may indicate why the empire chose to expand into certain areas and not others. And third, the establishment of boundaries beyond which the empire did not expand may be understandable only in macro-regional terms.

In sum, although many aspects of imperialism are not directly available for archaeological reconstruction and evaluation, many aspects are. To understand the processes of imperialism, indeed to even decide if a particular society was an empire or not, data from both the core and the provinces are critical. And it is useful to look beyond just the investigation of imperial sites, and look at local sites and settlement patterns to round out the picture. And, finally, it is in the provinces that we can best see the effects of imperial takeover, and the strategies employed by an empire to consolidate its control.

Now let us turn to the well documented case of the Inka empire as an example of some of these aspects of imperialism.

2

The Inka Empire
Imperialism in Andean Form

When Francisco Pizarro marched into the Andean cordillera in 1532, he found himself face to face with the ruler of the largest empire ever known in the New World. The Inka ruled a political empire that extended from their capital at Cuzco, in southern Peru, to Colombia in the north, and to central Chile in the south (Fig. 2.1). They called their empire Tawantinsuyu—the inextricably linked four quarters.

In this chapter, the Inka empire will be used as the primary example of a society that best describes an Andean empire. We know more about Inka society than any other indigenous Andean political organization, because it was still in existence at the time of the Spanish conquest, and we have eyewitness accounts of the Inka and their institutions. And, although it was perhaps not the only empire to exist in the Andes, it was certainly the largest, most extensive empire that ever existed in the Andes. From its inception as a small core polity, to the extension of its mosaic of control over a vast geographical region, the Inka empire looks in many ways like the ancient empires of the Old World. Yet there are some differences as well, some uniquely Andean aspects of imperialism, which may help us understand not only the Inka, but also political systems that came before the Inka.

Figure 2.1. Map of Andean South America indicating the distribution of Inka roads. These roads provide the best estimate of the extent of Inka imperial control at the beginning of the sixteenth century A.D.

ECOLOGICAL COMPLEMENTARITY

The most obvious aspect of the Andes that distinguishes it from other areas in which empires arose is the diversity of the geographical setting. No other ancient empire ever came to control as wide a range of vertical and horizontal environments, and the corresponding range of human adaptations, as did the Inka. No other empire arose and exercised most of its control in regions lying at elevations mostly in excess of 10,000 feet above sea level. Many aspects of Inka control were derived from basic Andean adaptations to this high altitude environmental diversity (Morris 1985:481). The following discussion considers this variability and its effects on the growth of complex political organizations.

The central Andean region can be divided from west to east into three major environments: the coastal desert, the high sierra, and the montaña (Fig. 2.2). Of greatest concern to this study are the coast and highlands of Peru, and each of these zones varies significantly along a north-south gradient.

Variations in weather patterns in part determine these major zones, while at the same time the juxtaposition of the zones creates some of these weather patterns. In general, there are two distinct weather patterns in the annual cycle. Between May and November, the austral winter, Pacific weather systems dominate the region. The coast (especially the central coast) is cloaked in a dense ground-hugging cloud cover; at the same time the highlands are clear and dry. During the austral summer the pattern shifts, and Atlantic systems dominate. The coast becomes clear, warm

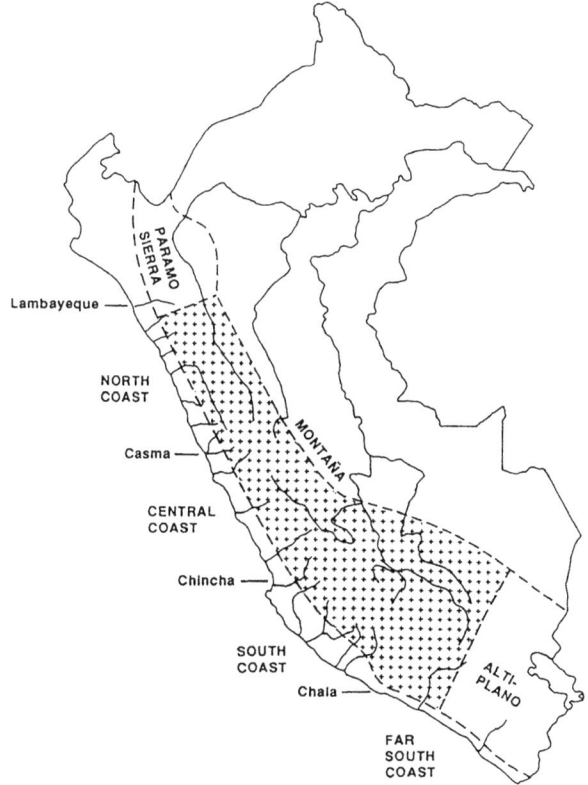

Figure 2.2. Map of Peru showing the division of the coast and highlands into major environmental zones. The shaded area is the puna sierra.

and dry, while rain falls in the highlands. The rain-bearing winds come generally from the east; as they rise over the Andes most of this rain is dropped on the montaña and the eastern ranges of the Andes. As a result, the western flanks of the Andes and the coast receive little to no precipitation.

Coastal Desert

The coastal desert includes some of the driest desert on earth, and increases in aridity as one moves from north to south, from northern Peru to Chile. In normal years, rainfall varies from up to about four inches in the north to barely a trace in the south. In no part of the coast is there sufficient rainfall for large-scale dry farming, and agriculture is almost entirely dependent on irrigation. Rain falling in the highlands flows down the western flanks of the Andes in a series of small rivers; where these rivers cross the coastal desert they form lush green linear oases. Coastal population, both modern and prehistoric, is largely concentrated in these river valleys.

The coast may be usefully divided into four major segments, based on environmental variability. The north coast extends from Lambayeque south to about the Casma Valley. The central coast extends from Casma south to about the Chincha Valley. Both the north and central coastal valleys are relatively well watered by rivers flowing out of the Andes, and they support high population densities. The south coast extends from Chincha south to Chala. Here the valleys are drier, owing to reduced rainfall in the southern highlands. The far south coast extends from Chala south into northern Chile, and is by far the driest sector of desert. Here essentially no rainfall reaches the coast, and the situation is exacerbated by corresponding aridity in the adjacent highlands. River valleys are fewer and farther between on the far south coast, but these valleys have a generally greater area of drainage in the highlands, as the Continental Divide is located at a greater distance inland than in other parts of the coast. Today, much of the population in this region is located well inland in the higher elevations of the western Andes.

One natural phenomenon has a profound periodic effect on the coast, especially in the north: El Niño-Southern Oscillation events (Nials et al. 1979). Although not fully understood, ENSO events involve interaction between the atmosphere and the ocean in the tropics, and have been linked with extraordinary variations in weather on a global scale (Thompson, Mosley-Thompson and Morales 1984). On the coast of Peru these events include a warming of ocean currents off the coast, and torrential rainfall on the normally hyper-arid desert. ENSO events occur at irregular intervals of three to seven years on the north coast of Peru. More serious ones affect the central coast as well. The south and far south coast valleys are rarely directly affected. (However, Mosley-Thompson, Thompson, and Morales [1984] have recently documented a correlation between ENSO events in the north, and reduced precipitation in the southern highlands, so ENSO occurrences may be felt indirectly in the south.)

Besides terrestrial resources, and the limitations on their exploitation imposed by the natural environment, the coast has also available a rich base of maritime resources (Moseley 1975a). The combination of the northward moving cold Peru Current, and southward moving warm currents in the north, and the upwelling due to the temperature differential between the currents, provides an incredibly productive environment for all manner of sea life. This is especially true with respect to the central and north coast. But when warmer currents invade normally cold waters during ENSO events, the maritime system is temporarily disrupted, and often takes several years to recover.

Complex social organization developed on the coast of Peru probably before it did elsewhere in the Andean region. The first evidence of complex organization appears at transition between the north and central coast, in the Casma Valley (S. Pozorski 1987; S. Pozorski and T. Pozorski 1987), where the combination of maritime resources and relatively ample water allowed the growth of population and the concomitant development of political control hierarchies. However, through time, the centers of complex cultures came to be located farther to the north and south: regions where environmental stresses may have called for more diverse and complex strategies of human organization. By the Early Intermediate period, the two most complex societies in Peru were located on the north coast (Moche) and the south coast (Nasca). Although we do not yet know at what level of complexity the Nasca polity was organized (Silverman 1986, 1988), the Moche polity was apparently organized at the level of a state, probably the most complex culture of its time in the Andes. And again in the Late Intermediate period, the most complex culture in the Andes was located on the north coast: the Chimú state. Thus, it seems that the coastal environment provided a subsistence base that gave the coast an advantage over the highlands in the development of early complex societies, and that the coast, especially the north coast, was repeatedly the locus of complex political developments.

Sierra

The Andean highlands are qualitatively different from the coast in terms of both environment and cultural developments. While the coast exhibited precocious cultural development, and produced a number of impressive polities, all three major archaeological horizons—Chavín, Wari/Tiwanaku, and Inka—were centered in the sierra. While coastal cultures rarely controlled sierra zones, highland cultures time and again exerted profound influence—to the point of direct conquest and political control in the case of the Inka empire—over the coast. These differences may be explained in part through a consideration of the highland environment, and the human adaptations developed to cope with the diversity of a mountain environment.

Like the coast, the sierra varies along a north-south gradient. Moving from north to south the sierra increases in elevation and aridity. The sierra can be usefully divided into three segments: the *páramo sierra* of the far north, the *puna sierra* of the central Andes, and the *dry puna/altiplano sierra* of the south. The páramo sierra lies largely in Ecuador, but also includes the northernmost portion of the Peruvian sierra. Lower and wetter than the Andes to the south, the topography is more broken and dissected as well.

Most of the sierra of Peru lies in the puna sierra zone. Here the Andes are dominated by broad expanses of high elevation plateau (puna), mountain ridges, and deeply incised river valleys. While the high puna is generally too high for agriculture, and serves mostly as grazing land, the deep valleys have more moderate environments suitable for intensive agriculture. As a result, most population is concentrated in the valleys. The puna sierra extends from Cajamarca to Cuzco, and gets progressively drier as one moves south.

Farther to the south lies the dry puna/altiplano zone. Here the Andes open up into a broad high plateau—the altiplano—ringed by high peaks and regions of very dry puna. In the center of the altiplano plateau lies Lake Titicaca, the highest navigable lake in the world. The altiplano has a drier climate and is not incised by river valleys like regions to the north. It comprises the Department of Puno in Peru, as well as northwestern Bolivia. Surrounding areas of dry puna include the highland portions of the Departments of Arequipa, Moquegua, and Tacna, as well as northern Chile, and northwest Argentina.

These three major highland zones are distinguished not only by differences in the natural environment, but, more importantly, differences in human adaptations. In 1972 John Murra coined the phrase "vertical ecology" to describe generally the division of the Andean environment into a series of ecological levels, and the different strategies developed by human groups to exploit a maximum of these zones. In recent years the more general term "ecological complementarity" has gradually replaced "verticality," extending its meaning to include cases of "horizontality" (cf. Shimada 1985: xiii-xiv; 1987:130).

Using the puna sierra as an example, in a typical valley as one moves upward in elevation, temperature decreases, the atmosphere becomes less dense, and humidity increases. As a result, the mountain environment comprises a series of diverse microclimes, arranged generally by elevation. At the lowest elevations in some valleys it may be possible to grow fruits and vegetables, including squashes, chili peppers, and coca. At higher elevations, typical of most highland valleys, is a zone called *kichwa* that is devoted primarily to the cultivation of maize. Above this is the *suni* zone, devoted to the cultivation of tubers, mostly potatoes. And the highest elevations, the broad expanses of grasslands above the limits of agriculture, are termed *puna*. The exact altitudinal ranges of each of these zones varies from valley to valley, but the same general sequence of zones is found throughout the Andean highlands (see, for example, B.J. Isbell 1978; Brush 1977).

In the puna sierra, villages are generally located in close proximity to those zones most exploited. Typically villages are located at the ecotone between the kichwa and suni zones, in order to maximize access to maize and tuber fields. Individual households own or have rights to land in each agricultural zone; puna grazing lands are generally held communally. As Brush (1977) points out, where the environmental gradient is steep, ecozones are located closely spaced; this he terms "compressed zonation." In this case each household or village or ethnic group directly exploits all the necessary zones. In other areas where the gradient is more gradual, ecozones are located farther apart; this is termed "extended zonation." In this case, rather than each household exploiting all zones, whole villages may specialize in the production of a single zone. These products are then exchanged for goods from other villages in other zones, through reciprocal relations, or redistribution. (Today, for example, the Urubamba Valley in Cuzco is characterized by an extended system of zonation; here small local markets have developed to facilitate exchange of products between regions.)

Another important variation on this adaptation exists, and was first pointed out by Murra (1972) who termed it an "archipelago" system. In this case, villages (or *ayllus*—ethnic groups) are located in a region that is lacking one or more important zones. To obtain goods from other zones, people may migrate to those zones on a temporary basis to exploit them, returning periodically to the home territory. Alternatively, permanent satellite communities may be established in the distant zones, and produce sent to the home territory.

This archipelago system is most clearly seen in the case of groups living in the altiplano region. The altitude of the altiplano (3,900 m) renders it unsuitable for maize agriculture, although tubers will grow at that elevation. Using ethnohistoric records, Murra (1972) documented the case of the Lupaqa, residents of the altiplano, who apparently maintained colonies in distant regions on the western flanks of the Andes, in order to acquire produce—maize and lower-elevation products—that was not available on the altiplano. There is evidence that this archipelago system had its roots back at least as far as the Middle Horizon: recent research in Moquegua has documented the presence of Tiwanaku settlements in that region (Moseley, Feldman and Goldstein 1985).

Thus, the three major segments of the sierra can be distinguished on the basis of human adaptation. The far northern Andes, the páramo sierra, never developed the vertical complementarity of the puna segments. As Murra has recently pointed out, there is a profound difference between puna and páramo, and the multiplicity of contrasting environments in proximity to the puna did not exist in the far north (Murra 1985:8). In the páramo sierra of Ecuador there developed a system of professional merchants, *mindaláes* (Salomon 1986:102-6); in contrast, in the puna zones of the central Andes, extensive systems of centralized storage and redistribution developed.

The puna segment can be distinguished on the basis of humidity and topography, as well as on the basis of exploitation patterns. While archipelago systems dominated the altiplano adaptation of the southern Andes, compressed zonation and direct exploitation are more typical of the puna sierra. While some groups in the puna sierra probably did maintain colonies in distant regions (see the discussion in Chapter 4 of possible colonies of Andamarca Lucanas), the more common pattern was for each village to directly exploit zones in the immediate vicinity. In contrast, the altiplano was lacking in critical resources, so all altiplano groups probably maintained colonies in distant regions.

Interestingly, the major prehistoric polities that emerged in the Andes did so within the puna zones to the south: Chavín, Wari and Cuzco, all located in the puna sierra; and Tiwanaku, located on the altiplano. This might suggest that an adaptation involving the exploitation of a variety of diverse ecozones might provide an organizational basis for the political control of diverse regions. As Murra writes, "ethnic groups and polities emerged in this region in whose success complementary access played a decisive role" (Murra 1985:5).

Montaña

Moving down the eastern slopes of the Andes, one enters the zone called the *montaña*. Here the Andes fall steeply off into the Amazon basin below, rainfall is abundant, and vegetation dense. Human population, at least until recently, has been relatively low in this region, and no major complex societies were centered on this region. Although this region was peripheral to many of the events taking place in the highlands (Raymond 1988), it lies outside the mainstream of complex political developments of concern here.

The Relationship between Andean Environment and Cultural Developments

First of all, there is a profound difference between developments on the coast, and developments in the highlands. While the coast was precocious in the initial development of complex organizations, the great horizons were all centered in the highlands. While the coast, especially the north, repeatedly developed highly complex states, none of these ever extended its control into the highlands. In contrast, the Inka, and perhaps earlier highland polities, extended their control down into the coastal valleys.

Second of all, there is a relationship between ecological complementarity and the expansion of political control. Highland groups, right down to the level of the household, had developed a subsistence system whereby diverse regions were controlled by a single social unit. These ecological zones were not necessarily contiguous, and were often great distances apart. Groups adept at controlling diverse regions for basic subsistence might not find it qualitatively different to control diverse regions for other reasons as well.

Third, there is a difference between the ecological adaptation and discontinuous political control, although these notions are sometimes equated in the Andean literature. As discussed in the preceding chapter, expanding empires establish a mosaic of control. Not all regions are under direct rule; some are ruled through local alliance, others may not be consolidated at all. The result is a discontinuous distribution of state facilities.

There is a tendency in Andean studies to view discontinuous political control as being a result of ecological complementarity. This may not be entirely appropriate, and it may be preferable to keep the two issues separate. Discontinuous territoriality is a common pattern in imperial situations, regardless of geographic origin. Only in the Andes do we seem compelled to try to cast it in the mold of ecological complementarity. There is certainly a relationship between the two concepts, and I suggest that the Andean ecology may cause political systems, especially those in the sierra, to be even more spatially discontinuous than they might otherwise be. It may be that the discontinuous territoriality of subsistence pursuits, at the village and household level, presaged more complex political strategies, even preadapted highland polities to large-scale expansions.

THE INKA EMPIRE

The Inka empire provides us with the best documented example of Andean imperialism. Rather than attempt to describe all aspects of Inka culture, this discussion will focus on aspects of Inka imperial expansion, particularly variations in strategies of provincial administration. In many ways the Inka example conforms to general expectations regarding the development and organization of an imperial system. Yet there are some subtle differences that warrant further discussion.

Much of what we know about the Inka is based on historical documents, descriptions of Inka institutions written by the Spanish in the sixteenth century. These early accounts of the collapse of Inka control are an invaluable resource in understanding Inka imperialism, especially those of Sarmiento de Gamboa (1960), Juan de Betanzos (1987), Molina de Cuzco (1942), and Cieza de León (1984). Archaeological investigations have also provided useful detail regarding particular aspects of Inka culture, and Inka provincial administration.

The best summary of Inka history and culture is still that compiled by John Rowe (1946) who worked his way through the various historical documents, weeded out the inconsistencies, and put together an Inka history, in the truest sense of the term. I generally follow his analysis of the sequence of events in Inka history, and rely on his absolute dating of the important events.

The Foundations of Empire

The Inka capital was at Cuzco, in the southern part of the puna sierra, and around this center grew the core polity that came to control the vast imperial holdings. We know very little of Inka origins, except for a variety of origin myths told to the Spanish that point to different locations for the mythical beginnings of the Inka dynasty. However, most versions agree that Cuzco was established by Manqo Qhapaq, and his descendants ruled Cuzco for many generations, beginning perhaps around A.D. 1200. Whatever the actual facts are, it is apparent that the Inka lived in and ruled the region around Cuzco for quite some time prior to the expansion.

The Cuzco region was occupied since at least the Early Horizon (Rowe 1944; Chávez 1982). During the Late Intermediate period, prior to the Inka expansion, the region around Cuzco was characterized by the presence of K'illke-style ceramics (Rowe 1946:199-200; Dwyer 1971). Settlement data are incomplete, so the configuration of K'illke society is yet unknown. This is probably due in part to the fact that the Inka occupation reorganized and obscured earlier remains, as well as the fact that limited archaeological research has been directed more at the Late Horizon, and not the Late Intermediate. Thus, we have no settlement pattern data that might show us the gradual development of Inka control in the core polity, but the distribution of K'illke ceramics probably indicates the boundaries of the pre-expansion core.

The Inka capital was at Cuzco. K'illke ceramics found at the Coricancha (the sacred "enclosure of gold") in Cuzco indicate that it was an important place in Early Inca times as well (John Rowe, pers. comm.). But even without the documents and historical descriptions, the archaeological evidence should also point to Cuzco as having been the Inka capital. The large size of the site, and the concentration of Inka styles of architecture and artifacts there and in the surrounding region, would distinguish it from any other Inka site. Unlike most Inka sites, Cuzco is not an intrusive, foreign site.

According to Inka oral tradition, the Inka expansion began after their defeat of the Chanka. During the rule of Wiraqocha, the eighth Inka, Cuzco was attacked by the Chanka, the traditional enemies of the Inka, who lived in a region to the northwest of Cuzco. Together with their allies, the Kichwa, the Inka fought a desperate battle to prevent a Chanka victory. Feeling all was lost, Wiraqocha and his heir, Urqon, fled the city and took refuge elsewhere. Another son of Wiraqocha, Yupanki, rallied the troops, and was able to definitively defeat the Chanka. With this great victory he had himself crowned ruler of the Inka, and took on the name Pachakuti, which means revolutionary or cataclysmic change.

Archaeological data from elsewhere in the central highlands indicate that the Late Intermediate period was a time of much warfare. Large hilltop fortresses are characteristic settlements in many parts of the highlands at this time. The data suggest that politically much of the highland population was organized at the level of complexity of chiefdoms and complex chiefdoms, and that there was much fighting among the various groups. The warfare between the Inka and Chanka seems typical of the general pattern of the time.

The Inka, however, went beyond defeating their traditional enemies, and continued to conquer and take over other groups.

The Expansion

The sequence of Inka conquests is known to us from the Spanish documents, and although there is some discrepancy in detail, the general outlines of the conquests are relatively clear. After defeating the Chanka, Pachakuti conquered the regions to the north and west of Cuzco, as far as Vilcas Guamán, and then regions to the southeast, to the altiplano. He sent Qhapaq Yupanki, probably a close blood relative, to conquer some regions farther to the north, but Qhapaq Yupanki had the misfortune to disobey orders and was summarily executed. Pachakuti continued to conquer (and reconquer, in some cases) groups in the sierra to the north and south of Cuzco. Soon his son, Thupa 'Inka, took over the task of extending the boundaries of the empire, but under Pachakuti's direction. Thupa 'Inka began the great expansion to the north, conquering up into Ecuador, and taking the Chimú state on the north coast of Peru. He continued back down the coast, eventually controlling the remainder of it.

At this point, Pachakuti stepped down, and Thupa 'Inka was crowned emperor. He then continued the expansion, this time to the south to central Chile, highland Bolivia, and northwest Argentina. Besides being a brilliant military leader and diplomat, like his father, Thupa 'Inka apparently had the organizational genius of his father as well. Between the father and son, nearly the entire extent of the Inka empire was conquered and consolidated in the space of perhaps 55 years. According to Rowe's estimates, Pachakuti was crowned in 1438 and led the expansion until 1463, when Thupa 'Inka took over under his direction. Thupa 'Inka became emperor in 1471 and ruled until 1493 (Rowe 1946: 203).

After the death of Thupa 'Inka, his son Wayna Qhapaq was crowned emperor. Wayna Qhapaq continued the process of consolidating new territories into the imperial administrative system, and also expanded the empire somewhat to the north. Wayna Qhapaq died suddenly in about 1528, a victim of new infectious diseases introduced by European invaders. The Inka expansion effectively ended with the death of Wayna Qhapaq. For the next four years the empire was wracked by a civil war between two of his sons, Waskar and 'Ataw Wallpa, each vying to become emperor. At about the time the civil war ended, Francisco Pizarro arrived in Cajamarca and put an end to the Inka empire.

The sequence of Inka conquests occurred so quickly that, using archaeological data alone, the expansion would seem to have been virtually instantaneous. No changes in artifact style can be used to distinguish between earlier and later Inka conquests. And radiocarbon dating is barely precise enough to distinguish events that took place within the same half millennium; events taking place within a single century simply could not be distinguished temporally from one another using this method. So, we are very fortunate in the Inka case to have the evidence of the documents to indicate the sequence, and the speed, of the Inka expansion.

The Inka conquests did not proceed in an orderly, linear fashion. Expansion went in one direction, then in the opposite direction. Thupa 'Inka's big push to the north skipped over less important areas, areas that were added to the empire later. The coast of Peru was conquered from north to south, rather than the expected order. And some groups, notably in the area around Lake Titicaca, needed subduing more than once.

While the military aspects of the Inka expansion are heavily stressed in historical accounts, it is evident that military solutions were not necessarily the rule. Certainly the armies were marched up and down the length of the empire, but time and again the historic documents indicate that particular groups submitted without a battle. The army seems to have been used most often in the case of more complex groups, such as those in the Titicaca Basin (Qolla, Lupaqa), or the Wankas of the central highlands. Likewise, military action was clearly important in the conquest of the Chimú state (Pease 1982). In any case, those groups organized at the level of complex chiefdoms or states provided sufficient (and repeated) threat to Inka rule such that military force was necessary in their subjugation. Other groups, such as those on the central and south coast, and in the south central highlands, did not seem to require military action. These groups were mostly organized at the level of a simple chiefdom.

In the next section some of the various strategies used by the Inka to consolidate their control over the diverse regions they conquered are discussed. The Inka were not only establishing political control over new regions, they were organizing local groups to provide labor to produce all manner of goods and services for the empire. The Inka were conquering people and resources that were economically useful. As Murra puts it, "[t]he major changes that followed incorporation into Tawantinsuyu had more to do with economics than politics" (1982:238).

THE INKA OCCUPATION OF THE PROVINCES

It is abundantly clear that the Inka revised their consolidation strategies depending on the conditions they encountered in each region (Menzel 1959; Morris 1972, 1982; Pease 1982). In some regions are found huge Inka centers, with thousands of storehouses. In other regions there is barely a potsherd, but documentary sources indicate that those regions were in fact incorporated into the empire.

The Inka mosaic of control becomes especially apparent when we compare the Inka occupations of a variety of regions. Because the central Andean region forms the geographic backdrop of later discussions of the Wari polity of the Middle Horizon, this section focuses on Inka strategies of control in the coast and central highlands of Peru (Fig. 2.3). Were we to consider strategies employed in the more distant portions of the empire, the variability in the Inka responses to diverse situations would be even greater. But even in just the central Andes, a wide variety of Inka strategies of control can be seen.

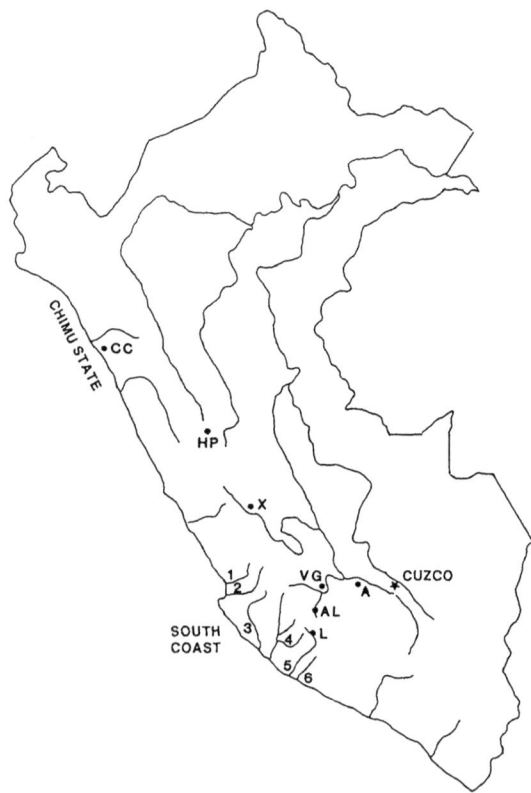

Figure 2.3. Map of Peru indicating areas of Inka occupation discussed in the text. On the south coast, the numbered river valleys are as follows: **1.** Chincha; **2.** Pisco; **3.** Ica; **4.** Nasca; **5.** Acarí; **6.** Yauca. The highland occupations are: **AL.** Andamarca Lucanas; **L.** Lucanas; **VG.** Vilcas Guamán. In the Río Pampas region, **A.** Abancay; **X.** Xauxa. In Wanka Wamaní, **HP.** Huánuco Pampa; **CC.** Chan Chan.

The South Coast

The first major analysis of differences in Inka occupations was that of Menzel (1959; 1977) who looked at variations in the Inka occupation of valleys on the south coast of Peru. She looked at archaeological remains as well as documents, and concluded that the Inka used different strategies of control in different valleys, depending in large measure on the level of political organization extant in each valley:

> The Incas took advantage of native centralization where it existed, constructing their own administrative headquarters in the native capital; elsewhere they established a new center, sometimes...taking advantage of an abandoned site which had dominated the valley in much earlier times. [Menzel 1959:129]

Both the Chincha and Ica valleys show evidence of some political centralization prior to the Inka conquest. In Chincha, a complex of Inka buildings is found in the local center, suggesting to Menzel that the Inka took over the local administration (see also Menzel and Rowe 1967:67-68). This valley was apparently organized at a level sufficiently complex for Inka purposes, but the uppermost level of control was removed and replaced with Inka administrators. In Ica, in contrast, only a single Inka building is found in the local center. This might indicate a situation in which local levels of control were sufficient for Inka purposes, and perhaps only an Inka overseer was imposed, leaving the local ruling elites in power.

But why the slight difference in the two cases, if each was organized at basically the same level? First of all, although both the Chincha and the Inka denied this in their own accounts of the conquest, neighbors of the Chincha said that the Chincha at first resisted Inka control (Menzel 1959:126). And second, the Chincha controlled resources, especially silver, useful to the Inka (Menzel and Rowe 1967:68). So for two reasons, potential threat, and useful economic resources, the Inka invested more in Chincha than they did in Ica.

The other valleys of the south coast showed no evidence of centralization, and in each is found an Inka site not associated with contemporaneous local occupation. In Pisco two Inka centers are found, suggesting to Menzel that this region was ruled as two administrative units, although I suspect the fact that one of the major Inka roads passed down this valley accounts more for the presence of multiple Inka sites. Likewise, in Nasca (actually seven small river valleys), two Inka centers are found, suggesting that the region was divided into two separate provinces, a northern one centered in the Ingenio Valley, and a southern one centered in the Nasca Valley.

My own survey work in Nasca suggests fairly high population in the Nasca Valley proper, but only one town significantly larger than other settlements. This situation may represent a society organized at the level of a simple chiefdom, insufficient for Inka purposes. In this case an additional administrative level was added over and above the local system to integrate the province into the imperial administrative system. If the adjacent valleys were organized at the same level, it makes sense that the Inka combined several valleys together to form a single province. The Inka administrative site (today called Paredones) in the Nasca valley has recently been subject to excavation by a Peruvian team, and some of the finest Inka stonework known on the coast of Peru has been exposed. Clearly, the Inka site in the Nasca valley was in some way special. I suspect that its strategic location at the junction of the coast road and a connector road into the sierra may have added to its importance.

The final two valleys, Acarí and Yauca, probably had very low populations relative to the other valleys, yet still we find an Inka facility in each valley. Both sites are called *tampu*, indicating that they may have been way stations along the Inka road. This may entirely account for their presence, although, despite low population, there may have been economic resources worth exploiting in those valleys as well.

In none of these cases do we yet have settlement pattern data to help verify the level of political organization in each valley prior to Inka occupation. But it is apparent, based on available data, that Inka strategies varied depending on local circumstances.

Andamarca Lucanas

In contrast we may look to the nearby highlands to a valley in which settlement pattern data are relatively complete. The Carhuarazo Valley was home to an ethnic group known as the Andamarca Lucanas, and the valley formed a separate province within the Inka empire. This valley will be discussed in much greater detail in the chapters that treat the Middle Horizon, but here it is relevant to point out aspects of the Inka occupation. An archaeological survey was undertaken in this valley with the specific goal of understanding both the Wari and Inka occupations (Schreiber 1987a).

At the time of the Inka conquest of the region there were four large towns in the valley, two in the central core of the valley, and one in each of two tributary valleys. Survey in the valley core indicates that each town was surrounded by several smaller villages. There is no evidence of political centralization of the entire region under a single center. Rather, the society present at the time of the Inka conquest appears to have comprised four small polities organized at the level of a simple chiefdom.

During the Inka occupation, no major changes were made in settlement location, but one of the towns was designated the capital of the province. An Inka road passes through the valley, and there is a small Inka way station associated with it. There is one Inka building in the capital town, and a second small Inka structure nearby. The only other Inka remains in the valley are a suspension bridge, and two small storage centers.

It appears in this case that the Inka created an additional level in the local hierarchy of control by manipulating the local system, by elevating one local ruler to a higher administrative position. Further, historic documents (Monzón 1881b:207) state that a single Inka, a member of the royal family, was located in the province. I suggest that this resident Inka was placed in the provincial center to supervise local elites who remained in power, and were elevated to positions of control over the entire province. His presence and association with those elites added legitimacy to their new status as rulers of more than just their own polity. The Inka was on hand to receive orders from Cuzco, and to supervise local operations, but he was not single-handedly directly ruling the province. If the Inka were directly ruling the province with their own people, certainly more than just a single individual would have been required. And the archaeological data and the documentary evidence are in accord in suggesting that the Inka presence was minimal.

Lucanas

The situation of the Andamarca Lucanas may be contrasted with their near relatives, the Lucanas. No systematic archaeological investigation has yet been undertaken in the territory of the Lucanas. No major Inka sites have been reported to me, or seen by me, in my numerous visits to this region. Zuidema (pers. comm.) reports having seen some Inca stonework in a cave near Lucanas, perhaps a small Inka shrine. In any case, historic documents indicate that the Inka investment in this province was even less than that of the Andamarca Lucanas. According to information collected in 1586 (Monzón 1881c), prior to the establishment of Inka control, there were a series of local rulers, three of whom are mentioned by name. This province was significantly larger, and contained many more villages and towns than the province of Andamarca Lucanas, and population was certainly quite a bit higher. It is also likely that the political organization of this region was more complex than that of the Andamarca Lucanas. When the Inka took control of the region, they designated a local leader, named Guáncar Illa, to rule in the name of the Inka.[1] It is also written that the Inka combined two *parcialidades*, Hanan Lucanas and Lurin Lucanas (upper and lower ayllus), into a single unit, Hatun Lucanas (Monzón 1881c:179).

In sum, the Lucanas were organized at a level nearly sufficient for Inka purposes. The Inka made only a slight change in organization, and they designated a single local leader to rule in their name. They did not rule this province directly. The Lucanas were fully consolidated into the empire, however; they paid tribute by serving as litter bearers to the Inka emperor (Monzon 1881c:188).

The Occupation of the Río Pampas Valley

The Río Pampas valley, in what is today the heart of Ayacucho, provides an interesting example of what may be a uniquely Inka strategy: the nearly complete removal of a local population, and their replacement by groups from various parts of the empire.

There is little archaeological evidence of pre-Inka political organization in the Río Pampas. From historic records we know that the people that lived in this valley were called Tanquihuas; in 1586 only four villages remained that were of this original ethnic group (Carabajal 1881:168). The Inka apparently removed each of the existing villages and towns, and moved the residents to other parts of the empire as *mitmaq* settlements. In turn, new groups were moved into the valley. In fact, even today the villages maintain oral traditions identifying the Inka emperor that moved them into the valley (Billie Jean Isbell, pers. comm.). By the time the Inka empire collapsed, this valley was a multiethnic, multilinguistic unit of unrelated groups of people.

What happened here that caused the Inka to take such drastic action? This is difficult to answer based on current data, but a few possibilities can be suggested. It may be that this region was one of complex political organization, and/or that it presented a direct threat to Inka control. Rather than try to establish control over the existing society, it was deemed preferable to entirely dismantle the society, disperse it to other regions, and establish an entirely new ethnic mix. This must have been a rather costly strategy to implement.

There is a major Inka center in this region, Vilcas Guamán, that served as the provincial capital. It was regarded by the Inka as the geographic center of their empire. Cieza de León reported that this was affirmed by Spanish travelers, who found it was the same distance, in travel time, to Quito in the north and to Chile in the south (Cieza de León 1984:252). Vilcas Guamán is also known for its finely built *usnu* platform. An *usnu* was probably a shrine of sorts, involving a sacred object, sometimes a pointed stone, sitting on top of a flat platform. The term *usnu* seems to refer both to the object, and to the platform (John Rowe, pers. comm.). Sometimes the platform had several levels; the one at Vilcas Guamán has four levels.

It is apparent that the Inka went to great effort to effect a total reorganization of the Río Pampas valley, and went so far as to remove most of the local population. The reasons for this are unclear. Little archaeological work has been carried out in the region, and no systematic surveys have been undertaken that can provide data on pre-Inka political centralization. The establishment of a major Inka center at Vilcas Guamán may have been in part for strategic reasons. The site lies along the main highland road, at the intersection of at least one, and possibly two, connector roads to the coast.

The Inka Occupation of Abancay

Abancay presents an interesting case in which the Inka controlled an important resource zone, but one that was largely unoccupied. A large tract of land was in Inka hands, and groups of *mitmaq* were moved in to farm these lands (Espinosa Soriano 1973). The assumption has been made (ibid.) that local residents were moved out of the region to make way for the newly imposed groups, but the documents make no direct mention of this. It seems reasonable to suppose either that the region was not occupied at the time of the Inka incursion, or that native population was very low, thus explaining the need to move laborers into the region. In any case, population was inadequate for Inka purposes, but the area was important because of the resources there. Therefore, the Inka established a production enclave to produce coca, ají and cotton in this zone (La Lone and La Lone 1987:51-53).

The Inka Occupation of Wanka Wamaní

For a case contrasting with those already described, we look farther to the north in the central highlands, in what is today the Department of Junín. At the time of the Inka incursion this region was occupied by a large ethnic group collectively called the Wankas. These were divided into three subgroups (*saya*): Ananwanka, Lurinwanka, and Hatunxauxa (D'Altroy 1987:80). Prior to Inka conquest, the Wanka were a series of hierarchically organized polities. The hierarchical settlement pattern was dominated by a series of large towns with houses numbering in the thousands. Sites were fortified and located on high defensible knolls (Earle et al. 1987:1). The evidence indicates that these competing polities can best be described as complex chiefdoms (D'Altroy 1987:81-86). Warfare was endemic to the region prior to Inka conquest, with ever-shifting alliances between the various small polities. As D'Altroy has shown, the Inka occupation of this province was one of relatively direct control, but that also integrated local elites into the ruling superstructure (D'Altroy 1981).

Certainly the Wanka were a threat to Inka control. They were populous, organized, and well skilled in military matters. The Inka strategy of consolidation of Wanka territory involved three processes. First, the local population was reorganized and settlements moved away from high defensive locations and down into the more productive valley bottom land. This had two important effects: the population was no longer in a strategic position with regard to military action, and agricultural production could be intensified. The second Inka step was to establish a major administrative center—one of the largest in the empire—at Xauxa. Unfortunately, this site is poorly preserved, and has not been the focus of intensive archaeological investigation, so this aspect of the Inka occupation is not yet documented archaeologically. The third Inka strategy was to include local elites in the political superstructure. This had the effect of leaving local leaders with some power and autonomy, but at the same time keeping them firmly under Inka control.

In sum, at the time of the Inka incursion, the Wankas were organized at a level of complexity conducive to Inka control, but they were perhaps too much of a threat for the Inka to leave the system intact. In this case the

Inka added an additional level of control—another level above that of the complex chiefdom—creating an administrative structure with three levels: two local, one Inka. This province lay along the major route to the north, to areas of active conquest, and some of the largest provinces in the empire, so it had paramount strategic importance to the Inka. Thus, local matters could not be left to chance, especially when the local group was not only organized, but hostile as well. (And there is evidence that the Inka fears were justified. The Wankas seem to have cooperated with the Inka during the occupation, but they were the first major group to side with the Spanish against the Inka.) Direct Inka control was imposed; and this was certainly one of the more costly Inka occupations in the empire.

Recent archaeological investigations by members of the Upper Mantaro Archaeological Research Project (UMARP), directed by Timothy Earle and his associates, have provided detailed data regarding the effects of Inka conquest on a local economic system. This body of data will be discussed in greater detail below.

The Inka Occupation of Huánuco

The case of Huánuco provides another scenario for Inka control. The site of Huánuco Pampa (Morris and Thompson 1985), one of the largest Inka centers, was built far from any centers of local population, and, indeed, far from regions of agricultural production. The site is located on the high plateau, at an elevation of 3,800 meters—suitable for limited potato cultivation, but better suited for camelid herding.

In this case it is apparent that the location was important, more so than the presence of people. Located along the main Chinchaysuyu trunk line (much like Xauxa farther to the south), this was a location of great strategic importance; location of the center in the populated valleys would have necessitated a major detour of the Inka road (Morris and Thompson 1985:57). Major centers were needed every so often along the road, not just as provincial capitals, but also as places to garrison the army. And as Morris (1972) has demonstrated, the population of this center was largely transient *mita* laborers brought in to pay their labor service to the state for several months at a time.

The site was provisioned by produce brought in from the Marañon and Huallaga valleys. Although those valleys were populous, and the local Chupaychu society probably organized at the level of complex chiefdoms, the Inka chose to locate their center some distance away. Like the situation in Wanka territory, the Inka were probably grafting on an additional level of control, due to the strategic importance of the location. Unlike the Wanka case, there is less evidence for Inka manipulation of local political structures. Perhaps the Chupaychu presented a less hostile attitude toward the Inka. In any case it appears that in Huánuco the empire did not go to the people, it brought the people, and the fruits of their labor, to the empire.

The Inka Conquest of the Chimú State

Finally, the Inka takeover of the Chimú state provides us with the only example of Inka conquest of another group that was undoubtedly organized at the level of a state, and perhaps was an empire in its own right. According to documents describing the Inka conquests, the north coast was conquered by Thupa 'Inka after his sweep northward through the highlands to Quito. He invaded the north coast from the north, along their least-protected border (Rowe 1946:207). This account is reinforced by that of the Anonymous History of Trujillo (reported in Rowe 1948), which states that the Chimú state was conquered by Thupa 'Inka Yupanki, during the reign of the local ruler, Minchanzaman. It is said in this document that the Inka killed many Indians, and did great damage in the valley of Chimor (Moche Valley). Military force was clearly used in subduing the Chimú state (Pease 1982:186-88).

Apparently, the Inka strategy on the north coast was to dismantle over time the overarching pre-Inka Chimú organization, and reduce the state to its component parts, each ruled separately. But at the level of these components, that is, each individual valley, local elites were allowed to stay in power, and the system was left largely intact. Again, the best data come from the Anonymous History. The first thing the Inka did was to remove Minchanzaman, and send him to Cuzco; he was replaced by his son, Chumun-caur, who ruled under Inka direction. He was succeeded by his son, who in turn was succeeded by his son.

> [I]n his time the towns of the above-mentioned coast were already divided in feudal holdings because as sons multiplied partitions were made between them to give each town its ruler with the consent and blessing of the Inka to whom they were subject. [Rowe 1948: footnote 2]

From this account it appears that the Inka let the system fragment into its component parts, each of which came to be ruled by a local elite who in turn owed allegiance to the Inka. By the time of the Spanish invasion, Chanchan, the old Chimú capital, was apparently abandoned.

Archaeologically, the evidence of Inka control of the north coast is minimal. It seems that the Inka may have established their own administrative center at the site of Chiquitoy Viejo, in the Chicama Valley. Conrad (1977) suggests that this site was established to supervise commerce along the coast road. It may also have served to provide an Inka presence in order to supervise the local puppet ruler left in place. In any case, despite the fact that the Chimú presented the greatest threat to Inka control, owing to their high level of political complexity, there is no evidence of direct Inka control. Rather, the archaeological data support the ethnohistoric record in indicating that Inka rule was very indirect, and carried out mostly through local elites. (It is possible that, if we were to rely purely on archaeological evidence, we might be tempted to suggest that the Inka never conquered the north coast, and that the collapse of the Chimú state was not the direct result of Inka conquest.)

Conrad (1977:17) suggests that the lack of Inka remains on the north coast is due to the fact that little fieldwork has been oriented toward the study of the Inka occupation in that region. I suspect that while this may be true, it is also true that we do not expect to find much evidence of Inka control—at least in terms of the presence of major sites and high quantities of imperial artifacts—given the rather indirect nature of Inka rule of the region. In archaeological terms, the collapse of the Chimú state, the collapse of centralized control from Chanchan, not the presence of Inka sites, is the best evidence of Inka conquest. Further, the Chimú example supports the suggestion that in some cases of imperial conquest of complex societies, we might expect less imperial presence in areas of greater political complexity, than in areas of lesser complexity.

The Inka Mosaic of Control

It should be clear at this point that Inka strategies of consolidation differed from place to place, and that one factor determining Inka strategy was the complexity of local political organization. Other factors seem to be strategic location along the road system, potential local threat to Inka control, and economic potential of the region. The Inka presence is greater in areas lacking sufficient political organization, particularly in areas organized at less than the level of a complex chiefdom. We see a range from minimal Inka investment in Hatun Lucanas, where local organization was adequate for Inka purposes, and where rule was entirely indirect, to valleys like Nasca, where direct control had to be imposed. In between we find a broad range of strategies: elevating local elites to a new higher level and supervising them, as in the case of Andamarca Lucanas; or, leaving the local system alone but supervising it, as in the case of Ica; or, finding local organization sufficiently complex, but taking over the upper level, as in the case of Chincha.

But we also see a greater-than-expected Inka occupation in such places as Junín and Huánuco. In Junín, the Wankas were organized at a level sufficiently complex, but they occupied a strategic location, and were a military threat to the Inka. So in this case, the Inka invested more heavily than might otherwise be expected, building a major administrative center, and creating an additional level of control over the extant system. And in the case of Huánuco Pampa, we see perhaps the most extreme example of the creation of an administration system: a center was needed, probably for strategic reason, in an area devoid of any significant population. Not only did the system have to be built from nothing, the people had to be imported as well. In a somewhat analogous situation, we consider the Inka occupation of Abancay. Here, as at Huánuco Pampa, people did not live in sufficient numbers, so they had to be imported. But here, unlike the Huánuco Pampa example, the reason was strictly economic: Abancay was a valuable resource zone whose exploitation was desired by the Inka.

The case of the Chimú provides us with our only clear example of the Inka conquest of a complex state. In this case, the level of existing organization was perhaps more than desirable. And, as we might expect, the Inka gradually let this system fall back to a lower, less centralized level, with each sector ruled separately.

And the case of the Río Pampas provides us with a situation that may be uniquely Inka: the entire dispersal of a local population and their replacement with groups from elsewhere in the empire. This certainly goes well beyond the expectations of simply establishing imperial control, and may be the result of unique symbolic or historical factors.

Imperial Infrastructure

The imperial infrastructure is a direct product of this mosaic of different levels of control. The distribution of administrative centers and other facilities throughout the empire enables us not only to see the Inka presence, but also which areas were of strategic or economic importance, and which areas required great effort by the Inka in order to create the administrative system. We do not see any size hierarchy of Inka administrative centers that directly represents levels of political hierarchy, however. For example, there is not one major center, larger than all of the rest, in each quarter of the empire. Rather, the largest centers are arranged along the road, especially along the highland road north of Cuzco, rather than being distributed spatially around the imperial capital. The size of the center has more to do with local needs and communications networks, than position in an imperial control hierarchy.

The Inka road system (Strube Erdmann 1963; Hyslop 1984) deserves special mention. A system of royal roads linked Cuzco with all parts of the empire, and especially with the chain of regional centers. There were two main roads, a highland trunk road that followed the Andean cordillera north through Ecuador, and south through Bolivia. A second major trunk line ran down the coast. The two roads were linked by a series of connector roads, running between the coast and the highlands. The Inka certainly did not build all the royal roads (an impossible engineering feat given the short duration of the empire), but rather made use of existing roads in many cases. What they did do was pave the roads, build bridges, and establish rest houses and small storage centers for state travelers and *chaski*, the runners who carried messages between imperial centers.

As discussed in the preceding chapter, roads are critical for empires. Not only must there be well-maintained routes for military purposes, but there must be communications systems that can bring information from various parts of the realm in the minimum of time. And certainly, the movement of tribute through the empire is made more efficient with a well-developed system of roads. The Inka were no exception in this regard.

Other administrative activities required means of keeping records, especially of economic matters. In the Inka case, such records were kept on the *quipu*, a series of knotted strings. These served as mnemonic devices for the *quipucamayoc*, those trained in their use and the keepers of the records. There was also created a special class of retainers, called *yana* (plural: *yanakuna*). Separated from their local support networks, based on kinship ties, they were supported by the state (Rowe 1982). Sometimes they have been regarded as slaves, but they might probably be better considered a newly created class of lower-level bureaucrats. The Inka nobility was hardly numerous enough to fill all administrative posts from within its own ranks, so the formation of this class of retainers served to supply many of the lower-level positions not entrusted to local elites.

In sum, when looking at Inka imperialism from a broad regional perspective, not only did imperial strategies differ from region to region, but the archaeological evidence of imperial control varies as well. In fact, archaeological evidence can actually be quite meager, even in important areas known to have been conquered. Inka imperial occupations did not always occasion the construction of major centers, nor did they disrupt all aspects of local traditions.

Economic Control under the Inka

Up to this point emphasis has been placed on Inka political control, the means by which the Inka established their control over the people in the empire. While the Inka expansion may have begun for political reasons, they quickly turned their concern to the economic reorganization and control of new territories. The expansion of political control necessitated the economic reorganization of conquered territories, as imperial motivations became increasingly economic in nature. The Inka devoted a good deal of effort to the exploitation of resources, and the acquisition of material goods.

A great deal of attention has been paid to Inka economic institutions, and the work of John Murra (1980) stands out especially in this area. These important analyses will not be repeated here, except in summary fashion, as they pertain to Inka imperialism.

The Inka were very concerned with economic control. The Inka manipulated nearly every aspect of the economic organization of the regions they conquered. As Murra has pointed out, the Inka did not collect tribute in kind, but rather required labor service of every adult, male or female, in the empire. This is an important distinction, and one that points out one of the most unique aspects of the Inka, in the face of general considerations of imperialism. The Inka acquired the goods and resources they wanted, but they did so not by directly collecting tribute in kind, but by collecting the labor of the people to make those goods.

The Inka labor tax was called *mita*, which simply means "rotation." Each married adult in the empire served the empire by providing their labor for a specified period, or by completing a specified task. In many situations, laborers were supported by the state—fed and clothed—while performing this service. At the local level, the typical tribute requirement involved working state lands, and producing textiles. When the Inka conquered a region they divided the lands into three parts: one for the *ayllu* (the local people), one for the Sun, and one for the Inka. This parallels the preexisting system of land tenure, and does not represent an Inka invention. Traditionally, lands were held communally, by *ayllu*, and people were given usufruct rights according to their need. In addition, certain lands were set aside as the lands of the local *huaca*, and were used to support the local cult. Other lands were set aside for the *curaca*, the local ruler. The lands of the *huaca* and the lands of the *curaca* were worked by the people, in addition to their own lands. The Inka simply revised this system and elevated it to the level of the state. In this case the local *huaca* and *curaca* sometimes kept some lands, but the lands of the Sun and of the Inka were to be worked by the people, and the products of those lands used to support the Inka religion, and Inka public works, respectively.

We can see that the Inka also followed traditional practices in the giving of gifts and hospitality to *mita* workers. As the workers served the state, so too did the Inka, literally, serve the workers. Workers were given food, drink, and clothing during their tenure of state service. This evokes the traditional patterns of reciprocity, and village-level rituals of solidarity (Morris 1982).

Women were largely responsible for textile production, and the state provided all the raw materials for the production of cloth. Again, what was required was just the labor to produce the cloth, not the cloth itself. In addition to agriculture and textile production, typical *mita* requirements might require men to serve for several months a year doing public works, mostly construction and repair of buildings and roads; other *mita* might require service in the army for a more extended period of time. There were other special *mita* that were required of some regions, where the people had some special skill useful to the Inka. For example, the Andamarca Lucanas of the Carhuarazo Valley served as the litter bearers of the Inka, because, it was said, of their very even pace. The Soras, reputed to be fast runners, provided *chaski* to carry messages through the empire. It is said that those groups that provided these special services were exempt from normal *mita* services, although archaeological data from the Carhuarazo Valley suggest that other forms of service were provided as well.

There is a tremendous amount of documentary information that treats the Inka economy. It part it received such great attention because the Spanish were interested in extracting as much as possible from the conquered populations. But in part, the Inka too were supremely concerned with things economic. The fact that they invested heavily in areas with important resources, such as Abancay or Chincha, indicates very clearly an economic focus on particular resource zones.

Archaeological Evidence of Economic Control

While ethnohistoric analyses have given us the best general overview of the Inka economy, the best archaeological evidence of the effects of Inka economic policies on a local group comes from the Upper Mantaro Valley. Earle and his associates have been able to document major changes in the local economy caused by the imposition of Inka control over the Wanka ethnic group. They found that while the local domestic economy went basically unchanged during the Inka occupation, there were major changes in the local prestige economy.

In terms of patterns of consumption, prior to the Inka incursion local elites were involved in serving large quantities of food, probably hosting ceremonial feasts. Local elite residences also yielded evidence of storage by the presence of large storage jars. Under Inka domination this pattern changed. Elites were serving less, and local storage jars decreased in proportion to new Inka aryballoid forms. Further, the construction of large numbers of *qollqa* in the region indicates that "the state may have assumed some of the functions previously met by local storage, such as buffering against poor harvests" (Earle et al. 1987:101).

But even under Inka domination, local elites continued to maintain their privileged access to preferred goods and foods. This offers archaeological support for the interpretations that they were integrated into the Inka power structure.

The Inka were interested in the production of maize, and this is evident in the data from the Upper Mantaro. The shift in settlement locations to areas of maize production indicates this change in focus quite clearly. Hastorf has shown that maize formed a greater part of the local diet during the Inka period, and, interestingly, that men were consuming more maize than women (Hastorf 1983). She suggests that the latter situation may be due to the fact that men were performing labor service to the Inka, and being fed maize products (perhaps largely in the form of *chicha*) by the state.

Incorporation into the Inka empire also affected local production, especially specialized production for exchange. The state may have been directly involved in the manufacture and distribution of valuable objects (especially metal products). In terms of exchange, most exchange was between local regions, both prior to and during the Inka occupation, with elites having preferential access to certain exchanged goods. This indicates that some aspects of local economic organization went largely unchanged (Earle et al. 1987:102-3). However, there is an apparent change in the distribution of certain exchanged wealth items, especially shell and metal, that indicates state intervention. The presence of imported shell items indicates the new participation of the local political economy in the larger exchange system established by the Inka. And the state was apparently controlling the import and export of metals, both raw materials and finished products. As is pointed out in Earle et al. (1987:103):

> It is hardly coincidental that the commodities most affected by the conquest were wealth goods involved in the political economy; in fact, this is precisely where state intervention should be most noticeable.

In sum, the Inka did not interfere significantly in the local domestic economy, leaving it largely unchanged. They did, however, increase local production (and consumption) of maize. The major effects of the Inka conquest are seen in the local prestige economy, where patterns of consumption, production, and exchange were significantly altered.

Inka Ideological Control

The Inka empire was also characterized by an ideology that served to maintain Inka political and economic control. The Inka certainly used religion to promote their cause, and they likewise manipulated traditional symbols of power to reinforce their own political and economic control. The Inka created among the conquered peoples the notion that Inka control was right, that it was appropriate, that it was deserved.

The Inka left local religions intact, but added a specific set of beliefs, particularly the worship of Inti, the sun, to the local system. In many ways this is analogous to their imposition of political control, a system based upon and grafted onto local traditional systems. Local huacas, sacred objects, were sent to Cuzco (as were the sons of local rulers). But in any case, Inka religion did not differ markedly from the local traditions, which regarded worship of the sun and moon as part of normal practice; so the system was not an alien one.

In addition, the Inka emperor was said to be the son of the Sun, and hence had divine right to rule. The Inka marriage structure was also in some ways equated with religious symbols: as the Sun was married to his sister, the Moon, so the Inka emperor's primary wife was supposed to be his full-blooded sister.

The creations of Pachakuti are also interesting. He elevated the creator god, Viracocha, to a higher position, supreme over the Sun and Moon. He put Viracocha in charge of the universe, much as he, himself, was in charge of the empire. There is some question as to the actual origin of this god (Demarest 1981), but it seems that Pachakuti enhanced the cult of a god who was in many ways the spiritual manifestation of himself. So, in many ways, Inka religion manifested the same patterns as Inka political structures. Religion was an important means through which Inka rule was legitimized.

While the Inka expansion involved establishing political and economic control over conquered territory and people, ideological means were also used to help maintain this control. Part of their success in expanding and imposing economic and political control throughout Tawantinsuyu was certainly due to their success in convincing the people (and themselves) that this was absolutely justified.

Summary

The Inka successfully established political and economic control over a vast region, stretching from the northern Andes of Ecuador, to central Chile and northwest Argentina to the south. They expanded rapidly from the core polity located in and around Cuzco, and within two generations created the largest empire ever to exist in the prehispanic New World. The descriptions of the Inka empire recorded in the documents of the sixteenth century, along with archaeological research, provide an unmatched set of data. We have no such detailed records of any other Andean polity. This chapter has outlined the history of the Inka empire, and focused most attention on the variety of Inka responses and strategies of control in the central Andean region. In many ways, the Inka empire is like other empires, occurring at other times, and in other parts of the world.

Yet there are also unique aspects of Inka imperialism that set it apart from other forms of imperialism. The Inka did not collect tribute in kind, but required labor service from all able adults. This is not unique in the Andes (Moseley 1975b), but it is a trait that is not generally seen in non-Andean empires.

It has been said that Andean polities are generally unique because of their discontinuous territoriality, and that this is actually the result of "ecological complementarity." Attempts to interpret Inka political organization in light of notions of "ecological complementarity" may have obscured the issue, not clarified it. The basic highland subsistence adaptation leads to a situation of discontinuous exploitation of vertically arranged ecological zones. Political expansion in the case of empires also results in what appears to be discontinuous territoriality, and this is commonly the case in empires. But this discontinuity of political control—the mosaic of strategies of control—is not the same as ecological complementarity.

The notion of ecological complementarity is useful in interpreting the Inka case in two ways. First, it may be true that the distribution of Inka control is even more discontinuous than we might expect, as a result of their subsistence adaptation, although it is not clear at all that this is the case. Second, it is possible that the adaptation to the vertical ecology gave the Inka, as well as other highland cultures, a qualitative advantage over other groups, especially those on the coast. That is, perhaps highland cultures were in some way preadapted to establishing political control over far-flung and diverse regions, given their long tradition of discontinuous control over ecological zones.

Highland cultures on several occasions exerted control over coastal cultures, but the reverse never seems to have occurred. In the Late Horizon, the Inka conquered the coast, but not even the powerful Chimú ever controlled the sierra. And this is not a pattern seen for the first time in the fifteenth century A.D. As we will see in the case of the Middle Horizon, highland centers influenced (or perhaps even conquered) coastal regions, but not the reverse. Even in the case of the Early Horizon, we see a highland center exerting influence over the coast, rather than the reverse. So there seems to be some significant difference between coastal and highland polities, and I suspect that the adaptation to the vertical ecology may be the key to this difference.

The resulting mosaic of different levels of political control, ranging from very indirect to entirely imposed and direct, is documented in the archaeological record. In some areas more visible remains of the imperial occupation are to be expected; in other areas the evidence may be minimal. There is no one set of expected evidence that can be relied upon in all regions to define an imperial presence. Ideally we need data from not only imperial centers (the usual focus of study), but also the data of regional settlement patterns, and excavation of local sites. Changes in local cultures may tell us a great deal about imperial control, even where such control was relatively indirect.

NOTE

1. "...y que en esta tierra y repartimiento obedecían a un curaca que el Inga señaló que se llamaba Guáncar Illa, y a éste obedecían y éste estaba puesto por el Inga, y lo que él mandaba en nombre del Inga obedecían todos los de esta provincia..." [Monzón 1881c: 188]

3

The Problem of the Middle Horizon

Having seen the case of the Inka empire, and aspects of Andean imperialism, in this chapter we address the problem of the Middle Horizon. During this period of Andean prehistory we find an artistic style with a distinctive iconography widespread throughout the central Andes. But the nature of this distribution, the point(s) of origin, and the mechanism(s) of dispersal are matters of some dispute.

Studies of the Middle Horizon have generally followed two different approaches. The first approach involves the study of the artistic traditions of the period, the study of iconography. Designs carved in stone, woven or embroidered into cloth, and painted or incised on pottery are studied, and compared. Similarities among different styles are identified, and explanations are proposed in terms of some sort of cultural contact. Differences between different styles are also identified, and explanations are proposed in terms of temporal or cultural differences.

Ideally, when studying style, the artifacts should come from known proveniences, with good temporal associations. But unfortunately, this is not always the case. Sample sizes are often extremely small, and artifacts without known provenience can form a major portion of the database. Interpretations are sometimes offered as if the sample were complete, with little allowance made for the fact that many examples of a particular style are certainly unknown. And many unsubstantiated assumptions can underlie the interpretations of similarities and differences in styles. (For example, in the case of the Middle Horizon, the implicit assumption that Wari styles ultimately derived from Tiwanaku has colored many interpretations of Wari iconography.) Interpretations of iconography tend to stress religious organization and ceremonial aspects of culture.

The study of iconography has produced a relative chronology for the Middle Horizon that describes changes in art style, and can be used to document temporal changes in other aspects of culture. Such chronologies are critical to the documentation of the growth of political and economic subsystems in all the major prehistoric civilizations.

The second approach to the Middle Horizon is one that has proceeded in earnest only within the past few decades. This approach uses the study of architecture and settlement patterns to document and understand the nature of cultural events of the Middle Horizon. Like ceramics and iconography, similar styles of architecture can indicate connections between different regions. However, while ceramics are portable, and can be distributed in a variety of ways, architecture indicates more direct connections. Likewise, the study of regional settlement patterns can be used to interpret the nature of Middle Horizon political organization on a regional level, and to discern local changes associated with the spread of the horizon style. These data provide more direct evidence of political and economic changes at the local level, which can then provide an interpretive framework for explaining distributions of different styles.

In this chapter, emphasis is placed on the second approach: the study of archaeological sites, their architecture, and their distribution in space. My interest is in understanding political complexity in the Middle Horizon. Settlement pattern data provide a less ambiguous set of data than do studies of iconography in trying to reconstruct political and economic change. However, this would not be possible without the chronological foundation provided by those researchers who have studied the iconography for so many years.

TIWANAKU AND THE DEFINITION OF THE MIDDLE HORIZON

While the focus of this study is the understanding of the nature of the Wari culture of the central Andes, it will be useful to include some brief discussion of the site of Tiwanaku, and its role in the definition of the Middle Horizon. Wari and Tiwanaku share certain aspects of their iconography, and are largely contemporaneous cultures. While it appears that Wari was the center of dispersal of the Middle Horizon styles of the central Andes, Tiwanaku was the center of dispersal of the Middle Horizon styles of the southern Andes (Fig. 3.1). For many decades the two cultures were confused, and this confusion still colors many interpretations of the events of the Middle Horizon.

Tiwanaku is a large urban settlement located on the altiplano at the south end of Lake Titicaca (Posnansky 1945; Ponce 1969, 1971, 1972; Parsons 1968; Kolata 1983). Interpretations of Tiwanaku, like those of Wari, have run from its being an influential religious center, to the capital of a conquest empire (Browman 1978, 1980, 1985). These issues will be discussed in greater detail below. For present purposes, the stylistic confusion between Tiwanaku and Wari is the issue of concern.

The site of Tiwanaku is known primarily for the monumental architecture and elaborate stone carvings found there. Perhaps its most famous monument is the so-called Gate of the Sun. This is a single (now broken)

Figure 3.1. Map of Peru showing locations of Wari, Tiwanaku, and places named in the text. The dotted line indicates the approximate boundary of the distribution of Wari-style ceramics.

slab of andesitic basalt that has a detailed series of mythical creatures carved across the top, above the doorway cut in the stone. Central to the scene is a large anthropomorphic figure wearing a belted tunic, and an elaborate headdress with numerous appendages. The figure stands with its arms out to the sides, and in each hand it holds a staff; it is generally referred to as the Staff Deity. The figure stands on a small stepped platform. On either side of the central figure are three parallel rows of winged creatures, some anthropomorphic with wings, others with the heads of birds, but still with anthropomorphic bodies. These are referred to as *profile attendants*. Below the main design is a series of disembodied heads, of the same sort as the head of the Staff Deity, all wearing the headdress with rayed appendages.

The site of Tiwanaku was well known to the Inka, who attributed their own origin to the region of Lake Titicaca, in some versions of their origin myth. The site may have functioned as a pilgrimage center during the Late Horizon. Likewise, the site was well known to early Spanish invaders; in fact Tiwanaku was one of the first sites known and reported in the entire Andean region. The Spanish were very impressed, as were later travelers, such as Squier, whose (exaggerated) etchings of the Gate of the Sun were published in the nineteenth century (Squier 1877:288-89). It is therefore not surprising that when materials were located in various places throughout the Andes, with depictions of this Staff Deity and the profile attendants, that the origin was attributed to Tiwanaku. This current still runs strong in interpretations of the Middle Horizon.

But very quickly, some important variations were noted, and different forms of the horizon style were defined. Working at Pachacamac around the turn of the century, Max Uhle uncovered artifacts depicting these icons in a style that had already been identified a few decades earlier at Ancón by Reiss and Stübel (1880-1887). But Uhle had recently worked at Tiwanaku (Stübel and Uhle 1892), and was quick to recognize that although the remains from Pachacamac were similar to styles there, they also differed in some significant ways. He called the Pachacamac style "Coast Tiahuanaco," to distinguish it from the southern highland form of the style (Uhle 1903).

Uhle undertook excavations in many different valleys on the coast of Peru, and sent the collections of pottery to California, where they now reside at the Lowie Museum of Anthropology, at Berkeley. These collections were studied by Kroeber and his associates, who confirmed the presence of the "Coast Tiahuanaco" horizon style in nearly every valley, and suggested the name Middle Period to refer to this time (Kroeber 1930). They also confirmed the fact that this style differed significantly from the Tiwanaku styles of the altiplano, as discussed in more detail below. However, it was still assumed by many that Tiwanaku was in some way the source of the coastal versions of the horizon style. Kroeber warned against such thinking in the absence of adequate data:

> The reason we tend to see ... other elements as Tiahuanacoid is that Tiahuanaco is well defined and well known, whereas the less focused and less specialized other highland elements are as yet very little known. [Kroeber 1944:106]

The first notice the English-speaking world had that a specific site had been identified that might be the highland point of origin of the coastal Peruvian styles, was a footnote in Bennett's (1946:129-30) summary of Andean archaeology in the *Handbook of South American Indians*. In his words,

> Many attempts have been made to explain the relationship of Highland and Coast Tiahuanaco, but none is completely satisfactory. One is that another site must exist somewhere between the Highlands and the Coast with materials which would account for the similarity. This is a good suggestion, but the hypothetical site has yet to be found.[2]
>
> [2]Recently, Dr. Tello has uncovered a site near Ayacucho which may well be the key to the problem.

The site referred to is Wari. In 1931, Julio C. Tello, accompanied by Toribio Mejía Xesspe and Lila M. O'Neale, had visited the site of Wari, and had discovered that this enormous urban site had an abundance of "Coast Tiahuanaco" artifacts on the surface. A small collection of sherds was taken back to Berkeley by O'Neale. Tello made some major excavations in the site, but never published any of the results of these excavations. (The locations of those excavations may be the two areas called "Canterón" at Wari. Each is a major excavated structure, surrounded by large mounds of excavated soil.) By 1939 Tello had realized the importance of the site and suggested that it played an important role in the dispersal of what he termed the "Wari culture," which included sites previously termed "Tiahuanacoid" on the coast and highlands (Tello 1942:682-84). This idea caught on quite quickly among Peruvian archaeologists, and in 1948 Larco Hoyle defined the horizon style appearing on the north coast as "Huari Norteño," suggesting that its means of dispersal was conquest from the Wari region (Larco 1948).

In 1946, John Rowe, Donald Collier and Gordon Willey visited Wari, and confirmed the earlier findings of Tello (Rowe, Collier and Willey 1950). They pointed out two critical attributes of Wari styles that further distinguished them from Tiwanaku, and helped eventually to establish Wari as the probable center of dispersal of the "Tiahuanacoid" styles. First, they noted that ceramics at Wari showed clear similarity to Coast Tiahuanaco styles, and that, to a lesser degree they also resembled Nasca styles (Rowe, Collier and Willey 1950:133). So Wari was clearly part of this "Tiahuanacoid" culture, related to but distinct from pure Tiwanaku styles.

And second, they provided the first description of the rather unique architecture at Wari, and noted its similarity to other sites they had seen that had this same odd style of architecture.

> When we saw the ruins of the La Capilla sector we were immediately reminded of two sites at opposite ends of Peru: Viracochapampa near Huamachuco and Pikillacta near Cuzco.... The similarities are: scarcity or absence of doors, windows and true niches, producing long stretches of blind walls; great height and tapering of the walls...; similar construction of fieldstones laid in mud; large size of the individual enclosures or "buildings"; use of "cornices" of projecting stones and rows of holes suggesting beam sockets; and absence of gables and rooftie pegs. [Rowe, Collier and Willey 1950:123]

This style of architecture not only provides a connection between Wari and other sites in the Peruvian Andes, it also further distinguishes Wari from Tiwanaku.

In 1950 Wendell Bennett conducted test excavations at Wari, digging a series of small stratigraphic soundings. He published a map of the site, showing little detail and only covering part of the site, but indicating its great size and complexity, nonetheless (Bennett 1953). He also recovered a great quantity of ceramics, and illustrated and described these remains in print. Unfortunately, Bennett's interpretation of the site chronology was exactly the reverse of the correct sequence. He dug fifteen pits, most of which were in disturbed deposits or areas without stratigraphic superposition of temporally significant styles. In only one of his test pits, Pit 4, did he find a stratigraphic sequence in the correct order. Because it differed so markedly from the evidence of the other pits, he could only attribute this sequence to reverse stratigraphy (Bennett 1953:33). Subsequent work by Lumbreras (1960) served to correct the sequence.

Soon thereafter, Dorothy Menzel undertook the most comprehensive study of Wari ceramics yet accomplished (Menzel 1964). She worked with existing collections, such as the Uhle collections at Berkeley, and Bennett's collections at Yale, as well as with published literature (e.g., Uhle 1903), and new collections made by herself and Rowe. Following the work of Rowe in establishing a master sequence of ceramic chronology based on the Ica Valley, she put together a detailed chronological sequence of Middle Horizon ceramics (Table 3.1), and described several distinct Wari (local and regional) styles for each epoch. Her chronology (Menzel 1964, 1968, 1977) still forms the basis of most chronological interpretations of Wari materials.

Following this chronology, the Middle Horizon is divided into four epochs (Middle Horizon 1-4), the first two of which are subdivided into two phases each (Middle Horizon 1A and 1B, Middle Horizon 2A and 2B).

TABLE 3.1
The Middle Horizon Relative Chronologies of Menzel and MacNeish,
with Pottery Styles Pertaining to Each Epoch or Phase in Ayacucho

Menzel 1964, 1968	MacNeish 1981
Middle Horizon 3-4 (A.D. 800-1000)	Huamanga phase (A.D. 900-1200)
Middle Horizon 2A-2B (A.D. 700-800)	Wari phase (A.D. 700-900)
Viñaque Black Decorated C	Viñaque Wari Robles Moqo
Middle Horizon 1A-1B (A.D. 600-700)	Ocros phase (A.D. 200-700)
Conchopata Chakipampa Ocros Robles Moqo Black Decorated A, B	Conchopata Chakipampa Ocros Acuchimay Ayacucho Cruz Pata
Early Intermediate period (200 B.C.-A.D. 600)	Huarpa phase (200 B.C.-A.D. 200)
Huarpa	Huarpa Caja Kumen Senqa

Middle Horizon 1A is defined by the appearance in Ica of stylistic influence from Ayacucho. During Middle Horizon epoch 1, the Chakipampa style is widespread in the highlands, and the Nasca 9 style is widespread on the south coast. Other styles include Ocros, Black Decorated, and Robles Moqo. An important offering was found in 1942 at the site of Conchopata, near Wari, and gives its name to another epoch 1 style. This offering has iconography similar in some respects to that of Tiwanaku, including depictions of several versions of the Staff Deity, and profile attendants. But for the most part, Wari ceramics of Middle Horizon 1, especially the Chakipampa style, are local Ayacucho developments, with close connections to the earlier Huarpa and Nasca styles. Working with materials excavated from a 2 by 2 m stratigraphic column at Wari, Pat Knobloch was able to confirm much of Menzel's epoch 1 chronology with stratigraphic associations (Knobloch 1983).

The great expansion of the Wari styles outside the Ayacucho region seems to have taken place in Middle Horizon 1B, when the Chakipampa B style is found widespread through the highlands, from Cuzco to Cajamarca. The large architectural complexes associated with Wari were probably built at this time as well: Pikillaqta, Viracochapampa, Wari Willka, Jincamocco, Honco Pampa, and others. A major offering deposit was also dated to MH 1B, the Pacheco offering from Nasca, with Robles Moqo–style ceramics. Because of the notable mythical component in the iconography depicted on MH 1 ceramics, especially in MH 1A, Menzel attributed the initial spread of the style to proselytizing missionaries of a religious cult (Menzel 1964:67).

In Middle Horizon 2, the religious iconography of Middle Horizon 1 continues, but in more abbreviated form. The Viñaque style is dominant in the sierra, while the related Atarco style is found on the south coast. On the central coast a Wari-related style emerged with a distinctive local iconography. The major ceremonial center at Pachacamac was founded, and this site gives its name to the ceramic style of the central coast. The similarity to Wari styles indicates a strong connection with Wari, but the differences in the Pachacamac style have been interpreted as indicating perhaps a greater degree of political independence of the central coast (Menzel 1964: 71).

According to Menzel, there was more reliance on secular themes in Middle Horizon epoch 2, suggesting that this signals a crisis in, and reorganization of, the Wari culture, and a focus on more secular pursuits (Menzel 1964:69-70; 1968:91-92). I hesitate to impute political changes from changes in pottery design, but other data suggest an increased distribution of Wari materials throughout the highlands at this time, and an increase in the number of sites with architecture similar to that at Wari.

Middle Horizon 3 signals the collapse of Wari, and an end to the spread of Ayacucho ceramic styles into the Ica Valley; together with Middle Horizon 4, Menzel suggests that this was a "Great Depression" that followed the Wari collapse (Menzel 1964:72).

Returning to the issue of connections between Wari and Tiwanaku, there is a clear distinction between the distribution of Wari styles, and the distribution of Tiwanaku styles. Although the two cultures shared certain aspects of iconography (Cook 1985), there are important stylistic differences between the respective depictions, and they are expressed in largely different media. The primary examples of Tiwanaku iconography are expressed in stone sculpture. In the case of Wari, such stone carving is unknown, and the iconography is expressed in an entirely different medium: ceramics. (Both cultures may have used the medium of textiles as well; this is clearly true for Wari.) Tiwanaku iconography was expressed in a nonportable medium; to see it, one had to go to the center. Wari iconography, on the other hand, was expressed in portable media; it could be transported long distances and seen by people who would never go to the center. The iconography of Tiwanaku also contrasts with that of Wari in that it is closely associated with medicinal (or drug-related) paraphernalia: snuff tablets, bone tubes, and so forth. These artifacts are unknown in the Wari sphere, and this aspect of Tiwanaku culture further distinguishes it from the Wari culture.

The best definition of the limits of the respective cultures is based on the distribution of ceramic styles. Wari and Tiwanaku ceramics are clearly distinguished on the basis of style, and their distributions are easily separated. Tiwanaku artifacts are found on the altiplano of Peru and Bolivia, the extreme southern highlands and coast of Peru, and northern Chile and northwest Argentina. Wari ceramics are found in fairly continuous distribution as far south as Sicuani in the sierra, and the Sihuas Valley on the coast (Lumbreras 1974:165). (There is an isolated site with Wari ceramics, Cerro Baul, located much farther to the south; this will be discussed in greater detail below.) In the north, Wari styles are found distributed through Cajamarca, in the sierra, and possibly to Lambayeque on the far north coast.

Despite the temptation to see Wari materials as derivative from the better-known Tiwanaku, it is useful at this point to regard them as separate entities. As Kroeber said, "[w]e should beware of making [Tiwanaku] stand for more than it actually represents, merely because it is convenient" (1944:106). For present purposes, discussions in this and the following chapters pertain to Wari materials and their interpretation. The issue of Tiwanaku and its relation to Wari will be treated later.

THE WARI HEARTLAND

The Site of Wari

The site of Wari is located in the central highlands of Peru, in the general environmental zone I have called the puna sierra. It was first reported in 1548 by Pedro de Cieza de León in his general description of the region around Guamanga (the old name of Ayacucho).

> The major river of the region is named Vinaque, where there are some large and very ancient constructions, and it is certain, given that they are worn and ruined, that many ages have passed by them. Asking the neighboring Indians who built that ancient place, they respond that it was other people, bearded and white like us, who came a long time before the Inkas ruled them, and they say that they came to these parts and made there their residence. And regarding this and other ancient constructions that there are in this realm, it seems to me that they are not of the same tradition as those things that the Inkas built, or ordered built, because this construction was square, and those of the Inkas long and narrow. And there is a tale that there was discovered writing on a stone slab of this construction. This neither confirms nor disproves anything, but in my opinion there arrived here in ancient times some people of great skill and reason, and that they built these things and others that we do not see. [Cieza de León 1984 (1553):249 (f. 114)][1]

In a later chapter, he compares the ruins of Wari with those of Tiwanaku, noting that both are very large sites, and both built long before the Inka period.

> For this reason, and because they report having seen on the island of Titicaca bearded men, and the construction of Vinaque having been made by similar people, I venture to say that it could have been that before the Inkas ruled, there must have been another people of wisdom in these realms, who came from some unknown place, who made these things, and they being few and the natives being many, they must have died in the wars. [Cieza de León 1984 (1553):284 (ff. 129-30)][2]

Cieza was not connecting the two sites because of any similarities in iconography or precise date, but simply because they were large and impressive, and predated the Inka empire. The legends of white, bearded men probably need not be taken too seriously. But he was astute in pointing out that the Inka were not the first to build a great civilization.

At the time of Cieza's visit, the ruins of Wari lay along the major Inka highland road, the road along which Cieza was traveling and recording what he saw. However, in the ensuing decades, the Colonial road was established in a new location, and travelers no longer passed near the site. In essence, the site was lost, and dropped from public view until the 1880s and 1890s, when the Sociedad Geográfica de Lima and local students took an interest in the site (Lumbreras 1981:167). But the first scientific reports of the site were forthcoming after Tello's investigation in the 1930s.

The site, as known today, is immense. The architectural core of the site, comprising diagnostic rectilinear compound–style architecture, measures some 200 hectares. Around this core is an area of dense surface scatter; including this scatter, the site covers perhaps as much as 300 hectares (Isbell et al. 1985). Since Tello's and Bennett's times, a number of excavations have been carried out in the site. In the 1960s, as part of the Ayacucho Botanical Project, under the direction of Richard MacNeish, sections of the site were excavated by MacNeish, Gary Vescelius, and Luis Lumbreras. Unfortunately, none of the results have been published in any detail.

In 1974 a new road was built through the site, providing direct and easy access, and new excavations were undertaken in areas along the new road in the ensuing years. In 1977 Mario Benavides excavated an area of small chambers made of large slabs of cut stone. He suggests that these were tombs (an interpretation supported by indirect evidence from the Carhuarazo Valley), but that they were looted long ago. He found them empty (Benavides 1985).

Additional excavations were undertaken nearby that same year by Abelardo Sandoval, and by Sandoval and Francisco Solano in a sector where a subterranean gallery, made of cut stone slabs, was excavated. Enrique Bragayrac excavated what he terms the Templo Mayor in 1982 (Bragayrac 1985).

From 1977 to 1981 William Isbell directed the Wari Urban Prehistory Project, and undertook extensive excavations in the Moraduchayoc sector, between the Peruvian excavations of the cut stone tombs and the subterranean gallery (Isbell 1987, 1988; Isbell et al. 1985; Brewster-Wray 1983; Spickard 1983). Part of his reason for selecting this sector, besides ease of access, was to demonstrate the benefits of excavating in sectors that did not have apparent unique monumental constructions. Isbell's excavations in this sector, along with those of Christine Brewster-Wray (1983, 1989), have exposed major sections of typical Wari-style architecture. This architecture, of the same odd style described by Rowe, Collier and Willey in 1950, is primarily open square patios, flanked on all sides by long narrow rooms, termed galleries. These "patio groups" form regular subdivisions or cells of larger rectangular compounds. This is the same form of architecture seen at various sites throughout the highlands of Peru, from Cuzco to Cajamarca.

But, unlike the provincial manifestations of this style, at Wari the architecture comprises more than discrete free-standing rectangular compounds. At Wari most of the interstitial areas have been filled in, and much of this architecture, although conforming to the same basic plan, is arranged according to the terrain. So the overall plan of architecture at Wari is one of discrete compounds following an internally consistent grid, with similar forms of architecture filling the interstices, following independent grids.

In the patio groups of Moraduchayoc the galleries were multistoried; two stories were preserved. The patios were ringed with low benches, and doors provided access between patio and gallery, and between patio groups. Remains in the patio groups indicated largely domestic activities, and some storage; no evidence was found of any major degree of ceremonial or religious function. The construction of this typical Wari architecture is dated on the basis of ceramic associations to Middle Horizon 1B, and it was probably occupied until the end of Middle Horizon 2.

Besides exposing the typical patio-group architecture at Moraduchayoc, deeper excavations revealed a feature entirely unique and unexpected. At a depth of nearly five meters below the surface was found a floor of cut and fitted stone blocks. Further investigation revealed a carefully planned and constructed feature, 24.11 m on a side, with cut stone floor and perimeter walls. Given the rough finish of the exterior of the perimeter walls it seems likely that the structure was semisubterranean. It is also apparent that the structure was carefully and intentionally dismantled. Clean sterile strata filled the floor, with the occasional cut stone block thrown in. What remained of the perimeter walls in some places formed the base of the foundations of the walls of the typical patio-group architecture above; the later patio groups follow the same grid plan as the earlier structure. Isbell has interpreted the cut stone structure as a semisubterranean temple (Isbell 1985, 1987, 1988).

Cut stone construction of this sort is unknown in the Ayacucho region, except much later in Inka times. The only other place that exhibits this form of construction at roughly the same time is Tiwanaku. The dating of the temple at Wari is problematic. Because of the sterile fill, no primary deposits remain to suggest a date of use or construction. Only six fragments of painted pottery were located in the fill outside the perimeter walls, and five of these are tentatively dated to Middle Horizon 1A. A single radiocarbon sample, on charcoal dispersed in this fill, is thought to date to the period of the construction of the temple. This sample was dated to A.D. 580 ± 60; calibrated to a 95 percent confidence level, this date falls between A.D. 560 and 770 (Isbell 1985:107-8). A second sample comprising small bits of charcoal found in fill above the cut stone floor was dated to A.D. 720 ± 60; calibrated to a 95 percent confidence level, it falls between A.D. 660 and 676 (Isbell 1985:108-9).

Making the best of the available data, Isbell (1988:181-82; Isbell et al. 1985) assigns a date of Middle Horizon 1A to the temple, and suggests, like Menzel, that there was a greater emphasis on religion early in the Middle Horizon. It is clear that this portion of Wari served a very different function at a time prior to the construction of the patio groups, that is, prior to Middle Horizon 1B. It is also reasonably clear that the temple was dismantled at about the same time the later patio groups were built, given that the old walls form the foundations of the newer ones, and that the later structures follow exactly the same grid plan as the earlier temple. So, regardless of the date of construction of the cut stone temple, which may significantly predate Middle Horizon 1B, it appears that its use continued up until Middle Horizon 1B when the patio groups were built. In other words, it probably was in use during Middle Horizon 1A, and possibly earlier as well.

Wari as the Center of Dispersal of the Horizon Style

As discussed above, Wari and Tiwanaku materials are distinguished both in terms of style and in terms of geographic distribution. Although both cultures pertain to the Middle Horizon, they have separate and discrete spatial distributions. Within the central Andes of Peru, the site of Wari is one of the largest sites occupied at that time. It is covered with many hectares of a distinctive style of architecture, the greatest concentration of this architectural style anywhere in the Andes. It is also characterized by the greatest concentration of the diagnostic horizon-style ceramics of any site in the central Andes. There seems little doubt now, more than fifty years after Tello pointed out the great importance of the site, that Wari was the center of dispersal of the Wari horizon style.

The distinctive Wari styles of ceramics are an intrusive, foreign presence everywhere they are found, except in the Wari heartland. Although the styles represent a new combination of traits, some borrowed from Nasca, others from the altiplano, there is a time depth to Wari ceramics in Ayacucho that indicates a strong element of local development. There is a direct connection between the Huarpa ceramics of the preceding Early Intermediate period, and the Chakipampa styles of Middle Horizon 1 (Menzel 1964).

Architecture is another story. The distinctive Wari architecture, the multistoried rectangular compounds comprising open patios flanked by long narrow galleries, has no direct antecedents in Ayacucho. Throughout much of the central highlands, typical architecture at the time was round in form. Data from Ñawinpukyo, a major Huarpa site in the Ayacucho Basin, suggest that irregular rectilinear architecture was present in Ayacucho in the Early Intermediate period, although it may have been limited to public buildings (Lumbreras 1981:182-84). In any case, the distinctive, rigidly planned, Wari architectural style appears almost as intrusive in Ayacucho, as it does elsewhere. I suspect that the Wari elites, much like the later Inka, found a style they liked, and modified it for their own purposes. The most direct similarities are seen in architecture of the north highlands, especially the Callejón de Huaylas and Huamachuco, an issue that will be taken up below.

The Regional Context of Wari

Over the years, numerous sites in the Ayacucho region have been reported, and various small surveys have been accomplished, especially by Luis Lumbreras and his associates, in the late 1950s and 1960s. The most extensive survey of the region was undertaken by the Ayacucho-Huanta Archaeological-Botanical Project, directed by Richard S. MacNeish, between 1969 and 1971. This project was devoted primarily to the earlier preceramic periods, with special emphasis on cave sites. However, many ceramic period sites were located as well. At present, only short descriptions and summary settlement pattern maps have been published for these ceramic periods (MacNeish 1981), and their interpretation is somewhat difficult at this time. However, since these are the most complete data, and were presumably recorded in a consistent and systematic manner, I shall rely primarily on these data here. In addition to these summary data, Mario Benavides has published a monograph that includes short descriptions of many of the sites in the region (Benavides 1976).

I suggest two productive avenues of inquiry: First, we need to define the limits of the Wari heartland, especially just prior to the time Wari styles erupted out into the hinterland. And second, we need to look at the distribution of settlements before and during the Middle Horizon, to see if we can detect evidence of changing political organization correlated with the expansion of the Wari horizon styles.

Defining the Wari Heartland

Prior to the emergence of the distinctive Middle Horizon Wari styles, there was a clearly defined ceramic style that characterized the region. The Early Intermediate period Huarpa style (Benavides 1971; Knobloch 1976) is largely a local development, with some input of design motifs and techniques from the south coast, especially Nasca 7. Huarpa ceramics are usually bichromes, black on a white slip, and sometimes (in its later phases) trichromes, black and red designs on a white slip. The designs are usually geometric: straight lines, wavy lines, stripes, and so forth. More representational designs are derived from Nasca, and provide a direct connection with the later Chakipampa style.

The distribution of the Huarpa style probably gives us the best approximation of the pre-expansion Wari heartland. Huarpa ceramics are found throughout the eastern portion of the drainage of the Cachi tributary of the middle Mantaro River (Fig. 3.2). The Ayacucho Valley is located along the Río Watata, which flows north to join the Río Cachi. At this point the Río Cachi forms the border between the Departments of Ayacucho and Huancavelica. All systematic archaeological survey has been carried on the eastern side of this border. The Cachi flows north, joining the Río Mantaro at a major bend in that river. Unfortunately, we have no survey data from the Huancavelica side of the Cachi drainage, so we do not know the western boundaries of the Huarpa style. But in Ayacucho, the distribution of Huarpa ceramics corresponds rather closely to the hydrographic unit formed by the Cachi drainage, at elevations below about 4,000 meters, an area of roughly 750 square kilometers. It is not unlikely that the Huarpa style is likewise distributed in the western half of the Cachi hydrographic unit.

The Río Pampas Valley across the divide in the Apurimac drainage, is sometimes included in the Wari heartland (e.g., Anders 1986:42). However, although Isbell (pers. comm.) reports having seen Huarpa sherds there, it does not appear that the Huarpa style was predominant, and hence this valley was probably not participating in the same sphere of in-

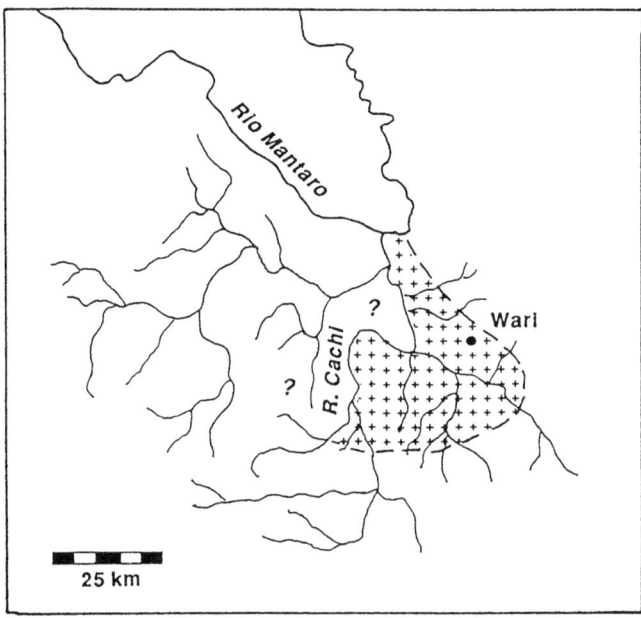

Figure 3.2. The Cachi hydrographic unit; the shaded area indicates the distribution of known Huarpa sites in the Ayacucho Basin. The distribution of Huarpa sites to the west of the Río Cachi is unknown at present. The distribution of Huarpa sites indicates the boundaries of the pre-expansion Wari core area.

teraction as the Cachi drainage. And certainly the lack of any major Middle Horizon Wari sites in the Pampas Valley, at least as presently known, indicates that it was not part of the core polity at any time.

In sum, at present the best estimate of the boundaries of the pre-expansion Wari core is that it conforms to the Cachi river hydrographic unit, certainly the Ayacucho portion, and perhaps the Huancavelica portion as well. This is the area of distribution of Huarpa ceramics, the style that immediately preceded the Wari horizon.

Evidence of Changing Political Organization

Perhaps the best evidence of changing political organization is the changes seen in settlement patterns in a region. The transition from simple egalitarian societies to small polities organized at the level of a chiefdom, to more centralized forms of control and state level organizations, can be detected in part by looking at the locations of sites of different sizes and types, and the apparent hierarchy of site sizes (Wright and Johnson 1975). We do not yet have complete settlement pattern data from the Cachi basin, but the results of the Ayacucho-Huanta Archaeological Botanical Project give us the best available approximation.

In 1978, Isbell and I presented some evidence suggesting that between the Early Intermediate period and the Middle Horizon, there developed a hierarchy of sites in the Cachi basin, indicating to us that by the Middle Horizon, Wari had attained the level of organization termed a state (Isbell and Schreiber 1978). We based this interpretation on the data published by Benavides (1976), as well as field observations made by Isbell. Here I shall use the data published by MacNeish, with some minor revisions, to reconstruct once again these changes in settlement patterns, and show the current evidence for the development of state level society in the Cachi basin (cf. Isbell 1985).

First a word about chronology. The periods in question are what MacNeish calls the Huarpa, Ocros, and Wari phases, and they are defined on the basis of ceramic associations (Table 3.1). The Huarpa phase is characterized by the presence of Huarpa, Caja, and Kumen Senqa type ceramics. The Ocros phase is characterized by the presence of Cruz Pata, Ocros, Acuchimay, Conchopata, Chakipampa, and Ayacucho styles. The Wari phase is characterized by the presence of Wari, Robles Moqo, and Viñaque polychrome styles (MacNeish 1981:224). The ceramic chronology was implemented largely by Luis Lumbreras, who has done probably more work in northern Ayacucho than any other researcher. Thus, the Huarpa phase corresponds generally to the Early Intermediate period, Ocros to Middle Horizon 1 (with perhaps slight overlap with the terminal part of the Early Intermediate period), and Wari to Middle Horizon 2 (with the possibility that some Robles Moqo material may be slightly earlier).

The absolute dates given by MacNeish for these phases are not precisely the same as general dates used by other researchers. For example, MacNeish's Huarpa phase ends in A.D. 200; most other researchers would put the end of the Early Intermediate period closer to A.D. 600. But while the issue of the absolute dating of the Middle Horizon will be taken up later, it is the relative dating that is of concern here.

MacNeish's survey did not cover the entire hydrographic unit, but, given the research goals of the project, most survey was concentrated in the eastern half of the region (MacNeish, Nelken-Turner, and García 1981:4-6). There are some minor problems with the published maps and tables, and occasionally the sites listed on the tables and depicted on the maps do not show an exact one-to-one correspondence. The environmental zones, while useful in interpreting ecological adaptations prior to the origins of agriculture, do not include divisions between agricultural production zones (see Anders 1986:50 for a map of the agricultural production zones). Thus, it is difficult to see changes in site location that may be correlated with changes in agricultural production. And the very abbreviated data presented do not include absolute site sizes, nor types of architecture present on each site. These data are yet forthcoming in future publications. With these caveats aside, let us turn to the data.

For this summary I am concerned with evidence of political organization, and especially site size hierarchies. Hence I do not include seasonally occupied microband or macroband camps in this summary; nor do I include nonhabitation sites such as terraces and irrigation features. What I do take into account are sites classed as hamlets, villages (of various types), towns (also of various types), and the one city. I assume the distinction between these classes was based on size.

The Huarpa phase of the Early Intermediate period was characterized by a broad regional distribution of sites, with no evidence of strong centralized control from any single site (Fig. 3.3). There were 6 towns, 20 villages, and 27 hamlets occupied during this phase. These may represent a series of small polities, perhaps organized at the level of a chiefdom or complex chiefdom.

Lumbreras's excavations at one of the towns, Ñawinpukyo, suggest to him that this site may have been the capital of a local Huarpa regional state, controlling the entire southern portion of the valley. He suggests that another city might have been located near Huanta in the northern part of the drainage, and may have been the capital of a corresponding northern polity Lumbreras 1981:183-84). Ñawinpukyo is characterized by both typical local architecture (irregular, circular to elliptical houses) as well as elite architecture (more rectilinear form, with large open patios, and distinctive stone masonry style), supporting the notion that this site forms a distinct settlement type. However, without comparable data from the other town sites, and comparison of their size with Ñawinpukyo, the existence of a Ñawinpukyo state remains a very tentative suggestion. I suggest that the overall settlement data indicate political organization no more complex than a series of complex chiefdoms during the Early Intermediate period.

This changed during the Ocros phase, or Middle Horizon 1 (Fig. 3.4). There was a shift in site location such that fewer sites were located in the north, along the lower Cachi River, and most settlements were located in the Pongor tributary valley. There was an increase in the number of towns (to 10), but a drop in the number of villages (to 8); hamlets stayed roughly the same (22). Inexplicably, MacNeish's scheme omits the site of Wari, classed as a village in the preceding phase. Wari certainly was the largest site in the region during the Ocros phase, forming a new settlement type: the city. The site size hierarchy in the environs of the new city included 9 towns, 6 villages, and 18 hamlets. Political organization in the valley would now seem to be at the level of a state, both by virtue of the

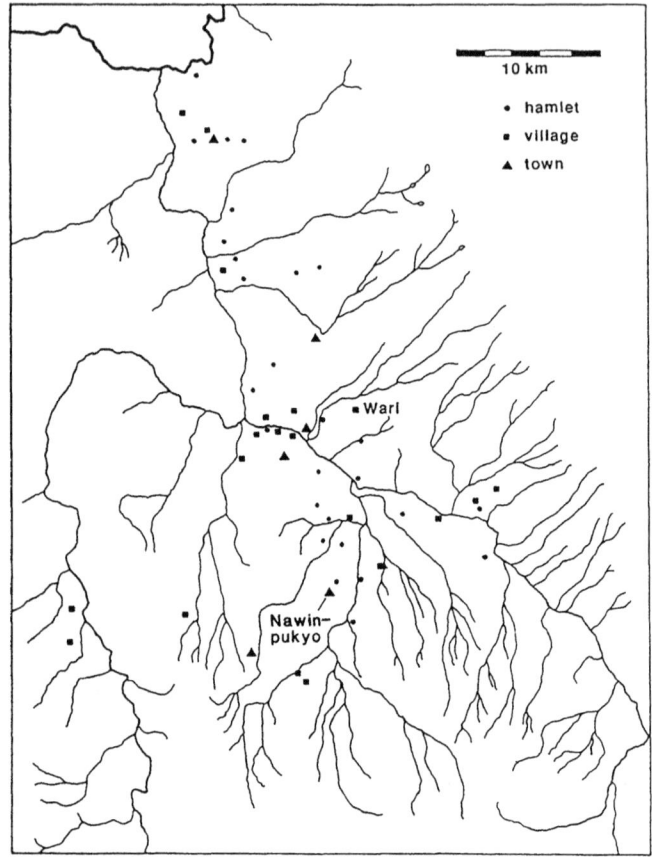

Figure 3.3. Map of the Ayacucho Basin showing the distribution of habitation sites occupied during the Huarpa Phase, Early Intermediate period.

growth of a major urban site, as well as the development of a (rather top-heavy) site size hierarchy with three levels above that of the minimum settlement.

A small cluster of sites (one town, one village, and three hamlets) remained in the north, nearer the Mantaro river, and was probably included within the Wari core polity. Another village and one hamlet lay in the upper Cachi valley, an area incompletely surveyed; the core polity prob-

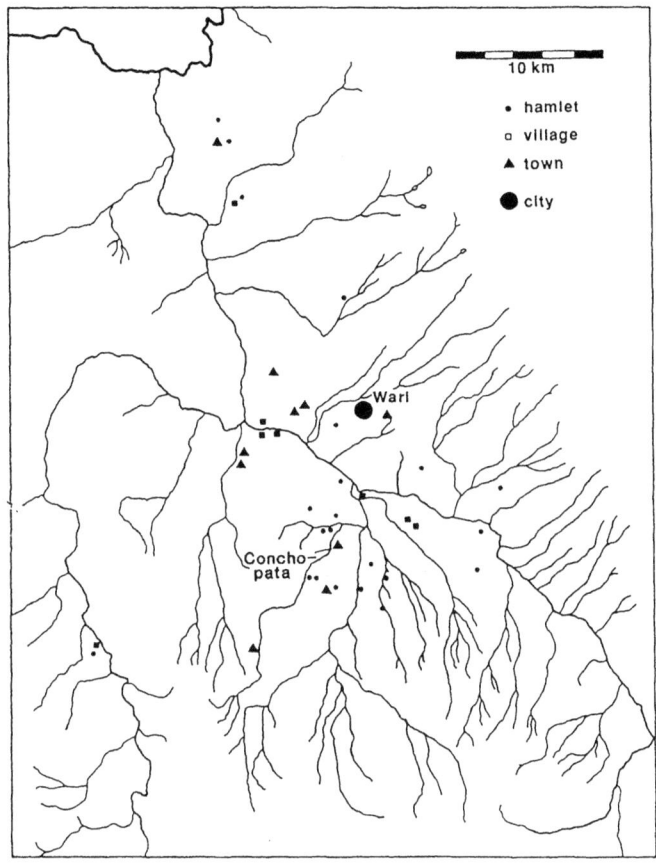

Figure 3.4. Map of the Ayacucho Basin indicating settlements occupied during the Ocros phase, Middle Horizon 1.

ably included this region as well. (And, as in the preceding period, we do not know the extent of the distribution of sites of this period into the Huancavelica portions of the Cachi drainage.)

A particularly important site during this period was the site of Conchopata, classed as an administrative town by MacNeish. Here two major offering deposits have been located: the 1942 Tello offering, dating to Middle Horizon 1A, and the 1977 offering, dating to Middle Horizon 1B. More will be said about these deposits below, in discussions of the Wari offering tradition. Unfortunately, a modern suburban housing project covers much of the original site of Conchopata, and the airport covers most of the remainder. But older air photos indicate traces of extensive architecture on the site.

In the following Wari phase, Wari grew even larger, and there appears to have been a depopulation of the hinterland (Fig. 3.5). The number of towns dropped to seven, and only two villages and eight hamlets were occupied. Apparently during this phase most population was concentrated in the capital city, and fewer people were living in the countryside.

In sum, with these changes in settlement pattern we see the emergence of state levels of organization centered around the site of Wari, during Middle Horizon 1, arising out of the chiefdom level society of the Early Intermediate period. During Middle Horizon 2, greater population was concentrated in the urban center, and the countryside experienced a degree of depopulation.

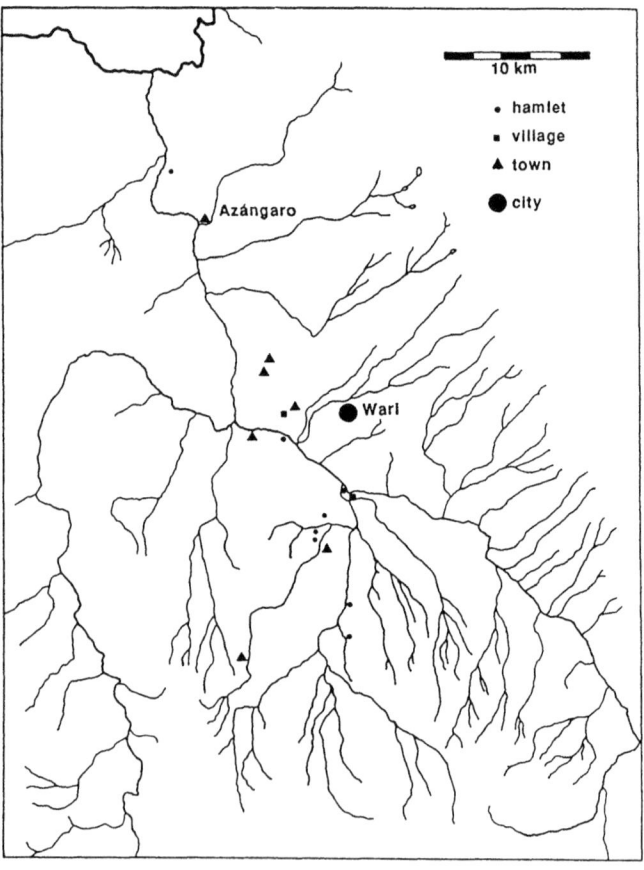

Figure 3.5. Map of the Ayacucho Basin indicating settlements occupied during the Wari phase, Middle Horizon 2.

One of the important pieces of data still lacking in this analysis is the evidence of architectural style, especially as it allows us to differentiate habitation from administrative buildings. The distinctive Wari style of rectangular compounds, subdivided into patio groups, emerged at Wari by MH 1B. Perhaps the best evidence of direct Wari connection with other sites is the presence of this architectural style at other sites, and the site-specific context of this architecture. For example, a large site that comprises a single major Wari compound may differ significantly in function from a large site that has numerous local non-elite–style buildings, plus a small Wari compound.

One site exhibiting predominantly Wari compound architecture is Azángaro. Situated in the northern part of the Cachi drainage, near the modern town of Huanta, this site has been excavated recently by Martha Anders (1986, 1989). She found that the site was built in Middle Horizon 2, and may have functioned in part as an effort by Wari to intensify agricultural production (Anders 1986:731-36). The location of the site in the low ecozone called *chaupi-yunga*, suggests an increased focus on exploitation of resources that could be grown there, but not at higher elevations, such as in the immediate environs of Wari. These products might include coca, chili peppers, and cotton, as well as several varieties of maize.

Azángaro comprises a large compound of typical Wari style, measuring 175 by 447 meters, divided into three major sectors. The northern sector is divided into numerous typical patio groups. The middle sector comprises long rows of small conjoined rooms. And the southern sector is a large open area within which are constructions of non-Wari style. The conjoined rooms are of special interest. Access to each row was restricted, and each room has a row of projecting corbels in the walls, about 80 cm above the ground surface. Anders argues that these were ritual habitations, and that the corbels supported very low ceilings. She suggests that they were occupied by mita workers; moreover, the number and arrangement of these rooms suggests to her that they represent an elaborate sidereal-lunar calendar (Anders 1986:812-906). This supports the association with intensified agricultural production, as scheduling is a critical factor in such production.

As interesting as this suggestion is, it seems more plausible that the conjoined rooms functioned as storehouses. Corbels around the perimeter of each structure, at a height of 80 cm, probably supported raised floors, rather than very low ceilings of habitations. The circulation of air under and through these floors provides better conditions for dry storage than storing produce directly on the ground surface. But this does not preclude the number and arrangement of the rooms from representing the calendar that Anders suggests.

Anders also defined an area that she interprets as non-Wari–style architecture, inside the Wari enclosure, that probably served as the homes of local rulers. She suggests that the local polity was ruled by dual chiefs, who in turn were integrated into the Wari political organization (Anders 1986:702-57, 1989).

Finally, we might also note the interesting changes in settlement patterns after the collapse of Wari, in the following Huamanga phase (Fig. 3.6). At that time the great urban capital was apparently abandoned. All that remained in the region were two towns, three villages, and seven hamlets. It is clear that the Wari polity had completely collapsed, and that

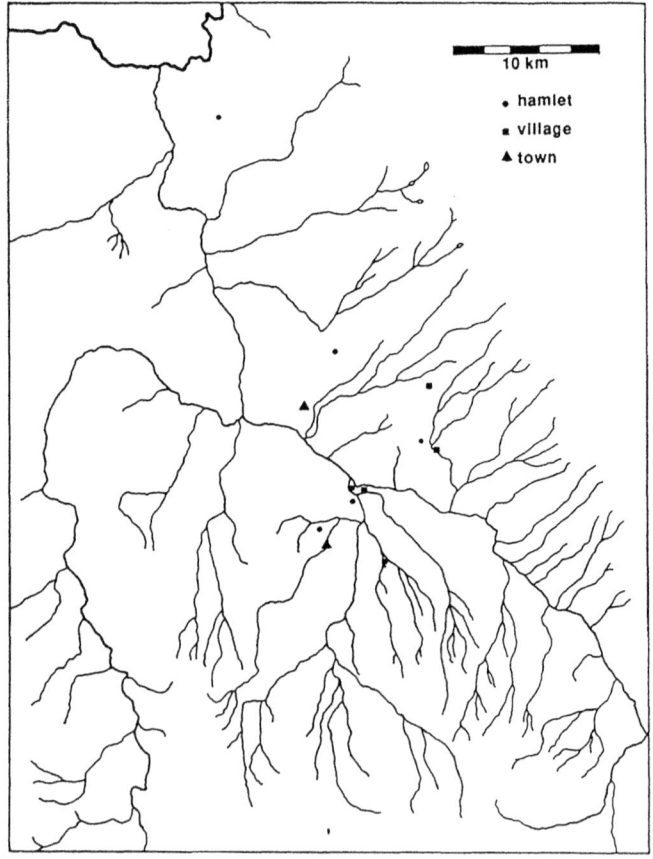

Figure 3.6. Map of the Ayacucho Basin indicating settlements occupied during the Huamanga phase, after the Wari collapse.

the valley experienced a major depopulation. The valley may have been characterized by three small polities at this time, two in the central part of the drainage, and one in the northern part of the drainage.

Wari in Spatial and Temporal Context

Wari was a major site that probably became a great city in Middle Horizon 1, the center of a core polity that was the point of origin for the Wari horizon styles found throughout the Peruvian Andes. The data from regions outside the Wari core region indicate that the expansion took place in Middle Horizon 1B. Current data from Ayacucho are not precise enough to indicate whether Wari was a state prior to this expansion (i.e., in Middle Horizon 1A), or whether the state was created at the time of the expansion (i.e., in Middle Horizon 1B). But the data do suggest that the Wari state emerged in Middle Horizon 1.

Before considering the situation in the provinces, a few words should be said about the cultural context in which the Ayacucho core operated late in the Early Intermediate period and at the beginning of the Middle Horizon. This was a time of cultural disruption in several parts of the Andean region. On the north coast, the Moche IV polity fragmented, and moved its domain northward. The southern portion of the Moche polity was abandoned by the Moche state, and a new capital established in the Lambayeque drainage, at the site of Pampa Grande.

On the south coast, the Nasca polity underwent some major changes in Nasca 5. The center at Cahuachi was abandoned (Silverman 1986, 1988), and a system of underground aqueducts was built (Schreiber and Lancho 1988). The ceramic styles of Nasca also changed radically, and Nasca 6 and 7 represent a major departure from the earlier tradition. As well, in Nasca 7, Nasca ceramics begin to show influence from other distant parts of the Andean region. Moche motifs, especially warriors, are depicted on Nasca 7 pots. Influence is seen from the Huarpa style of Ayacucho, and Nasca designs likewise were adopted by potters in Ayacucho. It appears that Nasca 7 was a period of interregional interaction between distant cultures, unlike anything that had come before. And it was at the close of this period, in Middle Horizon 1, that Wari emerged as a major state, and when the Wari horizon styles became distributed across much of the region.

Paulsen (1983) has suggested that the Nasca 8 site of Huaca del Loro, in the Nasca drainage, was a Wari colony—a colony significantly predating the Wari expansion. She bases this on what she sees as the distinctive style of architecture at the site, specifically a round stone building. Isbell (1988:90) has gone farther and suggested that this represents the earliest manifestation of a Wari vertical archipelago economy. I do not think that the data support these interpretations. Round stone buildings were the norm in the central highlands since probably the Early Horizon, so if they diffused to the coast they could have come from anywhere, not specifically Wari. Further, my own work in the Nasca region has shown that round houses were prevalent in the region since the beginning of the Early Intermediate period, if not earlier, so the presence of one at Huaca del Loro need not be explained by invoking an invasion from the highlands, much less from Wari (Schreiber 1989).

Climatic deterioration may have played a role in the cultural disruptions of the Early Intermediate period. Ice core data indicate a period of severe drought in the sixth century A.D. (Thompson et al. 1985). This may be roughly the time that the Nasca people built an irrigation system designed to tap new sources of water. Meanwhile the Moche, too, were disrupted, and a period of severe ENSO events may have contributed to this disruption (Moseley 1983); such events may be correlated with droughts in the south.

Thus, there is no evidence for direct Wari expansion out of Ayacucho in the late Early Intermediate period, although it is clear that there was an unprecedented level of regional interaction at that time. This provided at least part of the cultural context in which Wari emerged. The people of Ayacucho were certainly aware of people and events taking place in distant regions. And in Middle Horizon 1B Wari styles of art and architecture spread to far distant regions of the central Andes.

THE WARI HORIZON OUTSIDE THE HEARTLAND

Ceramics of the Wari horizon styles have been found widely distributed throughout coastal and highland Peru. This distribution ends, in the south, in the southeastern portions of the Departments of Cuzco and Arequipa. Beyond this boundary, Tiwanaku ceramics are dominant, and no Wari styles are reported. (The site of Cerro Baul is an exception, and will be discussed below.) This division between the distributions of Wari and Tiwanaku styles is the best evidence for defining the limits of the two cultures, as well as for establishing the fact that they were distinct separate cultures.

I shall not here provide an exhaustive list of every place in which Wari styles have been reported. Suffice it to say that Wari ceramic styles are found widespread, albeit often in very low proportions, in coastal valleys from perhaps Lambayeque in the north to the Sihuas Valley in the south, and in highland regions from Cajamarca to Cuzco. What is more important than the presence of Wari ceramics is the context in which they occur. Unfortunately, our state of knowledge in many regions is still limited to the data of mortuary remains, especially on the coast. In the sierra, however, there are a number of sites that appear to represent intrusive Wari occupations. In recent years investigations have been undertaken at a number of them, so we have additional contexts for Wari horizon styles in the sierra.

The Chakipampa style of Middle Horizon 1B is the first to be found widely distributed throughout the sierra, in Middle Horizon 1B. In Middle Horizon 2, Wari styles have a similar range of spatial distribution, but are found in greater frequency. There seems to be a regional differentiation of styles, with the Viñaque style prevalent in the sierra, Atarco style on the south coast, and Pachacamac style on the central and north coast. These three styles are very closely related, but differ in the depiction of certain icons, which are specific to particular styles.

This situation has been interpreted as evidence of some sort of Wari expansion in Middle Horizon 1B, and then the fragmentation of the Wari culture into three subcultures, represented by the three major styles of epoch 2. Menzel, in her study of the iconography suggests that there was a shift from religious to secular themes in pottery decoration, which indicates to her a similar shift in other aspects of Wari culture (1964:69-70; 1968:91-92).

Moving away from ceramics, and toward a consideration of architecture, we now turn to a discussion of the major intrusive Wari sites found through the highlands of Peru. Unlike portable artifacts, a foreign style of architecture may represent direct foreign intervention, especially if all the sites exhibit profound similarity to each other and are distinct from local constructions as well.

The study of Wari political organization has been based in part on the study of sites with distinctive Wari-style architecture, found throughout the sierra. As is too often the case, however, although we know something of these foreign sites, seldom do we have any local context in which to interpret them. They can be compared to Wari, and to each other, and the tenets of the style defined. But without seeing other changes in the local culture at the time of the imposition of the foreign sites, we have only a part of the regional picture.

Wari-style architecture is quite distinctive. As I described in the case of Wari itself, the overall diagnostic form of Wari architecture is the rectangular compound, varying in size, which is subdivided into a series of units, many of which are the diagnostic patio groups: roughly square open patios, with benches around the sides, and ringed by long narrow rooms called galleries. The galleries may be multistoried, up to three stories high. The outer wall of each discrete enclosure is thicker than the interior walls, and very tall. There are few doors into compounds, and are sometimes rare between patio groups. But doors are quite frequent between patios and their associated galleries.

The style is very austere and forbidding. For many years, before there was good evidence of any major culture preceding the Inka, these sites were thought to have been built by the Inka, despite the fact that they look very little like Inka architecture. The high walls and relative lack of doors and windows led people to think that these sites functioned as Inka prisons. However, Rowe, Collier and Willey (1950) noted the similarity between these odd sites and the architecture at Wari. And recent excavations at several provincial sites have confirmed this; Wari ceramics are characteristic of all of these sites.

The following discussion will summarize the major Wari sites known at present, especially those highland sites with diagnostic Wari architecture, but also including some other known occurrences of Wari materials. In the case of the coast, Wari sites with the diagnostic architecture known in the sierra have not been identified, although there is ample evidence of the Wari presence at a variety of sites.

This discussion will begin with the highlands, proceeding from north to south, and will proceed likewise down the coast (Fig. 3.7).

Highland Sites

Cajamarca

The northernmost sites with what may be Wari-style architecture are located in the Cajamarca Basin. A recent survey by Daniel Julien has reconstructed settlement patterns in this region, and has identified several sites with large rectangular enclosures that may pertain to Wari. The site of El Palacio is located about 10 km northeast of Cajamarca, and comprises a large rectangular enclosure. It had no diagnostic ceramics on the surface (Julien 1988:163), but on the basis of architectural form Julien feels that it is almost certainly a Wari site (ibid.: 241).

A second site, Yamobamba, is located southeast of Cajamarca, near the town of Namora. This too is a large rectangular enclosure, measuring 128 by 216 m (Hyslop 1984:61) and like El Palacio had no diagnostic ceramics on its surface (Julien 1988:163). Julien feels that it, too, was probably a Wari site (ibid: 241). Williams and Pineda (1985), based on their study of aerial photographs, have likewise suggested that this may be an intrusive Wari administrative site. The site is located immediately adjacent to the main Inka highway, and Hyslop also suggests a tentative Middle Horizon date (Hyslop 1984:61). The form of architecture at these two sites does

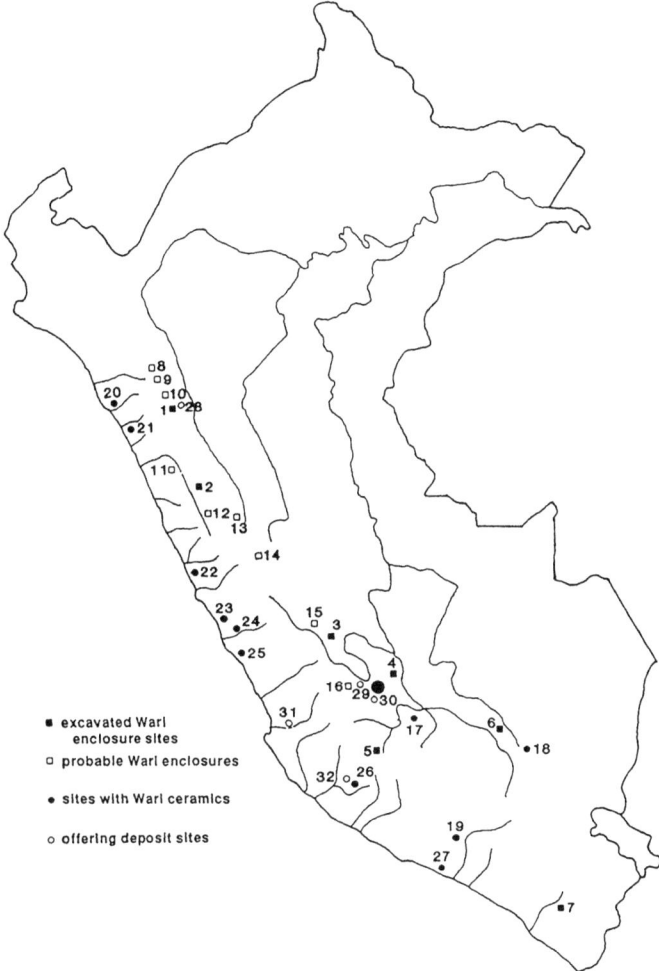

Figure 3.7. Map of the central Andes showing sites named in the text. Excavated Wari enclosure sites include: **1.** Viracochapampa, **2.** Honco Pampa, **3.** Wari Willka, **4.** Jargampata, **5.** Jincamocco, **6.** Pikillaqta, **7.** Cerro Baul. Probable Wari enclosure sites include: **8.** El Palacio, **9.** Yamobamba, **10.** Ichabamba, **11.** Pariamarca, **12.** Tocroc, **13.** Wisajirca, **14.** Yanahuanca, **15.** Calpish, **16.** Hatun Wayllay. Other Middle Horizon and related sites mentioned in the text include: **17.** Waywaka, **18.** Batan Urqo, **19.** Número Ocho, **20.** Chicama, **21.** Moche, **22.** Chimú Capac, **23.** Ancón, **24.** Cajamarquilla, **25.** Pachacamac, **26.** Huaca del Loro, **27.** Ocoña. The offering deposits are: **28.** Cerro Amaru, **29.** Ayapata, **30.** Conchopata, **31.** Maymi, **32.** Pacheco.

support the interpretation that they are Wari sites, although the lack of other diagnostic material on the surface makes this identification only tentative at this time.

Two other sites were found on which were built rectangular enclosures, amid extensive local architecture; they may be later constructions than El Palacio or Yamobamba (Julien 1988:163-66). Although Julien found no Wari-style ceramics in his surface survey, Wari ceramics have been reported by earlier investigators (Reichlen and Reichlen 1949; Terada and Matsumoto 1985). Julien concludes that there was a clear Wari presence in Cajamarca (Julien 1988:240).

We are fortunate in the Cajamarca Basin to have good settlement data, in addition to descriptions of major sites. Julien's extensive survey located major sites in the valley from the Initial period through Inka times. He found that in the period prior to the Middle Horizon, Early Cajamarca C, there may have been some political centralization, focused around the large site of Coyor, and that this trend continued in the Middle Cajamarca phase. In the following phase, this large site was abandoned, as were many other sites (Julien 1988:156-63). Later, perhaps five polities organized at the level of complex chiefdoms emerged, only to be conquered by the Inka empire (ibid.: 242).

Just to the southeast of the Cajamarca Basin is another site, Ichabamba, that may be a Wari enclosure. This site was identified by Williams and Pineda (1985), on the basis of its form, as being a possible Wari site.

La Libertad

Located near Huamachuco, the site of Viracochapampa is the second largest provincial Wari site known. It is a major compound, measuring roughly 540 by 570 meters, with a well-defined perimeter wall, and distinctive Wari-style patio groups inside. It also has a central plaza, and several architectural forms not seen at other Wari sites, but overall the architecture is distinctly Wari. It was investigated by McCown (1945) who mapped the site and undertook test excavations there. Local ceramic sequences in Huamachuco were defined by Thatcher (1972), with some special emphasis on the Early Intermediate period and Middle Horizon 1B (1975). He also located what may be an example of the Wari offering tradition (1977); this will be discussed in greater detail below.

For the past several years Theresa Topic and John Topic have been investigating Viracochapampa along with several other sites in the region, providing the first regional synthesis of cultural events surrounding the Middle Horizon. They have pointed out, for instance, that the site is not perfectly rectilinear, as indicated in most publications. Rather it measures 566 m along the north wall, 518 m along the south wall, 564 m along the east wall, and 574 m along the west wall (J. Topic 1985). They have also found that this site combined typical forms of Wari architecture, such as the patio group, but included distinctly Huamachuco-style forms as well, notably the niched hall. Thus Wari planners may have copied certain aspects of Huamachuco-style architecture in creating their own distinctive style (J. Topic 1985). One of the most significant of the Topics' conclusions is that construction of Viracochapampa was never completed. For some reason, construction ceased at the site and it was never occupied (T. Topic and Topic 1984; J. Topic 1985).

Wari horizon styles have turned up at several other sites in the region, but none that have Wari-style architecture. Wari-style ceramics have been located at Cerro Amaru, which may also have a number of round storehouses (Thatcher 1977; T. Topic and Topic 1984; J. Topic 1985). This site may have been an important shrine associated with water (J. Topic 1985).

The most notable local site is Marca Huamachuco, the largest site in the region, and probably the capital of the local polity. There is little direct evidence of the Wari presence at this site, except for the possible construction of a Wari mausoleum within the site (J. Topic 1985), although recently some additional Wari materials have been encountered (T. Topic, pers. comm.).

The Topics have concluded that a model based on trade and exchange of ritual information best explains the evidence from Huamachuco, rather than conquest or direct control from Wari (J. Topic and Topic 1985:47).

Ancash

There are three sites in the Callejón de Huaylas that may be Wari sites. The site of Honco Pampa is located on the east side of the Callejón de Huaylas, on the flanks of the Cordillera Blanca, overlooking one of the major passes through the Cordillera. The site has two parts. At the base of the site, on the edge of a marshy plain, are several large constructions, multistoried, and honeycombed with small rooms following a rigid plan; these structures were probably burial towers. This is a unique architectural style, found only in the Callejón. Above the burial structures on a sloping hillside, are a series of constructions in diagnostic Wari style.

Numerous researchers have visited the site, including myself, and have concluded that it is a Wari site, at least the portion of the site lying on the hillside. Excavations were undertaken by Vescelius and Amat, but never published, except in abbreviated form by Buse (1965). Recent excavations and mapping by Isbell (1989) have revealed details of the architecture. There are individual patio groups, along with a number of rounded or D-shaped structures. What sets this site apart from all other Wari provincial sites is the fact that the patio groups are not contiguous, and do not comprise cells of a typical Wari compound. Rather, they conform to the topography, and each follows its own grid pattern. This pattern is seen at no other Wari site, not even Wari itself.

Isbell (1989) suggests that this site is earlier than any other Wari provincial site, arguing that at the time Honco Pampa was built the Wari compound plan had not yet emerged. While plausible, this suggestion is difficult to support on the basis of extant data. Our sample of Wari provincial sites is still too small to attempt to try to seriate them on the basis of stylistic differences in architecture, and radiocarbon dating is not precise enough to distinguish this site temporally from other Wari provincial sites.

Two other sites have been identified by Williams and Pineda (1985), on the basis of their examination of aerial photographs, as possible Wari sites. Tocroc is located at the southern (upper) end of the valley, near the town of Recuay. The other site, Pariamarca, is at the northern end of the Callejón before the Santa River turns down toward the coast. Both of these sites are large rectangular enclosures.

Another site in the Callejón that has been attributed to Wari is Willka Waín, located near Huarás (Bennett 1944). This site, however, is not built in Wari-style architecture, and the associated remains indicate that it was more likely built prior to the Middle Horizon, although nearby tombs were found to have Wari (Coast Tiahuanaco) ceramics. One reason for attributing it to Wari is the similarity between its plan and that of typical Wari sites. I suggest, however, that the reason for the similarity is that Wari adopted certain aspects of this Callejón style, specifically (1) long, narrow, multistoried galleries, and (2) site layout following a rigid grid plan. Wari sites differ however, in having open patios (instead of closed rooms), and Wari galleries are wider (generally 2.2 m) than those of the Callejón style (generally about one meter wide). Another form that is seen at Wari, but occurs at earlier sites in the Callejón, is the stone slab tomb, although the ones near Willka Waín are smaller than those at Wari.

Huánuco

A site has been reported from near La Union that may be a Wari site (MacNeish, Patterson and Browman 1975:60), but no details have been published. Wisajirca is described as a large storage complex like Pikillaqta or Viracochapampa, which would suggest that it has typical Wari architecture.

Pasco

In his survey of Inka roads, John Hyslop found what may be a Wari enclosure at Yanahuanca, northwest of Cerro de Pasco (see Isbell 1988:186).

Junín

In the upper part of the Mantaro Valley recent work by Timothy Earle and his associates has not turned up any direct evidence of Wari constructions. Indeed, Wari horizon–style sherds are extremely rare, only a handful turning up in the surface survey (Christine Hastorf, pers. comm.).

Working farther south, David Browman found several sites he attributes to Wari, but none of these exhibit the diagnostic traits of Wari architecture, at least as I have defined them. But, despite these differences in interpretation, Browman did find very interesting evidence of a change in settlement patterns at the time of the Middle Horizon. He found that there was a shift from camelid herding to tuber cultivation, which he attributes to Wari influence (Browman 1976).

Farther south, near Huancayo are two sites of probable Wari affiliation. The first is Calpish, reported by MacNeish, Patterson, and Browman (1975:60) as being a large rectangular compound, with large rectangular rooms with peripheral galleries arranged according to a grid plan. Ceramics on the site indicate an occupation during epoch 2.

The second site is Wari Willka. This site was apparently a typical Wari compound, subdivided into patio groups, and Wari-style ceramics were found in the site, including the coastal Pachacamac style (Flores 1959:183-84). The full extent of the site is unknown, as it is obscured by later and modern constructions. The site, in Inka times, was a major shrine, related to the oracle at Pachacamac; this use of the site may actually date to much earlier times, given the presence of Middle Horizon Pachacamac ceramics.

Huancavelica

Tello reported a site near Lircay, called Hatun Wayllay, that he thought might be a Wari site (Tello 1942:683-84). He also said that there were many remains of Wari ceramics in Huancavelica. As I pointed out above, we do not know how far the Wari core extended into Huancavelica, as only the Ayacucho portions of the Cachi drainage have been surveyed. But Hatun Wayllay lies in the Urubamba tributary of the Cachi, so it and other possible sites may not be provincial sites at all, but part of the core polity.

The only Middle Horizon site excavated in Huancavelica is Ayapata, which will be discussed below in the section treating the Wari offering tradition. This site, too, lies in the Cachi drainage, in the Urubamba tributary.

Ayacucho

East of Wari, and only 25 km away, but across the high puna divide, is the small Wari site of Jargampata. Measuring only 25 by 40 meters (0.1 ha) at its maximum extent, it comprises two small patios (without peripheral galleries). This site functioned to organize local production, and was probably a point of collection and storage of local agricultural produce, which was then sent on to the urban capital at Wari (Isbell 1977). This site is probably not in the same category as most of the other major provincial sites discussed here, but I include it because it is one of very few Wari sites that have been carefully excavated.

Moving to the south of the Wari core region, no intrusive Wari sites have been identified in the Río Pampas valley proper. No intensive systematic survey has been undertaken of the valley, but there has been some general reconnaissance in the region. Near Cangallo, Isbell found a Tiwanaku-style vessel, the only one ever found in Wari territory. It is an incense burner with a modeled feline head, made in classic Tiwanaku style (Menzel 1968:98, note 32). Menzel suggests that it was not actually made in the Tiwanaku area, but might even be a local production (ibid.).

The Carhuarazo Valley is a southern tributary of the Pampas, in which one large (Jincamocco) and three small (Culluma, Anta and Willkaya) Wari sites are located. These sites and the region in which they are found are the subject of the following several chapters, so will not be discussed in detail here.

The Chicha-Soras Valley is another southern tributary of the Pampas, and has recently been surveyed by Frank Meddens (1985, 1989). This survey was extensive in nature, and only a ten percent sample of the region was intensively surveyed. No intrusive Wari sites were found in the valley, but there is ample evidence of occupation during the Middle Horizon. The valley was occupied briefly in the Initial period, and then abandoned. Occupation began again in Middle Horizon 1 (probably 1B, not 1A, as Meddens suggests), and is evidenced by a single site. The number of sites increased to seven in Middle Horizon 2, but only local architecture was present. One offering was found of local and Wari-style vessels in small pits, adjacent and partly under a large boulder (ibid.: 152-63). This probably represents a local practice, and has little in common with the Wari offering tradition (ibid.: 222). Meddens suggests that the valley was marginal to imperial control, and that perhaps it served only to support camelid herding (ibid.: 221-25).

Apurimac

In the Department of Apurimac the only evidence of Wari occupation so far comes from the site of Waywaka. Excavations of that site by Grossman revealed a long sequence beginning in the Initial period (Grossman 1983). The site is located on a hilltop adjacent to Andahuaylas, and Grossman excavated a series of small pits in a line across the top of the hill. In his excavations he located Wari horizon–style ceramics (MH 1B and 2), and in the Middle Horizon stratum of one excavation unit he exposed a piece of straight wall. Although the data are insufficient to say that there was a Wari provincial site at this location, there are clearly Wari ceramics on the site.

Survey by John Rowe in 1954 located no sites in the region around Abancay, but farther to the northeast, near Curahuasi, there was found evidence of several Wari cemeteries (John Rowe, pers. comm.).

Cuzco

The largest Wari provincial site is Pikillaqta, located in the Lucre Basin, southeast of the city of Cuzco (McEwan 1979, 1985, 1987, 1989). The site is an enormous rectangular compound, measuring 630 by 745 meters (47 ha.), divided into four major sectors. Like Viracochapampa it has a central plaza; in fact it has three central plazas. And, roughly similar to Azángaro in the Wari core area, Pikillaqta has one sector that comprises rows of conjoined rooms, with limited access.

Most of the remaining sectors are divided into patio groups. Here galleries are sometime three deep, rather than the single galleries seen at other sites. Further, in these cases the shared end walls of the galleries, at the corners of the patios, are sometimes diagonal. It is possible that the Wari builders were experimenting with different formal patterns at Pikillaqta, perhaps to speed up the rate of construction.

Some portions of some sectors were left open, while some were subdivided with walls outlining cells, and some of these have patio groups built in alternate cells. This gives the definite impression that some portions of the site were never finished. Pikillaqta differs from other Wari sites in that the entire site is not surrounded by a single compound wall. Rather, each of the four major sectors may have been built separately. The central sector was clearly completed, and McEwan's excavations have shown that it was occupied as well. But especially in the sectors flanking this one to the north and south, there appear to be areas that were still under construction at the time the site was abandoned.

Numerous small excavations were made at the site at various times in the past. One of these turned up two offerings of small turquoise figurines, perhaps the most famous finds from the site. In the 1960s William Sanders put together the first accurate map of the site (Sanders 1973). The most recent, and best reported, excavations at the site are those of Gordon McEwan (1979, 1985, 1987). McEwan's data suggest that the site, or at least the central sector, was built and occupied beginning in Middle Horizon 1B, and that the occupation continued through Middle Horizon 2.

McEwan has not only investigated the major site, but has taken a regional perspective, and looked at other Middle Horizon sites in the region. He finds a major Wari occupation, evidenced not only by Pikillaqta, but also by several other sites in the immediate vicinity. Following Schaedel (1966), he suggests that these several sites combined to form a single Wari community.

The great wall across the valley near Pikillaqta, with the later Inka Rumi Collca gateway cut through it, is well known. McEwan has located several other walls in the region that seem to block access to or from regions to the southeast.

Farther to southeast, no other sites with diagnostic Wari architecture have been identified, although there are numerous sites that have produced ceramics and other artifacts of Wari style. There is a large Wari offering, including large quantities of camelid bones, at Batan 'Urqo (Rowe 1956:142; pers. comm.). And at Cacha, in the area around the great Inka site of the Temple of Viracocha, there are abundant Wari surface sherds and burials (Rowe 1956:144; pers. comm.).

So while Pikillaqta in the Lucre Basin seems to be the last major Wari site in the southeast part of the central Andes, the distribution of Wari artifacts continues on for another 60 kilometers. Beyond this point, moving toward the altiplano region, Tiwanaku ceramics are found.

Arequipa

Many years ago Kroeber (1944) pointed out the presence of probable Wari remains in the Chuquibamba valley, a tributary of the Majes/Colca in Arequipa. A recent survey by Margaret Sciscento (1989) has shown that this highland valley was probably first occupied in the Middle Horizon, but she identifies no sites with diagnostic Wari architecture. However, one site, Número Ocho, did have poorly preserved rectilinear architecture, and Wari surface sherds.

In the Colca Valley, the upper portion of the Majes, a major Middle Horizon site called Achachiwa has been identified near Cabanaconde (de la Vera Cruz 1987:97-98). The site comprises a large walled area, some 500 by 700 m in extent, roughly rectangular in form, and delimited by a wall still standing 5 m in places. Remains inside the compound are poorly preserved, but ceramics are abundant, including Qosqopa style, a regional style thought to be related to Wari. This appears to be a local village with a defensive wall, rather than a Wari provincial site; but the wall construction is said to be of Wari style.

Moquegua

Although the Moquegua Valley lies outside the known distribution of Wari styles, there appears to be one Wari site in this valley, located in the midst of Tiwanaku territory. Cerro Baul is a Wari site, with Wari ceramics dating to MH 1B and 2A, located high on an isolated butte. The location is clearly defensive. The architecture is poorly preserved, but seems to comprise contiguous rectilinear structures, similar to Wari styles (Moseley, Feldman and Goldstein 1985; Feldman 1989). A related site is Cerro Mejía, which guards the access route to Cerro Baul. Cerro Baul gives us one of our only glimpses at the actual relationship between Wari and Tiwanaku, and the fact that the site is so clearly defensive suggests that relations were not entirely amicable (Feldman 1989).

Coastal Sites

The situation on the coast is rather different. No sites with diagnostic Wari architecture have been clearly identified. There are at least two reasons that can be suggested to account for this difference between the highlands and the coast. First, it is possible that direct Wari occupations did not occur on the coast. Or second, Wari coastal architecture may have been rather different from that of the sierra. The different climate of the coast, combined with different available building materials, may have resulted in different sorts of architectural forms. It may be that we just have not yet learned to recognize Wari coastal architecture.

The North Coast

On the north coast, Wari ceramics have been found in a variety of contexts, mostly isolated finds, as far north as Lambayeque. A small association of Middle Horizon 2A vessels was located by Donnan (1968) in the Chicama Valley. In the Moche Valley Wari ceramics have been found in elite burials, or perhaps offerings, on the Huaca del Sol, former capital of the Moche state (Menzel 1977:37-39; Mackey 1982:325). The summit of nearby Cerro Blanco may also have been used as a shrine for Wari offerings, according to Menzel (1977:37). Interestingly, most of the Wari remains found at Moche are of highland Wari style, not the central coast Pachacamac style.

In the Virú Valley, Gordon Willey (1953:235-38) noted that the Middle Horizon (Tomoval period) was a time of minor shifts in settlement location, a time of extensive road construction, and a period during which rectangular compound forms of architecture became prevalent.

In the Santa Valley, Larco (1966:160-61) reported finding Wari ceramics from elite burials. However, recent survey by Wilson located small numbers of Wari sherds, but nothing that could be called a Wari site. He did find an increase in rectangular compound forms of architecture, much as was the case in Virú (Wilson 1988:260). Wilson argues that there was no direct input from Wari, but that the Santa Valley was controlled by what he calls the Red-White-Black state, which extended at least from Santa to Casma (Wilson 1988:334-35).

For some time the murals of Pañamarca, in the Nepeña Valley, were considered to be of Wari style, but recent work by Donnan has cast doubt on this interpretation. In his film, *Discovering the Moche*, he demonstrates that the mural is part of an incomplete "presentation theme" depiction. It is interesting, however, to see a prominent member of this theme, depicted in Moche art, who is apparently dressed in Wari clothing. (This costume includes a sort of poncho and a square headdress with long rayed appendages, similar to depictions of the headdress of the Staff Deity, and is distinct from Moche styles of dress.)

The Central Coast

A large collection of Middle Horizon vessels was excavated at the site of Chimu Capac in the Supe Valley. Menzel (1977) has interpreted this collection as dating primarily to Middle Horizon 2, and suggests that it may represent a Wari outpost, designed to curb the northward expansion of Pachacamac influence.

Major collections of Wari ceramics have been located in the Ancón region, beginning with Reiss and Stübel (1880-1887). In the Rimac Valley is a major urban site called Cajamarquilla. Nearby is the cemetery of Nievería, which has produced many examples of Wari horizon–style ceramics. It has been thought by some that Cajamarquilla is a Wari city (Lumbreras 1974), even though the architectural forms and construction techniques are not typical of any known Wari sites. It seems more likely that this site is not a Wari site at all, but a major local site occupied during the Middle Horizon.

The biggest Middle Horizon site on the central coast is Pachacamac. This was the site of a major oracle during Inka times, and was the destination of pilgrimages made by people from all over the Andes. Excavations by Uhle (1903) turned up not only Inka, and immediately pre-Inka materials, but also a great quantity of Wari ("Coast Tiahuanaco") material. The major temple to the oracle was probably built during Middle Horizon 2, so it is not unlikely that the site functioned as a major pilgrimage center also at that time. The Middle Horizon layout of the site is impossible to know, as it is covered with later constructions. It is not unlikely that it was a site of major proportions, with a resident urban population, but we cannot know if typical Wari architecture was present or not. In any case, the variety of Wari pottery found at Pachacamac exhibits a strong regional style (the Pachacamac style) in Middle Horizon 2. Most distinctive are the depictions of a birdlike creature, called the Pachacamac griffin; other Middle Horizon 2 styles do not include this creature. The Pachacamac variant is found dominant on the central coast, and as far south as the Ica Valley; some limited examples of this style have been found in the highlands, at Wari Willka and Wari.

The South Coast

Aside from a number of important offering deposits in the Pisco, Nasca and Ocoña valleys, discussed below, no intrusive Wari sites are known from the south coast. Some writers have attributed such sites as Tres Palos II and Huaca del Loro to Wari (Paulsen 1983; Isbell 1987:90) but these sites do not have diagnostic Wari-style ceramics or architecture. However, numerous examples of Wari ceramics are found in the Ica and Nasca valleys, mostly from burial contexts. In the Nasca Valley was located the site of Pacheco, at which one of the major Wari offering deposits was found. Apparently associated with the offering deposit was a large habitation area measuring some 280 by 300 m (John Rowe, pers. comm.). Unfortunately, the site was bulldozed in the early 1950s, so little remains to be seen on its surface.

Also in the Nasca drainage is a large looted cemetery at Atarco. Ceramics in the Nasca region include the Nasca 9 style, which dates to the Middle Horizon 1. This is not a Nasca style at all, and perhaps should be better considered a part of the Chakipampa style. In Middle Horizon 2, the Atarco style emerged on the south coast. Similar to the Viñaque style of the highlands, and the Pachacamac style of the central coast, it also includes depictions of felines not seen in the other styles.

In my own surveys I have found Wari ceramics on local habitation sites dating to the Middle Horizon, as well as two hilltop redoubts with Wari ceramics. These latter sites have irregular rectilinear architecture, and are located high on a ridge top without direct access to agricultural land or water. They provide an excellent vantage point from which to observe any movement into or out of the adjacent highlands. Much work is still needed to clarify the nature of the Middle Horizon in Nasca.

South of Nasca, Wari ceramics have been found in burial contexts or as isolated surface remains as far south as the Sihuas Valley. A major deposit of intact Wari vessels was found in the Ocoña Valley, and is discussed in greater detail below.

Site Summary

The only sites with diagnostic Wari architecture so far identified are all located in the sierra. Besides numerous sites in the Wari core region, the best known sites are Pikillaqta, Viracochapampa, Wari Willka, Jincamocco, Honco Pampa, and Jargampata; numerous sites still lack even firm identification as Wari sites. It is useful to point out here that the sample of pure Wari (as defined by architecture) highland provincial sites is not only rather small, it is certainly incomplete. Most regions of the sierra have never been surveyed, so most extant data come from the urbanized (and civilized) regions around Cuzco, Ayacucho, Huancayo, and

Cajamarca. Regions that today are remote and of difficult access have been less systematically treated. It is not unlikely that we have located only a small percentage of the actual total of Wari sites. It cannot be assumed that we have a complete sample of Wari provincial sites.

The distribution of Wari sites in the sierra is also interesting in ecological terms. In Chapter 2, I defined several major highland sectors along a north-south gradient. No Wari sites have been found in the páramo sierra, nor have any been found in the altiplano, the zone of Tiwanaku horizon styles. All the Wari highland sites are found in the puna sierra, and the limits of the distribution of Wari sites conforms very closely to the limits of this zone. The transitional zone near Cajamarca between the puna sierra and the páramo sierra is the northern limit of Wari sites. And the divide between the puna sierra and the altiplano, southeast of Cuzco, is the area demarking the boundary between the Wari and Tiwanaku horizons. Thus, Wari sites are located in regions of generally direct exploitation of the vertical ecozones. Likewise, Tiwanaku styles are found in the altiplano and surrounding regions, regions characterized by the long-distance archipelago adaptations.

On the coast, the situation is less clear. While there are numerous sites dating to the Middle Horizon, none of them exhibits typical Wari architecture. Wari ceramics are quite abundant, however, especially on the south and central coasts. So here we see that in a radically different environmental setting—the dry coastal desert—the Wari occupation was also radically different.

The Offering Deposits

Up to this point I have stressed evidence of the Wari presence as evidenced through architecture and settlements, and to a lesser degree on the distribution of ceramic styles. However, there is another series of special sites that also deserve mention. These are the curious "offering deposits." There are so far known perhaps six major offering deposits of Wari-style ceramics, four in the sierra (two at Conchopata, one at Ayapata, one at Cerro Amaru), and two on the coast (in the Pisco and Nasca valleys). The basic outline of each is the same: a large quantity of elaborately decorated vessels were apparently intentionally smashed and interred. Some of the most distinctive Wari iconography is depicted on the ceramics of the offering deposits. Hence, the interpretation of these deposits has been primarily the focus of investigators with a primary interest in Wari iconography.

Conchopata

Conchopata is a site located adjacent to modern Ayacucho, in the Wari core region. Two offerings have been located at Conchopata. The first was excavated by Tello in 1942. Menzel has dated the remains to Middle Horizon 1A and has used them to define her Conchopata style (1964:19-21; 1968:49). Later restudy by Anita Cook has amplified Menzel's definitions, and defined additional icons not previously identified (Cook 1979). The iconography of the Conchopata style is closer to that of the Tiwanaku Gate of the Sun than any other Wari styles.

The 1942 offering was deposited in an unstructured pit, perhaps only 30 cm deep. Cook estimates that there were about 3,000 fragments recovered (1979:69). Although at least half of the vessels were unpainted, those with painted designs included depictions of mythical beings: two versions of the Staff Deity, five profile attendants, and various human forms. All vessels were oversized urns, and all appear to have been intentionally smashed *in situ*. The patterns of fracture suggest that the vessels were broken with a blow directed to the face of the mythical beings (Menzel 1968:49).

The second offering was recovered in 1977, in a salvage operation directed by William Isbell, and has been dated to Middle Horizon 1B by Cook (1979, 1985). Like the first offering, it was deposited in an unstructured pit, about 2 by 3 meters in size, of unknown depth. Unfortunately, the bulk of the ceramics had been removed from the pit before systematic investigation could begin, so the exact configuration remains unknown (Cook 1979:92). The offering comprises 22-25 oversized face-neck jars, and represents the first combination of Nascoid with Tiahuanacoid features in a ceremonial assemblage (Cook 1979:93-94). Furthermore, the modeled faces on the jar necks differ from vessel to vessel, so one might speculate that they were meant as portraits of individuals (Cook 1979:95).

Ayapata

This site is located 30 km northwest of Wari, near the village of Caja, in Huancavelica. The Ayapata offering was first defined in a limited (0.5 m square) excavation in 1967 (Ravines 1968). Five superimposed levels were defined in this tiny excavation, three of which contained massive densities of ceramic fragments. These data have been used to say that not all offerings were single events, and that Ayapata indicates re-use of the same offering several times, even though Ravines suggested that it really represented a single episode, or at least episodes not separated by significant lapses of time (ibid.: 39). Like the Conchopata offerings, the Ayapata offering was found in an unstructured pit. But unlike the Conchopata offerings, the Ayapata offering included a range of vessel shapes, not just a single form. The most common form, however, was an oversize urn. It seems that the vessels were broken *in situ*, but there is no reported evidence that mythical beings were singled out for the killing blows. Ravines makes the important point that no other remains were found that might suggest this to be habitation refuse, strengthening the supposition that this deposit was in some way special.

Ravines returned to the site in 1969 and opened up a 9 by 12 m excavation, in which he exposed seven more pits, all but one filled with high densities of ceramic fragments (Ravines 1977). These were unstructured pits, a meter or slightly more in diameter, and up to 75 cm deep. The mythical figures depicted include two forms of a staff-bearing anthropomorphic being, and two forms of the humpbacked animal. The same basic vessel forms were present in each pit, although in different proportions, and in a different stratigraphic order, strongly indicating that all the offerings were roughly contemporaneous (ibid.: 80).

Cerro Amaru

One possible offering deposit has been identified in the north highlands in the Huamachuco region (Thatcher 1977). This deposit was identified only on the surface, but hundreds of sherds were collected. Only the fanciest painted sherds were studied (ibid.: 101). Numerous vessel forms were found, and they appear to conform to the Chakipampa B style (ibid.: 104-5). All vessels were found broken, but the data are insufficient to indicate whether or not this was intentional. The fact that ceramics were found in such extremely high densities, and in such a restricted area (diameter about one meter), is reminiscent of Ayapata. We might therefore tentatively include Cerro Amaru in the list of known offering deposits. Thatcher, on the basis of this find, suggested that Cerro Amaru might have served as the Wari center of control in Huamachuco beginning in Middle Horizon 1B (ibid.: 104).

Pacheco

Probably the largest offering deposit so far reported is that recovered in the Nasca Valley at a site called Pacheco. In 1927, Tello excavated some three tons of sherds from the site; additional materials were recovered by Ronald Olson in 1930. The Pacheco offering includes a number of oversize urns, with two forms of the central deity depicted, like Conchopata. In contrast with the latter site, numerous other vessel forms were included as well. One distinctive aspect of the Pacheco offering is the variety of depictions of plants; these seem to be agricultural plants of highland origin (Menzel 1968:49). Analysis of the Pacheco materials provided Menzel with the basis for defining the Robles Moqo style of Middle Horizon 1B (Menzel 1964:26-28).

Pisco

Very recently, Martha Anders has uncovered another immense deposit of Wari ceramics, at Maymi in the Pisco Valley. This research is yet ongoing, and complete interpretation awaits the analysis of the material.[3] The fact that the pottery has very elaborate decoration, and is found in very high density in a limited area, indicates that it may conform to the offering deposit tradition.

Ocoña

Finally, there is a deposit of vessels found at La Victoria in the Ocoña Valley, that deserves mention here, but is not regarded as an example of the offering tradition. The remains include 10-12 intact oversize face-neck jars. The exact context is unclear, but it appears that they were not interred in any formal structure (Menzel 1964:86-87, note 196). The jars were filled with a number of rolled-up feather mantles, and artifacts that might be Inka in origin. Menzel defines the designs as being derivative of the Robles Moqo style, but pertaining to epoch 2 (ibid.). Ravines illustrates two of the vessels (1968:46).

Offering Summary

All these deposits seem to represent primary associations. They are very high in density, remains are generally reconstructible, and diversity of materials is very low. (In other words, not only are the range of ceramic forms limited—extremely limited in some cases— but there are generally no other kinds of materials directly associated with the deposits.) As Ravines pointed out, they are clearly not trash deposits.

The Conchopata offerings can be differentiated from the others on two bases. First, they have extremely low diversity of forms—each being characterized by many examples of a single vessel form. All the other offerings have a variety of forms present. And second, the Conchopata offerings are found in the Wari core region; the rest were interred in provincial regions. (Except possibly Ayapata; we do not know how far the Wari core extended into Huancavelica.)

The Ocoña material is not considered to be an example of the same offering tradition as the rest. In the other offerings, the fact that the vessels were smashed seems to be a significant part of the event. The Ocoña jars were found intact. They were not interred in a pit, but were found standing up in a line. And the presence of goods inside the jars—and artifacts of possibly Inka origin—indicates an entirely different cultural context. It is not unlikely that these jars were re-used at a later date by the Inka, and do not represent a Middle Horizon context at all.

A number of assumptions have been made about various of these deposits, and these assumptions have been generalized to described a Wari offering tradition. First, the fact that many of the vessels are oversize and depict mythical creatures indicates to Menzel that they had a ceremonial function (1968:69). The presence of an Andean tradition of buried offerings also lends support to the interpretation that these deposits are in fact offerings (Ravines 1968, 1977).

The depictions of the Staff Deity and profile attendants on oversize urns do seem to be religious (or ceremonial) in nature. But other depictions are defined as mythical (and hence indicating ceremonial function) that I suggest should not be interpreted as such. For example, one of the predominant mythical creatures is the hump-backed animal, seen on face-neck jars. I agree that the creatures are mythical, but they are secondary to the primary depiction: a human figure, whose facial features are modeled on the jar neck. The mythical creatures appear on the clothing of the personage. So the primary depiction is not mythical at all, but represents a human figure. So while the suggestion that these deposits represent ceremonial activities is certainly plausible, we might consider other interpretations as well.

It has also been assumed that the vessels were smashed and interred during the same period that they were made, thus indicating that the offering tradition had a good deal of time depth in the Middle Horizon. This is a perfectly reasonable suggestion, but there are no data that can directly support or refute such a conclusion, so perhaps this assumption should be questioned as well. It is equally plausible that the pots were smashed long after they were produced, and that differences between the different assemblages pertain to time of manufacture, not time of interment.

Finally, the sample of offerings is still very small, and most have rather poor archaeological contexts. Although one might argue for changes in political organization, changes in religious tradition, and relations with other sites such as Tiwanaku, on the basis of these offerings, the sample really is too small and incomplete to produce any really compelling interpretations.

Regardless of these problems, these deposits of smashed vessels are still a very interesting phenomenon. At some time and for some reason, some person or persons intentionally smashed and buried some outstanding examples of Wari art, and some of the clearest depictions of mythical and human personages.

EXPLANATIONS OF THE WARI EXPANSION

A variety of scenarios has been offered to explain this distribution of Wari materials in an extremely large region, and well away from the point of origin of the style (Schreiber 1987b). Menzel (1964) has suggested that the initial Wari expansion was the result of proselytizing missionaries. Certainly we see clear religious iconography depicted on Wari artifacts, and connections of this style both with Tiwanaku, and the earlier Pucara and Chavín cultures. Alternatively, but still in the same vein, rather than being spread by missionaries (who usually operate within the context of a larger imperial system), it might be suggested that the spread of Wari features might be the result of pilgrimages to Wari and to its related centers. Indeed, Pachacamac was probably a major pilgrimage center in the Middle Horizon, much as it was during the Late Horizon.

It has been suggested by some writers that Wari was just one of several small states that existed during the Middle Horizon, and that intensive interaction between these polities accounts for the spread of Wari horizon styles throughout the Andes (Shady and Ruiz 1979; Shady 1989; Czwarno 1989). This interaction may be in the form of commerce, or a shared set of religious beliefs. If this is true then we should see evidence of other state level organizations, contemporary with Wari, as well as evidence of reciprocal relations and interaction between them. Further, we need to document not only Wari materials in the spheres of these other polities, but materials from these other polities should be equally widespread.

Finally, it has been suggested that Wari was a conquest empire that established political control over the central Andes and the coast during the Middle Horizon (Tello 1942; Larco 1948; Rowe 1963; Lumbreras 1974, 1975). Arguments both for and against this position have not been very explicit in defining just what the archaeological remains of an empire should look like, and then demonstrating how the Wari evidence does or does not conform to these expectations. For example, arguments against this interpretation have been based largely on the absence of evidence of direct Wari control in particular regions. But as discussed in general terms, and in the specific case of the Inka, we do not expect to find evidence of direct control everywhere. Rather we expect to find a mosaic of different strategies of control. If we find evidence of only very indirect influence everywhere, then the notion of Wari having been an empire is not supported. Support for this position lies in finding regions in which more complex strategies were involved, and especially regions in which local political and economic systems were substantially altered during the period of Wari influence.

Let us turn now to the Carhuarazo Valley, and a more detailed analysis of the events of the Middle Horizon in a single region.

NOTES

1. Author's translation. Original text as follows.

   El mayor río dellos tiene por nombre Vinaque: adonde están vnos grandes y muy antiquíssimas edificios: que cierto según están gastados y ruynados deue auer passado por ellos muchas edades. Preguntando a los indios comarcanos quien hizo aquella antignalla [sic], responden que otras gentes baruadas y blancas como nosotros: los cuales muchos tiempos antes que los Ingas reynassen, dizen que vinieron a estas partes y hizieron allí su morada. Y desto y de otros edificios antiguos que ay en este reyno me parece, que no son la traa dellos como los que los Ingas hizieron o mandaron hazer. Porque este edificio era quadrado; y los de los Ingas largos y angostos. Y también ay fama, que se hallaron ciertas letras en vna losa deste edificio. Lo qual ni lo afirmo, ni de dexo de tener para mí que en los tiempos passados ouiesse llegado aquí alguna gente de tal / juyzio y razón, que hiziesse estas cosas y otras que no vemos.

2. Author's translation. Original text as follows.

   Por esto, y por lo que también dizen auer visto en la ysla de Titicaca hombres baruados, y auer hecho el edificio de Vinaque semejante gente, digo que por ventura pudo ser que antes que los Ingas mandassen, deuío de auer alguna gente de entendimiento / en estos reynos, venida por alguna parte que no se sabe, los quales harían estas cosas, y siendo pocos y los naturales tantos, serían muertos en las guerras.

3. Tragically, Martha Anders was killed in an auto accident in Peru in August, 1990. At that time she had not yet completed her investigation at Maymi.

4

The Carhuarazo Valley
The Natural Setting and Human Adaptation

Since 1974 a series of archaeological investigations have been carried out in the Carhuarazo Valley,[1] a rather small and isolated valley in the south central highlands of Peru, with the specific goal of understanding events of the Middle Horizon. This valley was never the center of any major cultural developments, but rather was marginal to events occurring elsewhere. However, those events had major effects on the people of this valley, effects that enable us to better understand some aspects of those events.

The archaeological projects carried out in the Carhuarazo Valley have been aimed at documenting the existence of a Wari presence in the valley, understanding the nature of the Wari occupation from the perspective of its major center in the region, and viewing the Wari occupation from the perspective of changes wrought on the local culture. As discussed in preceding chapters, if we are to document events of the Middle Horizon, and to evaluate the idea of Wari influence as having been the result of imperial expansion and control, then ideally we should pursue data from three complementary sources: regional settlement data, excavation data from imperial centers, and excavation data from local settlements. The archaeological investigations of the Carhuarazo Valley have included an extensive regional survey, and excavations at Jincamocco, a major Wari site in the valley. No excavations were undertaken specifically in local village sites, but deep excavations at Jincamocco revealed a long local occupation prior to the Middle Horizon, thus providing some limited data on a local settlement. This chapter presents the natural environmental setting of the valley, and modern cultural adaptations to its mountain environment. It concludes with some suggested differences between the modern adaptation and that which we might expect to encounter during the Middle Horizon.

THE GEOGRAPHIC SETTING

The Carhuarazo Valley lies in the upper portion of a tributary of the Río Pampas, in the south central highlands of Peru. This valley lies just on the eastern side of the Continental Divide, draining via the Pampas, Apurimac and Ucayali rivers to the Amazon. In terms of modern political boundaries, it is located in the southern half of the Department of Ayacucho (Fig. 4.1), in the Province of Lucanas. Today the valley comprises five districts: Huaycahuacho, Aucará, Cabana, Carmen Salcedo (Andamarca), and Chipao. As discussed in Chapter 2, during the Late Horizon the valley was ruled as a single province under the Inka; prior to the Inka conquest there were probably four small polities in the region.

The province of Lucanas (whose capital is Puquio), as well as neighboring Parinacochas to the south, is largely high plateau (*puna*): nearly half the area of the two southern provinces lies at elevations in excess of 4,000 meters above sea level. This high puna area is suitable for grazing animals, but is above the range of intensive agriculture. As such, few permanent settlements are located in the high puna zones. Overall population density today is quite low, with villages and towns concentrated in steep narrow valleys on either side of the Continental Divide. These two provinces comprise 60 percent of the total area of the Department of Ayacucho, yet have less than 30 percent of the total population. Based on population estimates of 1969 (INP-AG 1969), Lucanas and Parinacochas have population densities of 4.80 and 5.58 persons per square kilometer as opposed to an average of 19.06 persons per square kilometer for the five provinces comprising the northern half of Ayacucho (Victor Fajardo, Cangallo, Huamanga, Huanta and La Mar).

Overall, then, the modern topographic and cultural setting is one of relatively isolated, deep highland valleys (*quebradas*) separated by mountainous divides or broad expanses of high altitude plateau. Nearly all population is concentrated in these valleys, with only small groups occupying the puna on a permanent basis. The prehistoric distribution of population was probably very much the same as today, at least after plant cultivation was introduced. During the preceramic period, hunter-gath-

The Carhuarazo Valley

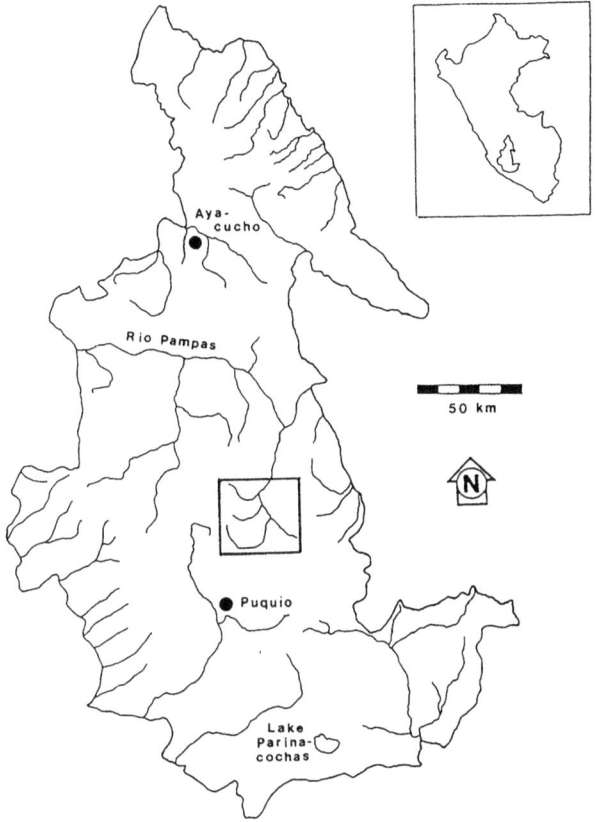

Figure 4.1. Location of the Carhuarazo Valley within the Department of Ayacucho.

erer subsistence may have been more focused on the high puna, where there was a greater abundance of animals, especially camelids, that could be exploited (see, for example, Rick 1980).

The Carhuarazo Valley takes its name from the major snow-capped mountain peak lying to the east of the valley, Señal Carhuarazo (Qarwarazu). According to local informants, this is an extinct volcano and the home of a most powerful *wamani* (mountain deity); it is believed to be the source of most weather, especially rain, in the area. Señal Carhuarazo reaches an elevation of 5,124 meters above sea level, with permanent snow fields at elevations above 4,800 meters; sulfur deposits are said to be found on its slopes. In Quechua, "qarwa" means discolored or yellowish, and "razu" means snow-capped peak (John Rowe, pers. comm.).

At the north end of the Carhuarazo Valley, the valley narrows abruptly and the river enters a deep chasm over 1,000 meters deep, with very steep sides. There is no agriculture or human occupation of the valley sides for about the next 10 kilometers. This provides a clear topographic boundary, which since at least Inka times has been an ethnic and linguistic boundary as well. The core of the valley is a relatively large area (about 52 km^2) of intensive agriculture, in which most of the modern population lives. In it are found the towns of Santa Ana de Huaycahuacho, Aucará, and Cabana, and the villages of Ishua, Queca, and Sondondo (Fig. 4.2). The towns are substantially larger than villages, and are district capitals. Except where noted, the descriptions of the geography of the valley pertain to this core. In the steep upland area to the northwest are three small villages, Santa Ana, Pampamarca, and Chacralla, each located in a small pocket of dispersed agricultural fields. From the south enter the two major affluents of the river, each the locus of intensive human occupation: the Negro Mayo branch from the southwest, in which is located the town of Andamarca, and the Mayobamba branch from the southeast, in which are located the town of Chipao and the village of Mayobamba.

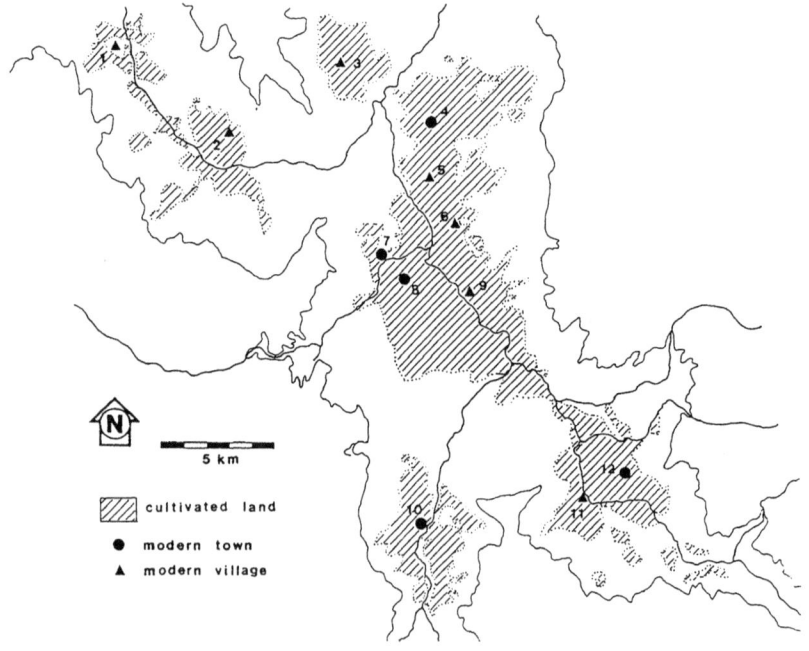

Figure 4.2. The Greater Carhuarazo Valley, showing modern towns and villages within areas of cultivation. The 4,000 m contour is indicated. The modern settlements are: **1.** Santa Ana, **2.** Pampamarca, **3.** Chacralla, **4.** Huaycahuacho, **5.** Ishua, **6.** Queca, **7.** Aucará, **8.** Cabana Sur, **9.** Sondondo, **10.** Andmarca, **11.** Mayobamba, **12.** Chipao.

ENVIRONMENT AND ECOLOGY

Geomorphology

The Carhuarazo Valley is located in an area that is predominantly Tertiary and Quaternary volcanic formations—mostly granites, diorites, andesitic basalts, and volcanic tuff—with older limestone and sandstone substrata exposed beneath these deposits by fluvial downcutting of the valley. The high elevations to the east of the valley comprise both gently sloping puna grasslands, and higher steeper mountain ridges, to elevations in excess of 5,000 m at Señal Carhuarazo. The area to the west and south of the valley is characterized by a broad, relatively flat puna grassland, averaging 4,400 m. This slightly undulating expanse of land, the Pampa Quilcata, is dotted with lakes and marshes, and small streams. It is underlain by deposits of andesitic basalt, laid down in thick horizontal beds. Where exposed by the downcutting of the river, there is a very distinctive layer of columnar basalt that rings the valley on all sides, but is especially prominent along the western and southern margins, at an elevation of almost exactly 4,000 m.

Except in the immediate vicinity of Señal Carhuarazo, where glacial features are prominent, tectonic and volcanic activity account for many of the visible features of the surface geology of the Carhuarazo Valley. This activity produced local deposits of metamorphic (quartzite, jasper) and igneous (obsidian) rocks that were exploited by human populations. The existence of hot mineral springs along the river near Huaycahuacho, Sondondo and Chipao also attests to this volcanic activity.

Within the valley core, the rock substrata are slightly inclined upward toward the northeast. On the west side of the valley the differential erosion of alternating harder and softer strata has produced a series of relatively wide horizontal shelves, some with marshy areas that have been dammed in modern times to form small lakes. On the east side, the valley flanks are steeper due to this inclination, and relatively flat areas are narrower. In general, volcanic deposits and limestone are found above 3,000 m a.s.l., and softer sandstones are located below this elevation. Once the river reaches this elevation its rate of descent increases markedly: above the 3,000 m contour, the river drops 50 m in approximately 6 km (8.33 m/km); below this contour, it drops 200 m in the same distance (33.33 m/km).

This geomorphological setting has important effects on both prehistoric and modern land use and settlement patterns. Abundant water sources on the puna to the west, and the relative lack of water sources on the puna to the east, provide a natural advantage to the exploitation of the west side of the valley core, in terms of potential irrigation. (The river is too deeply entrenched to serve as a source of irrigation water.) Further, the wider flat shelves on the west valley side provide natural areas for water accumulation; with some human modification these provide easily accessible sources of water to supply both villages and agricultural fields. The wider shelves also provide broad, relatively flat areas suitable for tuber cultivation. All things considered, the geomorphology of the core of the Carhuarazo Valley confers a slight advantage to the west valley side.

It should pointed out, however, that this pattern does not apply to the tributary valleys, especially that of Chipao. Above Chipao numerous small streams carry glacial meltwater from Señal Carhuarazo, so there is abundant water available on the east valley side in that tributary.

Natural Environment

The climate of the region is generally similar to that of other areas of the Peruvian highlands. It is characterized by two different seasons during the course of each year: a rainy season beginning in late November and ending in May, and a dry season for the remainder of the year. Most rain falls between January and late March. The valley is relatively dry as compared to other highland valleys due to a rain-shadow effect. Rain-bearing prevailing winds pass across the Amazon basin and drop most of their moisture as they ascend over the eastern ranges of the Andes. Valleys located toward the western side of the Andes, such as the Carhuarazo Valley, receive less rainfall than the eastern ones.

According to Troll (1968) and Pulgar Vidal (1987) this region comprises three natural biotic zones:

Janca or nival (above 4,800 m). This zone comprises the permanent snow fields on the slopes and summit of Señal Carhuarazo, and the tundra-like zone that immediately surrounds them. Where not glaciated or covered with snow, the land is very marshy, and vegetation sparse (Pulgar Vidal 1987:114-15).

Dry puna (4,000-4,800 m). Located below the snowline, the primary plant formations of this zone are subalpine scrub desert and humid alpine tundra (Tosi 1960: 124-31). Most of this zone is classed as the latter, and is dominated by a single species of bunch grass, *Stipa ichu*. Where overgrazed, *tola* (*Lepidophyllum*) shrubs have invaded. To the west and south of the valley there are regions of lakes and marshes; here there are some areas of subalpine humid puna, and very humid alpine tundra (Tosi 1960: 131-35).

Dry sierra scrub (2,700-4,000 m). Extending down to the base of the valley, this is a zone of thorny shrubs (fam. Berberidaceae), cacti (*Opuntia* spp., *Cereus* spp., *Trichocereus* sp.), and some native trees: molle (*Schinus molle*) and sauce (*Sambucus peruviana*). Between elevations of 2,800 and

3,600 m this zone has been extensively modified by human occupation such that few remnants of the natural plant community still exist. Most of this zone is classed as mountain steppe (Tosi 1960:80-87), with the lowest elevations classed as low mountain steppe (Tosi 1960:72-79). This zone, which is characteristic of all parts of the valley proper, may be further subdivided into several ecozones, based on human subsistence strategies.

MODERN CULTURAL ADAPTATION

As discussed in Chapter 2, vertical ecology is a term coined by John Murra (1972) to describe the division of Andean valleys into a series of levels, each of which is exploited in different ways by the native population. These ecozones correspond generally to vertical elevation, but there is a good deal of variation both within a single valley, and between valleys in different areas of the Peruvian highlands. The zones described here pertain to the core of the Carhuarazo Valley as it is exploited today (Fig. 4.3); slight variations occur in the more protected tributary valleys, where zones may extend to slightly higher elevations. Exploitation in prehistoric times was probably similar to that of today, but with some important differences that will be summarized below.

At present the inhabitants of the valley use only two terms to describe different ecological/topographical zones: *puna* and *quebrada* (valley). Lower portions of the valley are simply referred to as *más quebrada*. The zones described here are based on observations made in 1981, as part of the regional survey conducted in the valley core. Data recorded for each archaeological site included descriptions of both natural and domestic plants on and in the vicinity of each site. Based on these observations, the quebrada is divided into four discrete zones, each of which is characterized by a different mix of crops (Fig. 4.3). Given the extreme topography of the valley, there is a good deal of variation in different parts of the valley in terms of the extent of each zone, and the exact elevations at which it is found (Fig. 4.4). The elevations given here for each zone are averages for the entire valley core.

Puna (above 4,000 m). This corresponds more or less to the natural dry puna zone described above. Its lower boundary is sharply marked around most of the perimeter of the valley by an outcropping of andesitic basalt cliffs. The high puna ecozone is found at elevations in excess of 4,000 m, like the natural zone, and is used primarily for herding of native camelids (alpacas and llamas), and some sheep. Agriculture is rarely practiced in this zone, given the high probability of frost, although sometimes small fields of quinoa are seen.

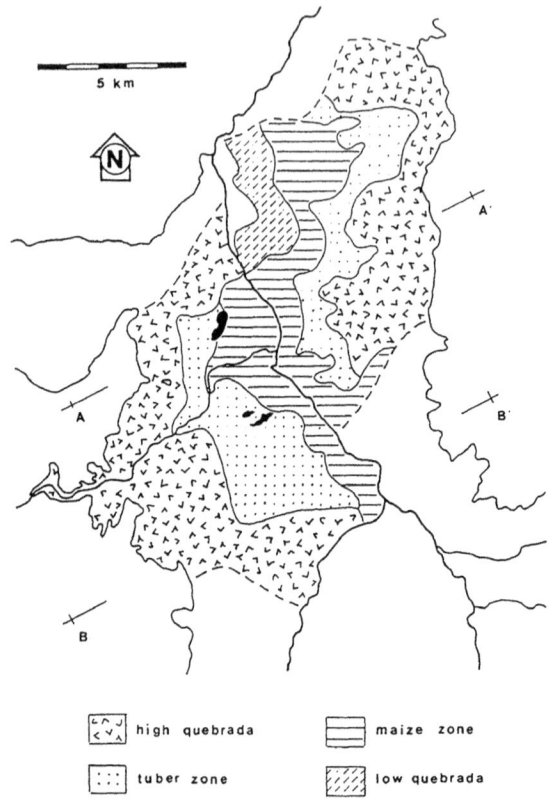

Figure 4.3. Ecological map of the core of the Carhuarazo Valley.

Large numbers of vicuña are found today on the puna to the southwest of the valley, an extension of the Pampa Galeras Reserve. In an effort to prevent the extinction of the species this reserve was created and the vicuña designated an endangered species. After just a few decades, the vicuña population has increased so dramatically that the pampa is badly overgrazed and some vicuña are being moved to other parts of the sierra.

Traditionally the puna has been a zone of communal use. At present there is no private ownership of this land (especially since the agrarian reforms of the late 1960s), although municipal maps indicate that the land is divided up between the various districts. People dwelling in the valley keep herds of animals on the puna, and go there on a temporary basis to tend the herds. No permanent villages are located in this zone today, although nuclear and extended family groups do live more or less permanently on the puna. These people have established reciprocal exchange relations with the villagers, trading salt and alpaca wool for agricultural

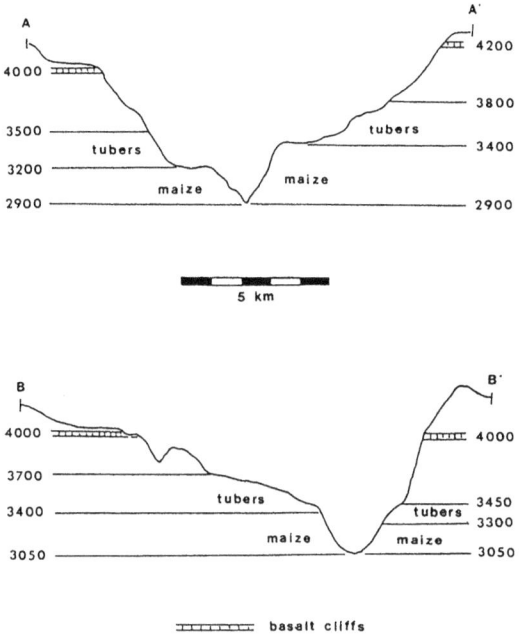

Figure 4.4. Two cross-sections of the Carhuarazo Valley indicating the agricultural resource zones present, their elevations, and detailing local variations in resource zone configurations.

produce. They return to the villages fairly regularly for major religious fiestas, and also in times of exceptionally severe weather. The puna is regarded as a savage place, a place in which supernatural (usually evil) creatures may be encountered. Behavior not permitted in the "civilized" valley may take place in this zone, an uncivilized place where normal social rules do not apply (B.J. Isbell 1978:57-59).

High quebrada (3,600-4,000 m). Below the puna is a zone of scrub vegetation and grasslands, transitional between the puna and the cultivated zones below. In some areas this is sharply marked by cliffs of andesitic basalt ringing the top of the valley, with large boulder fields in the talus below. Vegetation is dominated by the native thorny shrubs and cactus described above for the dry sierra scrub zone, and *ichu* grass. This zone is used for some grazing of cattle and sheep, along with the occasional llama. In general no agricultural fields are found in this zone, although there is some evidence of old (perhaps prehistoric) fields.

Tuber quebrada (3,300-3,600 m). This zone is devoted primarily to the cultivation of native tubers, and in some areas can extend as high as 3,800 m. All but the steepest portions of the valley between these elevations is devoted to the cultivation of numerous varieties of potato (*Sola-*

num tuberosa), and smaller quantities of ulluco (*Ullucus tuberosus*), mashua (*Tropaeolum tuberosum*) and oca (*Oxalis tuberosa*). Native grains include quinoa (*Chenopodium quinoa*) and cañihua (*Chenopodium canihua*); Old World domesticates include barley and some wheat, along with onions and garlic. Although some fields have been artificially leveled, most of the zone is unterraced. Tubers are typically grown on naturally flat areas, or on gently sloping hillsides; they are not grown on very steep hillsides. As can be seen in profile B-B' in Figure 4.4, the tuber zone on the east side of the valley is quite restricted, extending only up to an elevation of 3,450 m. Above this elevation the land is too steep for tuber cultivation.

In the lower portion of this zone, steeper slopes are terraced, and maize is grown on those terraces. As will be discussed in greater detail below, terraces create a microclime that reduces the danger of frost, especially on steeper slopes. Thus, the range of maize sometimes extends up into the tuber zone, to elevations as high as 3,500 m. For example, on the west side of the valley in profile A-A', Figure 4.4, the tuber zone is rather steep; here there are numerous sectors of terracing and maize cultivation. And on the east side of the valley, the maize zone extends up to 3,400 m; tubers are grown in the less steep areas above this elevation.

Especially on the southwest side of the valley, with its broad flat shelves of land, the tuber zone is quite large (see profile B, Fig. 4.4). Although numerous irrigation canals flow through this zone, they supply water from the puna to lower elevations; fields in the tuber zone are dry farmed. Today most land is privately owned, but traditionally the land was divided between *ayllus*, and farmed communally within each *ayllu*. No villages are located within this zone proper, but Cabana, Queca, and Aucará are all located at the boundary between this and the maize zone below. (Although Cabana and Aucará were moved to their present locations by the Spanish in the *reducciones* of the 1560s, neither was moved any appreciable distance from its original setting, so all reflect traditional site locations with respect to resource zones.)

Maize quebrada (3,000-3,300 m). This is the zone in which maize is the predominant cultigen, along with other grains and some tubers. In many ways, this zone is an artificial product of terrace construction. The upper limit of this zone is effectively defined by the upper limit of maize cultivation, which is in turn defined by the extent of terracing. This zone is extensively terraced, except in rare naturally flat areas. Prior to the construction of terracing much of this zone would have been unsuitable for maize cultivation, except in protected areas, and much of it was probably devoted to tuber cultivation.

In the upper third of the zone, terraces are dry farmed, but the need for irrigation increases at lower elevations, owing to the increased aridity and higher temperatures of the lower portions of the valley. The major crops grown in this zone today are wheat and maize (*Zea mays*); other products include alfalfa, field peas, and common beans (*Phaseolus vulgaris*). Tarwi (*Lupinus mutabilis*) is prevalent in this zone, but appears to grow untended around field margins, rather than being intentionally cultivated for food. Tarwi has an extremely bitter taste, and forms an effective barrier to keep grazing animals out of agricultural fields.

Some potatoes and quinoa are also grown in this zone. Although potatoes are predominant at higher elevations, in the tuber zone, they grow quite well at all elevations. In fact, in the maize zone when a field is put back into service after an extended fallow period, the first crop to be planted is potatoes. Only in the second year is corn or wheat planted. The fact that the tuber zone is used predominantly for potatoes is due primarily to the fact that maize will not grow there, rather than because potatoes do better at higher elevations.

A roseaceous fruit tree, locally called *níspero*, is grown for its fruit, and the native *molle* tree is used for its berries (from which an alcoholic beverage, *chicha de molle*, is made) and its bark, which has medicinal uses. A variety of cactus fruits are collected in this zone, especially *tunas* (*Opuntia exaltata*). Maguey (*Agave americana*) has been planted extensively in this zone, especially along stone walls.

As in the case of the tuber zone, most land is privately owned. Two settlements, Huaycahuacho and Ishua, are located at the base of this zone, in an area of transition between it and the lower quebrada zone. (Both settlements are in ecological settings very similar to their original, pre-*reducción* locations.) The village of Sondondo is also located at 3,000 m, but is not in a transitional zone between the kichwa and a lower zone—it is located on a small piece of valley bottom land at the base of the valley—the only such bottom land in the valley. (It was originally located farther to the north, at a somewhat higher location, making exploitation of higher zones more convenient; today the people of Sondondo must travel longer distances to tend their fields in the tuber zone.)

Low quebrada (2,800-3,000 m). Below 3,000 m there are only very limited areas of arable land. Lying at the northern end of the valley, this zone is hotter and drier and has poorer soil than other zones. The division between this and the maize zone above at 3,000 m is somewhat arbitrary; there is a gradual increase in aridity as one descends through these zones. However, below the 3,000 m contour, agricultural fields are notably sparse, while above 3,000 m most land is cultivated. All fields in the low quebrada must be irrigated. Cultivation ceases at or above 2,800 m, below which the land drops off steeply. Here the river begins its descent through a deep, high-walled canyon.

In this low zone it is still possible to grow maize and other crops of the kichwa zone, plus calabaza squash (*Cucurbita moschata*) and citrus trees. This very small zone is exploited by people living in Ishua and Huaycahuacho, who sell or trade squashes and lemons to people in other villages.

There is no zone in the Carhuarazo Valley equivalent to the mayopatan (literally, "river-place") zone of Chuschi, in the Río Pampas valley to the north (B.J. Isbell 1978:55), or the temple zone of Uchucmarca in the north Peruvian highlands (Brush 1977:74-77). The low quebrada zone in the Carhuarazo Valley is so limited in area that it cannot supply the quantities of squash, *ají* (chili peppers), fruit, and sweet corn characteristic of other Andean valleys. Today such products are acquired from the south coast, brought in by truck and sold in small *tiendas* in the towns and villages. In recent years there has been a great out-migration from the Carhuarazo Valley to the coast, especially to Ica and Lima. Coastal produce is also brought by migrants returning to the valley for fiestas or other important events, and distributed among family members.

Below the elevation of 2,800 m there is no more human occupation or exploitation of the valley core, as this lies at the natural topographic boundary at the north end of the valley. From this point on, until it meets the Río Pampas, the river (now called Jatun Mayo—the big river) is deeply entrenched. Groups living in small pockets of cultivated land high above the river, ten kilometers or more to the north, are quite distinct from those of the Carhuarazo Valley. Access to that region is by road from the north, and economically the area is tied with regions to the north and east; in contrast, access to the Carhuarazo Valley is from the south, and the valley maintains social and economic ties with areas to the south and west. There is little interaction between the two regions, and different dialects of Quechua are spoken. At the time of the Spanish conquest those groups living to the north were included in the same ethnic group as the valleys to the northeast and east; collectively they were called Soras. Inhabitants of the Carhuarazo Valley were called Andamarca Lucanas, and were related to groups to the south and west, called Lucanas.

This division of the valley into vertical ecozones is defined on the basis of the valley core, and the same pattern holds true for the tributary valleys with some slight exceptions. Narrower, more protected valleys are less subject to frost at the higher elevations, so each zone may extend to slightly higher elevations. The most striking case of this is the Andamarca tributary where impressive agricultural terraces are seen up to an elevation of nearly 3,800 m. This valley produces what may be the highest-growing maize anywhere in the world, due perhaps to its terraced microclime, as well as to the development of a variety of maize specifically adapted to local conditions. Andamarca maize is regarded as a very special strain, and is handed down from generation to generation, from mother to daughter (Tom Zuidema, pers. comm.).

Overall, the Carhuarazo Valley conforms to a pattern of vertical zonation that Brush has called the "compressed" type of zonation (Brush 1977:10). In this and similar valleys there is a relatively steep gradient of environmental zones such that the different zones are located close to one another. In this type of system each household generally has access to land in each zone, and directly exploits all zones, as is the case in the Carhuarazo Valley, where there is no well-developed local market system. Produce from lower, locally unavailable, zones is acquired from the coast through intrafamilial exchange networks, or via the cash economy.

As discussed in Chapter 2, the archipelago pattern of exploitation involves long migrations and the establishment of distant colonies to supply resources lacking in a region. While this pattern is most applicable to the drier puna highlands of the south, it does not apply well to the páramo highlands of the north (Murra and Wachtel 1986:5). Its existence in the central highlands is still open to debate, and the case of the Carhuarazo Valley might suggest that this pattern did exist prehistorically, but in modified form.

A document (Monzón 1881b) describing this valley in 1586 lists six villages of Andamarca Lucanas located in distant regions, outside the valley. One of these was the village of Uraguaci, located in the upper Nasca drainage—about a three-day walk from the Carhuarazo Valley. Ayapata, the pre-*reducción* site of Uraguaci, is located at an elevation of about 2,900 m, with direct access to the lower maize-squash-ají zone, which is of very limited extent in the Carhuarazo Valley. In addition, the village was located in a position suitable for establishing direct exchange relationships with coastal settlements of the Nasca valley. Indeed, Uraguaci was located on a route that the Inka used as one of their "royal highways" connecting the highlands with the south coast; the Inka built one of their *tampu* (way stations) near Uraguaci. (The modern village is called Tambo Quemado—burned *tampu*.) A brief investigation of Uraguaci in 1986 indicated that the village was probably established during the Late Intermediate period (LIP). Surface remains include sherds mostly of coastal styles of the LIP and Late Horizon. About 10 percent of the surface sherds are styles identified in the Carhuarazo Valley—styles dating also to the LIP. Hence Uraguaci was probably not an Inka *mitmaq* settlement, as it predates the Inka conquest by some centuries, but may have been a colony established outside the Carhuarazo Valley in order to gain access to goods not available locally.

Of the other five villages mentioned in the document, two (Alcamenga and Guamanquiquia) are located in the Río Pampas Valley. The fact that these settlements do not provide access to resources unavailable in the Carhuarazo Valley, considered along with the fact that the Río Pampas region was extensively resettled by the Inka, suggests that these two villages probably were *mitmaq* settlements. The other three villages (Colcabamba, Para, and Chicalla), however, are located in the upper Yauca Valley, which flows to the coast. I suspect that these, like Uraguaci, may be colonies located for access to lower ecozones.

Thus, data suggest that the archipelago pattern may have existed in the central highlands, although not at the scale that it did near the altiplano. The colony at Uraguaci may have facilitated exchange with the coast, as well as having direct access to a resource zone not available in the Carhuarazo Valley. Limited data suggest that this modified archipelago pattern was established during the LIP. But in earlier times, for example, during the Middle Horizon and earlier, local exploitation may have been limited to the zones in Carhuarazo Valley, and this archipelago pattern might not have emerged yet.

PREHISTORIC CULTURAL ADAPTATION

The modern exploitation of the mountain environment of the Carhuarazo Valley is based on the adaptation of the human population to the conditions of temperature, rainfall, and soils. Resource zones for the cultivation of different assemblages of plants tend to vary by elevation, and several zones can be defined on the basis of modern land usage. While the prehistoric agricultural adaptation may have been similar in many ways to the present, some aspects may have differed. These differences include the species of plants and animals exploited, possible differences in climate, and the effects of terracing.

Plants and Animals Exploited

First of all, the range of plants and animals exploited today includes a great number of species introduced by the Spanish. This has two important implications. The first is the obvious point that many crops grown today were not grown prehistorically: wheat, barley, field peas, alfalfa, onions, garlic, citrus fruit and others. Some nondomesticated plants exploited for food, fuel and industrial materials—such as tuna cactus, maguey, and Scotch broom (*Spartium junceum*)—likewise did not exist in the Andes. And animals such as sheep, goats, cattle, horses, burros and house cats were not present either.

The second implication, which is the more important, is that many native domesticates were probably cultivated to a greater degree prehistorically than they are today. Native plants including tubers such as oca, mashua, and ulluco, grains like cañihua and quinoa, and tarwi seeds may have made up a more substantial proportion of the prehistoric diet than they do today. Certainly potatoes were a major staple, but the modern cultivation of potatoes to the near exclusion of the other native tubers may reflect, in part, a modern preference for potatoes. The maguey plant, introduced to Peru in Colonial times from Mexico and today used for its fibers, has out-competed and nearly replaced the native *Furcraea*, which probably was exploited in much the same way before the introduction of maguey. In some parts of Peru sheep have replaced alpacas as the predominant species of herd animal. Although the alpaca still dominates the puna around the Carhuarazo Valley, sheep are increasing.

Climatic Differences

Certain aspects of climate may have varied prehistorically, especially temperature and rainfall. Such variations would have altered the arrangement of resource zones, raising or lowering the limits of cultivation of certain plants. For example, if the climate were significantly colder, the boundaries of the various ecozones would have been lower; conversely, warmer climate moves zones upward in elevation. In terms of long-term climatic change, certainly there have been some important shifts since the close of the Pleistocene—a gradual warming, then a slight cooling trend—not to mention shorter term events such as the Little Ice Age. For present purposes, it will be assumed that during the Middle Horizon temperatures were not significantly different from modern ones.

Rainfall is a different matter. Recent analyses of ice cores from the Quelccaya Ice Cap near Cuzco have produced estimates of changes in precipitation over the most recent 1,500 years (Thompson et al. 1985). These estimates show quite a bit of variation in precipitation over time. First of all, the current century appears to be wetter than average. Given that the Carhuarazo Valley is a rather dry valley by modern standards, the situation must have been even worse in the past. And second, there have been periods of significantly drier conditions, as well as periods of relatively greater precipitation in the span of time that includes the Middle Horizon.

Thompson et al. (1985: 973) identify the following wet and dry periods, occurring in the latter half of the first millennium A.D.:

540-560	drier
570-610	extremely dry
610-650	wetter
650-730	drier
760-1040	wetter

The Wari expansion of the Middle Horizon is generally considered to have occurred between A.D. 650 and 800, based on uncalibrated radiocarbon dates. Using calibrated dates, the beginning of the expansion would have occurred in the mid-eighth century, after an extended dry period. But regardless of the absolute dating (a problem that will be addressed below), it is clear that the periods before and during the Middle Horizon included periods of time that varied in terms of precipitation. It is therefore useful to consider the effects of differing precipitation on the local ecology of the Carhuarazo Valley.

Differences in precipitation have several effects on local zonation, affecting both the availability of water for dry farming, and the danger of frost. In a drier period, obviously, less water overall is available for dry farming. Given that aridity increases as one moves down in elevation, upper elevations can be dry farmed, while lower ones require irrigation. Thus in a dry period, the range of land suitable for dry farming narrows: the upper limit stays roughly constant, but the lower limit rises. However, during a wetter period, more land in lower zones can be dry farmed, hence the range of cultivable land increases as the lower limit moved down in wet periods.

The amount of water in soil also affects soil temperature. As water is a more efficient conductor of heat than soil, heat absorbed during the day will penetrate to a greater depth in wet soil than in dry. At night as the heat radiates back into the atmosphere, dry soil will cool more quickly than wet soil. Thus increased moisture in the soil may prevent killing frost in some circumstances. In effect, this moves the frost line slightly upward during wetter periods, and downward during drier ones.

Considering that the present century is one of wetter conditions, the general ecological conditions of wet periods in the past may have been roughly the same as they are today. However, during dry periods we expect to see a more limited range of elevations suitable for agriculture, with the lower elevations especially affected. Today most fields and terraces between the elevations of 3,200 and 3,600 m are dry farmed, so these were likely the limits of agriculture during wet periods prehistorically, prior to the development of irrigation systems. During significantly drier periods agriculture was probably more limited in extent, especially at the lower end of the range.

Terraces and Irrigation

The constraints of the natural environment on agricultural potential are significantly affected by human modification, especially the construction of terracing. Terracing serves a number of important functions, and in the central Andes allows the cultivation of maize in areas otherwise unsuitable. At a basic level, terracing allows the cultivation of steep slopes by providing a flat planting surface, allowing deeper soil formation, and preventing slope wash erosion (Donkin 1979:2-3). But the critical aspects of terracing in the cold, dry Andes are its effects on moisture and temperature (see, for example, Isbell 1974).

First of all, the flat surface provided by terraces increases water retention in the soil by decreasing runoff of rainwater. So terrace construction could increase the range of agriculture downward during dry periods, even without irrigation technology. Short of actual terrace construction, even the building of minimal water control features could increase the range of agriculture during dry periods. And further, irrigation systems could be more easily designed and implemented on flat surfaces like terraces, especially in the drier lower elevations.

A critical limit to maize cultivation is frost; therefore, ameliorating the threat of frost will increase the range of maize cultivation. Terraces have a number of thermal properties that serve to do just this, and allow maize cultivation at significantly higher elevations. The stone retaining walls of the terraces absorb more solar energy than soil during the day; at night, while soils cool off quickly, the greater energy stored in the stones takes longer to radiate out. Thus, terraces stay warmer at night than do unterraced hillsides. The steeper the slope, the greater the ratio of stone to soil, and the greater the effect. Terraces raise the *average* temperature of the agricultural fields, thereby increasing the rate of growth of maize, and they increase the *minimum* temperature, decreasing the chance of frost at higher elevations, thereby increasing the length of the growing season.

Prior to the construction of the extensive terracing in use today in the Carhuarazo Valley, the upper limit of maize agriculture was certainly much lower. The exact limit is not known at present, but it may have been as low as 3,000 m, or even lower. Only in protected areas, such as steep-sided, narrow ravines, does maize grow above 3,000 m in the absence of terraces. It is possible that maize cultivation was extremely limited in the Carhuarazo Valley prior to terrace construction, if indeed it was present at all.

Zones presently used for maize cultivation, especially the less steep portions of those zones, are also suitable for tuber cultivation, especially in the higher areas, which are cooler and have more moisture. The maize zone is essentially an artificial zone, created through the construction of terraces. Prior to terrace construction, then, what is today the maize zone was probably a lower continuation of the tuber zone. In fact, given the natural dryness of the Carhuarazo Valley, it is possible that maize was not produced in any substantial quantities at all, until the terraces were built, and the maize zone created.

SUMMARY: ENVIRONMENT AND ECOLOGY DURING THE MIDDLE HORIZON

The basic vertical zonation of the Carhuarazo Valley during the Middle Horizon was probably similar to that of the present, with some small variations. The mix of crops was certainly different, and there was certainly more reliance on certain native plants than is seen today. Precipitation may have been similar to the present during some periods, but significantly drier at other times. Changes in precipitation would have had important effects on agriculture. There may have been a long dry period prior to the Middle Horizon, and perhaps dry conditions at the time of the Wari expansion. At such times I expect that the upper zones, particularly the tuber zone, would have been more intensively cultivated, and lower zones, the maize and low quebrada, less intensively cultivated than they are today, especially prior to the construction of terraces and/or water control systems. During wetter periods the ecological boundaries were probably roughly the same as at present. Prior to the construction of terracing, the upper limit of maize agriculture would have been significantly lower, and, hence, the maize zone would have been much more limited.

NOTE

1. Although I refer to the valley here as the Carhuarazo Valley, this is not a name that is used locally. Today, the river that flows north through this valley has a series of names, including Mayobamba, Sondondo, Jatun Mayo, Yanamachay, and Pampamarca, derived often from the name of whatever local village it passes at a particular point. Older maps of the valley indicate the name Carhuarazo for the river; hence this name I use to refer to the valley. My use of the name stemmed from an attempt not to offend the residents of any one village by using the name of another to designate the entire region. It did cause some confusion, however, when I appeared with a permit to survey the "Valle Carhuarazo," a region whose existence local authorities did not recognize.

5

Analysis on a Regional Level
Settlement Patterns in the Carhuarazo Valley

This chapter and the two that follow present archaeological data pertaining to the events of the Middle Horizon in the Carhuarazo Valley. The goal of these chapters is to elucidate and reconstruct these events in order to understand the nature of the Wari occupation. This chapter begins at the level of the region, summarizing the data on settlement patterns and evidence of subsistence and political organization before and during the Middle Horizon. The following chapters move to successively more specific foci: first, the investigation of a single site, Jincamocco, and second, discussion of the artifacts uncovered at that site.

At the outset it must be noted that there is a definite Wari presence in the Carhuarazo Valley. This fact has been known since research began there, and has influenced much of that research and the interpretation of data recovered. The first archaeological investigation of the region was undertaken in 1974 when William Isbell organized a brief reconnaissance to the valley, in which seven sites were noted in the vicinities of Andamarca and Cabana Sur. The primary objective was to visit a site near Cabana Sur, thought to be a Middle Horizon site. Materials from the surface of that site, Jincamocco, in fact pertained to the Middle Horizon, and its architecture indicated that it was a Wari site.

In 1976-77 I returned to the valley and undertook excavations at Jincamocco, confirming this identification, and concluding that the site functioned as a regional administrative center within the Wari polity

(Schreiber 1978). However, the lack of any other research in or around this valley left Jincamocco without any regional context. So in 1981-82, a site survey and settlement pattern analysis were completed. The goal of the survey was to understand general processes of imperial consolidation in both the Wari and Inka cases (Schreiber 1987a). Shortly after the survey was completed, the region fell under control of the Sendero Luminoso, making additional fieldwork impossible. However, one final visit was made to the valley in 1987, during a period of relative calm, to clarify a number of issues that had arisen during the analysis of the data from Jincamocco and the regional survey.

Despite the chronological order in which research proceeded, I shall begin here with the results of the regional survey. Once a broad regional perspective is established, data from Jincamocco will provide more specifics regarding the major political center and evidence of political administration there. This chapter, then, treats the entire region as a unit of analysis.

In the regional chronology developed for the Carhuarazo Valley (Table 5.1) there are three ceramic phases that precede the Middle Horizon: the Accanta phase, the Sacrahua phase, and the Kancha phase. These correspond generally to the Initial period, the Early Horizon, and the Early Intermediate period, respectively. The Kancha phase may include Middle Horizon 1A. The Willka phase is the period of Wari occupation, dating from Middle Horizon 1b through 2. The Marke phase begins in Middle Horizon 3, after the Wari collapse. The periods of particular concern here are the Kancha phase and the Willka phase.

For the most part, in this regional analysis, I attempt to distinguish local sites and features from foreign ones. As will be seen, the foreign remains dating to the Willka phase are directly associated with Wari and events taking place in the Ayacucho Basin. Events of the Middle Horizon are seen not only through these foreign sites and artifacts, but also through changes in the local culture at the time of the Wari occupation.

FIELD STRATEGIES

From June to October of 1981, a systematic survey of the Carhuarazo Valley was undertaken. Subsequent laboratory analysis was undertaken at the Museo Nacional de Antropología y Arqueología in Pueblo Libre, Lima, from October, 1981, until February, 1982. Additional analysis was undertaken in November, 1985, also at the Museo Nacional.

The survey was concentrated in the valley core, as defined in the preceding chapter (Fig. 5.1; see also Fig. 4.3). The northern boundary of the survey corresponds to the natural topographic boundary of the valley; to

TABLE 5.1
The Master Sequence of Andean Chronology, and Temporal Phases in the Carhuarazo Valley

Dates	Standard Chronology		Carhuarazo Valley
A.D. 1533	Late Horizon		Jasapata
A.D. 1476			
	Late Intermediate period		Toqsa
A.D. 1000			
	Middle Horizon	3-4	Marke
		2	Willka
		1B	
		1A	Kancha
A.D. 600	Early Intermediate period		
200 B.C.			
	Early Horizon		Sacrahua
800 B.C.			
	Initial period		Accanta
1800 B.C.			
	Preceramic period		
?11,000? B.C.			

the east and west the survey extended up to the 4,000 m contour. The southern boundary on the west side of the valley was defined by the high ridge separating the valley core from the Andamarca tributary. The southern boundary on the east side of the valley was determined by time and access constraints; here the survey reached Sondondo, but did not extend appreciably south of that village. No survey was undertaken in the tributary valleys, but sites in the vicinity of Andamarca had been visited during the 1974 reconnaissance.

Within the valley core, an intensive systematic survey was undertaken. The general strategy was to walk transects along elevation contours, with survey team members spread about 50 meters apart. Aerial photographs were used in the field to locate survey transects, and sites recorded. The photos, however, are at too small a scale (average 1:40,000) to be useful for

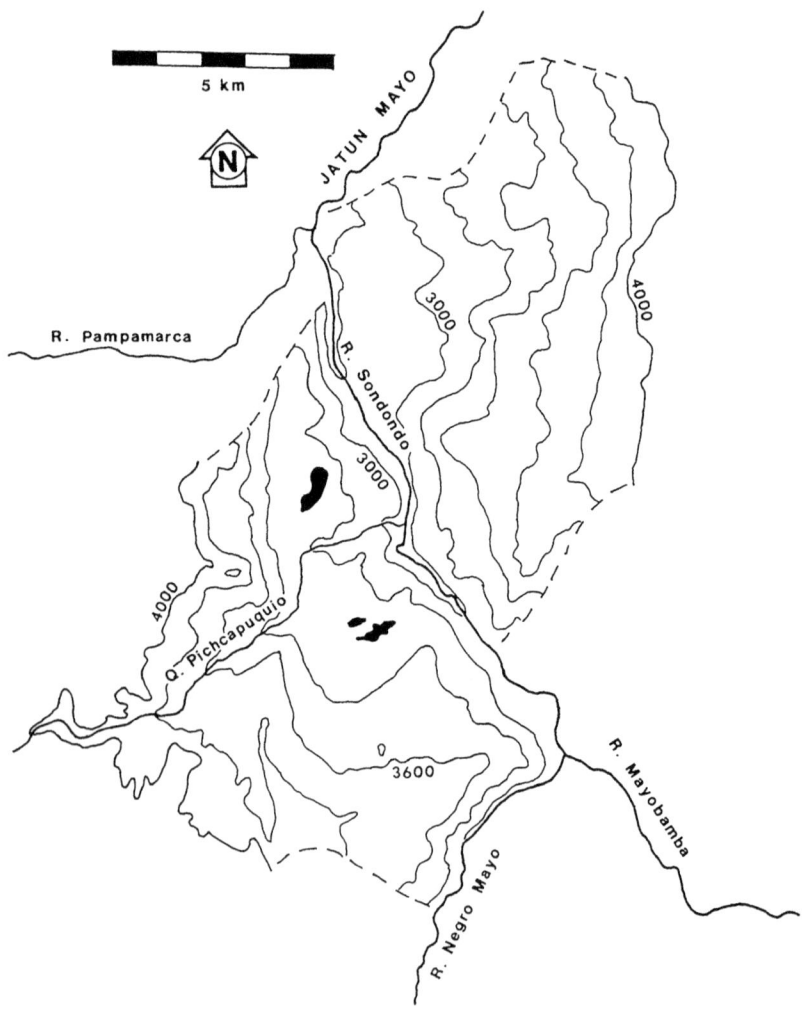

Figure 5.1. Map of the Carhuarazo Valley showing topographic detail within the surveyed portion of the valley core.

drawing site plans; further, the scale of features visible on the photos varies by altitude, so it was very difficult to make accurate measurements from the photos.

Isolated sherds and even small concentrations of sherds were not recorded as sites; indeed, the entire valley is one continuous low-density sherd scatter. Recorded sites included significant concentrations of artifacts (generally more than 20 in a restricted area), and remains of architecture. Information recorded at each site included: name and location, ecological context (including both natural and domestic plant associations), topographic setting, description of cultural remains, rough site plan, and a record of surface collections made and photos taken. Larger, more complex sites were divided into discrete loci and each locus was collected separately; smaller sites were generally collected as a single locus. When surface artifacts were sufficiently dense, two kinds of surface collections were made. First, a quantitative collection was made in an area of known dimensions (anywhere from 1 by 2 m to 3 by 4 m); the goal was to collect at least 100 diagnostic artifacts in such a sample. Then a general collection of diagnostic artifacts was made from the remaining surface of the locus. Often on smaller sites with low densities of artifacts, only diagnostic samples were collected.

Time constraints prohibited the drawing of detailed maps of sites, with just a very few exceptions. Maximum regional coverage was the highest priority, so most effort went into pedestrian survey. Once the crew members were acclimated to the altitude, it was not uncommon to traverse 20 kilometers horizontally, and 1,500 meters vertically in a day's work.

Sites were numbered consecutively, with prefixes denoting department and province. For example, Jincamocco is designated Ay5-6. "Ay" denotes the Department of Ayacucho; "5" denotes the Province of Lucanas (fifth in alphabetical order within the department); "6" is the archaeological site (numbered consecutively in order of discovery). Sites Ay5-1 through Ay5-7 were recorded by the 1974 reconnaissance. Five of these sites were re-recorded in 1981, and the survey continued until the last site, Oscconta, was recorded as Ay5-80. In all, 78 sites were formally recorded and collected in 1981; an additional 45 low-density artifact scatters were recorded in daily field notes. A total of 120 square kilometers was intensively surveyed, comprising most of the valley core, up to the 4,000 m contour.

SETTLEMENT PATTERNS OF THE KANCHA PHASE

Ceramic Definition of the Kancha Phase

Ceramic styles of the Carhuarazo Valley that are characteristic of the Kancha phase are part of a long developmental sequence beginning in the Accanta phase. These ceramics include plainwares, red-slipped wares and several types of local decorated wares. The Kancha phase can be separated from earlier phases on the basis of both diagnostic forms, and changes in relative frequencies of some types. The Kancha phase is defined not only on the basis of surface collections, but also on the excavations at Jincamocco. While surface remains were very fragmentary, and all sites were multicomponent, an unmixed Kancha component was identified in stratigraphic excavations at Jincamocco. This allowed the unambiguous separation of Kancha materials from those of earlier and later phases. The following discussion summarizes the temporal associations of the various ceramic types. As these categories of ceramics were found in great quantities in the excavations at Jincamocco, they will be described in detail in Chapter 7.

Separating Kancha from Pre-Kancha Phases

Plainwares can be divided into two categories, regular and polished. Regular plainwares show no diagnostic changes that can distinguish pre-Kancha from Kancha phases. However, there is a diagnostic polished plainware jar shape that occurs frequently in pre-Kancha contexts. This jar form is best known from the site of Hacha, an Initial period site in the Acarí Valley on the south coast.

Local decorated styles include incised bowls, which have a geometric design band incised on the exterior, just below the rim. While some designs are temporally diagnostic, incised bowls are small and thin-walled, and were not found well-preserved in surface collections. Thus, they were not useful in separating Kancha from pre-Kancha phases. Another local decorated form is a necked jar with an undulating, serpentine-like design on its neck. In the Kancha phase, the design is usually made with an appliqué fillet with almond-shaped punctations evenly spaced along it. In pre-Kancha phases the fillet is smaller, and thinner, and the punctations are very small. In addition, early forms may place the appliqué strip along the juncture of the neck with the jar body, rather than undulating around the neck. Other local decorated styles include a variety of plastic decorative techniques: stamping, fluting, punctation, and incised designs. Some designs are diagnostic of pre-Kancha phases, such as stamped circles, and circles with center dots, and can be used to distinguish earlier phases from the Kancha phase.

In addition to diagnostic designs and forms that can distinguish the Kancha phase from pre-Kancha phases, certain changes in the ceramic frequencies can be noted. In particular, incised bowls are relatively rare in pre-Kancha times, but can comprise as much as 20 percent of the Kancha phase assemblage. In contrast, polished plainware decreases markedly in the Kancha phase, and other tactile designs also decrease in frequency. Red-slipped wares occur in both phases, in low frequency.

Continuity from the Kancha to the Willka Phase

While incised bowls and necked jars with serpentine designs are the most common local decorated wares in the Kancha phase, they continue with only subtle changes into the Willka phase. Certain other tactile designs, such as dashes, gouges, and fluted ridges, also continue into the Willka phase.

Evidence of External Connections

Polychrome sherds are extremely rare in the Kancha phase, and do not represent a local style. When identifiable, these are pieces from the Nasca tradition, especially Nasca phase 4, of the south coast. Given their extremely low frequency, they probably represent the odd trade piece. These rare pieces do indicate, however, that there was some interaction with the south coast prior to the Middle Horizon.

Interestingly, there are no ceramic pieces from areas to the north; importantly, the Huarpa style of the Ayacucho Basin is not present in the valley. The Huarpa style is found throughout the Wari heartland, and I have suggested in Chapter 3 that the distribution of this style defines the pre-expansion core area of the Wari polity. The lack of Huarpa sherds in the Carhuarazo Valley is a strong indication that this valley lay well outside the pre-expansion core of the Wari polity, and that the valley did not become tied to Ayacucho until the Middle Horizon.

Sites of the Kancha Phase

All sites dating to the Kancha phase are multicomponent sites, most dating also to earlier phases, some continuing into later phases. Those sites having pre-Kancha and Kancha phase diagnostics, but that did not have any diagnostics of the following Willka phase are presumed to have been abandoned at the end of the Kancha phase (Table 5.2). (See Appendix A for tabular summaries of surface collections of ceramics for sites occupied in the Kancha and Willka phases.)

Two settlement types can be identified in the Kancha phase, villages and hamlets, distinguished on the basis of size and architecture. Villages are larger, ranging in size from one to two hectares; they are characterized by the remains of small (3-5 m diameter) round houses made of angular broken stone set in mud mortar. Hamlets, on the other hand, are quite small, ranging from a few hundred square meters up to a maximum of 0.4 hectares; they have no traces of architecture.

By the end of the Kancha phase, at least four local villages were occupied, all on the west side of the valley (Fig. 5.2); one other village, on the east side of the village, may also have been occupied at that time. And at least eleven hamlets can be dated to the Kancha phase. Throughout the pre-Kancha and Kancha phases, most settlements were located on the west side of the valley, which, as I have pointed out, had some advantages over the east side in terms of terrain and water availability.

Accanta Pata (Ay5-17)

This village is the highest village occupied during the Kancha phase. It is found at an elevation of 3,600 m, immediately adjacent to and above the tuber zone. Despite its altitude, it is located in a protected microclime that keeps it warmer than other areas at a similar altitude. Today there is a small garden adjacent to the site with crops that normally occur only at lower elevations. The site covers about 2.0 hectares, and the quantity of stone on the site indicates that it once had stone architecture; however, at present the stones have been rearranged to form low field walls, and little trace of the original architecture is visible. Surface remains included ceramics diagnostic of both pre-Kancha and Kancha phases, but did not include any diagnostics of the Willka phase. Accanta Pata was probably the first village site occupied in the valley, so it was the longest occupied of any of the pre-Middle Horizon villages.

Sacrahua (Ay5-35)

This village is located at the upper extreme of the tuber zone, at an elevation of 3,525 m. It is located in a rather open setting, with a broad expanse of grassland in the high quebrada above, and tuber fields immediately below. It covers 1.8 ha, and has abundant amounts of stone that must reflect remains of architecture. The stones have been piled up to

TABLE 5.2
Presence/Absence of Temporally Diagnostic Ceramics on Village Sites

Phase	17	35	5	6	63	67	50	41
Pre-Kancha		x	x					
Kancha		x	x	x				
Kancha/Willka	x	x	x	x	x			
Willka			x		x	x	x	x
Willka/post-W			x		x	x	x	x
Post-Willka					x			

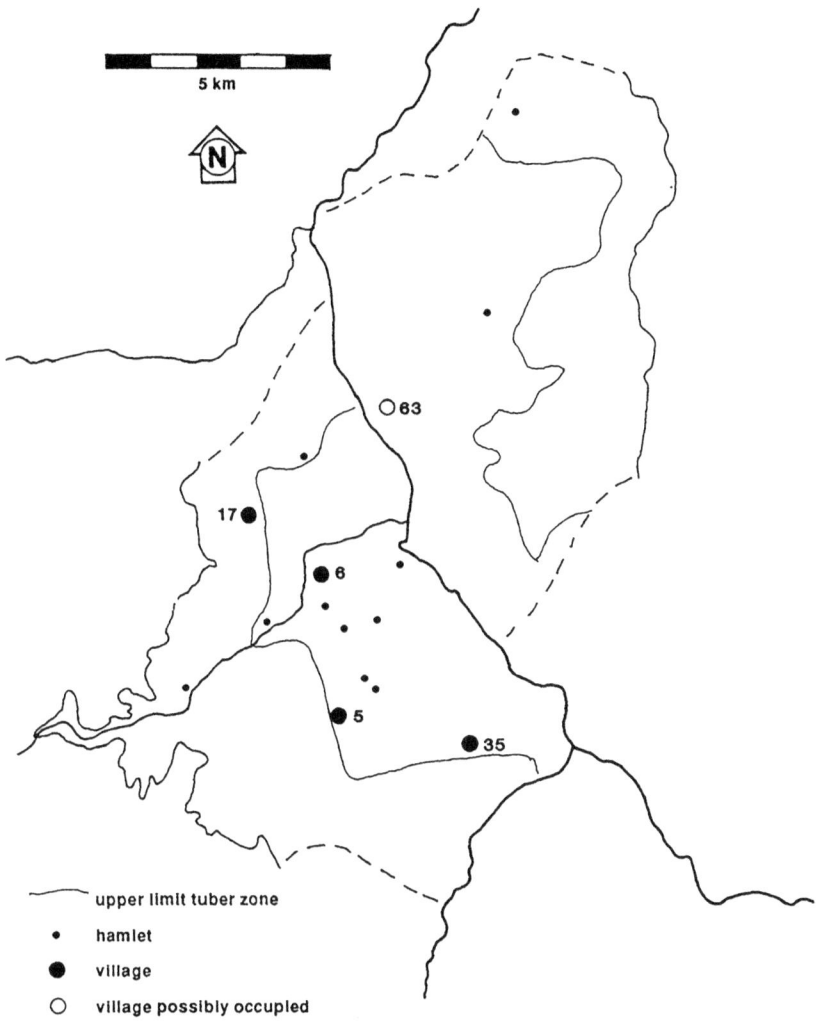

Figure 5.2. Settlements of the Kancha phase.

form low field walls, so original buildings are difficult to see, but there are traces of round structures. Surface remains included ceramics diagnostic of pre-Kancha and Kancha phases, but no diagnostic Willka phase ceramics.

There is one additional feature that warrants attention with regard to this site. Above the site, in what today is grazing land, is an expanse of hillside, at an elevation just below 3,700 m, on which parallel rows of rock alignments are found. Only one or two stones high, they are not formal agricultural terraces, yet they probably served an agricultural function. The increased water-retention behind these low walls might have allowed agricultural subsistence above the normal limits of cultivation, especially during wetter periods. These alignments are probably associated with Sacrahua, as no other sites are located in the vicinity.

Corralpata (Ay5-5)

This site, located at 3,500 m, is in the upper portion of the tuber zone, but adjacent to a small area of terracing where maize grows at higher-than-normal elevations. The site covers some 2.0 ha, and remains of round stone buildings still stand on the site. No pre-Kancha remains were present in surface collections, but diagnostics of both the Kancha and Willka phases were recovered. Thus, unlike the two preceding sites, Corralpata was not abandoned at the end of the Kancha phase, and it continued to be occupied through the Willka phase.

Jincamocco (Ay5-6)

Jincamocco is, of course, primarily a Middle Horizon site, and is characterized by extensive constructions of nonlocal style. However, under and adjacent to the foreign constructions are found traces of a local village dating to the Kancha phase. Obscured by the later construction, its total spatial extent is unknown. The architecture of the Kancha phase village comprises round stone houses. Located at an elevation of 3,300 m, it lies at the ecotone between the modern maize and tuber zones. Prior to the construction of terraces, however, the lower elevations may have been used for limited tuber cultivation.

Chaupi Urco (Ay5-63)

This site is the lowest village in the valley at this time, lying at an elevation of 2,975 m, and the only village on the east flank of the valley. It is characterized by round stone architecture, and covers 1.0 ha. It lies in the lower portion of the maize zone. The dating of this site to the Kancha phase is problematic; surface remains include diagnostics of the Willka phase, and post-Willka phases. There were also recovered sherds of incised bowls and necked jars with serpentine designs that may date to either the Kancha or Willka phase. While there are no diagnostics of the Kancha phase present, a Kancha phase occupation is a possibility. Interestingly, this was the only village not abandoned and relocated at the end of the Willka phase.

Hamlets

At least eleven, and possibly thirteen, hamlets can be dated to the Kancha phase. They are located widely dispersed throughout the valley, ranging in elevation from 2,950 to 3,650 m. Hamlets are small, have no architectural remains, and may have been only seasonally occupied farming settlements. At present, inhabitants of the region typically live in the villages and towns, but may move to small, temporary sites near their fields during times of sowing or harvesting. Alternatively, the Kancha phase hamlets may have been permanently occupied; surface remains do not very well indicate seasonality of occupation. In any case, all hamlets are very small, suggesting that they were occupied by very small groups, perhaps a single household.

Dating of the hamlets is sometimes problematic as artifacts are usually quite sparse, compounded by the fact that they are all multicomponent sites. Dating of hamlets relies primarily on the presence or absence of temporally diagnostic ceramics. Surface remains from eleven hamlets included ceramics diagnostic of both pre-Kancha and Kancha phases. Two other hamlets were found with local decorated ceramics that could date to either the Kancha phase or the Willka phase, or both.

Of the hamlets that clearly date to the Kancha phase, seven are located in the tuber zone, and one at lower elevation, near the river. The remaining three are located above the modern limits of cultivation, but in areas probably suitable for tuber cultivation. As in the case of the villages, nearly all hamlets were located on the west side of the valley.

Kancha Phase Settlement Pattern and Political Organization

The local settlement pattern during the Kancha phase, immediately prior to the Wari incursion, comprised four or five small local villages, and eleven to thirteen hamlets. All villages have evidence of architecture, and where preserved, the typical forms are round buildings made of broken stone. All sites are located in or adjacent to agricultural zones, and most are located in or adjacent to what is today the tuber zone. The three largest villages are located at the upper limit of the tuber zone. One village, Jincamocco, was located near the lower limit of the present tuber zone. Only one village, with a possible occupation in the Kancha phase, was located in the maize zone. The archaeological data from the valley as a whole suggest that the valley was not terraced at this time. Thus, all sites were situated with good access to zones of tuber cultivation.

The local subsistence was likely based on the cultivation of potatoes, oca, mashua and ulluco. Quinua and cañihua were probably also grown. Maize agriculture was probably very limited, if indeed it was present at all. Without terracing the upper limit of maize would have been quite a bit lower than at present, perhaps even below 3,000 m.

In addition to agricultural production, the local subsistence was probably also based on camelid herding. The largest villages, and hence most of the population, were located at the upper extreme of the tuber zone, with good access to the grasslands of the high quebrada and the puna.

In terms of political organization, the settlement patterns of the Kancha phase do not suggest any complex political organization above the level of the village. No villages stand out as significantly larger than any of the others, so no site size hierarchy is apparent among the villages. Nor are there architectural or artifactual data suggesting any kind of status differences within or between the villages. Although hamlets are distinctly smaller, they may have been occupied only seasonally by people who normally resided in the villages.

In sum, at the time of the Wari incursion in the Middle Horizon, the valley was occupied by four or five villages of tuber farmers and herders. They were not politically centralized, and were probably characterized by an egalitarian society, each village comprising a small segmentary unit. They may have had informal connections with the south coast, but they were not directly tied into any of the events taking place to the north in the Ayacucho Basin.

SETTLEMENT PATTERNS OF THE WILLKA PHASE

All of this changed in the Willka phase. During this period a foreign presence appeared in the valley. A major change in subsistence occurred, with concomitant effects on local settlement patterns. New artifact styles were introduced, new architectural forms were built, and I will argue that a new political order took hold in the valley.

Material Definition of the Willka Phase

The Willka phase can be distinguished from the earlier Kancha phase, as well as from later phases, on the basis of diagnostic forms, and changes in frequencies of ceramic types. Ceramics of the Willka phase include plainwares, red-slipped wares, and local decorated styles, like the preceding Kancha phase, but also include slip-painted pottery and new lithic forms. The Willka phase is defined on the basis of surface collections, and also on a well-defined Willka phase component based on materials excavated from Jincamocco. Ceramic categories of the Willka phase are described in detail in Chapter 7.

Separating the Willka Phase from the Kancha Phase

Plainwares show some subtle changes in the Willka phase, including changing proportions of some shapes, and the introduction of a new rim form. Unfortunately, these changes were not visible in surface collections, so plainwares were not a useful diagnostic of the Willka phase.

As discussed above, some local decorated styles continued with little change from the Kancha phase into the Willka phase: incised bowls, necked jars with serpentine designs, and some other tactile designs.

However, some tactile designs did not continue into the Willka phase, specifically the combined occurrence of incised lines with other techniques on the same vessel.

Most diagnostic of the Willka phase, however, is the introduction of slip-painted pottery. Less fancy painted pottery is not well polished and is painted only one or two colors, often black geometric designs on a red-slipped background. Black-on-red ceramics are also common in post-Willka phase contexts. Fancy polychrome pottery, painted in up to six colors, is very diagnostic of the Willka phase, clearly distinguishing it from the Kancha phase, in which polychrome pottery was extremely rare. The fancy polychrome ceramics of the Willka phase are of styles pertaining to Wari; fragmentary surface collections included some pieces that could be identified as being Chakipampa B or Viñaque style vessels. Painted ceramics also serve to distinguish the Willka phase from later periods.

In addition to these diagnostics, certain ceramic types changed markedly in frequency. There was a marked decrease in polished plainware, and in all local decorated styles (incised bowls, necked jars with serpentine designs, other tactile designs) in the Willka phase. At the same time, red-slipped wares increased in proportion, and slip-painted pottery made its first appearance.

Thus, changes in local styles, and in overall ceramic assemblage, not just the introduction of the Wari horizon styles, signal the change to the Willka phase. Based on stratigraphic excavations at Jincamocco, local artifact styles were found in clear association with Wari styles in Willka phase deposits. These same associations were seen in the surface collections at other sites. However, at those sites without the foreign horizon style, Willka phase occupations were identifiable purely on the basis of local styles. (In fact, one site with Wari-related architecture had no Wari sherds on the surface. It was identified on the basis of its architecture and the presence of local ceramics dating to the Willka phase.)

This is of critical importance, with broader implications for Andean research: it is possible here to identify the Middle Horizon in the absence of the horizon style itself. By documenting changes in the local styles, and not just focusing on the foreign intrusive styles, local sites can be identified as having been occupied in the Middle Horizon. Time and again we find local sequences that cannot firmly identify the Middle Horizon period because researchers have had to rely on the presence of the horizon styles for its definition. Where the horizon style is not found, the Middle Horizon is not identified—even though local styles show a long and continuous development before, during, and after this period. This has been a problem, for example, in identifying the Middle Horizon in the upper Mantaro Valley of Junín (Parsons, pers. comm.; Matos, pers. comm. 1982; Hastorf, pers. comm. 1989).

In addition to changes in the ceramic assemblage, there is a change in lithic technology that also signals a change between the Kancha phase and the Willka phase. During the Willka phase, blade technology was introduced into the valley. No blades have been found on earlier sites, but sites dating to the Willka phase and later have blades present. A new projectile point shape, diagnostic of the Willka phase, was identified from excavated material at Jincamocco, but no such points were found in any surface collections.

Changes in architectural forms also signal the Willka phase. Local houses prior to the Willka phase were round in form, and made of broken stone set in mud mortar. This style of local architecture continues without change through the Middle Horizon, and, indeed, up to Spanish Colonial times. But a new form is found in the Willka phase: rectangular compounds comprising contiguous rectilinear forms. This is a style clearly foreign to this valley, without local antecedent, and with a very limited temporal range: it occurs only in the Willka phase. Further, this style is typical of Wari, and diagnostic of Wari provincial sites; it is the clearest criterion for identifying Wari sites in areas such as this. In the Carhuarazo Valley four sites were found with this style of architecture, one very large (Jincamocco), and three very small.

Separating the Willka Phase from Later Phases

Finally, there are some clear diagnostics that can serve to separate the Willka phase from later periods. Polished plainware is extremely rare in post-Willka phases, and incised bowls and necked jars with serpentine designs do not continue after the Willka phase. Red-slipped wares and less fancy pottery continue to increase in proportion, while the fancy Wari polychromes are restricted to only the Willka phase. New styles of painted pottery are diagnostic of post-Willka phases. Interestingly, no projectile points were found in any surface collections from post-Willka phase sites, although blades were common. Local architecture, round stone houses, continued unchanged in form; only in the latest prehispanic phase did distinctive new forms appear, all of them Inka.

Local Sites and Settlement Patterns

Local sites of the Willka phase are of the same two settlement types as the Kancha phase: villages and hamlets. However, significant changes in settlement patterns occurred in the Willka phase (Fig. 5.3). Some earlier sites were abandoned, some new ones were established. While the periods up to and including the Kancha phase evince a gradual increase in population and numbers of sites, the Willka phase is a period of abrupt change. In additional to local villages and hamlets, we now find an intrusive nonlocal presence manifest at four new sites.

Analysis on a Regional Level

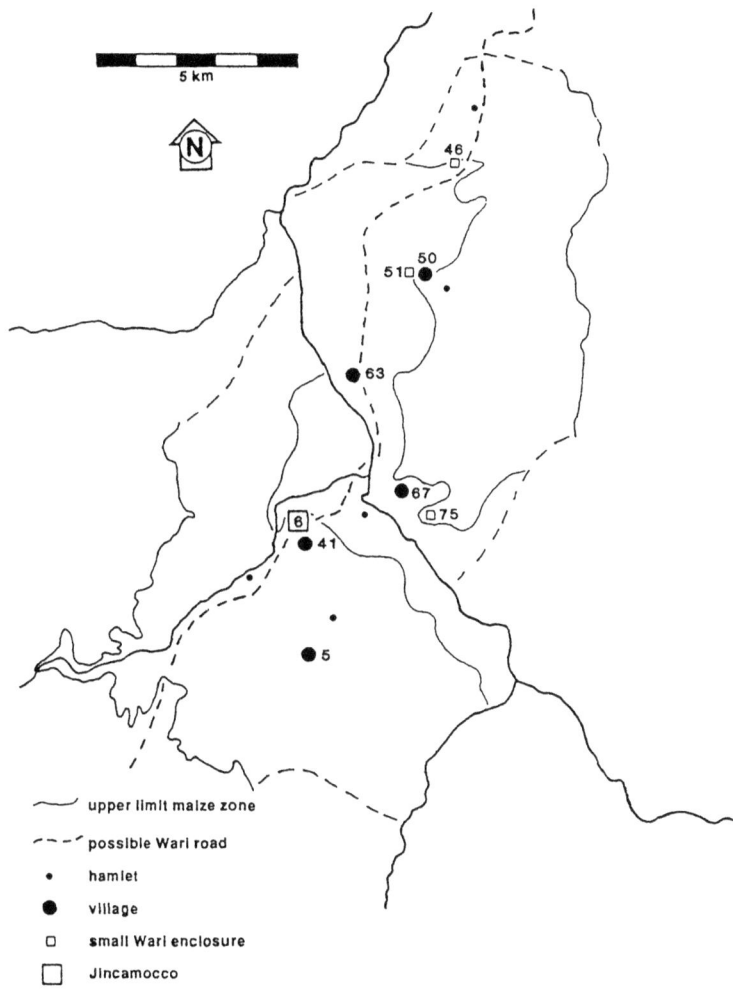

Figure 5.3. Settlements of the Willka phase.

At least five local villages were occupied during the Willka phase. Of the villages occupied in the Kancha phase, both Accanta Pata (17) and Sacrahua (35), two of the largest villages, both located near the ecotone between tuber cultivation and herding, were abandoned. The local village at the site of Jincamocco was razed to make room for new construction. Corralpata (5) continued to be occupied through the Willka phase. Chaupi Urco (63), possibly occupied in the Kancha phase, was certainly occupied through the Willka phase. Three new villages were established in the Willka phase.

Waillapampa (Ay5-41)

This site is located on a low hill at an elevation of 3,350 m, just to the southeast of Jincamocco. It is possible that the local village destroyed by the construction of Middle Horizon Jincamocco was simply moved to this adjacent hill. The site, lying immediately adjacent to the modern town of Cabana, is poorly preserved. Traces of architecture probably represent round stone buildings. The site covers at least one hectare; its total extent is probably obscured by modern houses. Surface collections at this site include ceramics diagnostic of the Willka phase, along with high proportions of red-slipped wares and slip-painted ceramics.

Millpu Pampa (Ay5-67)

Located at an elevation of 3,225 m on the east side of the valley, this village is just below the tuber zone, similar to the setting of Jincamocco. The site covers 1.5 ha, but is too poorly preserved to identify building forms. The quantity of stone on the site indicates that architecture was of stone, however. The dating of the site is somewhat tentative, as the number of diagnostics located was rather small, and no quantitative collection could be made. The only diagnostic ceramics on the site date to the Willka phase.

Pero Oyo (Ay5-50)

This village is located at 3,150 m, just below the tuber zone, near the upper boundary of the maize zone. It covers 1.5 ha, and architectural remains are of round stone buildings. Like Millpu Pampa, the dating of the site is somewhat tentative, as the number of diagnostics located was rather small, and no quantitative collection could be made. The only diagnostic ceramics on the site date to the Willka phase.

Hamlets

Surface collections from five hamlets included ceramics diagnostic of the Willka phase, and so can be securely dated to this period. Seven hamlets with Kancha and pre-Kancha occupations may have been occupied into the Willka phase, given the presence of local decorated styles that continued into the Willka phase; these sites have no clearly diagnostic Willka phase materials, however. And two other hamlets, discussed above, had very few diagnostic ceramics on them; only local decorated wares that can date to either the Kancha phase, the Willka phase, or both, were encountered.

The five hamlets securely dated to the Willka phase span altitudes from 2,950 m up to 3,450 m. This includes ecozones from the upper part of the low quebrada up into the tuber zone. Again, these may have been seasonally occupied farming settlements.

Changes in Local Settlement Patterns during the Willka Phase

Just in terms of local villages, both similarities and some major changes can be seen between the Kancha phase and the Willka phase. The local style of architecture in the Kancha phase—round stone buildings—continued to be the predominant form of construction on local sites during the Willka phase. The number of villages stayed roughly the same.

The biggest change was in terms of site location, especially with respect to elevation and ecological zone. In qualitative terms we see a downward shift in site location. Only one village remained in the upper portion of the tuber zone; the other two high elevation villages were abandoned. At least three new villages were established, one at the tuber/maize boundary, and the other two in the upper portion of the maize zone.

We can see this shift also in quantitative terms. In the Kancha phase the average elevation of a village site was 3,380 m; when weighted for site size, the average person lived at an elevation of 3,438 m. In the Willka phase the average elevation of a village site was 3,240 m; weighted for site size, the average person lived at an elevation of 3,262 m. This suggests a new subsistence focus, at lower elevations.

A downward shift in settlement location might suggest a period of colder temperatures, thus causing a downward shift in ecozones, but there are no data suggesting significant changes in temperature during the Middle Horizon. A significantly drier epoch would cause a slight lowering of the upper limits of cultivation, but would significantly *raise* the lower limits at the same time. This does not fit the observed data either. The downward shift in settlement location makes better sense if we consider a change in subsistence, specifically an increase in maize production.

Terrace Construction

Let us consider the evidence that suggests that agricultural terraces were introduced during the Willka phase. As discussed in the preceding chapter, terraces raise the upper limit of maize cultivation, and effectively create the maize zone. In the case of the Carhuarazo Valley, terracing raises the limits of maize agriculture up to at least 3,300 m in most areas, and even higher on steeper slopes. Prior to terracing maize cultivation was probably very limited.

As I have discussed elsewhere (Schreiber 1987a:271-73), there are several lines of evidence that can be considered in conjunction in order to estimate the date of construction of terraces. One line of evidence that is widely used to date terraces—the presence of potsherds on the terraces—can be particularly misleading. Artifacts present on hillsides prior to terrace construction become incorporated into terrace fill; their presence on the surface of a terrace therefore does not necessarily indicate dates of construction or use. Further, artifacts can be deposited at the time of construction, during the period of terrace use, and even after a terrace is abandoned and no longer used for agricultural production.

The presence or *absence* of artifacts on terraces, and the vertical distribution of artifacts within sectors of terracing, can indicate a date of construction in certain circumstances. One of the things that terraces do is limit erosion, the movement of material down a hillslope, by producing artificially leveled steps. Prior to terrace construction artifacts are free to wash down hillsides below abandoned (or occupied) sites; after terrace construction this movement is much more restricted. Hence, greater downward movement of artifacts is expected prior to terrace construction than after. And it is the case that artifacts from pre–Willka phase sites are often found broadly scattered down now-terraced hillsides. However, Willka phase artifacts are found in a much more restricted distribution—rarely more than two terrace levels down from a particular site. This strongly suggests a Willka phase date for the construction of terraces in the Carhuarazo Valley.

The relation of terraces to archaeological sites can indicate the relative date of terrace construction in several other ways. First, sites destroyed by terrace construction obviously predate the terraces. Second, sites or structures incorporated into terrace construction predate the terraces. Third, sites or individual structures built on terraces provide a date *ante quem* for terrace construction. And fourth, terracing that carefully avoids and winds around the perimeter of a particular site was likely built during the period that the site was occupied. In the case of the Carhuarazo Valley, the very few sites that were destroyed by terrace construction are all pre-Willka phase. The occasional structure built on a terrace is always post-Willka phase. And terracing encroaches right to the edge of, but not through, all the major sites occupied in the Willka phase. In all these cases, terrace construction might be dated to the Willka phase. In another instance, however, 16 Inka qollca were incorporated into a terrace; in this case the terrace was built, or repaired, in the Late Horizon.

The association between terraces and roads is also a good indication of relative date of construction. Roads in use at the time of terrace construction may be clearly visible and intact because the terracing left a clear path. Roads established after terrace construction are constrained by the terraces to follow more circuitous routes. If roads can be dated, then the relative date of terracing can be suggested (or vice versa). For example, the Inka road that extends from the river up the east side of the Carhuarazo Valley is barely definable as it winds around and between terraces; once it passes the terracing it is wide and paved, and easily definable. This indicates that the terraces predate the Inka road in this part of the valley. Another road, leading out of the valley toward the north follows a wide straight path up through the terracing. This road was likely in use at the time the terraces were built. This road was in use during the Willka phase.

And there are other lines of evidence that might suggest the relative date of terrace construction. Differences in construction style might indicate different periods of construction. In the Carhuarazo Valley there is one sector of terracing distinguished by a unique construction style. In this sector all sites date to the Late Horizon, thus suggesting a relatively late date for the terracing there. The use of terrace technology—cutting and filling, and the use of retaining walls to form artificially leveled areas—in other contexts may suggest the date of introduction of the technology. Beginning in the Willka phase, parts of sites were artificially leveled, further supporting the dating of the introduction of terrace technology to the Willka phase.

In sum, there are many lines of evidence that can indicate relative date of construction of terracing. Alone, no one line of evidence is convincing, but when taken together the evidence strongly suggests that a substantial portion of the terracing in the maize zone was built during the Willka phase (Fig. 5.4).

As discussed in the previous chapter, terracing produces a profound alteration of the ecological landscape. Terracing creates an artificial environment, a microclime, such that the upper limits of maize agriculture are significantly raised. This in turn creates the maize-producing ecozone. Prior to the construction of terraces, the alteration of the natural environment by human hands, the maize zone essentially did not exist in the Carhuarazo Valley. However, after the establishment of this new zone, human occupation was significantly altered in turn.

The downward shift in settlement location in the Willka phase may be related to the creation of a large zone suitable for maize cultivation. The majority of Willka phase sites are located in or immediately adjacent to the maize zone. Further, this pattern is also followed by the intrusive nonlocal sites: all four of these sites, discussed below, were located at the upper limit of sectors of terracing.

Nonlocal Sites

Four additional Willka phase sites are clearly distinguished from local sites by virtue of their distinctive architectural style. While local architecture features small round houses made of stone, the newly introduced architecture is rectilinear in form, and laid out in large subdivided compounds rather than individual structures. This is a clear and sharp break from the local tradition, easily distinguishable on the basis of sur-

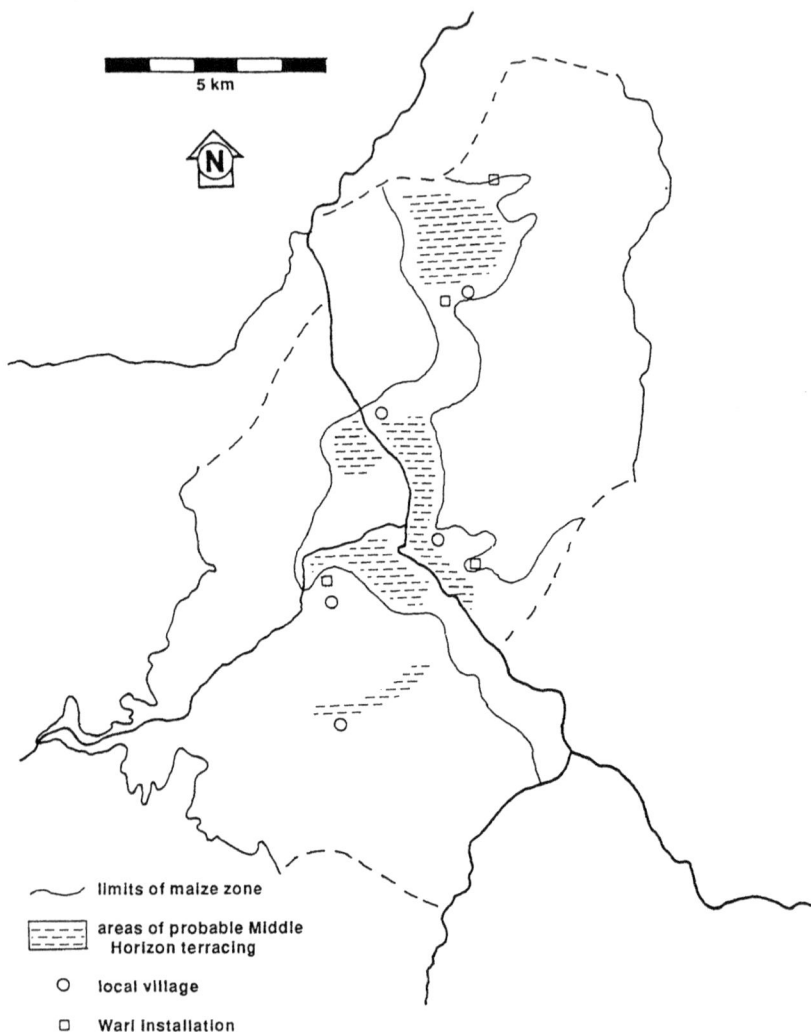

Figure 5.4. Areas of probable Willka phase terracing.

face remains at the sites. In most cases, as well, foreign ceramic styles—in particular the horizon styles that define the Middle Horizon throughout the central Andes—are found in greater proportion on these sites than on local sites.

Jincamocco (Ay5-6)

The most notable site in the valley at this time is of course Jincamocco. It is the largest site in the valley during the Willka phase, and much larger than anything in preceding periods; even in later periods only two other sites ever equaled or exceeded Jincamocco in size. Because of its central importance to this study, the following two chapters are devoted to the results of the excavations of Jincamocco. However, for the purposes of this chapter, with its broader regional focus, it is useful to briefly describe the salient features of the site, especially as it represents a foreign presence, distinct from local occupations.

Jincamocco is an exceptionally large site, by local standards, covering at least 15 ha. It may have been somewhat larger, but the modern town of Cabana Sur has encroached on the east margin of the site making its exact definition impossible. The site was first occupied by a local village, which, as discussed above, was razed to make way for new construction in the Willka phase. The Willka phase construction began as a single large compound, measuring 127 by 255.5 m, 3.24 ha. Its distinctive orthogonal plan clearly associates the site with Wari and distinguishes it from local constructions. The enclosure was built in Middle Horizon 1B, and occupied through MH 2. At some point during its occupation new constructions were added onto the original enclosure, greatly increasing the size of the site. After Middle Horizon 2 the entire site was abandoned.

The site is located at an elevation of 3,300 m, exactly at the ecotone between the maize and tuber zones. The location of Jincamocco on a small promontory overlooking the valley is not particularly defensible, nor is there any evidence of fortifications at the site. The site does command a good view of the valley, and of the roads entering the valley from the southwest. In fact, the name of the modern town, Cabana, derives from the Quechua *qhawana*, which means lookout.

The survey encountered three additional sites with the same foreign style of architecture. While Jincamocco is located on the west side of the valley, all three of the smaller sites were found on the east side. Despite poor preservation at all three, they clearly represent a distinctive new type of site. Smaller than local villages, their rectilinear compound style of architecture links them to Jincamocco, while also distinguishing them from local constructions. The presence of foreign artifact styles at two of them—diagnostic of the Middle Horizon—reinforces these interpretations.

Culluma (Ay5-75)

Also called Culluma Baja to distinguish it from a later village located nearby, this site is located at an elevation of 3,300 m. It lies on a ridge top, at the upper limit of the maize zone. Below it, on a relatively broad shelf, is some of the best agricultural land in the valley (at least by modern standards). This sector, whose terracing extends up to the edge of Culluma, is called Millpu. The local village of Millpu Pampa is located about 800 meters north of Culluma, in this agricultural sector. The location of Culluma is defensible, but there are no indications of fortifications. Its ridge top location distinguishes it from local villages, which are never found in such locations at this time. From this vantage point it has an unimpeded view of the valley to the north and south.

The site comprises a rectilinear subdivided compound measuring roughly 80 by 100 m; this style alone distinguishes it from local sites and associates it with the foreign architectural styles seen at Jincamocco. The site is poorly preserved, and all that remains on the surface are low mounds that indicate the locations of the buried walls. Running along the north side of the Willka phase compound, and extending farther up the ridge, is a row (and in one short section, a double row) of Inka *qollqa* (storehouses), numbering 46 in all. The qollqa are still preserved to a height sometimes in excess of 3 m. I suggest that the Willka phase compound provided a handy source of already broken stone, and that it was intentionally dismantled by the Inka when they had the *qollqa* constructed.

Artifacts were scarce on this site, in the area of the compound, but diagnostic local style Willka phase ceramics were identified, thus confirming the dating of the site.

Anta (Ay5-51)

Like Culluma, this site is very poorly preserved, but appears to comprise a rectilinear subdivided compound measuring about 80 by 100 m. Also like Culluma, it was probably intentionally dismantled, but at a much later date, in the sixteenth century, when the town of Huaycahuacho was reduced to its new location near the site. Its location on a ridge top is also similar to that of Culluma; again, the location is defensible, but no fortifications are seen, and it is in a good vantage point, much like Culluma. It lies along a trail leading out of the valley toward the east. The local village of Pero Oyo is located below the north side of this ridge just a few hundred meters to the east of Anta.

The site lies at an elevation of 3,125 m, making it the lowest of the Wari sites. This puts the site firmly in the maize zone, but it is similar to the other foreign sites in that it sits at the top of a major sector of terracing. The survey located mostly local ceramic styles on the site, with only a few examples of the Wari horizon styles. However, local residents from Huaycahuacho showed us *huacos* they had found there, including an intact tumbler with modeled face in the Viñaque style of Middle Horizon 2.

In addition to its foreign architectural style and ceramics, one other aspect of this site is especially notable. There is at least one (and possibly more than three) semisubterranean chamber built of large slabs of cut stone. The one chamber that was clearly visible measured 1.5 by 2 m, with a depth of at least 1.3 m. Entered through an opening in the north side, there seems to be a blocked doorway in the east wall. This chamber had been subject to local excavation—one of the only sites found with any modern disturbance—and its original contents are unknown.

Structures of large cut stone slabs are found at Wari, where it has been suggested that they functioned as tombs (Benavides 1985). However, these were plundered long ago, perhaps even in prehistoric times, and modern archaeological investigation found them empty. Thus, at Wari, the suggestion that they were tombs is still a matter of conjecture. There is some evidence in support of this interpretation, however, that derives from a sixteenth-century description of Jincamocco (see Chapter 6, below, for the text of this description). This passage states that near Jincamocco people remembered having seen tombs made of large slabs of cut stone (Monzón 1881b:210).

Although no such tombs were found in the vicinity of Jincamocco in the recent archaeological investigations, their presence at Wari and their association with Willka phase Anta in the Carhuarazo Valley indicates a Middle Horizon date for such structures. It is not improbable that they functioned as tombs, and documentary evidence from the sixteenth century might support this notion. To date, however, such structures have only very rarely been encountered outside Wari itself. Chávez Ballón reported some Middle Horizon slab tombs near Cuzco (Gordon McEwan, pers. comm.), but aside from these the only other ones known are in the Carhuarazo Valley: those at Anta, and purported ones at Jincamocco.

Willkaya (Ay5-46)

The third small Wari site encountered, Willkaya, is located at the northern end of the valley at an elevation of 3,325 m. This elevation is typically at about the ecotone between the tuber and maize zones, and the valley side below the site is intensively cultivated. However, today there is only very limited tuber agriculture above the site, and the region is used largely for grazing animals. The site is on a low rise near the edge of a broad flat shelf. The location is not particularly defensible, nor is there any evidence of fortifications.

Like Culluma and Anta, this site is characterized by a rectilinear subdivided compound measuring about 80 by 100 m. Artifacts on the site include both local and Wari styles of the Willka phase. The Wari sherds all seem to date to epoch 2 of the Middle Horizon. The site is very poorly preserved, but, unlike the other two sites, Willkaya was not stone-robbed—probably owing to its location far from any post-Willka phase occupation. There is a great quantity of stone still remaining on the site, but no original walls remain standing above the surface; only wall mounds yield evidence of the original site plan. The loose stones have been piled up into low walls crisscrossing the site in irregular arrangements.

Willkaya is not located near any local village, as are the other Wari sites, but the location of this site is particularly interesting. Despite the very broken topography of the valley, Willkaya has an unimpeded line-of-sight view of Jincamocco; it is located at the only point in the north end of the valley from which it is possible to see Jincamocco. Further, the site is located along a major road that enters the valley from the north. In fact, to enter the valley from the north, it is nearly impossible to avoid passing very close to this site. Thus, the vantage point of the site and its location along a major road and the only entrance into the valley from the north, suggest that this site's location may be due to a need to control access into and out of the valley.

There is one additional resource located near this site that may have been important: an obsidian source. Analysis of trace elements of obsidian from various archaeological sites in Peru was carried out by Burger and Asaro (1977). Most samples from Jincamocco, and several other sites in the Carhuarazo Valley, collected in 1974, were identified as having come from an unknown source thought to be somewhere in the Río Pampas drainage; they termed this unknown source the Pampas source. While the majority of samples from the Carhuarazo Valley were from this source, only a few artifacts made of this obsidian were found elsewhere: in Initial period contexts at Hacha, in the Acarí Valley of the south coast, and at Waywaka in Andahuaylas. Local informants in 1976 indicated to me that the obsidian source might be located near Huaycahuacho; this information was passed along to Burger and Asaro and published by them. Although the source was not located at that time, small obsidian nodules occurring in natural strata near Huaycahuacho were collected and subsequent analysis showed them all to be from the missing Pampas source (Burger, pers. comm.).

In 1981, the regional survey did finally locate the source of Pampas obsidian, and this source is renamed the Jampatilla source. The obsidian occurs in small nodules, up to about 10 cm in diameter, in a deposit of looser soil made up of mostly volcanic ash. The deposit is exposed around the flanks of the Jampatilla ridge, immediately to the southeast of Willkaya, between elevations of 3,250 m (at the western limit of the distribution) and 3,350 m (at the eastern limit). The deposit continues around past this ridge to the south for several hundred meters.

The large quantity of obsidian on all sites, of all periods, suggests that this source was exploited from very early times. The presence of Jampatilla obsidian at other sites dating to the Initial period indicates that it was being distributed outside the valley at that time. Samples from Jincamocco were nearly all of Jampatilla obsidian, so it is clear that the source was being exploited in the Willka phase. Jampatilla obsidian has not yet been identified at Wari or at any other Middle Horizon sites, but few analyses have yet been undertaken.

I suggest that the location of Willkaya indicates not only that the site functioned to limit or at least observe access into and out of the valley, but that the site might have been located in proximity to the Jampatilla source in order to extract obsidian for use at Jincamocco. It seems equally possible that Jampatilla obsidian was then distributed outside the valley, through the macroregional exchange system of which Jincamocco was a part.

Summary of Nonlocal Willka Phase Sites

Unfortunately, we have no excavation data from any of the three small Wari sites, and hence, no direct evidence of the function of these sites. The sites are so poorly preserved that we were not able to produce a detailed map of the surface remains at each site. Despite these limitations, a number of plausible interpretations can be offered.

First, the four Wari sites are clearly distinguished from local sites and represent a foreign intrusive presence. New styles of architecture were introduced, as were innovations in ceramic and lithic technology. The four sites are as clearly associated with one another as they are distinguished from local sites.

Second, there is a clear distinction between Jincamocco, on the one hand, and the three additional sites, on the other. Although they all share the same general architectural style, Jincamocco measures at least 15 ha, while the other sites are each less than 1 ha in size. This might be interpreted as a two-level site size hierarchy, with Jincamocco as the primary center. If the secondary, smaller centers also played some sort of administrative role, then we may be seeing here evidence of an administrative hierarchy. We do not have, however, any direct evidence of an administrative role played by any of the small centers.

Third, the three small centers may have served to maintain control over the local populace and over access into and out of the valley. Culluma and Anta are located in close proximity to local villages (as is Jincamocco, in fact); interestingly, these two villages were probably newly established in the Willka phase. And both Anta and Willkaya are located along major routes into the valley (again, as is Jincamocco).

Fourth, at least in the case of Willkaya, exploitation of special resources, in this case obsidian, may have been an important function.

Fifth, it is also possible that the small centers served as storehouses. In the case of the later Inka empire, great attention was given to the acquisition of subsistence and craft goods, and Inka storage centers were ubiquitous throughout their empire. If the same were true in the Middle Horizon, then we should expect to find storage facilities in the Carhuarazo Valley. In the Inka case, maize was the primary subsistence crop stored. Looking at the locations of the three small centers in the

Carhuarazo Valley we see that two of them are located at the ecotone between the maize and tuber zones, and the third is in the maize zone—and all have direct access to terraced sectors of the valley. The ridge-top locations of Culluma and Anta are appropriate for storage facilities, allowing good air circulation in and around those facilities. Further, the Inka chose the location of Culluma to establish their own storage center, suggesting that this was a good place to store things. Thus, it is plausible to suggest that the small centers may have functioned, at least in part, as storage centers.

Finally, the relative dating of the four sites may be important. Jincamocco was clearly built during Middle Horizon 1B, and occupied throughout MH 2. Beginning as a relatively small rectangular enclosure, at some time during its occupation it was greatly expanded until it reached its now visible size of over 15 hectares. Of the three smaller centers, limited ceramic evidence from two of them indicates a date of Middle Horizon 2 only. (The third was dated using local styles only, and these cannot be used to distinguish MH 1 from MH 2.) These data, taken together, suggest that there may have occurred a major change in the administration of the valley during the Middle Horizon. At some point Jincamocco became too small for Wari purposes, and was enlarged. The additional centers may have been built at that time, in MH 2.

Roads and Bridges

In addition to the major center at Jincamocco and three smaller centers elsewhere, remains of probable foreign influence may be seen in the presence of a major road, and a probable suspension bridge. There is some evidence that a major road connected this valley with Wari in the north, and Nasca on the south coast (Schreiber 1984). The Carhuarazo Valley lies midway between Wari and Nasca, 138 km from Wari and 124 km from Nasca, as the condor flies. Iconographic evidence suggests a strong connection between Ayacucho and the south coast beginning late in the Early Intermediate period, and continuing in the Middle Horizon (Menzel 1964).

Between Nasca and the Carhuarazo Valley is a major road that in the Late Horizon formed part of the Inka system of royal roads (Strube Erdmann 1963; Hyslop 1984). The presence of Nasca sherds on local sites in the Carhuarazo Valley indicates that at least informal connections were maintained between the valley and the south coast, so it is not unlikely that this road has a very great antiquity. In fact, the Jampatilla obsidian from Acarí indicates connections between the Carhuarazo Valley and the south coast all the way back to the Initial period, if not earlier.

From Nasca the road climbs to the northeast up the Tierras Blancas river valley past Tambo Quemado (location of a settlement of Andamarca Lucanas, discussed in the preceding chapter), up across the Pampa

Galeras and down to Lucanas, in the upper Acarí valley. From Lucanas it turns slightly northward and crosses the high puna of the Pampa Quilcata. Where I have observed this road on the puna, it is paved with slabs of volcanic tuff—paving probably dating to Inka times. The road descends into the Carhuarazo Valley along the south side of the Pichcapuquio quebrada. At the first point at which one can see into the valley, rounding a bend, the first sight is the promontory whose summit is entirely covered by the site of Jincamocco (Fig. 5.5). Not only is this an impressive view of the site for approaching travelers, but observers from Jincamocco also had a good view of anyone entering the valley on this road. Down the quebrada the tuff paving continues, except where the stones have been used to build modern walls; again, this paving probably dates to Inka times. Finally, the road leads directly to the edge of Jincamocco. A later Inka *tampu* (Ay5-39) is located on the hillside below Jincamocco, and the Inka road diverts to the north toward Huayhuay Puquio (Ay5-8) and Jasapata (Ay5-18), the Inka centers of control.

From Jincamocco the Middle Horizon road leads downward to the northeast, fording the Pichcapuquio quebrada, and merging again with the Inka road descending from Jasapata and Huayhuay Puquio. This

Figure 5.5. Photograph of the Carhuarazo Valley as seen from the major prehistoric road entering from the southwest. In the center of the photo is Jincamocco; it covers the two low hills and extends to the limits of agricultural terracing below. The original Wari enclosure lies in the saddle between the hills.

route leads down a steep incline cut through a vertical cliff face to a large rock outcropping towering some ten meters above the river below. Across the narrow gorge the pillars of the Inka suspension bridge can be seen. The fact that the Middle Horizon and Inka roads are coterminous here, and that the only means by which the river can be crossed at this location is on a suspended rope bridge, argues that Inka-style suspension bridges were in use in the Middle Horizon.

From the bridge two paths lead up the valley side. The one climbing to the east winds around and among the terraces, emerging above Queca as a wide paved Inka road leading east to Soras, Abancay and Cuzco. The one leading north is very badly eroded, and sections have eroded completely away along the rather steep slope near the river. This trail meets a major road that runs the length of the valley, and continues north. This road is not paved completely with slabs of tuff, as is the Inka road, but has large stone steps of andesitic basalt in steeper sections. This is quite distinctive, and different from Inka paving. This road climbs out of the valley to the north, passing immediately adjacent to Willkaya, the small Wari site. The road has a wide unobstructed path through the terraced valley side, indicating that the road was in use at the time of terrace construction (unlike the Inka road to the east, which postdates the construction of the terraces). Leaving the valley, the road passes through Soras territory to the north, across the Río Pampas, past Vilcas Guamán, and on to the Ayacucho Basin, the Wari heartland.

The fact that these roads provided access between the Carhuarazo Valley and both Ayacucho and Nasca, that they are directly associated with two Wari sites, and that they were in use at the time the valley was terraced indicates that they were used during the Middle Horizon. It appears, further, that portions of the roads were re-used by the Inka, and paved by them in a different style.

THE MIDDLE HORIZON IN THE CARHUARAZO VALLEY

To summarize the regional data from the Carhuarazo Valley, we see both continuity and change from the Kancha phase to the Willka phase. Local styles of ceramics and architecture continued with little change, and showed no significant influence from the foreign styles. New ceramic styles were introduced, along with a new architectural form; together these signal the beginning of the Willka phase.

Visible in the archaeological record is a change in settlement location, particularly in the case of the local villages. A downward movement of village locations, coupled with the massive construction of terraces throughout the valley, signals a major shift in subsistence focus. Whereas Kancha phase subsistence was focused on the cultivation of tubers, maize agriculture may have formed a major component of the subsistence pursuits beginning in the Willka phase. Most importantly, these changes occurred at the very time that a foreign presence, Wari, appeared in the valley.

In the Kancha phase there is no evidence of complex political organization, and the local culture was probably organized at the level of a simple tribal society. This, too, changed in the Willka phase. Considering the evidence of both local and foreign sites, we now see evidence of a complex political order, dramatically different from the preceding period. A very large foreign site comprised the primary center of the new order, and three smaller centers may have functioned to exercise control over local villages. At the local level, villages did not change appreciably; they remained in the same size range, with the same architecture, and lack evidence of social stratification. There is some evidence that suggests a further shift in political control later in the Willka phase. The major center, Jincamocco, was greatly enlarged; the smaller centers also may have been built later than the original enclosure at Jincamocco.

The picture that emerges in the Carhuarazo Valley is one of a small highland valley with a relatively low population engaged in tuber cultivation and camelid herding. The society was basically egalitarian, without complex political organization. Suddenly, in the Middle Horizon, a new culture appeared. A large center was built, after summarily destroying the local village that occupied the desired location. Terraces were built and maize cultivation increased. Some of the local villages were moved down to lower elevations, closer to the newly created maize zone. The increased labor inputs required to build the center and complete the terraces may have necessitated bringing in laborers from outside the valley. The large center was expanded, and three new centers built, all near the terraced sectors of the valley. Eventually the newly created maize zone would have produced large quantities of maize, collected by the new political rulers. The maize may have been stored at Jincamocco and in the smaller centers; some of it may have been shipped out of the valley. Some of the maize was probably used to support the local labor projects.

The valley was transformed from a simple tribal society with perhaps only intermittent ties to the south coast, to a small component of a macroregional political and economic system. The same foreign styles of artifacts and architecture seen in the Carhuarazo Valley are seen broadly distributed throughout the central Andes. As never before, the farmers of the Carhuarazo Valley were tied to, and controlled by, events taking place far from home.

Figure 5.6. Settlements of the Marke phase, the period following the collapse of Wari control.

And then it was over. We cannot know how quickly the collapse occurred, but the archaeological data indicate another major change in settlement patterns at the end of the Willka phase, equaled only by the change at the beginning of the Willka phase. The foreign political order disappeared, along with the distinctive styles that marked its presence. The foreign centers—Jincamocco, Culluma, Anta and Willkaya—show no evidence of occupation beyond epoch 2 of the Middle Horizon.

After the collapse of Wari control, in the ensuing Marke phase local ceramic styles continued to change, as local decorated styles disappeared and were replaced by red-slipped wares and painted pottery. Local round architecture continued as before, but now the occasional rectangular structure was built. But the local society was forever changed, and it never returned to the egalitarian society of tuber farmers that had existed prior to the Middle Horizon. Not only were the foreign sites abandoned, but every local village but one was also abandoned. Only Chaupi Urco (63), located down near the bottom of the maize zone, continued to be occupied. Three new villages were established, in or adjacent to the maize zone (Fig. 5.6). Of these, two were heavily fortified (49 and 55), and the third (18) was located in a defensible setting. Over time population increased, and in the Toqsa phase more villages and fortresses were established. Eventually several of these grew into large towns. By the Jasapata phase there were probably two polities organized at the level of simple chiefdoms in the core of the Carhuarazo Valley, and one each in the Andamarca and Chipao tributaries as well. And once again a foreign presence, this time the Inka, consolidated the valley under a greater political order.

6

Jincamocco
Analysis at the Level of the Site

In this chapter the focus narrows to a single site: Jincamocco. This is an intrusive Wari site in the Carhuarazo Valley, distinct from local sites by virtue of its great size, its architectural plan, and its artifact inventory. The regional settlement data presented in the preceding chapter suggest that Jincamocco was the focus of Wari political control during the Middle Horizon. While regional settlement patterns tell us a great deal about the effects of Wari control on the local culture, the excavation of Jincamocco gives us more detailed evidence of the actual Wari occupation.

This chapter will describe the 1976-77 excavation of Jincamocco, and some of the results of those excavations. First, the site is described, along with a history of research that guided the research. General field strategies are summarized, as is the typical stratigraphy uncovered throughout the site. After a consideration of archaeological formation processes, each excavated architectural unit is then treated separately. The nature of the deposits uncovered is evaluated, and the details of architecture revealed are described. Then the overall architecture of the site is briefly compared with that of other Wari sites. Chapter 7 will discuss the artifact inventory, and the evidence for specific activities carried out in the site, and the nature of the social groups that occupied the site.

THE SITE OF JINCAMOCCO

Jincamocco has the distinction of being one of the few pre-Inka archaeological sites described in some detail in sixteenth-century Spanish documents. The first description of Jincamocco was written in 1586, during a Spanish *visita*. Answering a questionnaire sent out from Spain, the local *corregidor*, Luís de Monzón, provided a wealth of information about the geography of the valley, its towns and people, local history, and the local resources exploited. One question asked for information on all other "notable and admirable features" not covered by other questions. His response was as follows:[1]

> Responding to article twenty one, next to the town of La Vera Cruz de Cahuana is a ruined town, seemingly a very ancient thing. It has walls of worked stone, although the work is rough; some of the doorways of the houses are more than two *varas* high, and the frames are of very large stones; and there are traces of streets. The older Indians, those who know something of their past, having heard about it, say that in ancient times, before the Inka became their lords, there came to this land another people that they called *viracochas*, that there were not many of them, and that the Indians followed behind them listening to their words, and today they say that they must have been saints. They [the Indians] built roads for them, which are still seen today, as wide as a street and with low walls on either side, and in the resting places they built them houses of which there are memories today, and they built this town for them; and some Indians remember having seen in this town some ancient tombs with bones, made of squared stone slabs with white plaster on the interior, but at present not a bone nor a skull is seen. [Monzón 1881b:210]

This is the only archaeological site that Monzón described in the region. In fact, in his descriptions of the adjacent districts of the Hatun Soras (Monzón 1881a), and the Hatun Lucanas (Monzón 1881c), he mentions no other ruins, so the remains at Jincamocco must have been particularly noteworthy in his eyes. The description is also very interesting in that it gives some specific details of the site. First of all, the site is described as a large town with houses and streets, and standing walls two *varas* high (slightly less than two meters). Second, it firmly identifies the site as a pre-Inka town (despite the fact that its modern name translates to mean "Inka hill"). Third, it records a legend of the founding of the site, that it was built by the local people for a small group of foreigners; a similar legend has been reported in the cases of Wari and Tiwanaku, as discussed in Chapter 3. Fourth, it states that roads and resthouses were built for these pre-Inka invaders, and that the roads still existed well after the Spanish conquest. And finally, as discussed in Chapter 5, it describes tombs made of stone slabs.

In his insightful summary of the history of settlement development in ancient Peru, John Rowe cited this passage when he wrote:

Jincamocco

A 16th century writer describes what appears to be another [large site like Huari] at Cabana in the province of Lucanas in the southern part of the modern Department of Ayacucho. [Rowe 1963:14]

Despite never having seen the site, it turned out that he was quite right in his suggestion that it might be a Wari site.

Based on Rowe's assessment, William Isbell organized the brief 1974 foray into the Carhuarazo Valley, discussed above, for the purpose of visiting the site to determine its cultural affiliation. The plan of the site—a large rectangular compound with numerous subdivisions—and the presence of Middle Horizon Wari ceramics on the surface, confirmed Rowe's interpretation. Using alidade and plane table, a rough map was made of the central core of the site; systematic collections of surface artifacts were also made. A sample of obsidian pieces from those surface collections was given to Richard Burger for trace element analysis.

The mapping of the site was made especially difficult by the fact that no standing walls remained on the site (Fig. 6.1). Shortly before the 1586 *visita*, the town of La Vera Cruz de Cahuana (modern Cabana Sur) had

Figure 6.1. Photograph of Jincamocco. The sites covers the entire uncultivated area, above the agricultural terraces, to the edge of the modern town of Cabana, in the upper right. The remains of the enclosure can be seen in the center of the photo; rectangular agricultural fields are bounded by prehistoric walls within the enclosure. The walled structure just above is the modern cemetery, which lies in the unsubdivided half of the Wari enclosure.

been "reduced" to its new location adjacent to the site. As the town grew, Jincamocco provided a source of building stone near at hand. All that was left in 1974 were long straight low mounds, with abundant growth of cactus and thorny shrubs, and an occasional trace of a stone wall at the surface of a mound. These wall mounds enclosed large rectangular spaces that were either depressions filled with loose rock (and the occasional venomous creature), or carefully leveled agricultural fields. Further compounding the problem of constructing an accurate map, each wall mound typically contained (as I found later) an average of three parallel walls. Bits of wall visible on the surface of each mound were mapped in, but when the dots were connected many of the resulting lines were oddly diagonal—the resulting of connecting segments of parallel walls as if they were a single wall. In actual fact, the plan of the site is extremely regular, and there are few walls that depart from the rigidly rectilinear plan. While the site core was quite apparent, despite problems with visibility and thorns, the total Wari enclosure is actually twice what was mapped. The unmapped (in 1974) half of the enclosure has no subdivisions, so was not very apparent on the surface, although one part of the enclosure wall clearly continued beyond what was mapped. And although we recognized and mapped some remains on a low hill immediately to the north of the enclosure, and some walls to the south, we did not realize the actual extent of architectural remains elsewhere on the site (Fig. 6.2).

In sum, based on the reconnaissance of 1974, Jincamocco was clearly a Wari-style rectangular enclosure. It appeared to be about 130 meters square in size, with a few adjacent structures, especially on the north hill. It was on the basis of these data that the excavations of 1976 were designed.

THE EXCAVATION OF JINCAMOCCO

Research Design

The 1976 excavation of Jincamocco was designed to elucidate the function of this Wari site and to provide a detailed study of its architecture. At that time it was thought that the various Wari sites identified throughout the Peruvian highlands were probably storehouses. In the report of their brief reconnaissance to Wari, Rowe, Collier, and Willey (1950) had pointed out the odd features of Wari architecture, and its similarity to Viracochapampa and Pikillaqta. A few years later, Rowe wrote,

> A striking feature of the Huari expansion was the construction of very large building complexes consisting of plazas, corridors and rectangular rooms laid out according to a formal plan. The walls are very high, with few doors and windows,

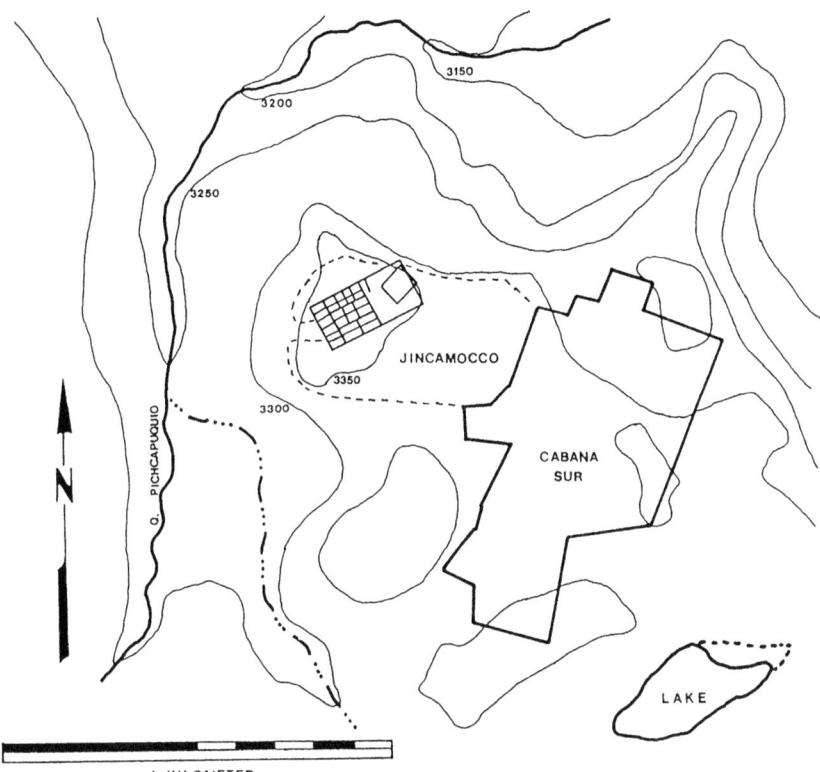

Figure 6.2. Map of the total extent of Jincamocco. The dotted lines indicate areas of rectilinear architecture that was too poorly preserved to be mapped.

and refuse is virtually absent. These elaborate complexes probably housed government stores rather than people....The existence of these formal storage complexes provides evidence that the expansion of Huari was not simply a matter of peaceful penetration or raiding. It represents the formation of an imperial state with a well organized administration. [Rowe 1963:14]

Isbell's excavations at the site of Jargampata in 1969-70 provided results that were consistent with this interpretation (Isbell 1977). Although the rectangular enclosure at Jargampata is quite tiny, and perhaps not representative of major provincial centers, excavation indicated that it may have served to organize local production, and was a locus of collection, storage, and trans-shipment of agricultural produce. Jargampata probably provided direct economic support to the great urban site of Wari, located only about 25 km away.

So when investigations began at Jincamocco in 1976, it seemed reasonable to expect that the site was probably a storage facility. Several other alternatives were considered as well (Table 6.1). A possibility suggested

TABLE 6.1
Possible Functions of Jincamocco and Archaeological Implications

General Site Function	Specific Activity Loci	Proportion of Site So Used	Empirical Data
storage facility	storage	most	remains of stored goods; large storage jars; empty space, minimal deposits
	permanent residence (retainers in charge)	some	household food preparation; habitation refuse
craft production	obsidian workshop	most	obsidian debitage; few finished tools or blanks
	temporary residence (workers)	some	communal cooking areas; habitation refuse
	permanent residence (bosses)	some	as above
	storage (to support all residents)	some	as above
	acquisition of raw materials	—	local obsidian source
waystation along road	storage	half	as above
	temporary residence (travelers)	half	as above
	permanent residence (retainers)	limited	as above
	animal care	some	corrals
	travel	—	associated roads, trails
political capital	permanent residence (retainers)	some	as above
	permanent residence (foreign elite rulers)	some	as above; high status items
	temporary residence (laborers, travelers)	some	as above
	storage	some	as above
	craft production	maybe	as above, also weaving tools, ceramic production, etc.
	ceremonialism	maybe	distinctive architecture; ritual items; religious iconography
	administration	some	distinctive architecture indicating "offices"; elite artifacts
	travel	—	as above

by the 1586 description was that the site functioned as a waystation along an ancient road. Such a site would probably be small (as Jincamocco seemed to be), contain some areas of storage, and provide quarters for travelers and animals.

Another alternative considered was that the site might have been a specialized craft workshop, specifically for the working of obsidian. The preliminary results of the Burger and Asaro analysis of obsidian samples had suggested that the then-unknown Pampas source might be located in the vicinity of Jincamocco. It was therefore possible that Jincamocco was established to exploit the source and produce obsidian blanks or tools, which could then be distributed throughout the Wari domain. If this were the case, one would expect to find immense quantities of obsidian debitage, resulting from this activity, and a relatively low proportion of finished tools.

Also considered was the possibility that the site might have functioned as a generalized administrative center, serving as a local political capital. This seemed unlikely, given the presumed small size of the site. However, if it were so, the site might be expected to yield evidence of all the prior activities—areas of storage, living quarters, specialized production—as well as evidence of "administration," including ceremonial functions, permanent residents, high status residents, and perhaps other kinds of craft production.

But the most likely function was, of course, storage. A storage facility could be expected to be largely empty of remains. Stored goods would have been used up long ago, or removed when the site was abandoned. Some areas might have been devoted to residence, for retainers in charge of the facility, but most of the site would be expected to be devoid of large quantities of remains, except, perhaps, for remains of storage jars.

Finally, in addition to evaluating the function of the site, a major goal of the project was to complete a detailed study of its architecture, and to compare this architecture with that of other major Wari sites. Although some of the unique aspects of the style had been pointed out by Rowe, Collier, and Willey (1950; Rowe 1963), and there existed published maps of Viracochapampa (McCown 1945) and Pikillaqta (Sanders 1973), no extensive comparisons had been made between these major Wari sites.

The Sampling Strategy

The excavation of Jincamocco was therefore designed to reveal a representative portion of the site in order to elucidate possible site functions, and to expose as much architectural detail as possible. Investigation was limited to just the enclosure, as this was the area of the site most representative of the Wari occupation, and the primary zone of diagnostic Wari-style architecture. The enclosure at Jincamocco, like those of other Wari sites, is extensively subdivided into small architectural units (Fig. 6.3). At Jincamocco, one half of the enclosure has no internal constructions, while the other half is subdivided into a variety of units. Except where noted, these discussions pertain to the subdivided half of the enclosure, the half mapped in 1974.

First, the enclosure is divided into four major sectors, each of which is then subdivided into four to eight room blocks. Within sectors the room blocks are of roughly equal size, but the size of room blocks varies between the sectors. Each room block comprises one or more patio groups, with access corridors around one or more sides of the perimeter of the room block. The patio group is the basic element of Wari architecture, repeated over and over again at each major Wari site. A patio group comprises a central open patio, flanked on one or more sides (usually all four sides) by long narrow galleries. Galleries at some sites may be two or three deep, but this pattern seems not to occur at Jincamocco.

This regular arrangement of architectural units, apparent even on the rough map drawn in 1974, formed the basis of a stratified random sampling design. Each sector of the enclosure formed a discrete stratum; within each stratum a 25% sample of room blocks was chosen for investigation. Within those sample room blocks, a 50% sample of all patios, galleries and corridors was to be excavated, resulting in a final sampling fraction of 12.5% for the subdivided half of the enclosure. Additional excavations were also made at our discretion both within the enclosure, and in structures outside it. These are referred to in this chapter as "judgment excavations."

Wall Trenching and Site Plan

Before excavations could begin in 1976, an attempt was made to more accurately define the exact architectural layout of the enclosure, especially in those room blocks designated as sample units. Given the condition of the site, a plan of wall trenching was undertaken to reveal subsurface walls. This involved digging a narrow shallow trench along the face of a wall, beginning where a trace of the wall could be seen on the surface, and then following it along. These walls trenches rarely encountered or disturbed underlying cultural deposits, with one important exception (excavation Unit T2/3) that will be discussed in more detail below. In all, wall trenching was completed along the northernmost third of the enclosure, and a much-improved plan was made of the architecture so revealed (Fig. 6.4). However, even with these efforts, many architectural details are still

Jincamocco

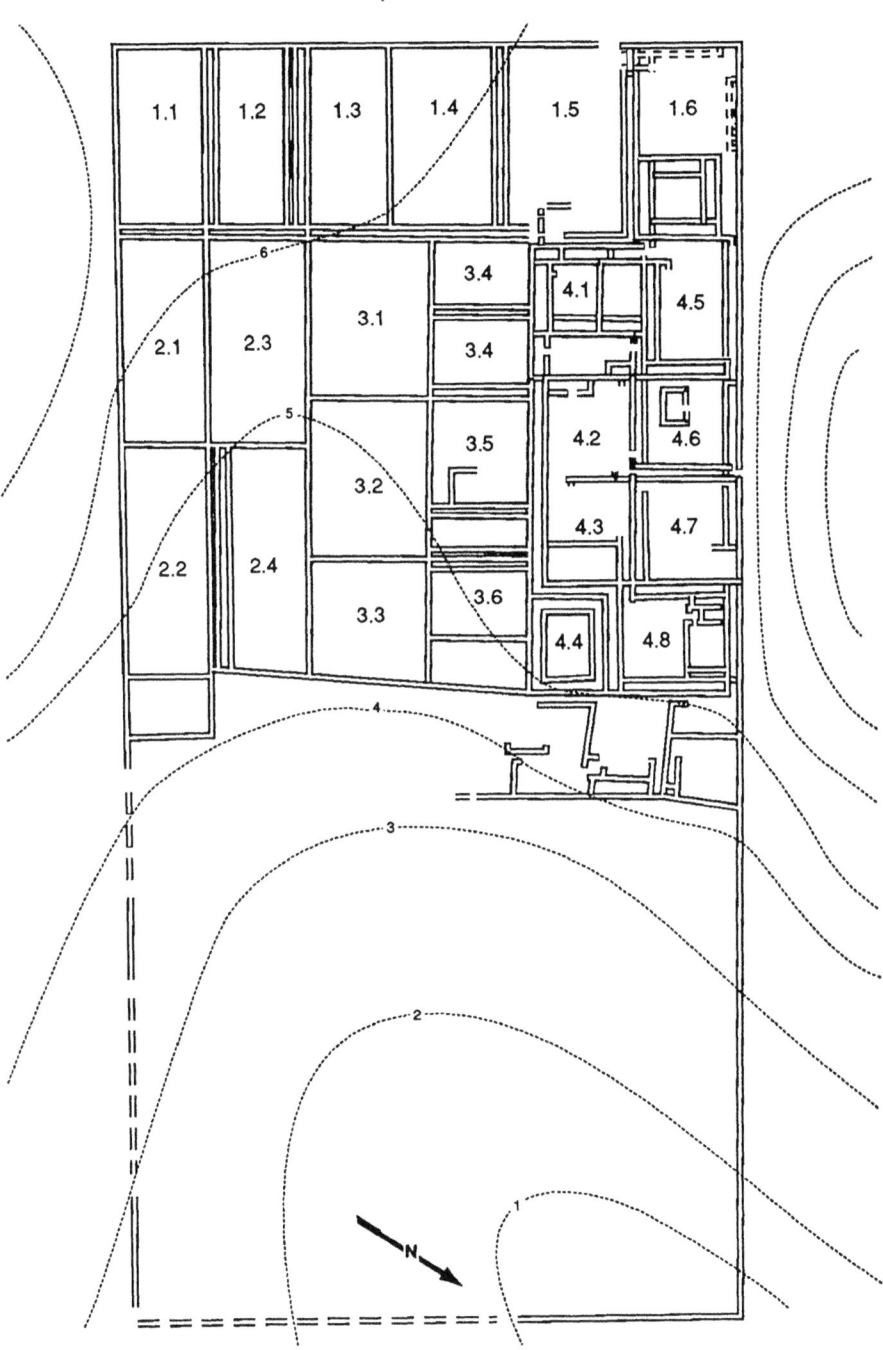

Figure 6.3. Plan of the enclosure at Jincamocco. The subdivided half of the enclosure comprises four sectors, each of which is divided into room blocks. Room blocks are numbered.

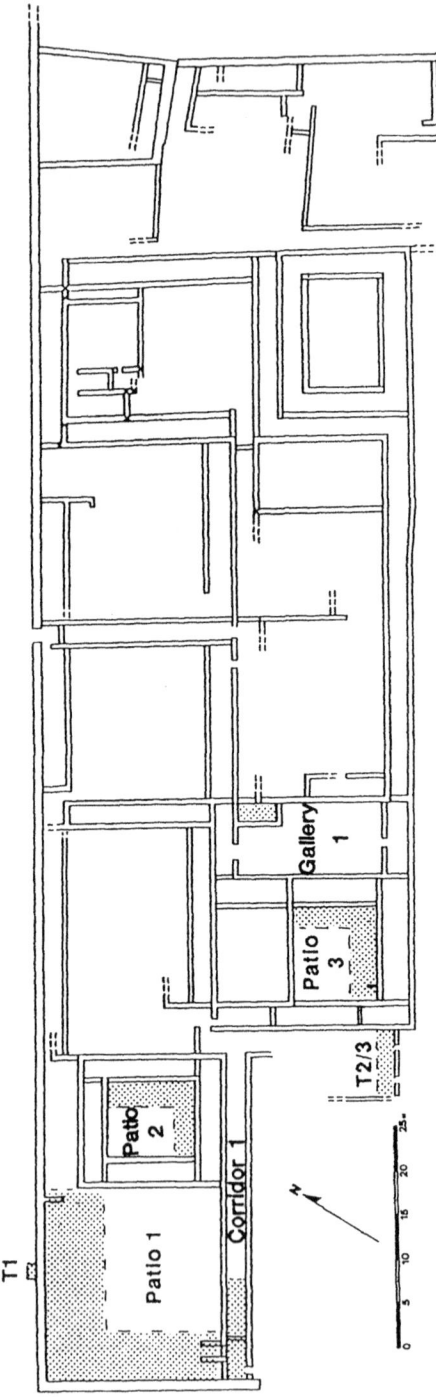

Figure 6.4. Results of wall trenching in northern third of enclosure. Shading indicates areas excavated.

missing or obscure, especially doors. Excavated areas provide the most accurate architectural plans, but even these are sometimes incomplete owing to the poor preservation of some walls.

An important result of the wall trenching was the establishing of the fact that the site has an extremely regular plan, with irregularly oriented walls encountered in only one sector—outside the planned subdivisions of the enclosure. So, it was possible to revise the 1974 plan, and indicate more accurately the outlines of the other room blocks. Wall trenching exposed the entire length of the enclosure, thus allowing its full dimensions (127 by 255.5 m) to be measured.

Around the enclosure, in all directions and especially to the south, are extensive traces of architecture. While the enclosure totals 3.28 ha, the total extent of architecture on the site is close to 15 ha. In fact, the eastern boundary of the site cannot be defined because of the encroachment of the town of Cabana; it may be larger than I have estimated here. Except for traces of round stone structures near the northwest corner of the enclosure, all of the architecture visible on the surface is rectilinear, and laid out in large compounds. Because it is so poorly preserved, no detailed maps have yet been made, except to indicate broad areas of architectural remains (see Figs. 6.1 and 6.2).

Excavation Strategy, Techniques, Areas Excavated

After walls were exposed through trenching, excavation of sample units began. In the case of the large open rooms (patios), each was divided into twelve units of equal size (four in length, three in width). Six of these (50%) in an L-shaped configuration were chosen as sample excavations units. In this manner architectural details were maximized by exposing two complete walls, parts of the other two, and three of the four corners. Further, differences in artifact distribution could be seen along both the length and width of the patio.

The Actual Sample

Only two of the six planned sample units were investigated. Three of the six sample room blocks, located in the southern portion of the enclosure, were privately owned and under cultivation. Only the northern third of the enclosure was available for excavation. (Fortunately, this was the best-preserved portion of the enclosure.) So investigation began first in one, and then in a second sample room block. An enormous quantity of cultural material was encountered in the excavations; the empty storage rooms I had anticipated did not exist. After the excavation of three patios, a portion of a corridor, and a gallery (some 420 cubic meters of excavated material), the artifact collection totaled well over 50,000 artifacts.

It seemed prudent to cease excavation at this point. As a result, sample excavations were limited to only two of the six planned sample room blocks, and both of these are located near the northwest corner of the enclosure. The sample excavated totals only 1.1% of the area of the enclosure—far less than the 12.5% anticipated.

By virtue of the small sample fraction, and the limited spatial distribution of the sample units, the sample cannot be regarded as representative of the spatial variability in the enclosure, or of the full range of activities that took place in the enclosure. However, the tremendous quantity of material recovered supplies evidence regarding a wide range of activities carried out in at least part of the site. In addition to a rich and diverse artifact assemblage, architectural details exposed in the excavations indicate a variety of spatially discrete activity areas. And the results of wall trenching and remapping of the site have yielded details of architectural planning and layout unavailable for most Wari sites. So, while knowledge of the full range of activities carried out at the site remains incomplete, there does exist evidence of a portion of that range of activities.

General Stratigraphy

Excavation was carried out with small hand picks and trowels, with shovels used to move away the backdirt; picks were used to remove larger rocks. Wall trenching was done with larger picks as well. Excavation proceeded by natural stratigraphy where possible, and arbitrary levels where no major changes were seen in natural strata, or where the natural strata were so thick that subdivision into thinner levels was warranted.

With some exceptions, the same general stratigraphic sequence was encountered in each excavation unit. The uppermost stratum, sometimes well over a meter thick, comprised mostly rocks and brown loamy soil, with very few artifacts. This stratum represents postabandonment wall fall and soil formation. No post–Middle Horizon occupation was identified, with the exception of some later intrusive burials found in the wall fall. The site was apparently used as the local cemetery for some time, and these late burials were encountered rather frequently. (Most often they were found during wall trenching, and nearly all were left in place.) In fact, the modern cemetery is located inside the unsubdivided half of the enclosure, so this practice continues today in a slightly altered form.

Beneath the wall fall was generally found a stratum of Willka phase cultural material, deposited on and above the floors and benches of the structure. On the benches, and especially in the corners of the patios, this stratum could be as much as 50 cm thick; on the floors toward the center of the patios the deposit was much shallower, typically 5-10 cm. This stratum usually contained a great quantity of grey ash, so was clearly definable during excavation. (The nature of these deposits will be discussed in detail below.) The next general stratum was one of architectural remains and artificial fill: benches, compacted earth floors, and subfloor features such as canals. Architectural details were generally of stone, and fill was brown clay soil with numerous artifacts mixed in; artifacts in these levels might be a mix of Willka phase and earlier materials. Some excavations did not continue past this point.

Deeper levels, excavated in some units, contained pre-Willka phase materials. As discussed in the preceding chapter, there was a small local Kancha phase village occupying this location at the time of the Wari incursion. Remains of a round stone house were found beneath one of the excavated patios. Beyond this stratum, some deeper excavations reached sterile deposits; others penetrated sterile deposits and exposed additional cultural material. Some of this may date to as early as the end of the Sacrahua phase.

THE ARCHITECTURE OF THE ENCLOSURE

Jincamocco occupies the top of a low promontory that commands a good view of the valley. The rectangular enclosure is nestled in the saddle between low hills to the north and south. The ground slopes down from west to east, dropping about five meters to the midpoint of the enclosure, and then dropping even more steeply through the unsubdivided eastern half. The overall site plan is so regular and so rigid that, beyond choosing a relatively level piece of land, no attempt was made to accommodate the architecture to the topography. This is in marked contrast to the later Inka, who designed their sites to fit in with and conform to the topography.

The enclosure measures 127 m from north to south, and 255.5 m from east to west, with a width-to-length ratio of almost exactly 1:2. Clearly the enclosure was carefully planned and laid out, perhaps by professional architects. As discussed briefly above, the enclosure is divided in half, and the western half is subdivided into four sectors, which in turn are subdivided into a total of 24 room blocks. The arrangement of sectors and room blocks is very regular. Sector 1 comprises the western third of the subdivided half, and Sectors 2, 3, and 4 are each about one-third of the remaining portion of the subdivided half. Within each sector, all room blocks are of roughly the same size. However, in terms of details within room blocks, no two room blocks are exactly the same. So the overall plan is rigid down to the definition of room blocks, and then variations were permitted.

A typical plan, with many variants, is the patio group. A central patio, roughly square in shape, is surrounded by four peripheral galleries—long narrow rooms—one on each side. Around the perimeter of the patio is a low bench, about 20-40 cm high, which sometimes has a plastered surface; hearths may be located on the bench in the corner of the patio. Galleries were probably roofed; bench areas were probably roofed as well, but opened onto the unroofed patio center. There may be one or several patio groups in a single room block. Along at least one side of each room block runs a corridor that provides access to the room block, and allows movement within the enclosure. Access patterns are still poorly defined, but there seem to be no long streetlike corridors that extend from one side of the enclosure to the other. Rather, corridors wind around and between room blocks. Corridors vary from 2.1 to 2.4 m in width, with an average width of 2.2 m (measured wall face to wall face). Galleries conform to this same dimension.

Doorways provided direct access between patios and galleries. Entrance to a patio group may have been through open doorways at the time of construction of the enclosure. As will be discussed in more detail below, there is evidence that these doorways were filled in at some point, and access patterns altered.

The eastern half of the enclosure is, for the most part, devoid of internal constructions. The ones that do occur are found in the northwest and southwest corners, contiguous with the room blocks of the west half: one room along the south wall, and a group of irregular structures near the north wall. While these have some details in common with the rest of the enclosure, they do not follow the same rigid plan. The remainder of the eastern half of the enclosure has no internal subdivisions; this is where the modern cemetery is located.

Walls are built of angular broken stone (maximum dimension usually about 40 cm) set in a mud mortar. Local materials are used: most stones are of andesitic basalt and limestone, with some sandstone, and some volcanic tuff, and an occasional red jasper stone. Walls are double-faced, and the core is filled with smaller stones and mortar. Walls average 65 cm thick, except the outer enclosure wall, which is about 110 cm thick. The outer wall was built on a foundation set into a trench, up to 1.2 m deep. Other wall foundations were set into trenches of varying depths, up to 80 cm deep. Short cross walls in corridors have no foundations and may postdate the initial construction of the site.

Careful planning is evident not only in the regular layout of the site, but also in the construction sequence. Certainly the first step was the excavation of the foundation trenches, and then the laying of the foundation stones. Foundation stones are generally larger and more irregular in shape than those stones used in the visible portions of the wall. The drainage system of small canals found under the floors was probably laid out and built at this time; canals extend through walls just at the juncture between the foundation and the wall itself.

The first wall built was the outer enclosure wall. All other walls are abutted onto it, and hence were built later. An occasional vertical seam is visible in the outer wall, along with several doorways, so the possibility exists that the wall was built in sections, perhaps by different labor parties (see, for example, Moseley 1975b). The next walls built were those defining each room block, and the outlines of the patio groups. Last built were the walls in the patio groups separating the peripheral galleries from the patio.

After the major walls were built, details such as benches, platforms, and plastering were added. Floors were typically of compacted earth, sometimes with a white plaster surface. Cross walls in corridors were also built later. These may have been built very late in the occupation in order to close off areas of the enclosure.

The irregular constructions in the northwest corner of the unsubdivided half do not touch the planned room blocks, but are oriented to them; thus, they were probably built after the adjacent room blocks. As for the rest of the site, wherever constructions outside the enclosure are contiguous with it, they are always abutted onto the enclosure walls. This indicates that these were later additions, added some time after the initial construction of the enclosure.

RESULTS OF EXCAVATION OF INDIVIDUAL UNITS

In this section each major architectural unit excavated will be discussed, and the results of the excavation summarized. In each case it may be prudent first to evaluate the nature of the deposits exposed, and to distinguish between primary associations, artifacts and features indicating specific activities taking place at specific locations, and secondary deposits of trash. This is a critical distinction. As will be seen, nearly all artifacts recovered at Jincamocco pertain to secondary trash deposits, and do not directly represent activities carried out where the artifacts were deposited. On the other hand, architectural remains constitute primary deposits, and provide some of the best evidence for spatial patterning of activities in the enclosure.

Archaeological Formation Processes

In order to understand the activities carried out at Jincamocco, it is necessary to consider the stratigraphy and the nature of the archaeological deposits excavated. The distinction between primary and secondary deposits is an important one, and, unfortunately, one that is all too often ignored. Artifacts in primary context are found where they were used, associated with other artifacts and features pertaining to the same activities. Artifacts in secondary context have been redeposited some distance from where they were actually used; tertiary deposits may have been moved several times. Michael B. Schiffer (1983, 1987) has written in great detail about processes that can and do affect the archaeological record, and points out that the nature of the deposits and the processes that formed them are critical to the interpretation of past behavior. The presence of artifacts in a particular location does not necessarily mean that the artifacts were actually used there. Reconstruction of prehistoric behavior at a particular location requires remains found in their primary context. Artifacts found in secondary context, in redeposited trash, tell us little about discrete activities at a particular location. However, they can tell us something of the range of activities reflected in that trash, and perhaps something about the social units that produced the trash.

In the case of Jincamocco, an important goal of the analysis is to identify prehistoric behavior, to identify activity areas and functional differences within the site. If all deposits are secondary trash deposits, then little can be inferred about discrete activity areas. However, identification of primary deposits can direct the analysis toward more fruitful avenues of investigation, and indicate areas in which discrete activities may be identified. Therefore, some effort is devoted here to evaluating the depositional context of the materials excavated at Jincamocco, in order to determine which lines of analysis will be most valuable, and to avoid those that will produce invalid results.

Following Schiffer (1983) several lines of evidence were considered in evaluating the depositional context of each of the provenience units excavated at Jincamocco. Of the many and various properties of artifacts and deposits discussed by Schiffer, the following are particularly applicable to the case of Jincamocco.

1) *Fragmentary nature of the remains.* Whole or reconstructible vessels are more likely to indicate primary context (for example in burials, in caches, or left on benches or floors). In secondary refuse little is left intact, and fragments usually cannot be reconstructed into whole or even partial vessels.

2) *Spatial distribution of remains.* Clustering of remains can be produced by activity areas. However, trash can also appear in discrete clusters, so other criteria must be considered together with this one.

3) *Artifact diversity.* Primary deposits of certain activities (for example, lithic production) have very low diversities; that is, a very limited range of types will be present. On the other hand, secondary trash has high diversity.

4) *Artifact density.* Discrete activity areas may have relatively low densities of remains, as well as low diversity of artifact types. On the other hand, secondary deposits, such as trash or architectural fill, may have very high densities of artifacts.

5) *Soil matrix.* In particular, high concentrations of ash may be mixed in with secondary trash deposits. On the other hand, ash found with other evidence of burning (including *in situ* burned beams, etc.) may be present in primary deposits as well.

6) *Architectural context.* Primary deposits are more likely to be found in contact with a floor surface, or a bench, or in features such as hearths, storage pits, or burial chambers.

Following these lines of evidence, the depositional context of each excavation provenience was determined, and these are discussed below in the case of each excavated unit. Of the 130-plus provenience units, only two are clearly primary deposits, while a few other provenience units have limited remains in primary context (the occasional burial, or a few pots sitting on a bench). The vast majority of artifacts recovered at Jincamocco were found in secondary deposits. While they can indicate a range of activities, we cannot associate those activities with the locations of the artifacts recovered. On the other hand, architectural remains represent primary associations, and provide direct evidence of activities carried out at specific locations.

Excavation Summary

Excavations were undertaken in seven discrete units: three patios, one corridor, one gallery, one platform, and one refuse deposit. Each area was divided into excavation units, and excavation proceeded level by level. In all, over 130 provenience units were excavated. (See Appendix 1 for summary tables of artifacts and artifact densities in each provenience.)

Sample excavations were undertaken in two room blocks, and judgment excavations were undertaken in a third (Fig. 6.4). The first sample, room block 1.6 (located in Sector 1), comprises a large patio (Patio 1) with no peripheral galleries, a smaller patio (Patio 2) with four galleries, an undefined long narrow room, and a corridor (Corridor 1). Fifty percent of each patio was excavated as planned, and the west end of the corridor was excavated; no galleries were excavated in this room block.

The second sample, room block 4.1 (located in Sector 4), comprises three small patios, with one, two and three galleries, respectively, and one corridor. Fifty percent of one patio (Patio 3) was excavated, as was one gallery (Gallery 1). A substantial judgment excavation (T2/3) was opened up in Room Block 1.5 to the south and west of the sample room blocks; in this case wall trenching had disturbed cultural deposits, so the excavation was undertaken to clarify the nature of the deposit. One other test excavation (T1), only 1 by 2 m in extent, was undertaken outside the enclosure wall adjacent to Patio 1.

Patio 1 (Room Block 1.6)

This is the largest patio excavated, measuring 20.3 by 22 m; it is also unique in that it has no peripheral galleries, and it is located immediately inside the outer enclosure wall in the extreme northwest corner of the enclosure (Fig. 6.5). It was divided into twelve units of equal size, and the six along the west and north walls were excavated. After removing the stratum of wall fall, which was quite voluminous, traces of new walls were uncovered. The remainder of the patio was excavated in two major

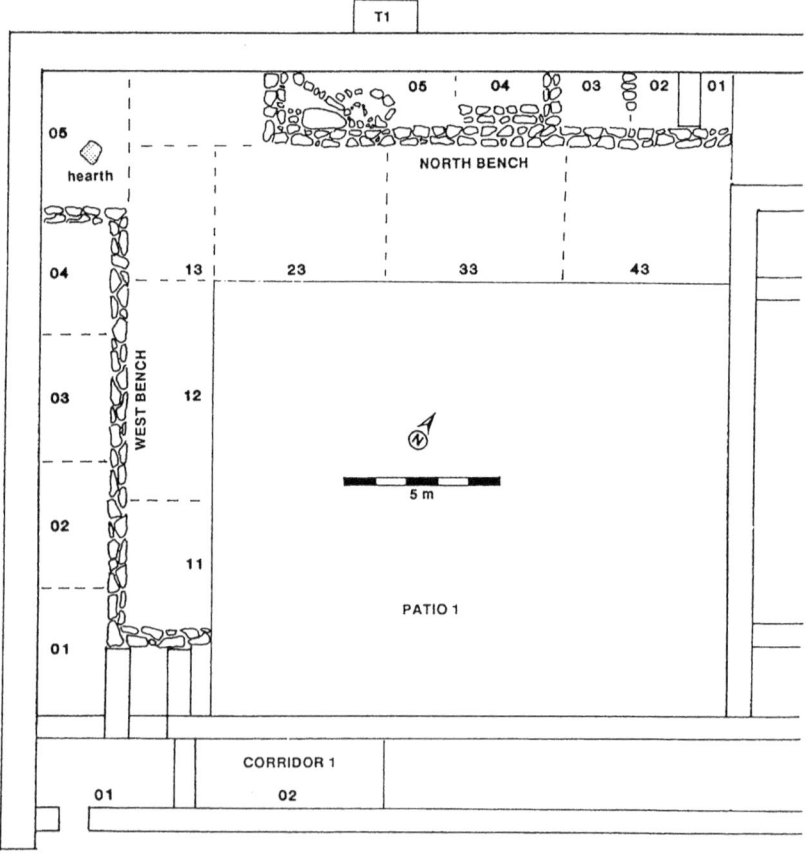

Figure 6.5. Plan of Patio 1 and Corridor 1. Excavation units are indicated by the dashed lines, and identified by number.

segments, the west bench and the north bench, each divided into five excavation units. The excavations continued below Willka phase materials, through a deep deposit of Kancha phase materials, and exposed the foundations of the outer enclosure wall.

This patio has benches along the south, west, and north walls. Two short walls protrude into the room, to the edge of the bench, from the south wall near the southwest corner of the patio; there was originally a doorway between these walls, providing access from the adjacent corridor. This doorway was found filled in, but with stones smaller than those of the rest of the wall; this suggests that the opening was not filled in at the time of construction of the enclosure. A single short wall protrudes into the patio, also to the edge of the bench, near the northeast corner. Near it is evidence of a filled-in opening in the outer enclosure wall. However, this opening has irregularly finished edges, and probably was just an opening left in the wall during construction.

The surface of the benches was poorly defined, having no clear layer of plaster or any other material to distinguish it. The benches had double-faced stone retaining walls, one or two stones high (about 25-40 cm), and the surface of the bench was probably about 5-10 cm below the level of the top of this retaining wall; the interior of the bench was filled with stones and earth.

The north bench of the patio has trash deposits above the bench, architectural fill in the bench, and pre-Willka phase secondary deposits below the bench. The only primary association here is in Unit 05 at the west end of the bench. Inside the bench was found an arrangement of large stones, surrounding a smaller circle of stones. In the smaller circle a skull was placed; this skull was that of an adult female of advanced age, and there were three small (unhealed) holes in the cranium (Figs. 6.6 and 6.7). This may represent some sort of offering deposit, made at the time of construction and embedded in the bench structure.

The west bench of the patio also has deposits of trash above the bench, and artificial fill in the bench itself. All these are secondary deposits. However, in Unit 01, on the surface of the bench was a large nearly intact jar adjacent to two intact bowls; inside the jar was found a small gold disk. Another nearly intact jar was found a few meters away (Fig. 6.8). These vessels and the bench surface represent a primary association. (The vessels are described and illustrated in the following chapter.) However, all other remains from the west bench are secondary deposits. Beneath the bench were low frequencies of artifacts predating the construction of the enclosure; these, too, are secondary deposits.

In the northwest corner of the patio, beyond the end of the west bench (which apparently did not extend all the way to the corner) and below the level of the floor, is a hearth. This hearth rests on what was probably the

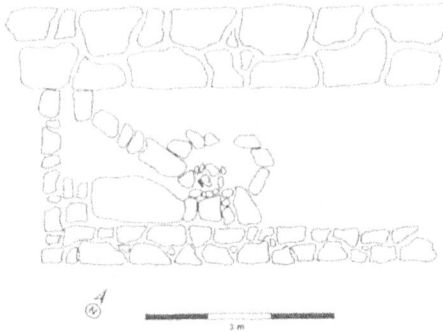

Figure 6.6. Plan of the skull offering in the north bench of Patio 1.

Figure 6.7. Photograph of the skull offering in the north bench of Patio 1. Note the small (unhealed) holes in the cranium, and the small tabular shaped stone placed upright next to the skull. The arrow indicates the north-south axis of the enclosure, not true north.

ground surface at the time of construction, below the stratum of architectural fill. It is clearly associated with Willka phase artifacts, so probably was used at the time of construction of the enclosure. No primary deposits were identified in this unit.

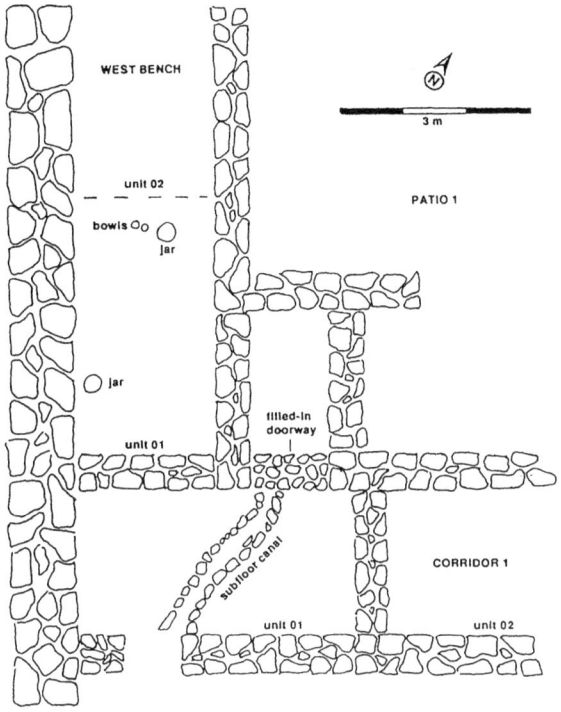

Figure 6.8. Detail of the southwest corner of Patio 1, west bench, indicating the location of the primary association of four plainware vessels with the surface of the bench. Also, detail of unit 1 of Corridor 1, including the remains of a subfloor canal. Note filled-in doorway between Corridor 1 and Patio 1.

Patio 2 (Room Block 1.6)

Adjacent to Patio 1 in the same room block is a smaller patio, measuring 8 by 10 meters, with four peripheral galleries (Fig. 6.9). Patio 2 was divided into twelve units of equal size, and the six units along the south and east sides were chosen for excavation. The patio has a bench along all four sides; it has a retaining wall one stone high (20 cm), and earth fill. In the southwest corner the bench retaining wall is double faced, and the surface of the bench lies 5-10 cm below the top of the wall. Along the east side and in the north east corner the retaining wall has only a single face, and the surface of the bench is even with the top of the retaining wall. In the southwest corner a small hearth was located on the bench surface. This hearth has a roughly oval shape, measuring some 40 by 50 cm, and is

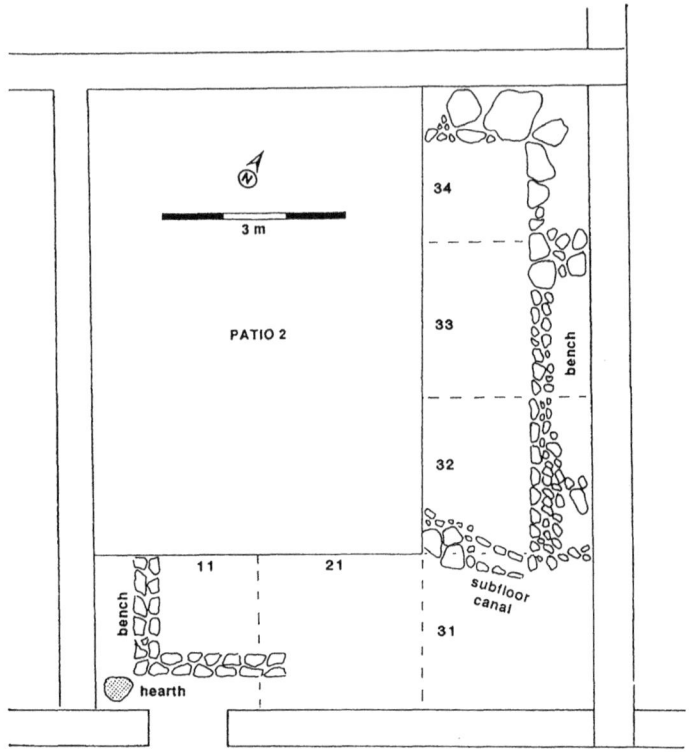

Figure 6.9. Plan of Patio 2. Excavation units are indicated by the dashed lines, and identified by number. Note the large stone slabs covering the subfloor canal; these could be lifted for access into the canal. The patio bench was poorly preserved in Units 21 and 31.

8 cm deep, on average. The soil under and around the hearth has been fire hardened, and is slightly orange in color. The bench in Units 21 and 31 was poorly preserved.

Doorways provided access between the patio and the peripheral galleries, at least along one excavated side of the patio. The base of the doorway is even with the level of the bench. The other walls are poorly preserved, and the patio may have contained more than the one doorway shown in the plan. Access into the patio group from the outside was likely through a doorway into one of the galleries, and then through a second doorway between gallery and patio.

A canal runs under the floor of this patio. It has a sandy bottom, stone sides, and stone cap stones. Access into the canal was through a circular opening in the patio floor, covered with flat stone slabs. This canal probably connects with one that passes under Corridor 1, and thence under Patio 1. Canals most likely served for drainage purposes, especially during the rainy summer months. It is unlikely that they supplied the site with fresh water, as there is no water source at a higher elevation directly accessible into the site.

Deposits in Patio 2 include wall fall, Willka phase secondary trash, architectural fill, and some pre-Willka phase secondary remains. The only primary associations in this patio are architectural features: the hearth in the southwest corner, and the canal under the floor. No artifacts were found in primary context.

Patio 3 (Room Block 4.1)

This patio is only slightly larger than Patio 2, measuring 9.6 by 10.8 m. Like the other patios, it was divided into twelve units of equal size; the six units along the south and east walls were chosen for excavation. This patio has peripheral galleries along two sides, the south and east, and benches were found along these same sides of the patio (Fig. 6.10).

The benches in this patio have single-faced retaining walls, and the surface of the bench is even with the top of the retaining wall. The bench along the south wall had a well defined surface at the west end, where it was finished with white plaster; it originally extended all along the south wall. Doorways into the peripheral galleries could not be defined, as the walls are very poorly preserved.

Access into the patio was through a doorway near the southwest corner, directly from the adjacent corridor. At some point this doorway was filled in, and a niche was constructed on the interior face of this fill (Fig. 6.11). The base of the doorway was even with the top of the bench, and white plaster is still preserved along the base of the original opening. This suggests that the door was open for some time while the patio was occupied and not closed up immediately at the time construction was finished. And the presence of the niche on the interior face of the closed door suggests that the patio continued to be used after the doorway was closed. Perhaps when the doorway was closed, access was gained by climbing over the wall. There is a short wall that extends into the patio as far as the edge of the bench, also near the southwest corner of the patio. There is also a cross wall in the adjacent corridor only one meter from the doorway.

Excavation of this unit extended well below floor levels, and remains of a round stone house, about 8 m in diameter, were found. Clearly predating the construction of the enclosure, this house was intentionally dismantled, and the stones used to level the ground in and around the older structure. A human burial was found in this level (see Chapter 7), but was probably interred during the Willka phase.

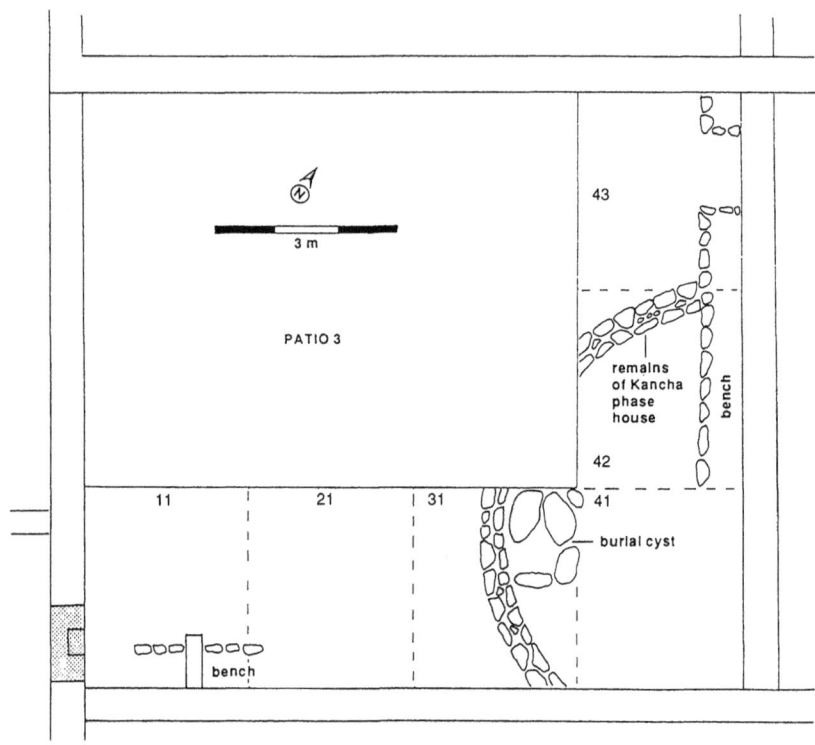

Figure 6.10. Plan of Patio 3. Excavation units are indicated by the dashed lines, and identified by number. Note the remains of a Kancha phase house, located beneath the Willka phase floors; and the burial cyst against the interior house wall. The patio bench was poorly preserved in Units 21, 31 and 41.

Like Patio 2, this patio included trash accumulation and architectural fill in the Willka phase levels. However, beneath the poorly preserved bench near the southeast corner of the patio, was found a nearly intact lyre cup, in what was otherwise architectural fill. This vessel represents a different depositional context than the rest of the remains in the provenience—perhaps a small offering, or perhaps just a vessel that was lost during construction. The lyre cup is described and illustrated in the following chapter.

Gallery 1 (Room Block 4.1)

This is a small room, measuring 2.15 by 4.35 meters, located in Room Block 4.1, adjacent to an unexcavated patio. It does not have a typical gallery shape, in that it does not run the full length of the patio side (see Fig. 6.4). But the fact that it is peripheral to a patio, is the same width as all

Figure 6.11. Photograph of filled-in doorway near the southwest corner of Patio 3, with niche. Note the remains of plaster flooring at the base of the doorway.

other galleries, and is clearly not a corridor, leads me to term it so. This room had no internal features, and, indeed, very few artifacts. Its southern wall has no foundation, which is also atypical. (However, it is possible that the gallery was originally intended to run the full length of the patio, and the south wall was built to truncate the gallery.) There may have been a door into this gallery from the patio, but it was not visible. The interior walls of this gallery were faced with a layer of clay. The surface of the floor was not well defined. No primary deposits of artifacts were identified; in fact, artifacts were rather rare in this unit.

Corridor 1 (Room Block 1.6)

Only one corridor was partially excavated, and this one is located along the south side of Room Block 1.6. The corridor opens at its east end to connect with several other corridors, which in turn provide access to the three adjacent room blocks (see Fig. 6.4). At the west end it is entered through a small doorway in the south wall. Immediately adjacent is a large doorway through the enclosure wall, providing access into and out of the enclosure. Also at the west end, in the north wall, is visible a filled-in doorway that originally provided access directly into Patio 1, as discussed above (see Figs. 6.5 and 6.8).

There is a cross wall in the corridor, 4.4 m from the west end, which would seem to block access through the corridor. This cross wall has no foundation, and is not bonded to the corridor walls; it was built some time after the corridor walls. Perhaps related to the closing of the doorway into Patio 1, it may have served as the base for steps used to climb over the wall to gain access into the now-closed patio.

Running under the corridor, from under the small doorway in the south wall, and thence under the filled-in doorway into Patio 1, is a segment of a subfloor canal. Its construction is the same as that described for the canal in Patio 2, and, as discussed above, is probably connected to that canal segment. There was no means of access into the canal from the corridor.

The floor to the west of the cross wall is very well defined, and shows evidence of burning, especially near the door in the south wall—the soil is very hard, and slightly orange in color. On the other side of the wall, the floor level is not nearly as distinctive, and there is no evidence of burning.

On the west side of the cross wall is a typical secondary trash deposit. Above the floor was found a deposit of materials averaging about 50 cm in depth. This included moderate to high densities of sherds, ground stone, and animal bone, as well as lithics, and other artifacts—a deposit of high diversity as well. All of the remains were fragmentary, and no reconstructible vessels were found. The soil matrix was very ashy. No discrete spatial patterning was apparent. In sum, this is clearly a secondary trash deposit, and the artifacts do not represent specific activities carried out in the corridor. Likewise, remains on the east side of the cross wall are secondary deposits. This portion of the corridor was excavated to very deep levels, but the deposits exposed were all secondary in nature. It is likely that the trash was deposited after the cross wall was built, and after the doorway in Patio 1 was closed up.

Unit T1 (Exterior Side of Enclosure Wall)

This unit was just a small test excavation undertaken on the exterior face of the enclosure wall, just outside Patio 1 (see Figs. 6.4 and 6.5). The purpose of this excavation was to reveal the stratigraphy outside the enclosure, and the exterior face of the enclosure wall. The only remains exposed were deposits of secondary trash, both Willka phase and earlier.

Unit T2/3 (Room Block 1.5)

This is a rather special unit. Not only is it the only substantial judgment (nonsample) excavation made at the site, it also provided the only major primary association of artifacts. This unit was selected for excavation because wall trenching along its east side had turned up quantities of white plaster, along with fragments of fancy Wari polychrome pottery. In this regard, the unit was unique, like nothing excavated elsewhere on the site. Since cultural deposits had been disturbed by wall trenching, it seemed prudent to do some test excavation. One 2 by 4 m unit (T2) was opened, and then a second unit (T3) of the same size was opened, resulting in an exposure measuring 2 by 8 m (Fig. 6.12).

This feature is apparently a raised platform at the east end of Room Block 1.5. (This accounts for the disturbance during wall trenching—it lies much closer to the current ground surface than other floors.) No adjacent units were excavated, so the exact configuration is unclear. From east to west it measures about 8 m long. At the west end of the test excavation is what is probably a retaining wall. It extends up only to the surface of the platform, and the ground surface drops off sharply just beyond it (an area not excavated). The ground surface over the unexcavated portion of the platform lies about 1 to 1.5 m above the ground surface in the remainder of the room block. The surface of the platform, where well preserved, is covered with a thick layer of white plaster, overlying a prepared surface of small stones covered with a layer of mud mortar. This plaster floor is well preserved at the east end of the excavation, but plaster traces were found all the way to the west edge of the platform.

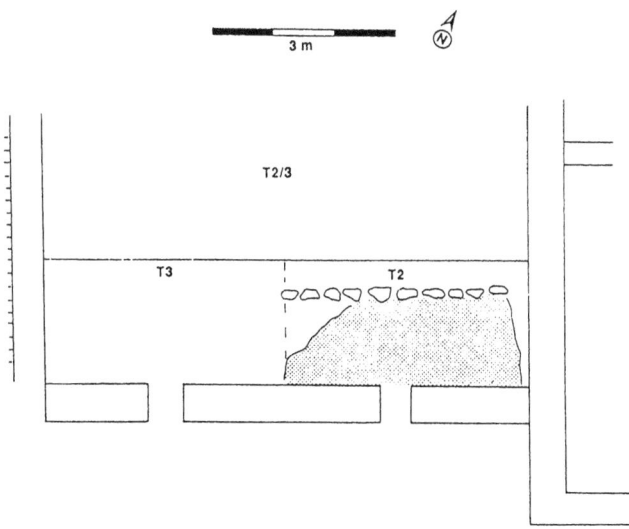

Figure 6.12. Plan of T2/3, and division into two excavation units. The shaded area indicates a well-preserved plaster floor.

A wall borders the platform to the south, and two doorways open through this wall. These doorways have the most finely finished jambs of any seen in the site. The east end of the platform is flanked by the wall that forms the east side of the room block. (It was the trenching along this wall that yielded the suspicious remains.) The north side of the feature remains undefined; the excavation was only 2 meters wide.

A clear primary association was located in this unit. Here twelve reconstructible vessels—all imported, and most with fancy polychrome painting in Wari style—were found in contact with the plaster floor. This deposit exhibits very low diversity of artifact types: few other artifacts or habitation debris were encountered. There is discrete spatial patterning apparent in the deposit: ten vessels were found along the east wall of the unit, one was farther west along the south wall, and the remaining vessel was broken on the floor a short distance away. This is clearly a primary deposit, with the vessels remaining where they were left at the time the site was abandoned. Their presence in this unit, and their association with each other, indicates that some special activity took place in this location.

Summary of Deposits

In sum, there are few primary deposits of artifacts at Jincamocco, and very little that can indicate specific activities carried out at specific locations. However, there are numerous architectural features in their original position. The locations of hearths, canals, the skull offering, and the group of pots on the west bench of Patio 1, all indicate activities and behaviors that took place at those locations. The primary deposit in T2/3 is especially important, since it includes an association of fancy Middle Horizon vessels with architectural features found nowhere else on the site. However, the vast majority of the artifacts from Jincamocco are from secondary or tertiary deposits of trash and architectural fill.

ABSOLUTE DATING OF THE WILLKA PHASE OCCUPATION OF JINCAMOCCO

Two charcoal samples, each a single chunk of burned wood, were located in contexts that should provide an absolute date for the construction of the enclosure. Sample 1 was found in the plaster floor of T2/3, the platform feature, between the plaster layer, and the mud layer below it. It was therefore deposited at the time that the plaster floor was laid down. Sample 2 was found in the mortar between the stones of the canal under

Corridor 1. This canal was well-sealed under a very hard floor, and there was no evidence of later canal repair in this location. Thus, the sample was most likely deposited at the time the canal was built.

The results of the assays are as follows:

Sample 1 (GX-4758): 1405 ± 135 (A.D. 545 ± 135)
Sample 2 (GX-4759): 1070 ± 125 (A.D. 880 ± 125)

When calibrated (following Klein et al. 1982), these dates are as follows:

Sample 1: A.D. 642 (one sigma range: A.D. 540-767)
Sample 2: A.D. 983 (one sigma range: A.D. 780-1148)

Although intuitively these dates seem rather distinct, a t-test comparing them indicates that they are not significantly different dates. Since both likely represent the date of construction of the enclosure, it is therefore reasonable to average the two dates:

averaged and uncalibrated:

A.D. 712 (one sigma range: A.D. 582-842)

averaged and calibrated:

A.D. 794 (one sigma range: A.D. 673-939)
(two sigma range: A.D. 640-1000)

Hence, the best estimate of the absolute date of construction of the enclosure at Jincamocco is the late eighth century A.D., plus or minus a century or so.

A third sample was collected from the cultural deposits in Patio 3. This particular deposit was secondary trash of Willka phase materials. So while this sample does not date the beginning or the end of the occupation of the enclosure, it should pertain to the period between those events. The result of the assay is as follows:

Sample 3 (GX-4761): 1220 ± 115 (A.D. 730 ± 115)

calibrated:

A.D. 793 (one sigma range: A.D. 670-977)

This date is not significantly different from the prior samples, and cannot be used to distinguish occupation from construction.

RELATIVE DATING OF THE OCCUPATIONS AT JINCAMOCCO

Clearly Jincamocco was occupied for an extended period of time. The small local village established at the site was occupied throughout the Kancha phase, perhaps beginning at the end of the Sacrahua phase. And the Wari enclosure was built and occupied during the Willka phase. Given that most of the deposits of artifacts are secondary in nature, it is not possible to subdivide Willka phase deposits into temporally meaningful strata. Likewise, the Kancha phase deposits are secondary or tertiary trash that may have been redeposited from elsewhere, and thoroughly mixed. Given these considerations, along with the evidence of stratigraphic associations, it is possible to separate deposits that probably represent pure Willka phase remains, from those that probably represent pure Kancha phase remains; in turn, these deposits can be separated from those that might be mixed.

Each of the provenience units that contained artifacts was assigned a temporal designation based on stratigraphic context and cultural associations (Table 6.2). The purpose of this designation was to distinguish de-

TABLE 6.2
Temporal Designations of Provenience Units

Temporal Designation	Description	# Proveniences
7	probably Willka phase some later material possibly mixed in	27
6*	Willka phase minimal possibility of mixing	33
5	probably Willka phase some earlier material possibly mixed in	14
4	mixed Willka phase and earlier	11
3	probably Kancha phase some Willka phase material possibly mixed in	4
2*	Kancha phase minimal possibility of mixing	25
1	distinctly earlier material possibly terminal Sacrahua phase	6

*These unmixed deposits are the only ones used in deriving interpretations of temporal changes.

posits that might be mixed from deposits that should represent pure temporal associations. This is especially important in trying to assess changes in artifact styles through time: only "pure" proveniences are considered, and proveniences with probable mixing are not. After assigning each provenience to its category based on stratigraphic context, this designation was checked and revised by checking for the presence or absence of known temporal markers, especially ceramics decorated with motifs of the Wari horizon styles. When there was any doubt, the more conservative designation was always chosen.

Seven possible designations were defined as follows:

7. This indicates deposits that are probably Willka phase, but may have later materials mixed in. The uppermost level of each excavation unit was automatically classified 7 because of the possibility of contamination by later occupations. No clearly later artifacts have ever been identified, but the presence of post–Willka phase burials throughout the site indicates the need to be cautious in any case. Twenty-seven provenience units were given this designation.

6. This indicates deposits that are of Willka phase date, with minimal possibility of mixing of earlier or later materials. These deposits occur on and above floor and bench surfaces. Thirty-three provenience units were given this designation.

5. This indicates deposits that are probably Willka phase, but may have earlier materials mixed in. These deposits include certain floor deposits where construction fill may be included with the Willka phase materials. Fourteen provenience units were given this designation.

4. This indicates deposits that are very likely a mixture of Willka phase and earlier materials. These are primarily architectural fill: bench fill, and floor leveling fill. Eleven provenience units were given this designation.

3. This indicates deposits that are most likely Kancha phase in date, but may have some Willka phase materials mixed in. In these cases the interface between the Willka phase surfaces and material below was not clearly defined in the stratigraphy, so some Willka phase material may be included in what are predominantly Kancha phase deposits. Four provenience units were given this designation.

2. This designates deposits that are unmixed Kancha phase materials. They occur under well-defined surfaces, below architectural fill. No Wari-style sherds are found in these deposits. Although the Kancha phase spans a broad period of time, in the case of Jincamocco all the deposits from this period are secondary trash, so no attempt was made to subdivide this period based on stratigraphic level. This certainly obscures some temporal variation, but still serves to draw a contrast with the Willka phase, the focus of this study. Twenty-five provenience units were given this designation.

1. In a few limited contexts, deposits were found that were given this designation, which indicates a period distinctly earlier than 2. In all cases these deep deposits were separated from Kancha phase levels by sterile soil. Differences in artifact style are clearly apparent, reinforcing this separation into a separate temporal designation. It is likely that this phase dates to terminal Sacrahua phase times. Only six provenience units were given this designation.

THE ARCHITECTURE OF JINCAMOCCO

Overall Plan

To summarize, the enclosure at Jincamocco is located in a relatively level location, but for the most part topography was ignored in planning the site. The enclosure was laid out as a single unit, with a well defined and continuous outer wall. The enclosure was divided in half, and the eastern half left empty except for a few irregular structures. The west end exhibits a tripartite division, having been subdivided first into thirds, east to west, with the westernmost third becoming a separate sector (Sector 1). The remaining two thirds was divided into three equal portions, from north to south (Sectors 2, 3, and 4). These four sectors were in turn divided into room blocks: six in Sector 1, four in Sector 2, six in Sector 3, and eight in Sector 4. Room blocks within each sector are roughly the same size.

Below this level of subdivision the plan becomes less rigid. Details of construction vary from room block to room block, and no two seem to be the same. A distinctive pattern is the patio group: a central, open patio surrounded by peripheral galleries. The normal pattern finds galleries on all four sides, but fewer are seen in some cases. Where clearly visible, galleries are only one deep.

Patios have low benches around their perimeter; benches always occur along those sides of the patio flanked by galleries, and sometimes along other walls as well. Some patios have short walls extending into them, the width of the bench, near one or more corners; these may be associated with entrances. Hearths may be located on benches, in the corners of the room. Access between the patios and galleries is through doorways. No evidence remains of roofing, but it is probable that the galleries were roofed, and that porticos were built over the benches to roof them as well. The center of the patio was probably left open. A system of canals runs under the floors, and probably served to drain water from the patios. On the basis of size and configuration, Patios 2 and 3 are quite similar, but are distinct from Patio 1; this may or not reflect differences in function.

While there are no well-defined streets running through the enclosure, there are many corridors. These are located between room blocks, on one or more sides of each room block. Access into patio groups is sometimes directly from corridor into patio via doorway. Other times, doors may provide access from corridor to gallery, and another door may then open into the patio.

There is no evidence remaining to suggest whether the enclosure was single-storied, or multistoried. Walls are not preserved to a sufficient height at present, since the stones were used for construction in Cabana, since the sixteenth century. The removal of most stones from the surface of the site also precludes estimating the volume of original construction— and hence the number of stories.

Spatial Patterning

The architecture of Jincamocco indicates that there are several functionally discrete forms present. The first form is the patio group, a central patio with peripheral galleries. Access into the galleries is generally limited to entrance from the patio; together the patio and its galleries form some sort of functionally related unit. The patio group includes an open central area, sheltered areas, and enclosed roofed spaces. The presence of a hearth in Patio 2 suggests that food preparation was one activity carried out on the sheltered benches of the patio; certainly a variety of activities might have been carried out on the sheltered benches, around the edge of the open patio. The functions of the galleries is so far unknown, from the excavations at Jincamocco, but the lack of remains in Gallery 1 might suggest activities that do not leave many material remains: perhaps storage, perhaps sleeping areas, perhaps something else.

Based on the primary architectural remains, we cannot know what sort of social units occupied the patio groups, but we might draw a distinction between the very large Patio 1, with no galleries, and the smaller patios, with galleries. The smaller patios are of a size possibly suited to a smaller, generalized group. The open areas may have been used for most activities, while the enclosed galleries served as areas for sleeping, or household-level storage. The presence of the hearth in Patio 2 might support this interpretation. On the other hand, these units might have served as administrative units, where low-level bureaucrats stationed in each patio controlled access to the peripheral galleries. In this case, valued items might have been stored in the galleries, and the patios served in a manner analogous to that proposed for the *audiencias* of the Chimú (Day 1982: 64).

The large Patio 1 might represent an entirely different set of activities. Probably too large for a household unit, and without galleries to be controlled by some official, perhaps it served some more communal or public function, or perhaps it served a larger, more specialized group than the smaller patio. Access into Patio 1 was originally relatively direct and unimpeded, from the outside of the enclosure. It might have served as some sort of receiving hall, or perhaps as an area of communal food service. Numerous other possibilities might also be suggested.

In sum, it seems clear that the patio group forms some sort of functionally interrelated unit, and that there are distinctly different kinds of patio groups—even given the very small sample from Jincamocco. On the basis of architecture and immovable features, however, we cannot be specific about activities performed in them.

The second functionally distinct form of architecture at the site is the corridor. Numerous corridors wind through the site, providing direct access to the various room blocks and patio groups. Given the poor preservation of Jincamocco, we cannot yet map out these circulation patterns in any detail. The corridors also indicate that an alteration of the original circulation patterns occurred sometime during the occupation of the site. Near both Patios 1 and 3, corridors were blocked with cross walls, and doorways into the patios were closed off. The evidence of Patio 3 suggests that the patio was still occupied even after the doorway was sealed. The evidence of Corridor 1 suggests that its use as a place to dump trash did not begin until after the cross wall was built. These data suggest, rather than an abrupt abandonment of the site, that parts of it were gradually closed off, and only later used for trash disposal.

If patios were still used after doorways were blocked (as suggested in Patio 3) and cross walls erected in corridors, then access to patios must have been from above. Either some sort of steps or ladders were used to climb over the walls, or else the corridors had a second story that served as a walkway.

The third architectural form defined at the site is the raised and finely finished platform of T2/3, in Room Block 1.5. Excavation of this feature was limited, and access to it from the north is unknown; there were two doors onto the platform along its south margin. To the west, the ground slopes down a meter or more; no excavations were carried out in the remainder of the room block. Along with the fine architectural detailing, the primary association of exotic imported polychrome vessels further indicates that this feature served a very special function. One is first tempted to suggest some sort of ceremonial function for this feature; indeed, the depictions of mythical creatures on several of the vessels (described in detail in Chapter 7) would tend to support this interpretation. But this area might equally well have served some purpose rather more political in nature, perhaps a base of operations for a particularly high-status official. The elaborate ceramics in the unit, complete with their ideological symbols, might be expected in the presence of such a personage. The fact that the feature is raised at least a meter above the floor of the remainder of the room block could conform with both ceremonial and political interpretations: the platform, and the people and things on it, were visible to those standing below. And this is the only room block directly accessible from the exterior of the enclosure: a doorway in the outer enclosure wall opens into this room block. Regardless of its exact use, it is clear just from the architectural remains that this was a very special place.

Temporal Variation

In addition to the change in access patterns within the enclosure, a second major change that took place during the occupation of the site was that more buildings were constructed outside the enclosure. It can only be assumed that when the site was first laid out, Wari planners had in mind certain needs, and designed a site of the proper size, and with the appropriate facilities, to carry out these needs. It would seem that these needs changed, and that the site was greatly enlarged. Given that the site quadrupled in size, this must have been a major change in strategy. The vast majority of the architecture that can be detected on the remainder of the site is rectilinear, and laid out in contiguous compounds, unlike the local style of architecture, which is always round in form. This does not seem to be a great influx of local peasants to the center, building squatter settlements on its periphery. Rather, the architecture is like that of the enclosure, in general configuration, and represents additional Wari construction.

We have no excavation data from outside the enclosure, and the poor preservation of the surface architecture precludes seeing details of plan. What is especially interesting, however, is the fact that two large areas were left open. One area lies immediately to the west and slightly to the north of the enclosure. In this area, no new constructions were built. In fact, traces still remain of local round houses, remains of the village located on the site prior to the construction of the enclosure. The second area left open was the eastern half of the enclosure. Now why should this be? If new room blocks were needed, why not build them inside the already existing enclosure? Given that this was not done, the open area must have served some important purpose. This is the lowest part of the site, which may be relevant, perhaps having something to do with water and drainage. In any case, there must have been something that this part of the enclosure was used for, something that continued to be important.

The open half of the enclosure may have served as a large, protected llama corral. Given that Jincamocco was located along a major road between Wari and the south coast, and was probably part of a long- distance exchange system, it is very probable that llama trains carrying state goods passed frequently through the region. And though Jincamocco may have changed through time, it would still need facilities to corral llamas, and to protect the goods they were carrying. Thus, the eastern half of the enclosure continued to serve as a llama corral, while the new facilities were built outside the enclosure. If this were so, then the irregular structures in this half of the enclosure may have served as temporary quarters for the animal handlers.

Comparison of Jincamocco with Other Wari Sites

Jincamocco clearly conforms to the tenets of the distinctive Wari architectural style, and is similar both to Wari and, especially, to other major Wari provincial sites, such as Viracochapampa, Pikillaqta, Azángaro, and Honco Pampa (Fig. 6.13). Wari architecture has been discussed in some detail elsewhere (Schreiber 1978; Spickard 1983; Isbell et al. 1985), and I will not here repeat all the details of this style. Rather, I shall point out some of the major points of similarity between Jincamocco and other sites of this style.

First of all, general masonry styles are the same at all Wari sites. Walls are made of broken stone, are double faced, and set in mud mortar. (Local materials were used, so different sites are made of different kinds of stone.) The general plan is orthogonal, sites are usually large subdivided compounds. Sites may be multistoried, and drainage canals are commonly found below floors. Jincamocco conforms to this pattern of construction, although it may have been just a single story in height.

One particularly distinctive characteristic of Wari provincial sites is the single, well defined rectangular enclosure with a thick outer wall, inside divided into repeating units of similar size. Beyond a general attempt to locate the enclosures on relatively flat land, the plan is oblivious to topography. The rigidity of the overall plan is a striking feature of the provincial enclosure. Jincamocco likewise conforms to this pattern.

Two sites are exceptions to this general situation. Honco Pampa, discussed in Chapter 3, is located on a steep hillside—perhaps too steep even for Wari planners to ignore. Here room blocks are separate, or occur in small groups, and they are oriented to the topography; no single contiguous rectangular enclosure occurs at Honco Pampa. The second exception is, of course, Wari itself. While large rigid rectangular enclosures occur with great frequency at Wari, intervening areas are filled with Wari-style constructions as well, but planned within the confines of available space.

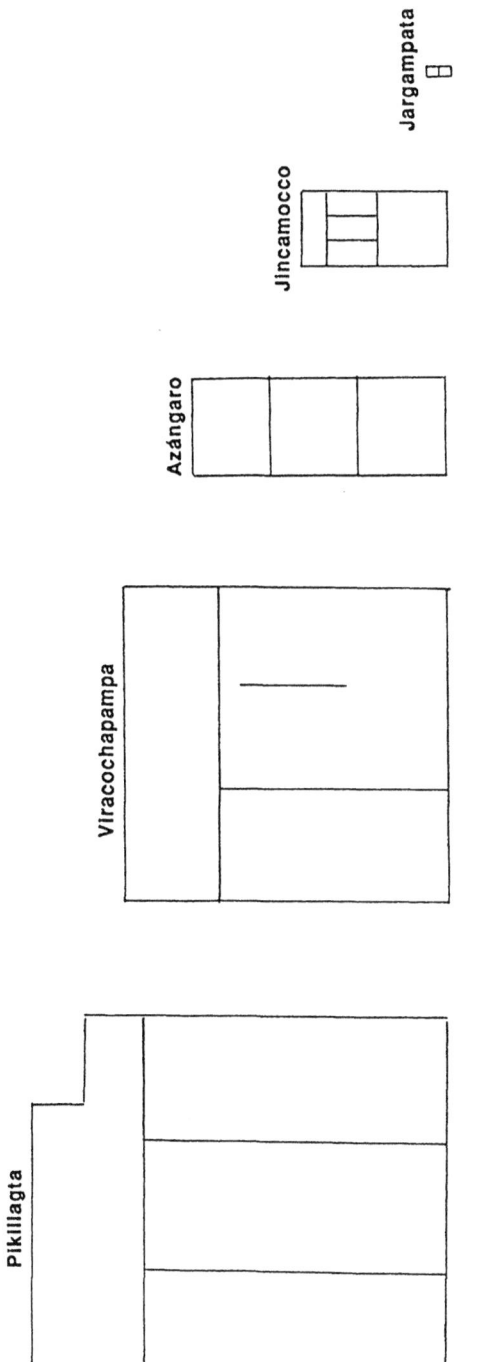

Figure 6.13. Schematic outline plans of Pikillaqta, Viracochapampa, Azángaro, Jincamocco, and Jargampata indicating variations in size and layout of Wari enclosure sites.

Another distinctive aspect of Wari rectangular enclosures is the division of the enclosures into three or four large sectors (Fig. 6.13). Azángaro is clearly divided into thirds. Pikillaqta, Viracochapampa and Jincamocco are divided into four major sectors, one along one side, and the other three perpendicular to the first.

And finally, the most diagnostic aspect of Wari site planning is the patio group: a single open patio, surrounded by peripheral galleries. Doorways provide access between patios and peripheral galleries, and patio perimeters are bordered with low benches. There are some variations here, but the typical plan can be seen at all known Wari sites, including Wari itself. As I have shown, the enclosure at Jincamocco also exhibits this most diagnostic characteristic. There are some variants at Pikillaqta that so far have not been identified at other sites: there patios sometimes have galleries three deep, with diagonal end walls.

CONCLUSION

Jincamocco represents a foreign presence in the Carhuarazo Valley, and the focus of political control during the Middle Horizon. There is no question but that Jincamocco is a Wari site, simply by virtue of its architecture. It conforms to the same rules of construction, plan, and form as Wari, as other known Wari sites. Furthermore, this style is foreign to the Carhuarazo Valley, where local structures were small round buildings. The site as a whole clearly represents an intrusion from outside the immediate region.

Variations in architectural forms within the site indicate several functionally discrete areas within the enclosure. Two kinds of patio groups, corridors, and a finely finished platform feature—all probably were put to different uses, although these uses might have involved some overlap in functions. Temporal variations are apparent as well. Access patterns within the site were changed, and major constructions were added outside the enclosure, quadrupling the size of the site. And as noted in the previous chapter, additional Wari sites, three small compounds, were built elsewhere in the valley. All of these indicate possible changes in Wari strategies of control over the region.

Now let us turn to a discussion of the remains recovered during the excavation of Jincamocco: the evidence of the artifacts.

Jincamocco

NOTES

1. Author's translation. Original text as follows.

   Respóndese al capítulo veinte y uno, que junto al pueblo de *La Vera Cruz de Cahuana* está un pueblo derribado, al parecer, antiquísima cosa. Tiene paredes de piedra labrada, aunque la obra tosca; las portadas de las casas, algunas de ellas algo más de dos varas en alto, y los lumbrales de piedras muy grandes; y hay señales de calles. Dicen los indios viejos, que tienen noticia de sus antepasados, de oidas, que en tiempos antiquísimos, ántes que los Ingas los señoreasen, vino á esta tierra otra gente á quien llamaron *viracochas*, y no mucha cantidad, y que á estos los seguian los indios veniendo tras ellos oyendo su palabra, y dicen ahora los indios que debian de ser santos. A éstos les hacian caminos, que hoy dia son vistos, tan anchos como una calle y de una parte y de otra paredes bajas, y en las dormidas les hacian casas que hasta [hoy] hay memoria dellas, y para esta gente dicen que se hizo este pueblo dicho; y algunos indios se acuerdan de haber visto en este pueblo antiguo algunas sepulturas con huesos, hechas de losas de piedra cuadradas y enlucidas por de dentro con tierra blanca, y al presente no parece hueso ni calavera destos.

2. A fourth date was run on a sample (GX-4760) of charcoal from an early Kancha phase context, in the deepest level excavated in Patio 1. This yielded a date of 530 ± 160, or A.D. 1420 ± 160. A note from the laboratory stated: "This sample was very tiny. It was counted for two full days, the two counts were essentially concordant and the average is reported." Given the small size of the sample, and the fact that, on stratigraphic grounds, it should significantly predate the Middle Horizon, this date is disregarded.

7

The Evidence of the Artifacts from Jincamocco

This chapter moves to a more specific level of analysis: the artifacts recovered during the excavation of Jincamocco.[1] The ultimate goal of the artifact analysis is to understand past lifeways at the site, and then to draw conclusions regarding the overall function of the site in the past cultural system. In order to accomplish this goal, relevant patterns in the artifact assemblage recovered from Jincamocco are sought, and then the evidence of such patterning is used to answer our questions.

The artifacts recovered in greatest abundance are ceramics: over 55,000 sherds. As a result, most of the analysis has been devoted to the ceramic remains, the presentation of which forms the bulk of this chapter. Chipped stone artifacts were the second most abundant remains, totaling over 4,000 pieces. In addition, the assemblage includes 124-plus ground stone artifacts, some 87 kg of animal bone, 134 ceramic spindle whorls, and rare items including bone, shell and metal artifacts. Several human burials were encountered, as well. Due to poor preservation conditions, no textile fragments were recovered, and no botanical remains were collected. Tables of artifacts recovered in each excavation provenience can be found in Appendix B.

The specific goals of the artifact analysis involve detecting temporally and spatially significant patterns within the overall assemblage. However, as discussed in some detail in Chapter 6, nearly all the artifacts recovered from Jincamocco were found in secondary or tertiary context. Only one good primary association was located, in Unit T2/3, along with a few vessels found in limited primary context on the west bench of Patio 1. With these few exceptions, trash deposits do not indicate the location of the activities that produced the remains. But, the general content of the assemblage can indicate something of the range of activities carried out in the enclosure. Weaving tools indicate textile production, even if not found where this production occurred. Cooking vessels likewise indicate food preparation, even if not found associated with the hearths where the cooking took place.

Differences in the trash deposits may indicate different constellations of activities. For example, remains from one patio may include weaving tools, while those of another patio do not. This does not mean that weaving took place in the first patio (although it might have), but rather that this activity was carried out in the source of the trash deposited there, but not in the source of the trash in the second patio. Not only does this indicate that weaving took place in the site, but it also suggests that weaving was a spatially discrete activity.

And while we can distinguish deposits that are clearly Willka phase from those that are earlier, it is not possible at this time to subdivide these time periods into shorter discrete spans of time. But we can contrast the artifact assemblage of the Willka phase with that of the Kancha phase, both in general terms, and in terms of specific changes within particular artifact classes.

This chapter will describe the various classes of artifacts, from the most abundant (ceramics) to the rarest (a single gold artifact). Each class will be described, variations in decoration and morphology pointed out, and temporal changes noted. Temporal changes between the Kancha phase and the Willka phase will be summarized, and interpretations of the reasons for some of these changes will be offered. Evidence of spatial patterning in Willka phase deposits will be outlined. Finally, the evidence of specific activities will be summarized, and the overall role of Jincamocco discussed.

CERAMIC VESSELS

Most of the material recovered from Jincamocco was ceramic remains. Of the 55,000-plus sherds excavated, some 8,000 were diagnostics, 6,200 of which were recorded in detail. Diagnostics include all decorated sherds, and all sherds representing a particular morphological part of a vessel, including rims, jar necks, handles, bases, and appendages. Undecorated body sherds were divided into bowls and jars, based on shape and interior surface finish, and counted. No further analysis was undertaken of the nondiagnostics.

The unit of analysis was the vessel, so each diagnostic sherd was treated as a separate vessel. However, where two or more sherds were from the same vessel, they were coded together as a single vessel. The diagnostic sherds were subjected to a detailed recording of attributes, coded in such a form that they could be directly transformed into a computer database. Up to 42 distinct attributes (80 columns of data) were recorded for each vessel; the resulting data set comprises over two megabytes of information.

The attribute coding system was designed to be flexible and could be revised and expanded at any point in the analysis to add new variations as they appeared in the data. Some codes were hierarchical in nature; general characteristics could be recorded, and more specific details could be included where they were visible. One disadvantage of this sort of attribute recording system is that it encourages the recording of perhaps too much detail. Another disadvantage is that it is sometimes difficult to categorize each attribute objectively and discretely.

Not all diagnostics were coded. In about half of the proveniences, all broken jar necks (without rims) and strap handles were coded. These yielded minimal useful data, so in the other half of the proveniences they were counted but not coded. This accounts for the discrepancy between total number of ceramic diagnostics (8,000), and number of recorded diagnostics (6,200).

In addition to the attribute recording, drawings were made of sherds with clearly visible decorations, and sherds with relatively complete morphology, especially rim sherds. All decorated sherds were photographed in black and white, and color. These data provide some more subjective data that complement the objective observations of the coded attributes. And, importantly, these data allow us to reassess some attribute codings and typological ascriptions.

Attribute Recording System

The attributes coded addressed first the construction of the vessel, its decoration, and its shape. Then, depending on what part or parts of the vessel were present, attributes of the rim, neck, base, handles and appendages were recorded. Then some additional measurements and observations were recorded. The details of the coding system are presented in Appendix C. Here I shall discuss the parameters of the coding system.

Manufacture. Attributes of manufacture include paste color, inclusion size, surface finish (interior and exterior), presence of slip, and slip color (also interior and exterior).

Decoration. A three-digit code indicates a general category of decoration, a more specific subcategory of that particular decorative technique, and the location on the vessel. Up to four codes could be coded per vessel, two interior, two exterior. For example, the code 112 indicates an incised design in a band below the rim; 213 is an appliqué strip with punctations on the neck of a jar; 436 is a fine polychrome painted design covering the entire surface of the vessel. Drawings and photographs are critical here, and provide details of decoration that go beyond the computer codes. During later stages of the analysis, more detailed design categories were developed for each class, and added to the computer database.

Vessel shape. In general, most vessels were allocated to either a bowl category or a jar category. A few specific vessel forms were designated as well, including lyre cups, tumblers, spoons and bottles. Within the bowl category two additional digits distinguished incurving from open forms, and wall shape (concave, straight, or convex). In the case of jars, necked jars were distinguished from neckless ones: 210 indicates a necked jar, 220 indicates a neckless jar, and 200 indicates a jar whose neck (or lack of one) was not evident, and so could not be put into the more specific category. Necked jars have a well-defined angled juncture between the neck and body of the vessel. Jars whose necks are formed by an upturned rim or an everted lip are classed as neckless.

Attributes of rims. Measurements were made of rim diameter (in centimeters), and the angle of the vessel at the rim (usually in 15° intervals). An angle of 90° indicates a vessel with vertical sides; a rim angle of less than 90° indicates an incurving closed form; and rim angle greater than 90° is an open form. A five-digit code indicates the profile of the vessel at the rim, and the curvature of the rim with respect to the vessel profile. A four-digit code gives details of the rim form.

Attributes of necks. Both the diameter and vertical height of the neck were measured in centimeters. The angle of the neck with respect to the body, and the general form of the neck were recorded as well.

Attributes of bases. The diameter of the base was measured (in cm) as was the angle of the vessel at the base juncture (15° intervals). One digit indicates the vessel profile at the base juncture, and two digits indicate the form of the base.

Attributes of handles and appendages. In the case of both handles and appendages a two-digit code indicates the form and location of the feature.

Other attributes. Other measurements were made, including wall thickness, total vessel height, and maximum vessel diameter (the latter two measurements rarely made, since they required nearly complete vessels). If the vessel was represented by more than one sherd, the number of sherds comprising the vessel was recorded. Space was left to code temporal epoch, and style, as well as type, but these were rarely used. Finally, a code indicates whether the vessel was drawn, photographed, or both. This latter record is especially useful as it can be used to produce an inventory or catalog of the hundreds of drawings and photographs.

Ceramic Classes

The ceramics from Jincamocco were classified on the basis of surface treatment and decoration into four basic classes: plainware, local decorated styles, red-slipped ware, and polychrome ceramics. Plainware is the most common category, and comprises undecorated utilitarian vessels without pigmented slip. Local decorated styles are divided into three subcategories: incised bowls, jars with serpentine designs, and other tactile decoration. Red-slipped wares are vessels in many ways similar to plainware, but with a red pigmented slip. Finally, polychromes include all painted ceramics with two or more colors. On the basis of surface finish, number of colors, and depictions, these are subdivided into less fancy wares, and fancy polychromes. The fancy polychromes include the Wari horizon styles of Ocros, Black Decorated, Chakipampa B, and Viñaque.

In this section I shall describe the general attributes and range of variation of each class of ceramics, pointing out the differences between the Kancha phase and the Willka phase in each case. In Chapter 6, a series of temporal designations that distinguish pure from possibly mixed deposits were defined. In my analysis of temporal changes I rely only on pure deposits (T = 6, T = 2, and sometimes T = 1); mixed deposits are not considered in the temporal analyses.

Finally, the special case of Unit T2/3 will be taken up separately. In this unit a primary deposit of twelve vessels was found. These include Wari polychromes, as well as some pieces that are less fancy, but are foreign imports. This primary association has implications for the relative dating of Wari horizon styles, as well as for specific activities taking place within Jincamocco.

Plainware

Plainware makes up by far the largest portion of the ceramic assemblage, totaling 3,937 coded vessels. Five basic vessel shapes make up the plainware category: necked jars, neckless jars, in-curving bowls, straight-sided open bowls, and convex-sided open bowls; given the fragmentary nature of the remains, not all pieces could be classified into one of these shapes. Plainware vessels have no pigmented slip; they are generally smoothed on the surface, with some polished pieces. For the most part the paste is brown to dark brown, and inclusions are medium to coarse in size. Some pieces have a lighter colored paste, and these pieces also have finer inclusions, suggesting greater care went into the production of these pieces; likewise, fine inclusions are correlated with polished surface, and thinner wares, also indicating greater care in production. There is an interesting temporal correlation here: within the plainware category, the percentage of polished plainware decreases from 38% in the Kancha phase to 23% in the Willka phase, and there is an increase in coarse inclusions as well, in the Willka phase. This suggests that less care was going into the production of plainwares in the Willka phase.

While the percentage of plainware in the entire assemblage remains unchanged from the Kancha phase to Willka phase (Table 7.1), staying at roughly 63%, there is a significant change in the proportion of bowls to jars. Jars decrease in proportion from 71% to 61% of the plainware vessels, with a concomitant increase in the percentage of bowls (Table 7.2). However, this is matched by an increase in jars in other categories.

Jars

Jars (n = 2,394) are divided into two general forms, based on the presence or absence of a well-defined neck; not all jars could be classified into one or the other form, given the fragmentary nature of the remains. Neckless jars (n = 140) are in-curving vessels with a constricted neck; there is usually some special rim treatment: thickening and turning out or up. Neckless jars are generally lighter in color and more highly polished than other plainware forms. Rim diameters range from 4 to 34 cm, with most vessels within the range between 17 and 26 cm; the mean rim diameter is 20.1 cm. Rim angle ranges between 0° and 75°, with an average of 41.9°; Kancha phase vessels are slightly more in-curving than Willka phase ones. There are three general rim forms. The first is a rim that is noticeably thickened, and sharply everted. This is the most common form in the Kancha phase, and it continues through the Willka phase. The second rim form is one that is thickened, but not everted. It first appears in the

TABLE 7.1
Frequencies and Percentages of Ceramic Classes During the Kancha and Willka Phases

FREQUENCIES							
Phase	Plainware	Local Decorated Styles*					
		IB	JSD	OT	Redware	Painted	TOTAL
Kancha	585	189	81	30	42	6	933
Willka	1513	189	150	43	295	167	2357
PERCENTAGES							
Phase	Plainware	Local Decorated Styles*					
		IB	JSD	OT	Redware	Painted	TOTAL
Kancha	62.7	20.3	8.7	3.2	4.5	0.6	100
Willka	64.2	8.0	6.4	1.8	12.5	7.1	100

* IB = incised bowls, JSD = jars with serpentine design, OT = other tactile decoration.

Evidence of Jincamocco Artifacts

TABLE 7.2
Frequencies of Plainware Vessel Shapes During the Kancha and Willka Phases

Phase	Jars				Bowls					TOTAL
	unk	nkls	nkd	Total	unk	inc	sso	cso	Total	
Kancha	106	27	276	409	6	14	83	61	164	573
Willka	333	53	509	895	30	37	314	195	576	1471

Kancha phase, but becomes more common in the Willka phase. Finally, the third rim form is one that is upturned, but not thickened. This form appears first in the Willka phase (and continues into later periods). Overall, neckless jars decrease slightly in proportion to total plainware from the Kancha phase to the Willka phase.

Necked jars ($n = 1,442$) have a well-defined and angled juncture between body and neck. The typical form, at least in the Willka phase, is relatively large (perhaps 40 cm maximum diameter), with a flaring neck, two vertical strap handles, and a pointed base. Rim diameters range from 4 to 60 cm, with most vessels having rim diameters between 12 and 30 cm; the mean diameter is 22 cm. In the Kancha phase levels, no pointed bases were located, so Kancha phase jars may have had rounded bases. As was the case with neckless jars, the local Kancha phase forms continue on through the Willka phase, but there is a wider range of variation in Willka phase forms. The range of rim diameters increases in the Willka phase, as does the range of neck heights. Generally the jar necks are straight-sided, and flaring; Kancha phase forms are less flared than Willka phase forms. Some jar necks have a convex rounded profile. This form is rare in the Kancha phase, but increases in proportion in the Willka phase (and continues through later periods). Most rims have no special treatment; some are flattened slightly, but most are just left rounded. In the Willka phase there is an increase in rims that are slightly thickened. (This pattern continues after the Willka phase, when thickened rims become a dominant form.)

Several new forms, which are basically subcategories of jars, are introduced in the Willka phase. These include bottles, and jars with spouts. These are very rare, even in the Willka phase levels, but are never found in Kancha phase levels.

Bowls

Bowls ($n = 1,436$) may be divided into three types: in-curving bowls, straight-sided open bowls, and round-sided open bowls; not all bowls could be classified into one of these shapes given the fragmentary nature of the remains. While plainware bowls increase in proportion to jars, from the Kancha phase to the Willka phase, the relative proportions of these three bowl shapes do not change significantly.

In-curving bowls ($n = 101$) have convex rounded sides, and a constricted mouth. Their mean rim angle is 64° (range = 30-75°), and mean rim diameter is 19 cm (range = 6-46 cm). They do not change in shape or size through time, and they generally have no special rim treatment. However, in the Willka phase, some in-curving bowls have rims that are slightly thickened. This was also the case with necked jars, and like them, foreshadows a form that becomes more common in periods after the Willka phase.

Straight-sided open bowls ($n = 771$) likewise exhibit little change from the Kancha phase to the Willka phase. They have straight sides and flat or rounded bottoms. These bowls have a mean rim angle of 123° (range = 95-165°), and no special rim treatment. Mean rim diameter remains constant at 24 cm, but the range of sizes increases from 9 to 40 cm in the Kancha phase, to 9 to 50 cm in the Willka phase. The only change that is seen is, like the preceding cases, the appearance in the Willka phase of rims that are slightly thickened.

Round-sided open bowls ($n = 494$) comprise two slightly different forms, differentiated on the basis of rim angle. Vessels with convex sides, but a rim angle of 90°, are roughly hemispherical, and differentiated from bowls that are more open. In general, the hemispherical forms tend to have flattened rims, while the more open forms have rounded rims. The mean rim diameter is 20 cm (range = 9-48 cm), and this does not change through time. Rim angle averages 114°, but the range of angles increases from 90-135° in the Kancha phase to 90-165° in the Willka phase. As in the case of other shapes, rims that are slightly thickened appear in the Willka phase.

A Primary Association of Plainware Vessels

Let me describe in a little more detail the four nearly intact plainware vessels (Fig. 7.1) found in primary context sitting on the west bench in Patio 1. Near the south end of the bench was found a large plainware necked jar, set into a small depression in the bench, and adjacent were two small round-sided open bowls. The jar was upright, and the two bowls were upside down. The jar originally had a neck, but it had been broken off, so its exact form is unknown; the jar had a pointed base. The maximum diameter of the jar was 31 cm; preserved height was 33 cm. There were two vertical strap handles on the sides of the jars; these were not placed symmetrically on each side, but were closer to each other on one side of the pot. Strap handles on modern jars have this same asymmetrical placement of handles. In the modern case these jars are meant for carrying on one's back, with a rope passing between the handles. In this jar was found a small gold disk.

Evidence of Jincamocco Artifacts

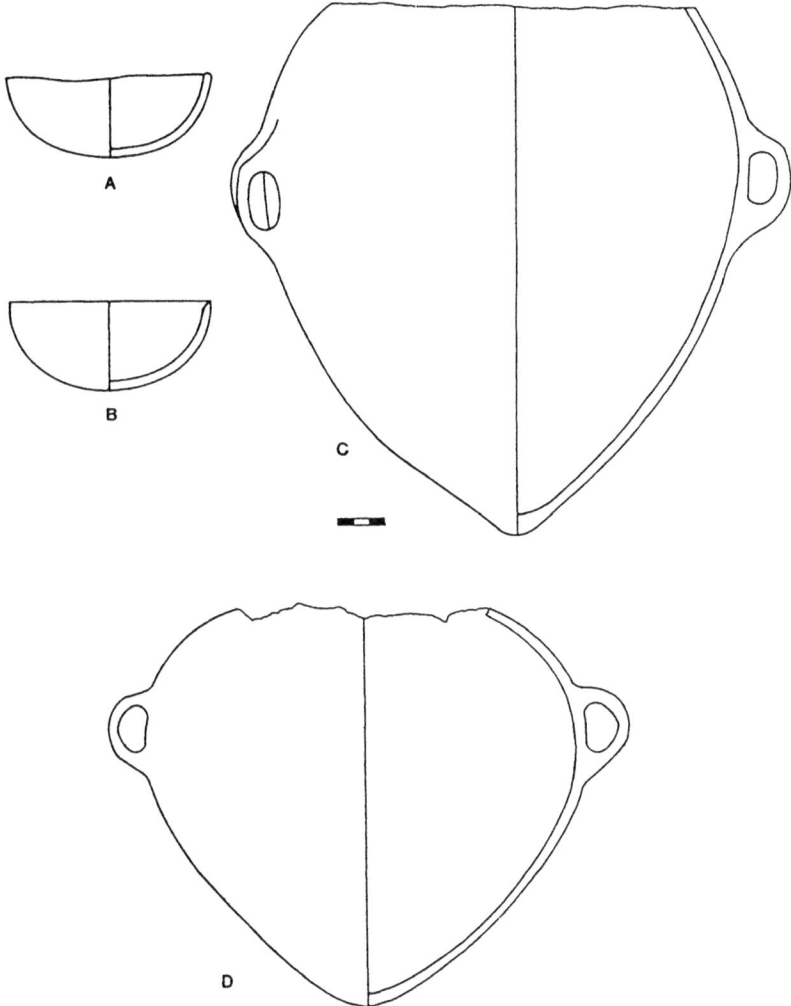

Figure 7.1. Profiles of four intact plainware vessels found in primary association on the west bench of Patio 1. The vessels above were found together, and the jar below was found a short distance away (see Fig. 6.8).

The two bowls found next to this jar are small round-sided open bowls. One measured 13 cm in diameter, and 5.5 cm deep, with a slightly tapered rim. The other measured 13.5 cm in diameter, and 5 cm deep, with a rounded rim.

The other jar was found nearer to the southwest corner of the patio, also sitting on the bench. This jar rested in a nest formed by three small cobbles. Like the first jar, this one had had its neck broken off. The maximum diameter of the jar was 28 cm, and preserved height was 24 cm; it has a shorter, squatter profile than the first jar. The two vertical strap handles were symmetrically placed; this jar also had a pointed base.

Plainware Summary

We see several temporal changes in the case of plainware. First, the proportion of bowls to jars changes markedly, with a much higher proportion of bowls in the Willka phase, and a lower proportion of jars. The second notable change is the decrease in the quality of the ceramics in the Willka phase. Less care was being taken with the production of each vessel. This may indicate one of several possibilities. Much more pottery was being used in the Willka phase than earlier, and if made by local production units as in the Kancha phase, there was less time to devote to each vessel. Furthermore, the locals were being forced to make pots for foreigners, not for their own use; the incentive to put in the extra effort to finely finish a vessel may have been lacking.

The third change seen is an increase in variability in Willka phase vessel forms. While all the Kancha phase shapes continue, new shapes are added, and the range of sizes increases. Most of the shapes that become dominant in the Willka phase have roots in the Kancha phase shapes, and probably do not represent outside introductions. Many of the shapes, both old and new, continue on in the local styles after the Willka phase as well.

The fourth change, apparent in the case of necked jars and bowls, is the change in rim forms in the Willka phase, with the first appearance of thickened rims. After the Willka phase, this rim form is increasingly common on local styles. Pointed bottomed jars also may be a new feature in the Willka phase, as no pointed bases were found in Kancha phase levels.

The most important conclusion to be drawn from the plainware ceramics is the fact that while the range of plainware forms was more diverse in the Willka phase, the local tradition experienced no sharp break. Most Willka phase shapes have antecedents in the Kancha phase, but a few forms are new: neckless jars with unthickened out-turned rims, bottles, thickened rims on other shapes, and pointed bases on necked jars. It has been argued in some cases that continuity in local utilitarian pottery indicates a lack of foreign influence. It is absolutely clear in the case of Jincamocco that local domestic utilitarian ceramics were not sharply affected by the foreign presence. Rather, local shapes continued, and new variations became more prevalent; many of these continued on in the local tradition in later periods. Change is characterized more by adding on a few new forms to existing styles, rather than mixing with and causing major transformations in the local styles. After the collapse of foreign control, these same local styles continued on without major change, right through to the Spanish conquest. Were we to look only at local utilitarian pottery, we would find no sharp break in the Willka phase, and we would see little direct evidence of any foreign presence.

In terms of spatial patterning in Willka phase deposits, especially high proportions of plainwares are found in Patio 2, while low proportions are found in Corridor 1. Plainwares are absent from T2/3.

Local Decorated Styles

The local decorated styles (n = 1,120) are more finely finished than plainwares, and they have plastic decoration: incision, appliqué, appliqué with punctation, punctation, stamping, gouges, and the application of small bumps and nubbins. Two subclasses are very distinctive: incised bowls, and jars with serpentine designs. The remaining pieces are classed simply as "other tactile."

In the Kancha phase levels, 32% of the ceramics were local decorated styles (Table 7.1). Painted pottery was virtually unknown; only six painted sherds were found in Kancha phase levels. There was no local tradition of painted pottery, and even pigmented slips were rare until the Willka phase. So, prior to the Willka phase, ceramics were mostly plainwares, plus these local decorated styles. However, in the Willka phase, the proportion of local decorated types dropped to 16%, half that of the preceding period. (This corresponds to an increase in red-slipped and painted pottery, discussed below.)

Within the local decorated styles, the proportions of the three subclasses changed with respect to each other, from the Kancha phase to the Willka phase. In the Kancha phase incised bowls were more than twice as common as jars with serpentine designs. In the Willka phase, the proportion of jars increased such that they made up 39% of the local decorated types; incised bowls dropped to 50%, and other tactile stayed about the same, at 11%.

Incised Bowls

Incised bowls (n = 651) are one of the more interesting and distinctive categories of ceramics (Fig. 7.2). Typically these are shallow open bowls, with a design band incised around the exterior just below the rim. The designs within this band are geometric, and sometimes have traces of red, yellow and white resin paint within the design band. Rim diameters range from 8 to 40 cm, with a mean diameter of 22 cm. The body is typically dark brown to black, and is often well polished. There are some important similarities between the Jincamocco incised bowls, and the Paracas pottery of Ica, and possibly Pukara pottery as well.

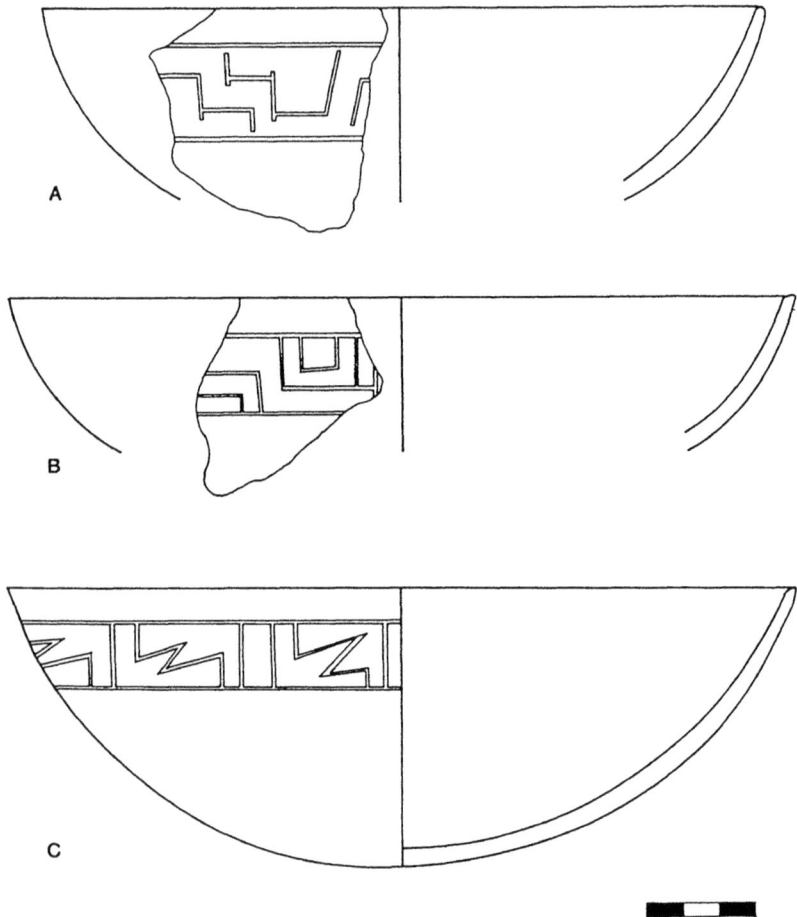

Figure 7.2. Incised bowls from Kancha phase levels of the north bench in Patio 1. A and B: Unit 05, level 4; C: Unit 03, level 5.

Within the entire ceramic assemblage from the site, incised bowls dropped from 20% in the Kancha phase, to 8% in the Willka phase. This is due to the drop in local decorated styles, as well as the decrease in proportion of incised bowls within that category. This change foreshadows periods to follow, when these local decorated styles disappeared from the local tradition, and were replaced with painted pottery.

Paste color of incised bowls ranges from buff to dark brown; most have orange to brown paste. The paste is rarely black, and never has grey tones. This suggests that the incised bowls were not fired in a reducing atmosphere, but rather were oxidized (cf. Shepard 1954:103). Surface color is darker than paste color, and ranges, with rare exceptions, from brown to black. The clear black on some well-polished vessels may be the result of intentional smoking (cf. Menzel, Rowe and Dawson 1954: 179). From the Kancha phase (n = 189) to the Willka phase (n = 189) the proportion of brown increases from 53% to 66% as black decreases from 44% to 33%. In the earliest period (T=1) we see the highest proportion of black vessels (52%). The sample from this period is extremely small (n = 21), but I include it because it will be relevant in later discussions of the Paracas style of Ica.

Three wares may be defined on the basis of inclusion size and surface finish. Wares are divided into three types: fine (fine inclusions, good polish), medium (medium to coarse inclusions, good polish), and coarse (medium to coarse inclusions, smoothed only). There is a strong correlation between fine inclusions and good polish, both attributes that indicate greater time and care in production. Fine ware decreases through time, while coarse ware increases, indicating a drop in the quality of the incised bowls in the Willka phase. There is, further, a strong correlation between fine ware, black surface color, and resin paint within the incised design. It seems clear that greater care went into production of highly polished black bowls with painted designs.

Incised bowls can be divided into four basic vessel shapes: straight sided open bowls, in-curving bowls (vessel angle less than 90°), hemispherical bowls (vessel angle about 90°), and round-sided open bowls (vessel angle greater than 90°). (The division between the latter two categories is somewhat arbitrary, based on vessel angle; the distribution of vessel angles is unimodal through the two categories.) Due to the fragmentary nature of the remains not all vessels could be classified into one of these forms. The only change in vessel shape through time is a decrease in in-curving bowls (Table 7.3). Willka phase bowls tend to be more open than Kancha phase ones.

Rims were subdivided into four categories: pointed, rounded, flat and thickened. These evidence some clear changes in rim forms through time: pointed rims decrease markedly, along with a decrease in rounded rims, while there is a corresponding increase in the percentage of flattened rims. Thickened rims are quite rare (n = 6) and occur only in Willka phase contexts, as we have seen in the case of plainwares.

TABLE 7.3
Frequencies of Incised Bowl Shapes During the Kancha and Willka Phases

Phase	in-curve	str-open	hemisph	convex	unk	TOTAL
Kancha	15	33	28	64	49	189
Willka	4	32	27	72	54	189

General correspondences between rim form and overall vessel form can be noted. Straight sided open bowls have all types of rims, with no apparent preference. However, in-curving bowls are more likely to have pointed or rounded rims than flattened ones. The decrease in these rim forms through time may be related to the decrease in in-curving bowls. Hemispherical and round sided open bowls tend to have flat rims rather than pointed or rounded rims.

All incised bowls have an incised design band around the exterior of the bowl, just below the rim. This band is generally 2-3 cm wide. The top of the band may be demarcated by two, one, or no incised lines. (In the latter case, the rim itself forms the upper boundary of the design field.) The bottom of the band is demarcated by one or two parallel incised lines. Most often there is a single line, both above and below the design band. All combinations of lines occur in all periods, with no clear patterns of temporal change.

The designs incised in the bands are always simple geometric figures, repeated around the circumference of the vessel. (On more complete specimens, it was always the case that the same design was repeated, and no combinations of different designs were ever seen on a single vessel. It is therefore assumed that this is the case with all vessels.)

Only about half of the incised bowl fragments were complete enough to define the design. Designs were divided into six basic categories: rectilinear, diagonal, jagged, zigzag, horizontal lines, and curvilinear. Specific designs within each category, where discernible, were given more detailed codes (Fig. 7.3).

Rectilinear designs (codes 10-14) are more common in earlier periods, and are rare in the Willka phase (Tables 7.4 and 7.5). All of the relatively complete rectilinear designs had single border lines above and below the design band. Diagonal designs (20-28), on the other hand, increase in proportion in the Willka phase, probably related to the decrease in rectilinear designs. Diagonal design 21 is by far the most common design and occurs in roughly the same proportions in the Kancha phase and Willka phase. Diagonal design 22 likewise does not change appreciably in proportion through time; diagonal design 24 is slightly more prevalent in the Kancha phase. Diagonal designs are more likely to occur with double bottom border lines than other designs.

The jagged designs (30-34) are interesting. In the earliest period they are the most common design; even despite the very small sample, this is striking. Jagged designs occur in roughly the same proportions in both the Kancha phase and Willka phase, but jagged design 31 is more common in the Kancha phase, and also occurs in the earlier period. Zigzag designs (40-42) are generally restricted to the Kancha phase. Horizontal

Evidence of Jincamocco Artifacts 219

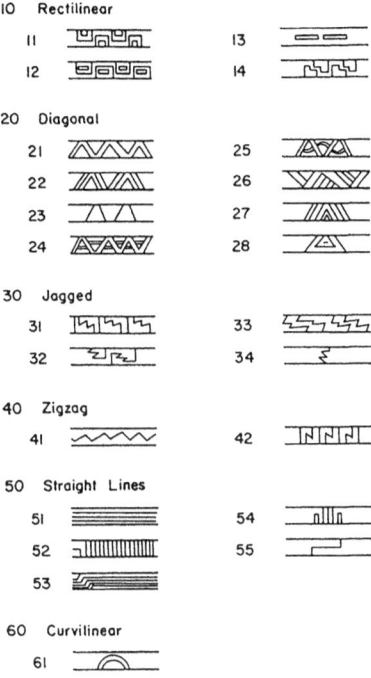

Figure 7.3. Designs and codes for incised bowls.

TABLE 7.4
Frequencies of General Incised Bowl Designs During the Kancha and Willka Phases

Phase	rect	diag	jagged	zigzag	horiz	TOTAL
Kancha	12	67	24	5	5	113
Willka	1	63	19	1	6	90

Note: Not all incised bowls could be assigned to one of these design categories.

lines (50-55) stay roughly the same through time. And the only curvilinear design (61) was found in a deposit probably Willka phase but possibly with later materials mixed in.

TABLE 7.5
Frequencies of Specific Incised Bowl Designs During the Kancha and Willka Phases

	11	13	14	21	22	23	24	26	27	31	32
Phase											
Kancha	6	1	1	29	6	1	7	1	2	5	2
Willka	1	0	0	26	5	0	4	1	0	2	2

	33	34	41	42	51	53	54	55	TOTAL
Phase									
Kancha	8	0	3	2	4	1	0	0	79
Willka	5	2	1	0	4	0	1	1	55

Interestingly, there is no correlation between design and ware: no particular designs were reserved for better-made pots. Nor is there any strong correlation between design and vessel shape. The only slight exception is that jagged designs tend to be depicted on less open forms. Rectilinear design 11 and jagged design 31 are painted more often than expected; diagonal designs tend not to be painted.

In sum, there are clear temporal changes in the quality of incised bowls, with quality declining in the Willka phase. In-curving bowls decrease in proportion, and there is a slight increase in round-sided open bowls. Some designs show changes through time: rectilinear designs tend to be early, as does jagged design 31. But the overall diversity of designs, 16 in the Kancha phase and 13 in the Willka phase, stays roughly the same.

In the case of the incised bowls, although they represent a local style with a long local history, we need to draw some comparisons with other regional styles, particular the Paracas and Pukara styles. Paracas pottery is known from the south coast, primarily the Ica Valley, and has been described in detail by Menzel, Rowe and Dawson (1964). Dating to the Early Horizon, the sequence has been divided into ten phases. The overall form of the Jincamocco incised bowls is reminiscent of the Paracas incised wares, especially those of Ocucaje phases 9 and 10. The Jincamocco bowls are the same shapes and sizes as those of Ica, and they have the same incised design band configuration as the Paracas bowls. The dark color of the bowls is similar to many of the Paracas examples, as is the correlation between a glossy black surface and fine resin painted designs (ibid.: 179).

But there are major differences as well between the two traditions. The Jincamocco examples are all small shallow bowls, while in Ica the Paracas tradition includes a wide range of decorated vessels: bowls, bottles, waisted vessels, dippers, large vases, etc. Likewise, in the case of designs, the Jincamocco examples all have simple repeating geometric designs. In contrast, a wide variety of forms were depicted on Paracas vessels: geometric designs, animal figures, birds, serpents, mythical beings, trophy heads, etc.

While form and design are clearly similar to those of the late Ocucaje phases, the style found at Jincamocco is a very simplified subset of the range of the Ica style. The Carhuarazo Valley was not closely related to Paracas, nor did it share a great many aspects of ceramic styles. But there was clearly some limited connection. As discussed in Chapter 5, this valley had indirect ties to the south coast since at least the Initial period. It is therefore not entirely surprising to find this similarity between the incised bowls from Jincamocco and the Paracas pottery of Ica.

The incised bowls of the earliest period at Jincamocco bear the closest similarity to those of Ica, which is why I have included them in the previous descriptions of the style, despite the small sample size. The only bowls with thick well-preserved resin paint are from the earliest period; these include colors (pink, tan) not occurring later. We also see well-made, glossy black bowls with painted designs more prevalent in early periods; these are more similar to the Paracas forms than are later developments. Rectilinear designs and the jagged design 31 are more like Paracas designs; these occur more frequently in the earlier part of the Jincamocco sequence.

In sum, I suggest that the incised bowl tradition at Jincamocco derived ultimately from the Paracas style of the south coast, but that only an extremely limited subset of that style was adopted. While the Paracas tradition changed, and slip painting became the dominant decorative technique in the ensuing Early Intermediate period on the south coast, in the Carhuarazo Valley the old style continued on. Painted pottery was not introduced until the Middle Horizon, when it spelled the end of the older incised designs.

Before leaving this topic, it should be noted that there is also some remote similarity between the incised bowls and the Pukara style of the Peruvian altiplano of the Early Intermediate period. There are similarities between Pukara and Paracas pottery that give the impression that the two styles may be in some way related. In particular, incised and painted designs on fine black ware occur in both traditions. These attributes are shared by the Jincamocco bowls as well.

The similarities with the Pukara style are very limited, at least based on the available literature. But one simple design stands out: jagged design 31. This incised design occurs in a band below the rim on the interior of a bowl from Pukara. (See the photograph of the vessel illustrated by Kroeber 1944: Pl. 41c; see also the drawing of this same vessel in Rowe and Brandel 1970: Pl. XII-51.) The vessel is otherwise slipped red, further differentiating it from the Jincamocco bowls. But the design is distinctly similar. Rowe and Brandel (1970) and Franquemont (1986) illustrate several other geometric design bands that, while not the same, are reminiscent of those at Jincamocco.

I do not suggest any direct connection between Jincamocco and Pukara. Rather, I argue that Jincamocco had some connection with the south coast, and adopted a simplified and limited range of the Paracas style. The Pukara style may or may not have similar origins. In addition, it is most closely similar to phases 1-3 of the Nasca style which certainly did develop out of the preceding Paracas style (Rowe and Brandel 1970:3). The similarity in origins of the Early Intermediate period Jincamocco and Pukara styles may account for their stylistic similarities, rather than any sort of direct connection between the two sites.

Jars with Serpentine Designs

The second major subclass of local decorated styles is what I have termed "jars with serpentine designs" ($n = 353$). These are unpigmented necked jars that have an appliqué strip of clay with punctations, or simply a line of punctations, undulating around the circumference of the neck (Fig. 7.4).

As is the case of all local decorated styles, jars with serpentine designs decrease in proportion to other types in the overall assemblage in the Willka phase, but increase significantly in proportion to the other local decorated styles in the Willka phase. In terms of paste, inclusions, surface finish and color, jars with serpentine designs are indistinguishable from the local plainware. The only temporal change seen in construction is an increase in coarse inclusions in the Willka phase. As is the case with plainware and incised bowls, this may indicate that less care was going into their production.

In terms of vessel shape, all identifiable vessels are necked jars, with necks ranging in height from 3 to 10 cm, with most falling between 5 and 7 cm. No complete profiles were found, so the overall size of the jars, and the form of the base is unknown. I suspect the bases were rounded.

Rims of jars with serpentine designs generally turn out, forming a small lip on the exterior. They are slightly more angular in the Willka phase, and more rounded in the Kancha phase. Rim diameter averages 19 cm, with no difference between the Kancha phase and Willka phase. The neck may slope inward, be vertical, or open, and is usually straight, not curved. Inwardly sloping necks are more common earlier, and Willka phase forms tend to be slightly more open, but all forms are found in all periods.

The most common design configuration is an appliqué strip of clay that undulates from near the rim to near the neck-body juncture, around the circumference of the neck. Regularly spaced punctations, usually almond-shaped, are made in the appliqué strip. On about 15% of the jars

Evidence of Jincamocco Artifacts 223

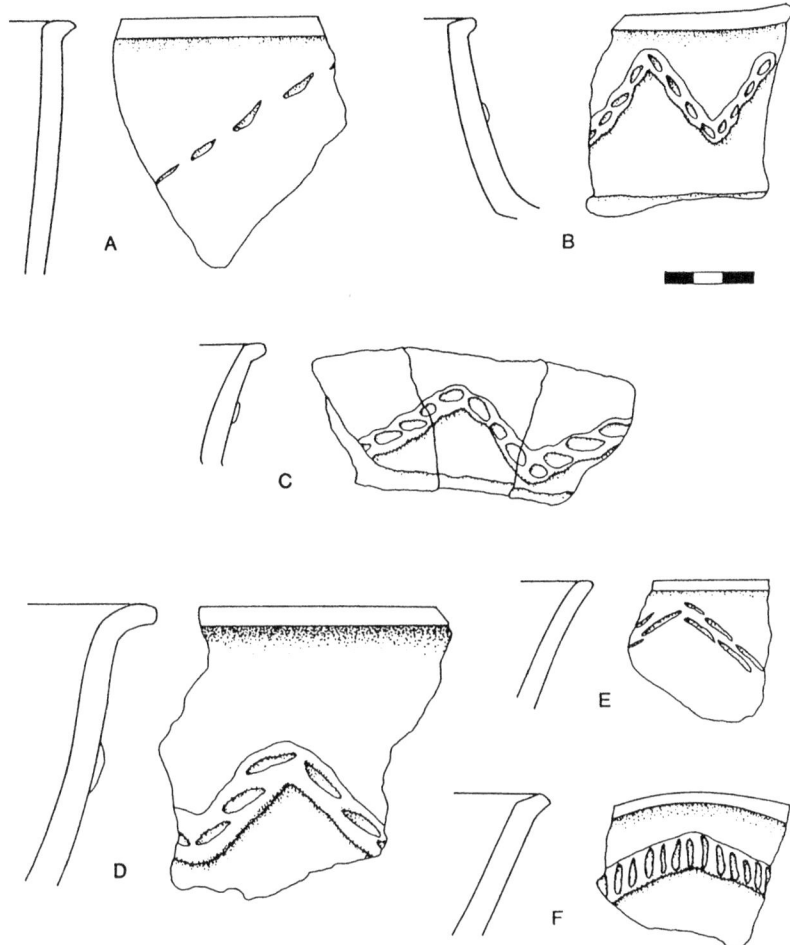

Figure 7.4. Jars with serpentine designs. **A-C** Kancha phase. **A**: Corridor 1, Unit 02, level 6, rim diameter = 18 cm; **B**: T1, level 6, rd = 10; **C**: T1, level 7, rd = 13. **D-F** Willka phase. **D**: Patio 1, Unit 43, level 2, rd = 28; **E**: Corridor 1, Unit 02, level 3, rd = 14; **F**: Corridor 1, Unit 01, level 2, rd = 24.

the designs lack the appliqué strip, and are made with punctations or short incisions alone. The only temporal difference seen in decoration is an increase in non-appliqué designs in the Willka phase. Given that non-appliqué designs were probably quicker and easier to execute, this may suggest that less time and care was going into the production of jars with serpentine designs in the Willka phase.

In sum, jars with serpentine designs undergo only subtle changes from the Kancha phase to the Willka phase, and in terms of vessel form and appliqué decoration, the two periods are nearly indistinguishable. The only slight changes might suggest a decline in quality in the Willka phase, along with a slight increase in variability within the style. This is the same pattern that emerged in the cases of plainware and the incised bowls.

Jars with serpentine designs are a local style, developed in a long local tradition that began in the Initial period. Early ceramics, including appliqué designs, were similar to both the south coast Hacha style, and to Muyu-Moqo styles of Andahuaylas. However, in the Carhuarazo Valley this decorative technique continued on through later periods in unique local form, disappearing only after the Willka phase when local plastic decoration was finally replaced by painted pottery. I am not aware of any other regions in which this Early Intermediate period/Middle Horizon style has been identified.

Other Tactile

Finally, the last subclass within the local decorated style includes miscellaneous pieces with plastic decoration that fall into neither of the preceding two categories. These "other tactile" pieces tend to be very fragmentary, and do not occur in large numbers ($n = 116$; Kancha phase $n = 30$, Willka phase $n = 43$). Thus, only some general observations can be made. Within the overall assemblage, other tactile vessels decrease in proportion from 3.2% to 1.8%, from the Kancha phase to the Willka phase. Among local decorated styles they stay roughly equivalent in proportion, 10% in the Kancha phase, and 11% in the Willka phase.

Other tactile vessels are unpigmented, and are otherwise indistinguishable from local plainwares or jars with serpentine designs. There are no apparent changes in construction technology through time. Designs are of four basic types: incision, appliqué, modeling, and punctation. Most other tactile vessels are jars (72%). While there may be some slight changes from the Kancha phase to the Willka phase, the sample is so small that these changes are difficult to discern. The various forms of other tactile designs, like incised bowls and jars with serpentine designs, fall within a local tradition of great time depth. These decorative techniques were used in the region since the Initial period. Few tactile designs continued into periods after the Willka phase, as painted decoration replaced plastic design.

Evidence of Jincamocco Artifacts

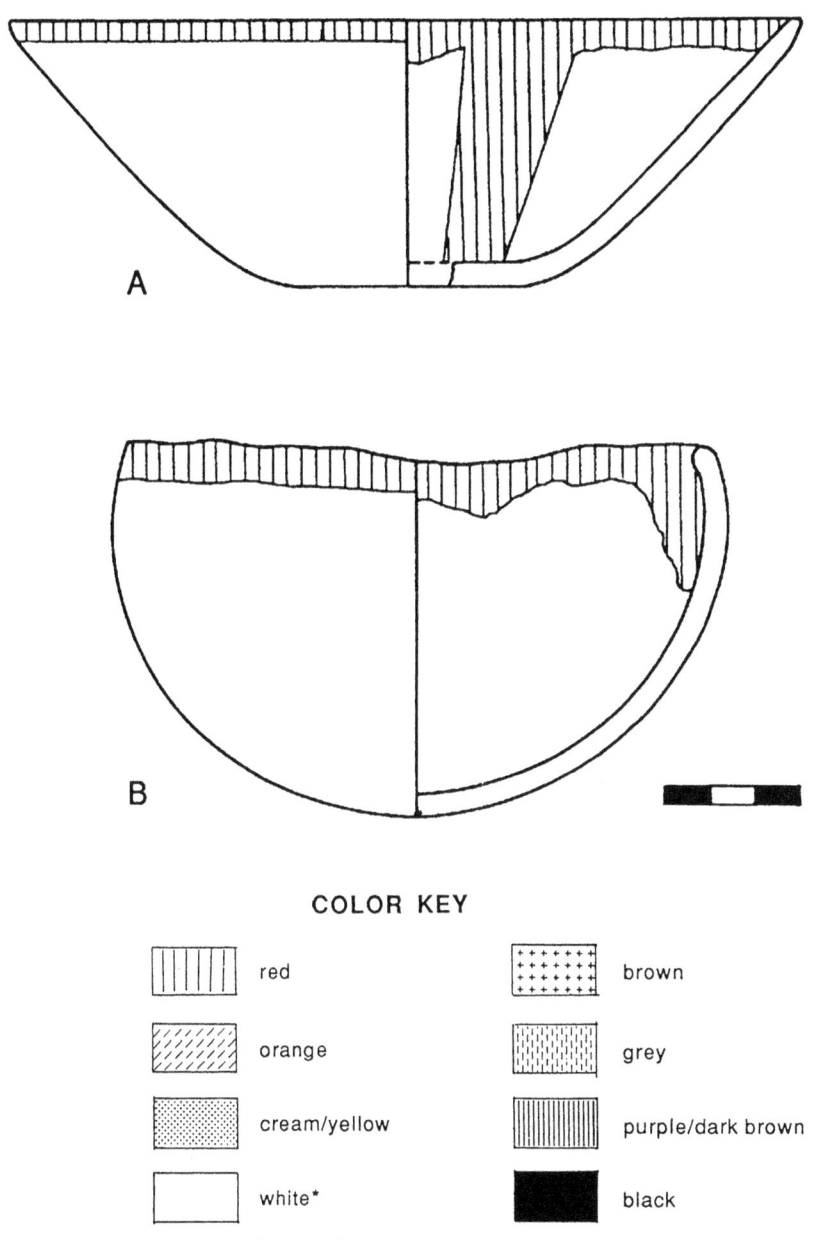

Figure 7.5. Red-slipped ware bowls. **A**: probably Kancha phase, Gallery 1, level 4; **B**: Willka phase, Patio 1, west bench, Unit 01, level 3.

Spatial Patterning in Local Decorated Styles

In Willka phase deposits, local decorated styles comprise 16.2% of the assemblage. However, especially high proportions occur along the south side of Patio 2, and on the west bench of Patio 1. Very low proportions are found in Corridor 1, and no local decorated styles are found in T2/3.

Red-Slipped Ware

The third major class of ceramics is red-slipped ware (n = 710). Red-slipped vessels comprise basically the same inventory of shapes and sizes as plainwares (with two exceptions), but are distinguished by the presence of red slip in various configurations (Fig. 7.5). Red-slipped vessels are relatively rare in the Kancha phase (4.5%; n = 42), but increase significantly in proportion in the Willka phase (12.5%; n = 295). The increase in red-slipped wares corresponds to the decrease in local decorated styles (Table 7.1).

In terms of paste and inclusions, red-slipped wares are indistinguishable from plainware, and other local styles. While more than half are polished in the Kancha phase, this drops to less than a third in the Willka phase. This may indicate a decline in quality, as has been seen in other cases. But, the sample from the Kancha phase is so small that it is difficult to discern meaningful temporal patterns.

Interestingly, bowls are found in unusually high proportions in this category: 85% in the Kancha phase and 73% in the Willka phase. The range of red-slipped vessel shapes is roughly the same as the range of plainware shapes, with two exceptions. First, a tripod bowl was found in Corridor 1; tripods are extremely rare at Jincamocco, and are not a local form. The second unique shape is a single-handled closed vessel, found along with fancy painted pots in the primary association on the platform of T2/3. This will be discussed in detail below. Both of these unique vessel shapes pertain to the Willka phase, and both of these vessels were probably imported from elsewhere.

Red-slipping of the surface of these vessels can occur in one of several major configurations. One or both sides of a vessel may be completely slipped red. When one side is completely red, the other side may have a red band around and below the rim. Some vessels have plain unpigmented surfaces on both sides, but with red bands around the rim on one or both sides; sometimes just the top of the rim is slipped red. And finally, red-slipped designs may be painted on otherwise plain unpigmented surfaces; these designs are usually wide straight lines extending vertically down from the rim.

Red slip configurations vary somewhat by vessel shape. Interior slipping is more common on bowls than jars, as expected; likewise, exterior slipping occurs more frequently on jars. Straight-sided bowls differ from rounded ones in that the former rarely have banded designs, but are slipped on the interior or on both sides. Round-sided bowls are more likely to have banded designs. And in-curving bowls have less interior slipping than more open forms, as is to be expected.

The most interesting temporal pattern emerges with respect to rim forms. Thickened rims are common on red-slipped vessels, usually bowls, of all time periods. In the earliest period red-slipped wares are rare, but most of them have thickened rims. In the Kancha phase, 7 thickened rims are found, or 18% of all red-slipped wares; this proportion continues roughly the same in the Willka phase (16%). So while red-slipped wares overall are rare in the early periods, the thickened rim is clearly present, and clearly associated with this category of ceramics.

As I have shown above, thickened rims are not common in other ceramic categories until the Willka phase. The red-slipped ware data demonstrate that this form was not a new introduction in the Willka phase. It had been present in the local tradition for a very long time, but was restricted to the relatively rare red-slipped vessels. It was not until the Willka phase that it was used more widely on other ceramic types, in addition to red-slipped wares. Not only did thickened rims continue on after the Willka phase, as I have said before, but the thickened rim became the predominant rim form.

While red-slipped ware makes up 12.5% of the Willka phase assemblage, especially high proportions of red-slipped ware occur in Corridor 1. Low proportions of red-slipped ware occur in Patio 2, and only one red-slipped vessel, of unique shape, was found in T2/3.

Slip-Painted Ceramics

The smallest class of ceramics are those that have slip-painted designs ($n = 400$). With very rare exceptions, all painted ceramics pertain to the Willka phase; those exceptions are imported Nasca 4 sherds from the south coast. There was no local tradition of painted pottery in this valley until the Middle Horizon (Table 7.1). Overall, bowls make up 55% of painted ceramics, jars 45%.

Painted vessels were subdivided into two general categories based on construction, surface finish, and painted design: less fancy, and fancy polychrome. The latter includes the Wari styles of Chakipampa B, Ocros, Black Decorated, and Viñaque, as well as an occasional imported Nasca sherd.

Less Fancy Painted Ceramics

Less fancy painted pottery ($n = 160$) in many ways resembles local styles in terms of construction and surface finish. Paste is usually orange to brown, rather than pink to buff, inclusions are generally medium to fine, with some coarse inclusions. Highly polished pieces are rare, and nearly half are not polished at all. Designs are painted in one or more colors, on a slip that may be pigmented or not. Most pottery in this category (60%) has no pigmented slip, and designs are simple black or red lines. Twenty percent has a red slip which is painted in black, or black and white; again the designs are simple: straight lines, or simple geometric patterns. Ten percent of it has a white slip, with either red or black painted design; the remaining 10% include odd pieces that fall into no major category.

Fancy Polychrome

Fancy painted pottery ($n = 240$) usually has pink to buff paste and fine inclusions; the surface is highly polished. The slip is usually pigmented, usually red, and designs painted in up to five colors. Nearly all fancy polychromes are decorated on the exterior of the vessel, regardless of vessel shape. Round-sided open bowls are rare; most bowls have straight sides in this category.

About 25% of the vessels in this category have a red slip, usually painted in black and white, or occasionally just black. These are like the less fancy vessels, except that the fabric and surface finish are much finer. The designs are simple geometric forms or straight lines. This style of decoration, both fancy and less fancy, continues on after the Willka phase, when it becomes the most common form of decorated pottery in the region. It is difficult to classify this style as either local or foreign. While painted designs first occur in the Willka phase, red-slipped pottery was present in low proportions in earlier phases. Painted designs may have been introduced by Wari peoples, or they may have developed independently in the local style. The paste and inclusions of the black-white-red ceramics are indistinguishable from local ceramics, and it is likely that these styles were produced locally. In any case, it is instructive that after the Willka phase none of the fancy styles associated with Wari continued in any form; these black-white-red styles did continue in the local tradition.

The remainder of fancy polychromes are usually slipped red, but also may be slipped in white, cream, orange, red-orange, black, or left unpigmented. These wares are fancy Wari polychromes, with an occasional Nasca sherd. Where the Wari sherds can be assigned to a particular style, most pertain to the Viñaque style of Middle Horizon 2. Some pieces of Middle Horizon 1B Chakipampa style are present, as well as the 1B Ocros style, and Black Decorated styles from Middle Horizon 1B and 2A. These styles are distinguished from local products by their distinctive fabric, as well as decoration. All the fancy Wari polychromes, especially the Chakipampa and Viñaque styles, were almost certainly imported from outside the valley.

Evidence of Jincamocco Artifacts   229

The mix of temporally diagnostic ceramics in the Willka phase adds final confirmation to the interpretation that the deposits are in are secondary or tertiary contexts, and reflect no reliable, temporally significant, stratigraphy. Styles dating to Middle Horizon 1B are found mixed with styles dating to MH 2; MH 1 materials are also encountered above MH 2 materials in some cases, indicating mixed secondary or tertiary deposits.

Ocros pieces (n = 18) have the diagnostic orange slip that defines this style, and designs painted in black; black and white; black and red; or black, white and purple. Remains were too fragmentary to define classes of designs. Where vessel shape could be determined, forms are mostly bowls; one Ocros-style spoon was recovered, the only spoon in the sample. Ocros-style pottery is thought to pertain to Middle Horizon 1 only. At Jincamocco all Ocros probably dates to no earlier than MH 1B, and I suspect it may have continued in use into MH 2.

Black Decorated pieces (n = 33) are, like Ocros, easily identifiable based on their distinctive slip color and painting style (Fig. 7.6). Unlike most other fancy polychromes Black Decorated never has pink paste, and fine inclusions occur in lower proportions. In general the fabric is coarser than other fancy polychromes. The surface of these vessels, while generally black, grades to various shades of brown. Indeed, one under-fired piece was still cream-colored. The paste of these vessels ranges from buff to dark brown, but is rarely black, and never grey. These characteristics of the paste indicate that these vessels were not fired in a reducing atmosphere, but in an oxidizing atmosphere. The under-fired specimen reveals that the slip color began as an entirely different color—cream—and that the final black color resulted from reduction late in the firing process.

Black Decorated pieces are painted in either a translucent red or white, in simple geometric or linear patterns. Parallel straight lines, cross-hatching, filled in simple shapes, and rows of zigzags are the most common patterns. Black Decorated vessels are only rarely jars; bowls usually have straight sides. A new vessel form occurs in this style, the tumbler. This vessel has straight sides, opening at an angle usually about 105°, and the vessel is taller than it is wide. The mouth diameter can range from as little as 12 cm to nearly 20 cm. The only other ceramic style that includes tumblers is red-slipped ware; red-slipped ware tumblers are indistinguishable from Black Decorated ones in shape.

The majority of Black Decorated designs pertain to phase C of the style, falling in Middle Horizon 2A; less than 20% of the vessels date to MH 1B.

The remainder of the fancy polychromes (n = 120) are quite distinctive in terms of fabric and decoration. They are all highly polished, with a buff to pink-colored paste, and fine, micaceous inclusions. They are painted in three to six colors, and pertain to either the Chakipampa or Viñaque styles. Because of the fragmentary nature of the remains, it was not al-

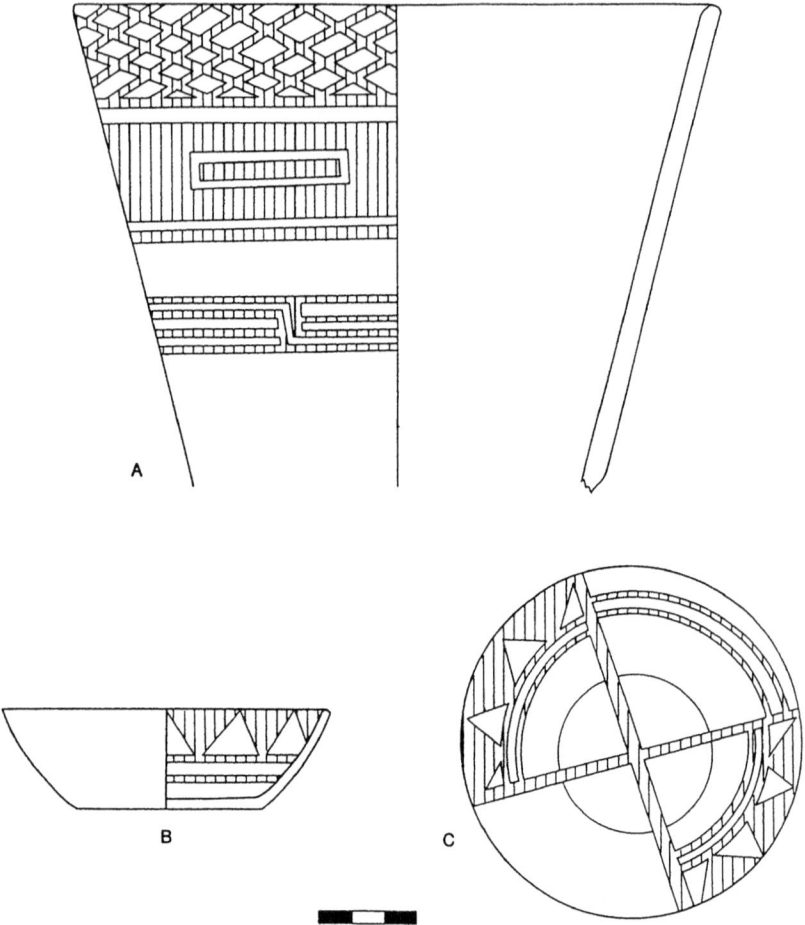

Figure 7.6. Black Decorated vessels. **A**: red slip-painted design on black background, Patio 1, west bench, Unit 05, level 2; **B**: light red design painted on background grading from cream to dark brown, Corridor 1, Unit 01, level 1; **C**: interior view of **B**.

ways possible to classify each sherd as pertaining to one or the other style, but where identification was possible, Chakipampa sherds comprised about 20% of the assemblage.

Chakipampa-style pieces are all examples of the phase B style, which dates to Middle Horizon 1B. These are found only as small fragments, with one exception, and usually have a red slip; designs are painted in white, cream, red-orange, grey, and purple, with black outlining. The recurved ray is a common design motif. Two lyre cups probably pertain to this style. One of these, found nearly intact, is discussed in detail below.

Chakipampa B is the style that seems to be associated with many other Wari provincial sites, suggesting that the Wari expansion took place in Middle Horizon 1B. While most of the trash deposits inside the enclosure at Jincamocco included predominantly MH 2 materials, quantities of MH 1B refuse was found on the surface below the site to the north. It would seem that in the early part of the occupation of Jincamocco, trash was deposited outside the site by tossing it down the hill. It was not until later in the occupation that trash was deposited inside the enclosure itself.

Most of the remaining fancy polychromes that could be identified can be attributed to the Viñaque style, the style typical of the sierra during MH 2. Viñaque vessels from Jincamocco (Fig. 7.7) have a wide variety of slip colors, but red is the most common. Designs are painted in up to five colors: white, cream, grey and purple, with black outlining. A number of reconstructible Viñaque-style vessels were recovered in the primary association in T2/3, and are described in detail below. Most remains were too fragmentary to reconstruct whole design configurations, but typical designs include the split face design, horizontal rows of S-shaped elements, step frets, rosette designs, plant motifs, the recurved ray "octopus" (a conservative design derived from Chakipampa), and various geometric de-

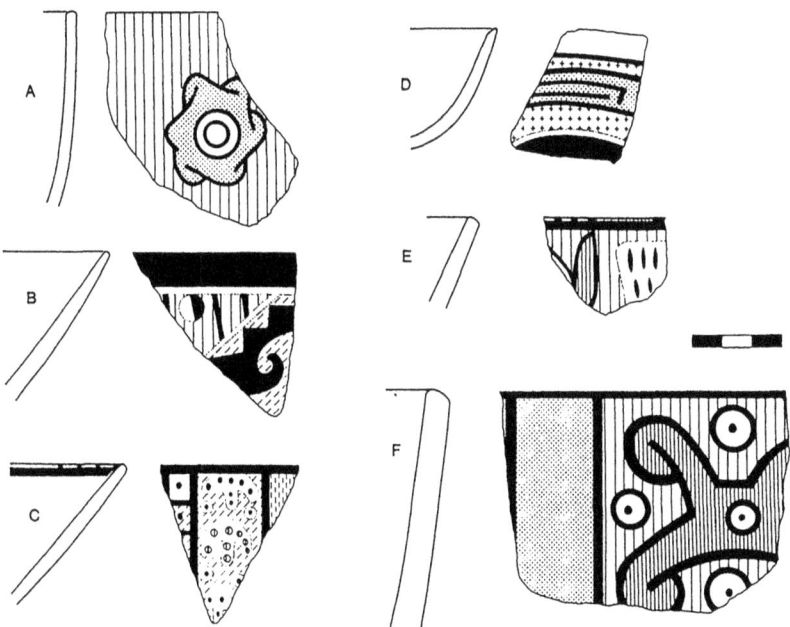

Figure 7.7. Viñaque sherds. A: Patio 3, Unit 42, level 3, rd = 9; B: Corridor 1, Unit 02, level 1, rd = 16; C: Corridor 1, Unit 02, level 3, rd = 20; D: Patio 3, Unit 41, level 1, rd = 12; E: Corridor 1, Unit 02, level 1, rd = 22; F: Corridor 1, Unit 01, level 1, rd = 19.

signs. Typical filler elements include a white dot outlined in black with a black center dot, or an un-outlined white dot, with black dot and line inside. Vessel forms include roughly equal proportions of bowls and jars, and a number of lyre cups. A few more comments should be made about the latter.

Fragments of twelve lyre cups were found in good associations in the excavations, and fragments of three more were found on the surface of the site. Menzel wrote that lyre cups were rare in the provinces (Menzel 1968:89), but that apparent pattern may be due to the fact that in 1968 little research had been carried out in the provinces, especially in the highlands. The evidence from Jincamocco (Fig. 7.8) indicates that lyre cups are not uncommon at highland provincial sites; perhaps they are rare only on the coast.

Decoration on lyre cups, where it can be discerned, is often the bodiless mythical front face deity, one on each side of the cup, separated by vertical chevron bands. This occurs on at least six of the lyre cups. Other designs include geometric designs, wings, a butterfly, and a split step fret design. All but two, or possibly three, of the lyre cups probably date to MH 2. Most of the lyre cups are represented only by single sherds; only four were reconstructible. Three of those were found in the primary deposit in T2/3, and are described in detail below.

The fourth reconstructible lyre cup is of special interest as well. This lyre cup (Fig. 7.9), mentioned in Chapter 6, was found nearly intact in the architectural fill, under the bench in Patio 3. It was broken into only three pieces, probably due to the weight of soil deposited over it. This vessel has a number of conservative features that suggest that it belongs to the Chakipampa B style of Middle Horizon 1B.

This lyre cup is more slender and less curvilinear than other lyre cups; the paste is buff colored, and the inclusions are fine. The interior surface is smoothed, and partially slipped red; the exterior is highly polished and entirely slipped red. The design is painted in white, yellow, grey, and black; the execution is somewhat crude. The design field is demarcated by white bands with black outlines, above and below. On each side of the cup is a depiction of the bodiless mythical front face deity. The eyes are round, outlined in black, and with a black center dot. The face is bordered by a yellow band. The rayed appendages include tail feather designs to the top, and off the two corners; the side appendages are small square elements, with an out-curving pendant element looking vaguely like some form of vegetable. Filler elements are un-outlined white dots, with black center dots that nearly fill them. On each side of the cup is a vertical chevron band, separated from the head designs by vertical white bands with black outlining. The chevrons are paired grey, white, and yellow chevrons, separated by pairs of red chevrons.

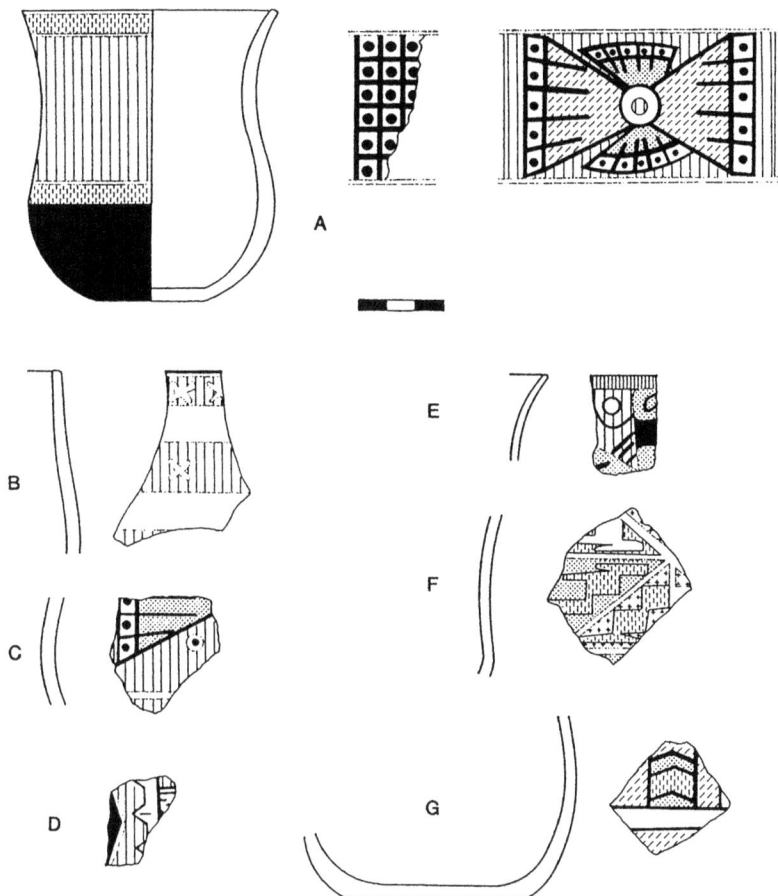

Figure 7.8. Lyre cup fragments. A: unprovenienced, Room Block 1.6; B: Corridor 1, Unit 01, level 1, rd = 13; C: Corridor 1, Unit 01, level 1; D: Patio 1, north bench, Unit 02, level 2; E: Corridor 1, Unit 02, level 3, rd = 13; F: Corridor 1, Unit 02, level 3; G: Patio 3, Unit 21, level 1.

The shape of this cup, the filler elements, and the chevron band are all features typical of lyre cups of MH 1B, in the Chakipampa B style. This cup anticipates the Viñaque-style lyre cup form that becomes common at Jincamocco in MH 2. The dating of this cup is further supported by the stratigraphic context of the vessel. Found in architectural fill, it probably dates to the period of construction of the enclosure. In fact, it is probably the only artifact encountered *in situ* from the period of the initial occupation of the enclosure.

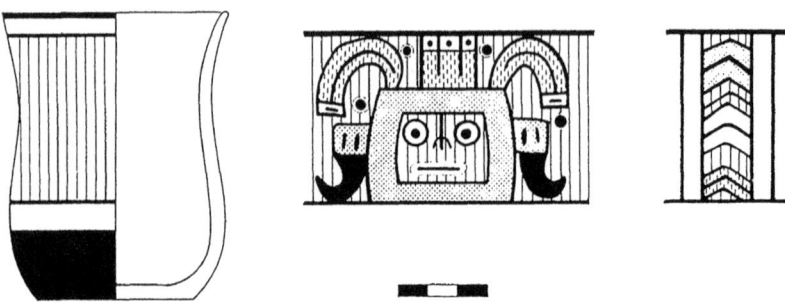

Figure 7.9. Chakipampa B lyre cup from Patio 3, Unit 41, level 3.

Non-Wari fancy polychromes found at Jincamocco include ten fragments of the Nasca style of the south coast. Of these, six date to Nasca phase 4, four to Nasca 8. Most of these were found in deposits that were mixed. The Nasca 8 pieces were all found in deposits that probably date to the Willka phase, but might be mixed with earlier or later materials. The Nasca 4 pieces were usually found in deposits that are most likely Kancha phase remains, but two were found in what should be an unmixed Willka phase deposit. These two pieces were located in the trash deposit in Patio 2. As pointed out in Chapter 6, occasional early Nasca trade pieces have been found on sites dating to the Early Intermediate. Nasca 4 was the period during which the Nasca civilization reached its maximum extent before its collapse at the end of this period. Interestingly, no earlier Nasca pieces have been found, nor were there found remains of Nasca phases 5 through 7 at Jincamocco. Nasca 8 is usually thought to date to the end of the Early Intermediate, just prior to the Middle Horizon, but my own work in Nasca leads me to suspect that this style continued in use into the Middle Horizon. The presence of Nasca 8 sherds in refuse that should be from the Middle Horizon may lend some support to this notion.

A Primary Association of Twelve Exotic Vessels

In Chapter 6 I described the excavation of Unit T2/3, a judgment excavation, that revealed part of a raised platform with a finely finished plaster surface, and other fine architectural details. On this platform was found the only major primary deposit of artifacts uncovered during the excavation of Jincamocco. The lack of any other refuse in this deposit indicates that no other materials or habitation refuse were mixed into this deposit after the site was abandoned. Why this deposit should have been so protected is not known, but it is likely that the platform was roofed.

When the roof fell in, it may have protected the remains below from both looting and mixing with other materials. It seems logical to consider the association of twelve reconstructible vessels contemporaneous.

The deposit includes three lyre cups, three straight-sided open bowls, three smaller bowls, a small jar, a red-slipped ware closed vessel, and an oversize face-neck jar. Seven of the vessels are Wari polychromes; the origin of most of the other vessels can probably also be attributed to Wari. One small bowl may have been imported from Junín. Importantly, none of the vessels in this association is of local manufacture or design; all represent exotic imports. These factors suggest the association dates to Middle Horizon 2A.

All but three of the vessels were located along the east wall of the platform, within two meters of the southeast corner. Unfortunately, this is the portion of the deposit that was disturbed during wall trenching, so the exact spatial arrangement of the remains cannot be known. One small bowl was found about a meter away, along the south wall; one straight-sided open bowl was found more than four meters from the corner, also along the south wall. The oversize face-neck jar was found smashed on the surface of the platform, centered about three meters west and one meter north of the southeast corner.

Lyre Cup 1 (Fig. 7.10)

This vessel was almost completely reconstructible; nine fragments were located. Paste and surface finish distinguish this vessel from local productions; the paste is light buff with extremely fine inclusions. The fabric is micaceous, which may be due either to naturally micaceous clay, or to the inclusion of mica in the temper; probably the latter. The surface is highly polished and slipped orange; the design is painted in white,

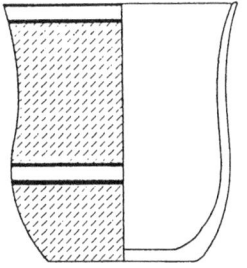 

Figure 7.10. Lyre cup 1, T2.

cream, purple and grey, with black outlining. This vessel preserves certain conservative features that resemble Chakipampa B forms. The form is less curvilinear than most MH 2 examples, and it lacks typical filler elements. The design field is bordered by a single white band. The design includes two bodiless mythical front face deities, separated by vertical chevron bands. The chevron bands are demarcated by single vertical cream bands on either side; the chevron bands include pairs of orange chevrons (also a conservative feature), separated by single cream or purple chevrons. The face of the deity has round eyes with center dots, a cream band with black dots outlining the face, and five tail-feather appendages. The conservative features of the vessel form and design argue for a date either in Middle Horizon 1B or early in MH 2, probably 2A.

Lyre Cup 2 (Fig. 7.11)

This vessel was also almost completely reconstructible; 14 fragments were recovered. Like Lyre Cup 1, this vessel is distinguished from local styles by virtue of its paste and surface finish. The fabric is pink in color, micaceous, with very fine inclusions; this fabric is typical of other fancy Wari polychrome vessels at Jincamocco. The surface is highly polished; the background slip is red-orange, and the design is painted in white, cream, orange, purple and grey, with black outlining. The form is more curvilinear than Lyre Cup 1, and more typical of MH 2. The design field is bordered by a single white band, and two bodiless mythical front face deities are depicted. These have faces with round eyes with center dots, the faces are bordered by a fret band, and the appendages have feather designs to the top and sides, with long rays with circular elements at the ends on the corners. Filler elements are white circles with dot and line. The mythical heads are separated by chevron bands, which are bordered on each side by a pair of white and purple bands. The chevron bands

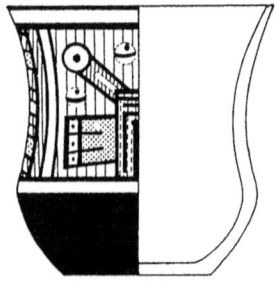

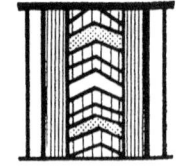

Figure 7.11. Lyre cup 2, T2.

include pairs of orange chevrons, separated by single cream or white chevrons. While this lyre cup is typical of Middle Horizon 2 examples of the Viñaque style, the slightly conservative chevron bands argue for a placement early in MH 2, probably in 2A.

Lyre Cup 3 (Fig. 7.12)

Only about two-thirds of this vessel was reconstructible; eight fragments were recovered. This vessel has typical fine paste: pink, micaceous, very fine inclusions. The vessel shape is slightly broad and squat, a conservative feature, but generally curvilinear like MH 2 forms. The surface is highly polished, and slipped red; the design is painted in white, cream, purple, and black. The design is geometric, bordered top and bottom by a band with black and cream or white, S-shaped elements; these are quite angular. The central design field is separated from the border designs by

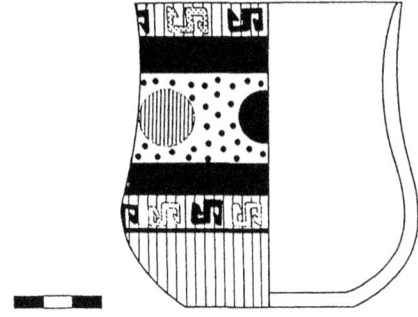

Figure 7.12. Lyre cup 3, T2.

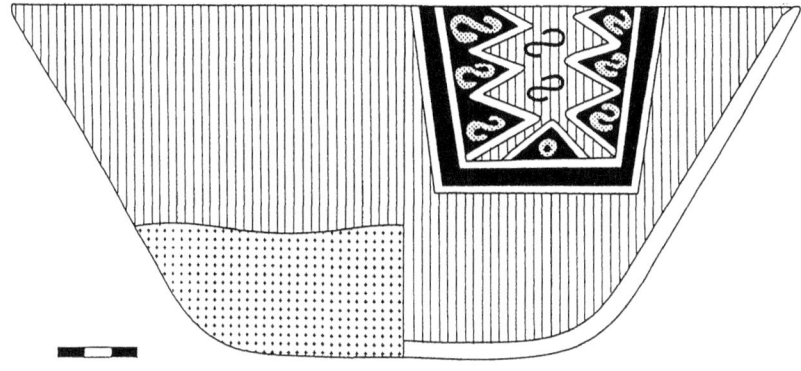

Figure 7.13. Straight-sided open bowl 1, T2.

wide black bands. The central panel has a white background, large dots alternating black and purple, and small black dots as filler elements. The design suggests a date of Middle Horizon 2, while the broad proportions are slightly conservative, so a date of MH 2A might be suggested.

Straight-Sided Open Bowl 1 (Fig. 7.13)

This bowl was almost completely reconstructible; 51 fragments were recovered. The paste is buff in color, with fine inclusions; the surface is highly polished. The entire interior of the bowl is slipped red, as is about two-thirds of the exterior; the exterior above the base is left unpigmented. The design is painted in black and cream. The vessel is a straight-sided open bowl, with a slightly tapered rim; it measures 28 cm in diameter, and stands 13 cm high. The base is nearly flat, but has no sharp inflection where it meets the sides. The design is a pendant rectangle, surrounded by a wide black band outlined in cream. In the design field a wide cream line zigzags toward the center from the border, forming small fields; these have horizontal S elements or circles, painted in cream on a black background. The center of the field is left red, with two horizontal S elements. This pendant rectangle is repeated three times on the interior of the vessel; the only difference between the three design fields is variation in the placement of S and circle elements in the small black triangles. Paste, vessel shape, and design distinguish this vessel as an import from elsewhere. Nothing about this vessel suggests a date of manufacture.

Straight-Sided Open Bowl 2 (Fig. 7.14)

This bowl is smaller and of finer proportions than the preceding bowl. Only half of this bowl was reconstructible from the seven fragments that were recovered. The vessel is a straight-sided open bowl, with a flat bottom; it measures 19 cm in diameter, and stands 8 cm high. While this vessel has fine inclusions, it has more typical paste, orange in color. The surface is polished, but not highly so; the finish is a matte white slip, inside and out. On the exterior are painted four narrow lines, alternating

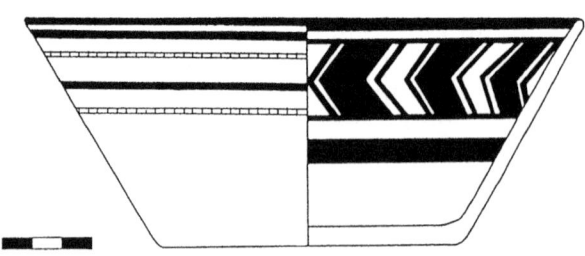

Figure 7.14. Straight-sided open bowl 2, T2.

black and red. On the interior, in a band below the rim, is a black-on-white chevron band. The execution of this band is quite unique. Wide black chevrons alternate with white ones; but a narrow black line is painted to either side of each black chevron, in the white chevron. The chevron band is bordered by narrower white and black bands. Chevron bands are found on the south coast in the Middle Horizon, but these had antecedents in the Ayacucho region. Black and white chevron bands are known from Wari, as well as the Ayapata offering, especially in Middle Horizon 2, but none are painted exactly as they are on the Jincamocco chevron bowl. A tentative date of MH 2 might be suggested.

Straight-Sided Open Bowl 3 (Fig. 7.15)
This is the bowl that was located some distance from the other vessels, along the south side of the platform. It was mostly reconstructible, and eleven fragments were recovered. Its fabric is not exceptional, being orange in color, with medium inclusions; the surface is highly polished and slipped red inside and out. The vessel is a straight-sided open bowl, with a base that is basically flat, with slight rounding. It measures 20 cm in diameter and stands 10 cm high. The rim is decorated, being outlined just to the interior and exterior with a black line; the open space along the top of the rim is subdivided by small black lines; the spaces so defined are painted white or cream, or left red. This type of rim design is typical of MH 2 Viñaque vessels. The design is painted on the exterior, in a band around the vessel, located just below the rim. The design band is demarcated by black lines, and it is divided into triangular fields by a zigzagging black line. In each small field are three horizontal cream lines. This particular design has not been described for any Wari style, but the rim treatment suggests a date of Middle Horizon 2.

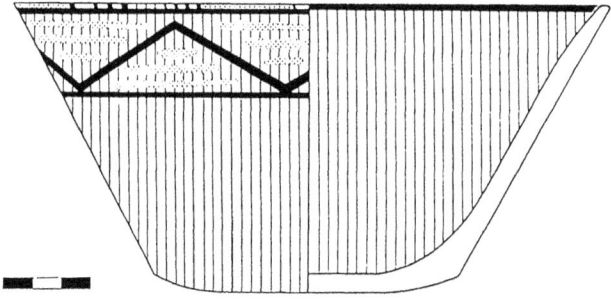

Figure 7.15. Straight-sided open bowl 3, T3.

Small Bowl 1 (Fig. 7.16)

This vessel comprises only a single fragment, but it represents about one-third of the entire vessel. This is a round-sided open bowl, with a slight inflection where the vessel side meets the rounded base; the vessel measures only 13 cm in diameter, and stands probably 5 cm high. While the paste is orange in color, the inclusions are very fine and micaceous, and the surface is highly polished. The bowl is slipped brown on the interior, and dark brown on the exterior. The design is painted in white, cream, brown, grey, and black. The design comprises a band around the exterior of the bowl just below the rim, and its major features are a fret band, and a series of small wavelike elements. The fret band indicates that this vessel probably pertains to the Viñaque style of Middle Horizon 2.

Small Bowl 2 (Fig. 7.17)

This is a Black Decorated bowl. Only two fragments of this bowl were recovered, and only about one-third of the vessel could be reconstructed. It is a round-sided open bowl, 20 cm in diameter, and standing probably 7 cm high. The fabric is typical of other Black Decorated vessels, orange in color with medium inclusions. The surface is polished and slipped black; the design is painted in red. The interior of the bowl is decorated with various straight lines, dividing the design field into various bands. The band below the rim is filled with parallel zigzag lines. This design is characteristic of Black Decorated C, which dates to Middle Horizon 2A.

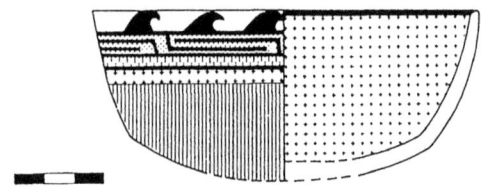

Figure 7.16. Small bowl 1, T2.

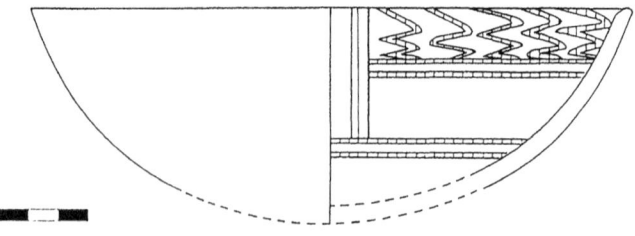

Figure 7.17. Small bowl 2, T2.

Evidence of Jincamocco Artifacts 241

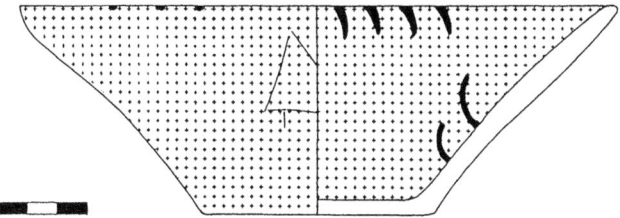

Figure 7.18. Small bowl 3, T2.

Small Bowl 3 (Fig. 7.18)

This bowl is not like anything in the local styles, nor is it like the painted styles known from Wari. This vessel was about two-thirds reconstructible from the thirteen fragments recovered; it was located about a meter away from the bulk of the other vessels in the deposit, along the south wall of the platform. The paste is pinkish, but not the pink of typical Wari polychromes; this pink paste has a slight lavender cast to it. The inclusions are fine. Overall, the paste is very hard, and has an almost chalky feel to it. The slip is a light reddish brown, very washy, and poorly preserved; it has been worn off the surface in several places. The vessel shape is also unique: it is an open bowl, with slightly flaring concave sides and flat bottom. The painted design consists of irregular short curved black lines on the interior of the vessel, some of which extend over the rim just to the exterior. On the exterior of the vessel is a post-fire incision, roughly triangular in form; perhaps this represents some sort of owner's mark. While this vessel is clearly not local, and just as clearly not a Wari vessel, it may be an import from elsewhere in the Wari realm. Sherds collected by Jeffrey Parsons and Ramiro Matos in Junín, and thought to date to the Middle Horizon (Parsons, pers. comm.), are roughly similar to this vessel.

Small Jar

Seven fragments of a small, necked jar were also recovered, but its exact form could not be reconstructed. The paste is typical of Wari polychrome, pink in color and with fine inclusions. The exterior is highly polished and slipped red. The design, whose details cannot be made out, is painted in white, grey, and black.

Red-Slipped Closed Vessel (Fig. 7.19)

This vessel was almost completely reconstructible; 17 fragments were recovered. The vessel is red-slipped ware, with orange paste, and coarse inclusions. The surface is smoothed, and slipped all over with a matte red slip; it has no painted design. The vessel is a closed, globular form, with an everted rim; it measures 17 cm in diameter, and stands 15 cm high.

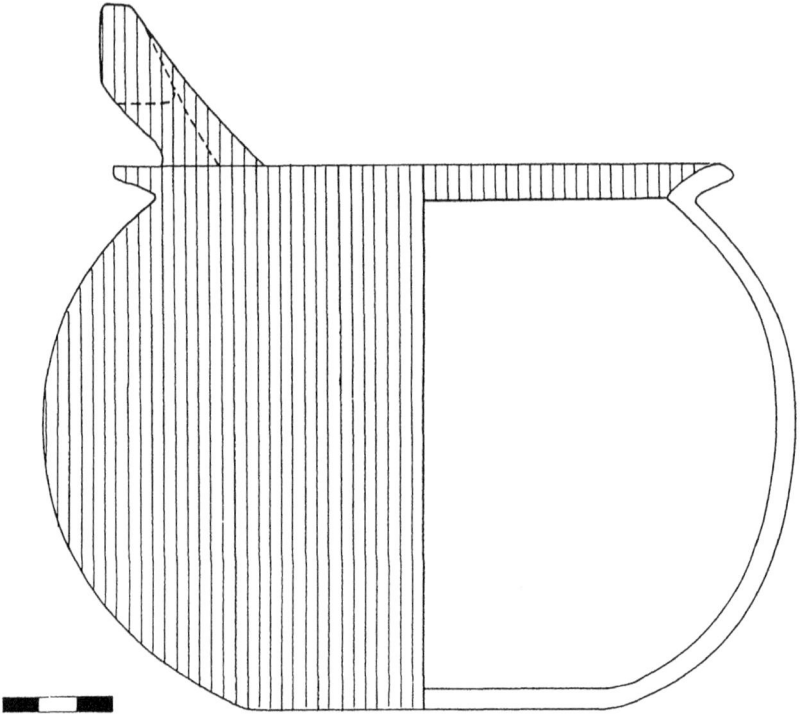

Figure 7.19. Red-slipped closed vessel, T2.

The vessel has only a single handle, a wide flat strap that arches up and outward from the rim; such handles have been called basket handles (Bennett 1953:42). Compared to most of the other vessels in this association, this vessel is not very fancy, but its shape is unique, and it is clearly not a local product. In fact, this shape may be typical of Wari. A nearly identical handle and rim is illustrated in Bennett (1953:43, Fig. 9f); that vessel, too, is slipped red. A vessel similar in shape and handle form, but with a different rim treatment, was found at Pikillaqta and is illustrated by McEwan (1987:108). It seems likely that this vessel form, with the distinctive single handle, is a Wari form.

Oversize Face-Neck Jar (Figs. 7.20, 7.21)

The biggest and fanciest vessel uncovered in this deposit was an oversize face-neck jar. This jar was found smashed on the center of the floor; the pattern of breakage indicates that it was broken with a blow to the chest. While 241 fragments were recovered, only limited pieces of the vessel could be reconstructed. The paste is orange in color, with medium-

Evidence of Jincamocco Artifacts 243

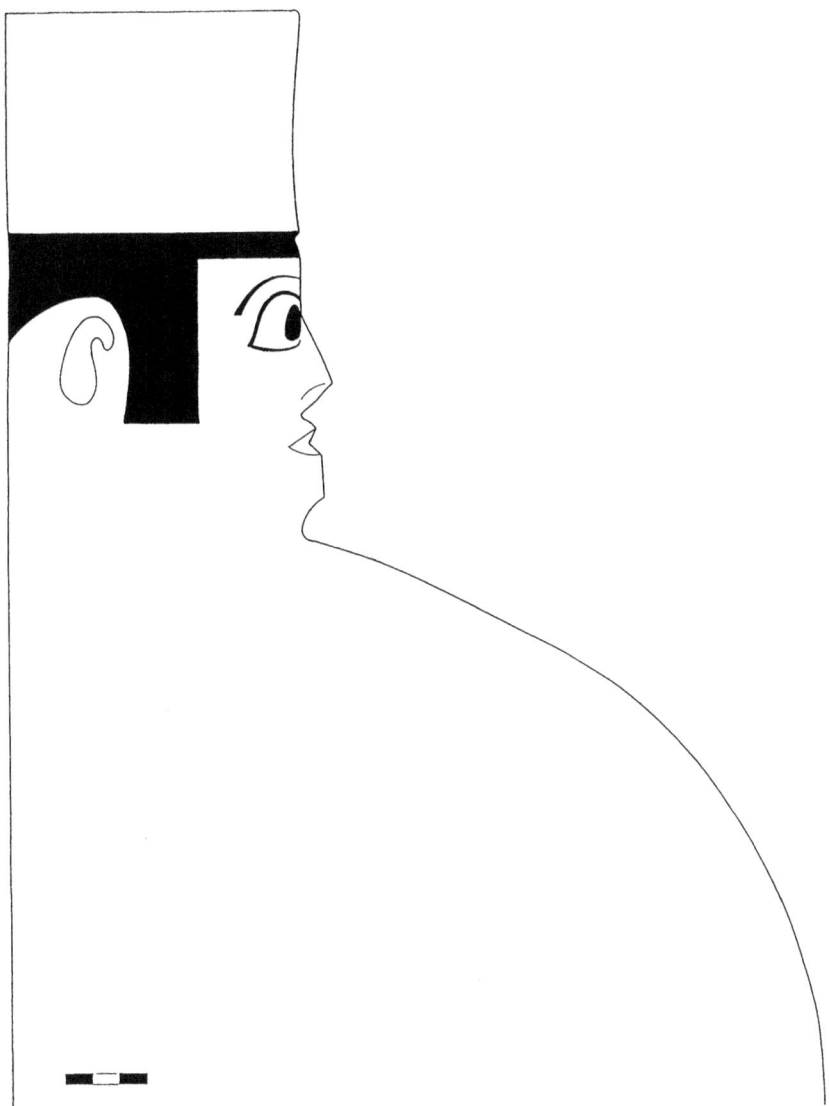

Figure 7.20. Profile of oversize face-neck jar, T2/3.

sized micaceous inclusions; the exterior is highly polished, and slipped red. The design is painted in white, cream, orange, grey, purplish-brown, and black. The jar neck is 22 cm in diameter at the mouth, with a vertical profile. The body of the jar has sloping shoulders, and extends to a maximum diameter of about 60 cm. I estimate the total height of the jar to have been 80 to 85 cm; the height of the neck is 19 cm. The jar has two vertical strap handles, placed toward the back side of the vessel.

Figure 7.21. Front view of oversize face-neck jar, T2/3.

The face has modeled eyes, nose, mouth, chin and ears; the eyes and eyebrows are outlined with black lines. The hair is painted black, with thick sideburns, and with streams of black hair extending down over the back of the jar. Above the face is a headdress on which is depicted a small mammal; the tail curves forward over the back of the animal, suggesting perhaps a vizcacha, or perhaps a domesticated dog. Overall, the execution of the modeling and painted design is simple, but well done.

The design on the body of the vessel is restricted to the upper portion of the body, and the front of the vessel, and is demarcated by a white band with black outlining. The design field is divided into two panels, one to either side of a vertical center design band. The center band is divided into three squares, each divided in half diagonally with a zigzag line, with a triangle in each half; this is reminiscent of the split face design, but much more regular and geometric. The vertical panel is bordered to each side by a white and a grey stripe, outlined in black. On each side panel is a three-banded humped animal, facing center. The animal has almond-shaped eyes, N-shaped incisors, and a low bump with center dot nose; the heels of the feet are rounded, and the knees are bent. Filler elements are white dots with black outline and center dot. It was not possible to fully reconstruct either panel.

This vessel is a Viñaque-style face-neck jar, dating most likely to Middle Horizon 2A. The arrangement of the design field on the upper front of the vessel is typical of MH 2; MH 1 jars often had designs over the entire body (Menzel 1968: 72). The white outline band is typical of MH 2, and can be seen on one of the Ocoña jars illustrated by Ravines (1968: lám. xxvii, Fig. 87). The humped animal is a mythical being depicted on MH 2A jars (see Fig. 88 in the Ravines illustration); according to Menzel this creature does not continue into MH 2B (1968:75).

Discussion

These twelve vessels together form a primary association, and, therefore, suggest a unit of contemporaneity dating to Middle Horizon 2A. In the case of those vessels with temporally significant attributes, all probably date to MH 2; where finer distinction is possible, all date to phase A.

What does this association indicate about the nature of the Wari occupation of Jincamocco? The location of the deposit on an atypical architectural feature, one so finely finished and lacking in domestic refuse, indicates a carefully ordered and defined, and therefore presumably ceremonial or ritual activity. Without further examples and a better knowledge of the contexts of deposits such as that in T2/3, we cannot say whether the ceremony or ritual was predominantly religious, relating people to supernatural powers, or predominantly secular, relating people to their rulers; indeed, the two are often closely correlated in early empires. Images such as the front-face design and the humped animals have been cogently interpreted as mythical creatures (Menzel 1964, 1968), and a use of mythically sanctioned iconography in such contexts would certainly reinforce the importance of the ritual.

The spatial patterning of the deposit indicates that all the vessels were found where they were left when the site, or this part of the site, was abandoned. The large face-neck jar would appear to have been intentionally broken with a blow directed to the chest. I suspect that the other pieces were intentionally broken as well, in the Middle Horizon. The number of fragments of each vessel, the size of those fragments, and their slightly scattered distribution suggests perhaps intentional breakage. Breakage caused by the pressure of the weight of the soil accumulated above the remains should result in fewer and larger pieces, and less scattering, as in the case of the lyre cup in Patio 3.

If the vessels were intentionally broken in the Middle Horizon, we might suggest two possible interpretations of this act. First, given the presumed existence of a Wari offering tradition, as discussed in Chapter 3, involving the smashing of pots for ceremonial purposes, we might suggest that this association represents some sort of ceremonial behavior. This is not like the offering deposits in that these remains are not interred, but the images depicted do suggest ceremonial associations. The second possible interpretation is a bit more violent. It is possible that the vessels were intentionally destroyed when the Wari empire fell, when the site was abandoned. The vandalism of the site, and the destruction of the symbols of Wari power might be an expected reaction of the local people against the remembered tyranny of Wari control. While the oversize jar may have been smashed where it stood, the locations of the smaller vessels against the walls might suggest that they were smashed by having been thrown against the walls.

NONCERAMIC ARTIFACTS

Lithics

After ceramics, the second most common type of artifact, numerically, is chipped stone. A total of 4,054 lithics were recovered in the excavations. Lithics were divided into categories on the basis of both raw material and artifact type. Raw materials fall into one of six classes. Red jasper is by far the most common material used, comprising over 75% of all lithic artifacts. The source is local, and located only a few hundred meters south of Jincamocco. Obsidian tools are common, and most probably derive from the Jampatilla source at the north end of the valley, near Willkaya. Some red obsidian was also observed; this color is not present in the local source, as far as we know, and Burger and Asaro (1975) indicate that red obsidian is probably from the Quispisisa mine in Huancavelica. A fine-grained basalt, probably related to the local Jampatilla obsidian source, is also used. Light grey quartzite, grading to both a yellowish color, and to nearly white, is also common. The source of this material is also local, located about 2 km north of Jincamocco, on the side of a mountain named Cristalnioq. The remaining lithics did not fall into any major recognizable category, so they were classed as either "other silicate" or "other non-silicate." Individual materials did not appear in any abundance, and the sources of these materials have not been located. It is not unlikely that most come from small local sources.

Tools were divided into eight types: cores, unutilized flakes, use-modified flakes (irregularly flaked), unifacially flaked pieces, bifacially flaked pieces, projectile points (always bifacially flaked), blades (always unifacially flaked), and drills.

The most common artifacts were use-modified flakes. These flakes show irregular chipping that results from use, rather than from intentional modification. Actual finely finished tools were rare, and most of these were made of obsidian. All projectile points ($n = 54$) were made of obsidian. Points are typically triangular in shape, both before and during the Willka phase. However, during the Willka phase a leaf-shaped form was introduced. (Seven leaf-shaped points were recovered, six of which were in deposits firmly dated to the Willka phase, or in which mixing should have been minimal. The seventh was found in a mixed deposit.) Unifacially flaked blades appear first in the Willka phase.

There is a change in the use of different raw materials from the Kancha phase to the Willka phase (Table 7.6). Quartzite, fine-grained basalt, and especially obsidian increased in proportion in the Willka phase, and red jasper correspondingly decreased in proportion. If we consider cores and unutilized flakes to represent remains of production of tools, and utilized flakes and tools to indicate use (consumption) of lithics, red jasper shows

TABLE 7.6
Frequencies and Percentages of Lithic Raw Materials in the Kancha and Willka Phases

	Jas	Obs	Bas	Qua	Sil	Oth
FREQUENCIES						
Kancha*	925	45	20	19	83	12
Willka**	825	148	43	62	79	30
PERCENTAGES						
Kancha	83.8	4.1	1.8	1.7	7.5	1.1
Willka	69.5	12.5	3.6	5.2	6.7	2.5

*$n = 1,104$
**$n = 1,187$

no major change in either production or consumption from the Kancha phase to the Willka phase. However, in the case of obsidian we do see a slight change. In the Kancha phase no cores and only 4 unutilized flakes were found; most remains indicate tool use rather than production. In contrast, in the Willka phase, cores and flakes increased in proportion. Interestingly, while the proportion of utilized flakes stayed about the same, the proportion of manufactured tools dropped by half. This demonstrates that there was more production of obsidian tools in the Willka phase, relative to consumption.

No lithics were found in primary deposits; all come from secondary trash. Many of the finished tools were found broken. Lithics are sparse in Patios 1 and 3, as well as in the corridor and the gallery. They are nearly absent from the primary deposit containing the 11 reconstructible vessels. Lithics are found in moderately high density, however, in Patio 2, especially along the south side of the patio, and in the test pit outside the north wall.

In the Kancha phase deposits, there are very high densities of lithics located near the north wall of the enclosure: under the north bench of Patio 1, and in the test pit outside the wall. As these same deposits have very high densities of all artifacts, they were probably a trash deposit associated with the Kancha phase village, possibly accumulated in a low spot at the base of the hill, or perhaps the result of intentional filling at the time that the enclosure was built.

The temporal distribution of red obsidian deserves note. Red obsidian, as discussed above, is probably not local, but comes from the Quispisisa source in Huancavelica. Red obsidian occurs in deposits of all periods at Jincamocco, not only the Willka phase and Kancha phase, but also in the earliest pre-Kancha phase deposits. Red obsidian has also been found on sites in the region dating to the Initial period, and Early Horizon, indicating that this material was being exchanged since much earlier times.

Ground Stone

Of the 124 ground stone artifacts recorded, most were manos and metates. Manos are made of small river cobbles, and are of two types: rocker manos, and slab grinding manos. Some larger rocker grinders were recovered as well; all but one were broken. Metates are usually basin metates; all were found broken. A fragment of a slab grinding stone (*batán*) was found in the earliest levels (T = 1), and an intact *batán* was found on the west bench of Patio 1.

Forms and frequencies of ground stone artifacts show no changes through time. However, two unique artifacts were found: a broken axe head or hoe was located in a Willka phase context, and a broken donut-shaped mace head was found in a deposit that is probably mixed Kancha phase and Willka phase remains. (A star-shaped mace head, purportedly from Jincamocco, and currently in the collection of the local Colegio, was shown to me. Such forms are more commonly known in Late Horizon contexts.) In terms of Willka phase spatial patterns, ground stone was found in high frequency on the west bench of Patio 1, and in moderate frequency on the south side of Patio 2, and in Corridor 1. Ground stone was absent from the north bench of Patio 1, Patio 3, Gallery 1, and T2/3.

Animal Bone

Some 87 kilos of animal bone were recovered. All pieces were fragmentary, and no articulated remains were found. Most bones were long bones, and no skulls or vertebrae were located (except for guinea pigs), indicating that primary butchering took place elsewhere. No detailed analysis of the bone has been undertaken, but gross morphology indicates the presence of deer, camelid, and guinea pig.

The density of bone is another good indicator of trash deposits. In Willka phase levels, the highest densities of bone came from trash deposits in the corridor, and in Patio 2. In earlier strata, high densities of bone fragments were found below the north bench of Patio 1.

Human Remains

Several burials were recovered in the uppermost strata of the excavations, as well as in wall trenches (Burials 1-4, 7-8; mni = 10). As discussed in the previous chapter, the site was apparently used as the local cemetery for quite some time. All these burials are intrusive, post-Willka phase remains, and so will not be discussed here.

Only two proveniences yielded Willka phase human remains, both in primary context. The first is the small skull offering (Burial 5) in the north bench of Patio 1, discussed in the preceding chapter. This skull was that of an old adult female.

The second burial (no. 6), probably dating to the Willka phase, was encountered beneath the floor of Patio 3, adjacent to the remains of the pre-Willka phase round stone building. The burial chamber was a small cyst, flush against the interior wall of the old stone building, and was apparently lined with stones on the remaining sides. The cyst was covered with flat stone slabs. It contained two individuals in a seated flexed position. No other associated items were observed. The burial was only partially exposed, but one skull and some postcranial remains were removed from the burial, and the stone slabs were replaced. The skull removed was that of an adult male; it had no obvious deformation. We saw no evidence of any pit dug through the floor, so the burial may have been interred at about the time the Wari enclosure was built.

Ceramic Disks and Spindle Whorls

Some 121 ceramic disks were recovered. These are worked sherds, 4-6 cm in diameter, with rounded off edges. Half of these pieces had no hole drilled through them, one third had a hole drilled entirely through the center, and the rest had the beginnings of a hole drilled on one or both sides. Some of these certainly were broken at the time of drilling, for many of these pieces were found broken in half. The disks with holes drilled all the way through probably were spindle whorls; the remaining disks may have been intended for the same purpose.

Thirteen artifacts were recovered that were certainly spindle whorls. This form is modeled, with a biconical profile. These are nearly exactly the same as the spindle whorls in use in this region today. While worked sherd disks occur in all temporal levels, the modeled whorls occur only in Willka phase contexts.

The distribution of ceramic disks and spindle whorls corresponds to the distribution of other artifacts. The highest proportions in Willka phase levels are found in the corridor, and in Patio 2, and they are present in all other units. Interestingly, in Patio 1, although deposits on both benches are secondary trash, with similar densities of ceramics and lithics, there are more ceramic disks and spindle whorls on the west bench. This might suggest that spinning was a more common activity in the source of this trash, than in the source of the trash on the north bench. In earlier levels, ceramic disks are densest under the north bench of Patio 1, as is the case with other artifacts.

These ubiquitous artifacts indicate that spinning was a common activity both before and during the Willka phase occupation of the site.

Special Objects

Worked bone. Fourteen worked bone artifacts were located, and nearly all came from Kancha phase contexts. Artifacts include tools associated with textile production: two needles (one broken), two weaving tools, and two awls. Three bone tubes of unknown function, and one perforated disk, of a size similar to the worked sherd spindle whorls, were located. Four other fragments of worked bone were recovered, but their form is unknown; one piece had a single straight line engraved on it. Only two pieces came from Willka phase contexts: one tube, and one weaving tool. The latter was found in the corridor, along with higher densities of spindle whorls.

Evidence of Jincamocco Artifacts 251

Shell. One piece of worked marine shell was found, spatulate in form, 7 cm long, ranging from 1.2 to 2.2 cm wide, and 0.9 cm thick. It was found above the west bench of Patio 1, in secondary trash. This unit is defined as of probable Willka phase date, but with some possible mixing of later materials. Broken at the time of excavation, the inside of the piece is a light pink color; the exterior was eroded, and white in color with dark adhesions. This has been tentatively identified as *Spondylus* shell, the nearest source of which are the warmer waters of coastal Ecuador. The presence of marine shell at Jincamocco indicates that the site participated in some sort of long-distance exchange network.

Metal artifacts. Four objects of metal were located, two of which were small sheet fragments of badly corroded copper or bronze. One of these fragments was located in Kancha phase levels in Patio 1, the other was from the Willka phase or later level (T=7) of Patio 3. In the corridor, in the same deposit as the bone weaving tool and higher densities of spindle whorls, was found an unbroken needle, 9.1 cm long, and 2.6 mm thick, of cuprous metal. The eye of the needle was formed by thinning the end of the needle, and curving it around, with the end inserted back into the body of the needle. The presence of the needle in this particular deposit adds further support to the notion that the source of this deposit included more textile production than did the sources of most other deposits.

The last artifact is a small gold disk. Extremely thin, less than 1 mm, and measuring only 1.5 cm in diameter, it is perforated by a small hole, below which is a narrow slit. The gold disk was found inside one of the large plainware jars that were in primary association with the west bench of Patio 1. Being both valuable and portable, normally we should expect that items such as this one would have been removed from the site at the time of abandonment. In all likelihood it was lost, and was unintentionally left behind.

Overall, the presence of shell and metal artifacts, especially the gold disk, indicates a departure from earlier periods. Not only was Jincamocco tied into a system of long-distance exchange, as evidenced by the presence of warm-water shell, but it also had access to (probably specialized) people who crafted metals. The paucity of metals on the site suggests that metal production did not take place at the site, but rather that certain finished items were used there.

TEMPORAL PATTERNING OF THE ARTIFACTS

In the preceding sections I have pointed out numerous temporal changes in artifact inventory. I shall not repeat those here, except to point out some of the more important patterns. The biggest pattern that is seen is that local styles continued through the Middle Horizon without major change. Some new vessel forms were introduced, as were some rim treatments, but the older local forms continued as well. One interesting pattern that emerged is the fact that apparently local ceramics declined in quality during the Middle Horizon. This may be due to the fact that production was greatly increased, and there was less time to devote to the production of each vessel. But this decline in quality may also have had something to do with the fact that the local residents were no longer making pots for themselves, or their family, or people they knew; they were now making them for the occupying foreigners.

Local decorated styles decreased in proportion in the Middle Horizon, as red-slipped wares and painted pottery increased in proportion. Simple painted designs in black, or black and white, on red appeared first in the Middle Horizon, and continued on in the local tradition after the end of the Wari occupation. By the Late Intermediate, the local decorative tradition of incised and appliqué designs had given way almost entirely to the newer painted tradition. Some of this may be attributed to the introduction of painting technology by Wari, but for the most part the shift in decorative styles was gradual, with no sharp break at the Middle Horizon. And in terms of utilitarian plainware pottery, change during the Middle Horizon was very slight; the tradition continued virtually unchanged in later periods.

Other general patterns of importance at Jincamocco include the increase in the manufacture of obsidian tools. Given the presence of a local source, and a Wari site near that source, at the very least the source was being exploited for material to be used at Jincamocco. It will be interesting to see, after future analyses, if Jampatilla obsidian turns up at Wari, or at any other Wari provincial sites.

While we do not know if Jampatilla obsidian was being exported during the Middle Horizon, the presence of red obsidian indicates that Quispisisa obsidian was being imported into this region. Other materials appearing at Jincamocco during the Middle Horizon, such as exotic shell, gold, and fancy ceramics, indicate that this site was tied into long-distance relationships unlike anything that had come before.

SPATIAL PATTERNING IN THE WILLKA PHASE DEPOSITS

Given that nearly all the deposits at Jincamocco are secondary or tertiary in nature, we can say little directly about activities carried out at particular locations, with the possible exception of T2/3. Secondary and tertiary trash deposits can show only the broadest of activity patterns, and can say little about the locations at which those activities occurred. But I

Evidence of Jincamocco Artifacts

TABLE 7.7
Composition of Twelve Discrete Willka Phase Deposits

Unit	Ceramic Percentages				Relative Densities				
	Plain	Local	Rdw.	Ptd.	Cer.	Lith.	G.S.	Bone	Whorls
C1-01	54.3	4.7	30.7	10.7	mod	low	mod	high	mod
C1-02	64.9	4.0	13.3	17.8	mod	low	mod	high	mod
P1w	60.4	29.5	4.7	5.4	low	low	high	—	low
P1nw	67.4	17.9	7.4	7.4	mod	low	low	mod	low
P1n	58.8	17.2	15.6	8.4	low	low	—	low	low
P2s	69.5	24.3	4.1	2.0	high	high	mod	high	mod
P2e	82.4	2.8	6.3	8.5	mod	mod	—	mod	mod
P3s	58.0	2.9	34.1	5.1	low	low	—	low	low
P3e	50.6	16.5	25.9	7.0	mod	low	—	mod	low
G1	(80)	0	0	(20)	low	low	—	low	—
T1	28.9	8.9	53.3	8.9	?	high	?	high	?
T2/3	0	0	(n=1)	(n=11)	low	—	—	—	—

have been pointing out that there are some variations in the spatial patterning of particular classes of artifacts. We can divide the Willka phase assemblage of deposits into eleven discrete units of secondary remains, and one primary deposit (Table 7.7; see Appendix B for counts and densities of materials in each excavation provenience). Differences in the composition of the different trash deposits suggest some differences in the activities and behaviors that produced them. Further, differences in inventory suggest differences in the social status of the groups producing the trash. However, the latter suggestions must be regarded as very tentative. Evidence of activities is more reliable and somewhat less speculative than the evidence of status differences.

For example, a deposit with high proportions of fancy polychromes might be contrasted with one containing only local decorated styles. This might indicate that the first deposit was produced by people of higher status, perhaps foreigners; the second deposit might have been produced by people of lower status, perhaps local residents. Likewise, a deposit with weaving tools might be contrasted with one lacking such tools; this indicates a difference in a specific activity that produced the deposit. A summary of such differences can suggest some general parameters of the range of activities carried out in the site, as well as the range of social classes present in the site. But, given the secondary nature of the remains, we cannot associate those activities with the specific locations in which the trash was located.

Corridor 1 was excavated in two units, Unit 1 on the west side of the short cross wall blocking the corridor, Unit 2 to the east. Each of these represents a separate spatial deposit, but deposits that are more similar to each other than they are to most other deposits on the site. Both units have exceptionally high proportions of fancy polychromes, but very low proportions of local decorated styles; weaving tools are present, animal bone is high in density, but lithics are low. Both of these units represent high status trash, with Unit 2 perhaps from a group of exceptionally high status. The activities apparent include food preparation and consumption, spinning, and weaving. An activity conspicuously lacking is lithic production or consumption.

Patio 1 is characterized by low density of all materials, and can be divided into three spatial units: the west bench, the northwest corner, and the north bench. On the west bench, where the small primary association of plainware vessels was recovered, exotic ceramics are lower in proportion, while local decorated styles are high. All nonceramic classes are very low in proportion, but the gold and spondylus were found in this deposit. While the only activity clearly present was food preparation, and perhaps some low level storage in plainware jars, the social unit that produced this deposit was perhaps of local origin, but perhaps also of some elevated status.

The northwest corner is not distinctive in any way, except that it has higher than normal proportions of animal bone. This may have come from an area of more specialized food preparation, or may be the results of food consumption. The north bench has low densities of all artifact classes, and no exceptional proportions of any particular artifact class. Trash deposition here was minimal, and we cannot infer anything about activities or social units. Interestingly, however, just below the bench, this unit produced the highest densities of pre-Willka phase trash. Unit T1, just on the other side of the enclosure wall likewise produced high densities of early trash. This area may have been a low spot where trash accumulated prior to the Willka phase, or it may have been fill intentionally deposited at the time of the enclosure.

Patio 2 is very different, and is subdivided into two units, the south patio, and the east patio. The south side of Patio 2 has the highest densities of trash anywhere on the site, and the east side is of only slightly lower density. The two units are more similar to each other than to any other units, but they do exhibit some differences as well. The south patio, despite extremely high densities of all artifact classes, has the lowest proportion of fancy ceramics of any unit on the site. It does have a high proportion of local decorative styles, however. The preponderance of all manner of artifacts indicates a wide range of activities that produced this deposit: food production and consumption, lithic production and consumption, and spinning. This appears to be dense habitation refuse, but from a rather low status group, probably local residents.

The east patio has moderate densities of all artifacts, with higher than average plainware vessels, but lower than average local decorated styles; it has more fancy polychrome than the south patio. This assemblage is difficult to interpret. It may represent normal habitation refuse, but of nonlocal residents, or at least of people with access to fancy ceramics. Interestingly, two Nasca 4 sherds were found in this deposit; everything else about this unit indicates that it is an unmixed Willka phase deposit. I can only suggest that the Nasca vessels were already antiques in the Middle Horizon.

Patio 3 is likewise divided into two units, one along the south side, and one along the east. Overall, the trash in this patio was low in density, although slightly higher on the east side. The south side of the patio is high in red-slipped wares and polychromes, but low in local decorated styles; it has only low densities of all other artifact classes. This would appear to represent food preparation and consumption by a social unit of relatively high status; other activities seem to be lacking. Perhaps this unit represents typical foreign occupation, of not exceptionally high status. The east side of the patio likewise has unusually high proportions of red-slipped ware, but has normal proportions of local decorated styles and polychromes. Other remains are low in proportion, except animal bone which is moderate in density. Again this refuse would appear to have resulted from food preparation and consumption, but the social unit involved had access to both local and nonlocal artifacts.

The gallery had extremely low densities of all artifacts, and was, in fact, nearly empty. It is possible that this room served for some function that produced minimal remains, such as storage. But it was certainly not used for trash disposal like the other excavated units.

T1, the small test pit outside the enclosure wall, is similar in most respects to the corridor units. It has mostly high status trash like the corridor units, but it lacks weaving tools. Here it would appear that trash was just dumped against the outside of the main enclosure wall, but that this trash came from locations of higher status residence.

In sum, the range of activities present at Jincamocco certainly included food preparation and consumption, the production and consumption of lithics, weaving, spinning, and perhaps storage. High status remains are found in the corridor units, and T1; other high status remains were found in Patio 3, but in low density. Remains in Patios 1 and 2 would seem to have pertained to groups of lower social status. The extreme high density of remains in Patio 2 indicates that this space was used more intensively than other areas for trash disposal. While we cannot associate these activities and social units with the specific locations of the trash deposits, it is apparent that the enclosure at Jincamocco included a wide range of activities.

The residents of the enclosure probably included both high status foreign residents and low status local residents, at the extremes. The diversity of social groups was probably quite high, and some groups may have been permanent residents, while others lived at the site only temporarily, if they lived there at all. While the fancy polychromes were probably all imported from outside the valley, the vast majority of the artifacts were local products in local styles. It is probable that a substantial number of local residents were living in the site.

THE FUNCTION OF JINCAMOCCO

As demonstrated in Chapters 5 and 6, Jincamocco is a foreign, intrusive site, built in the style of Wari architecture. It is undoubtedly a Wari site. Compared to such provincial sites as Pikillaqta and Viracochapampa (see Fig. 6.13), Jincamocco is not a particularly large site, especially when we consider just the original rectangular enclosure. It ranks in size with sites such as Honco Pampa, and Wari Willka, moderate size Wari provincial sites. But relative to sites in the Carhuarazo Valley, it is enormous.

This chapter has addressed the artifacts recovered during the partial excavation of Jincamocco. Excavations were restricted to only one corner of the enclosure, and exposed only 1.1% of the area of the enclosure. While the remains uncovered cannot begin to reveal the full range of activities carried out in the enclosure, nor the broader spatial patterning of remains within the site, it is possible to elucidate a part of that range and that patterning.

In terms of spatial patterning, the fact that nearly all remains were found in secondary trash deposits precludes associating specific remains with specific locations, with rare exception. But the various trash deposits do exhibit spatial patterning, suggesting that there were spatially discrete activities carried out in the enclosure. The differential distribution of certain kinds of artifacts indicates spatial patterning of such activities as food preparation and consumption, weaving, and lithic manufacture. Differences in classes of artifacts indicate that perhaps some areas of the site were occupied by low-status people, perhaps local residents, or perhaps temporary residents brought in from outside the valley. Other parts of the site may have been occupied or used by higher status foreign personnel, perhaps including elites directly from Wari.

It is now possible to return to the original list of possible site functions, and eliminate some of those possibilities, and offer support to others.

Storage. If Jincamocco were devoted primarily to storage, we should expect most of the area of the enclosure to be devoted to storage, with some evidence of permanent residence. While most remains reflect residence, no storage areas were defined on the basis of architecture or lack of artifacts, with the possible exception of Gallery 1. Large plainware jars, commonly used for storage, actually decreased in proportion in the Willka phase, as compared to the Kancha phase. Jincamocco was not primarily a storage facility, as I had expected, although it is possible that small portions of the site might have been set aside for storage.

Craft production. There is limited evidence of craft production: textile production and lithic manufacture. But neither of these activities is represented in great proportions, so were not the primary focus of the site function. The obsidian source was located in the valley, but we do not find large amounts of obsidian debitage in Jincamocco indicating large-scale lithic production. Further, although Jampatilla obsidian is the most common at Jincamocco, it has not yet been identified at other Wari sites. Lithic production may have served only the local center, rather than supplying other regions.

Waystation along a road. Jincamocco is simply too large to have served only as a *tampu*, judging from the size and layout of Inka *tampu*. While the site was located along a road, and probably had facilities for travelers and animals, it was certainly much more than just a waystation.

Political center. The size and layout of the site, the location of the site, the diversity of social groups within the site, and the range of activities evident in the site indicate quite clearly that it was a regional administrative center, the focus of foreign political control. The site was built in the Wari style, like the capital city and like other provincial centers, and it was very different from local constructions. There is ample evidence of residence, perhaps both commoner and elite; the data are insufficient to distinguish temporary from permanent residence, never an easy task even with primary deposits. There may have been some limited storage and craft production in the center. There was certainly a significant ceremonial component, judging from the primary association of fancy imported ceramics and a unique architectural feature, the plaster covered platform. The presence of foreign exotic goods—ceramics, metal, shell—indicates that the site was part of a macroregional exchange system; further, these goods were consumed at the site but not produced there. The location of the site along a major road, with facilities for travelers and animals, is also to be expected in the case of a regional center.

But direct evidence for "administration" is still rather elusive. We have not yet been able to identify particular forms of architecture that might represent administrative facilities, like the *audiencias* of Chimú sites. It is possible that certain goods were stored in galleries and controlled by administrators who operated out of the associated central patios, but without primary deposits this is impossible to know.

Based on the total assemblage, the architecture, and the form and location of the site, there is little question but that Jincamocco was a regional administrative center, the focus of Wari control over this valley.

NOTE

1. The artifacts excavated from Jincamocco now reside in the collections of the Museo Nacional de Antropología y Arqueología, Pueblo Libre, Lima, under the jurisdiction of the Instituto Nacional de Cultura. At the request of the village authorities of Cabana Sur, several intact and reconstructible vessels were left in the collection of the local Colegio.

8

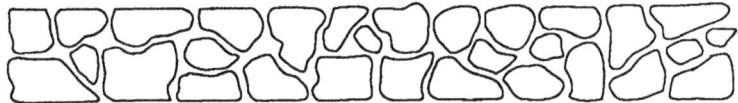

The Middle Horizon and Andean Imperialism

Beginning with a summary of the Wari occupation of the Carhuarazo Valley, this chapter views the problem of the Middle Horizon from the perspective of those data. Other remains of Wari occupations from the central Andes are reviewed in light of those data, and the nature of Wari imperialism considered. Finally two other areas are discussed: the relationship between Wari and Tiwanaku in the Middle Horizon, and the relationship of Wari to the later Inka empire.

THE WARI OCCUPATION OF THE CARHUARAZO VALLEY

The Middle Horizon was a time of major change in the Carhuarazo Valley. The Wari occupation of this valley resulted in an alteration of local lifestyles so revolutionary that some of those changes still affect life there today.

During the Kancha phase, prior to the Wari presence, the Carhuarazo Valley was occupied by a few small villages of people whose subsistence was probably based on tuber cultivation and camelid herding. There is no evidence of any sort of centralized political organization above the level of the single village, nor is there evidence of status differentiation within villages. For centuries the people of this valley had maintained indirect con-

259

tacts with the south coast. However, they were not tied into the sphere of interaction in the Ayacucho Basin; the Carhuarazo Valley lay well outside the Wari heartland.

In the Willka phase we see a new and foreign presence in the valley: Wari. A major administrative center was built at Jincamocco, and three smaller centers were built on the other side of the valley. These sites are distinguished from local sites by their distinctive architecture, and artifact inventory. All the sites are rectangular compounds, while local buildings are small round structures; three of the sites had Wari-style ceramics on their surfaces.

One effect of the Wari occupation on the local culture is seen in a change in subsistence focus. During the Willka phase much of the valley was terraced, and the artificial kichwa ecozone created. The shift to maize agriculture also occasioned a shift in local settlement locations: villages moved to lower elevations in or adjacent to the new kichwa zone. Even after the Wari collapse, when most local villages were also abandoned, they never returned to the higher elevations. Today village locations follow the same pattern introduced in the Middle Horizon, and maize agriculture on terraces still forms a most important focus of subsistence. The modern adaptation is certainly one of the most enduring Wari legacies.

But while local lifestyles changed, other aspects of the local culture did not. Local plainware utilitarian pottery continued with only subtle change during the Wari occupation. While less time or care was taken in the production of each vessel, and there was a slight increase in variability in vessel forms, the local styles continued on through the Willka phase and after. A greater change is seen in local decorated styles. A trend beginning centuries earlier, the decoration of pots with a red slip rather than plastic decoration, became more predominant in the Willka phase, and simple painted designs were added to the repertory. After the Willka phase, local styles with plastic decoration disappeared altogether, having been replaced by the newer slipped and painted forms.

The evidence of artifacts and architecture indicate not only that Jincamocco was a foreign site, but that a variety of spatially discrete activities took place at that site. The predominant activity evidenced in the limited excavations of the site was certainly human habitation. Nearly every deposit included remains of food preparation and/or consumption. Other activities included limited craft production of lithics and textiles, and perhaps some limited storage. The finely finished platform structure with its primary association of exotic pottery indicates perhaps some ceremonial activity as well.

Data from Jincamocco, along with settlement data, suggest that there were some changes in the Wari occupation during the Willka phase. The ceramic evidence indicates that the enclosure at Jincamocco was built in

Middle Horizon 1B, and that the occupation probably continued through MH 2. At some point in the occupation, Jincamocco was greatly enlarged, indicating very definitely some shift in the Wari occupation of the region. Limited data suggest that the three smaller Wari sites at Culluma, Anta and Willkaya, may have been built during MH 2.

Why was there such a major Wari occupation of this rather small and seemingly obscure valley? While this valley was occupied, and certainly had a much higher population than the adjacent Chicha/Soras valley, it was not exactly a major locus of high density occupation. And the local society was not organized at such a level as to be a threat to Wari. The initial occupation probably had much to do with the strategic location of the valley—probably its location relative to the south coast. This valley lies halfway between Wari and Nasca; similarities between Nasca and Wari ceramics indicate strong ties between the two regions, especially during the Middle Horizon. Further, given that this valley was already peripheral to south coast interaction spheres, it may have served in some sense as the Wari gateway to the south coast. So, a moderate size administrative center was established in this valley, along the road connecting Wari and Nasca. The local culture was not politically centralized, so a new administrative apparatus was created. Jincamocco site was the focus of direct political control over the local populace. It was also a convenient stopping point for travelers, being four to six days from each location. And perhaps goods moving between the two regions were controlled by this Wari outpost.

But we need to consider also the expansion of Jincamocco, the building of three smaller centers, and the construction of the terracing. The construction of the terraces, especially in such a relatively short span of time, must have been tremendous undertaking. It is unlikely that the terraces were built at the instigation of the local residents, and more likely that the construction was planned and directed by some greater organization: Wari. The terracing not only greatly increased the spatial extent of agriculture in the valley, it also increased yields per unit of land, and it drastically altered the focus of production from tubers to maize. All of a sudden this valley could produce far more than was needed locally. This marks a shift from minimal political control to the intensive economic exploitation of this valley.

Why should this be? During epoch 2 of the Middle Horizon, Wari grew into an enormous urban site. Population not only resulted from an influx of people from the countryside, as seen in the changes in settlement patterns in Chapter 3, but it is not unlikely that people from all over the Wari realm were living permanently or temporarily at Wari as well. The subsistence base of Wari would have needed significant expansion and intensification in order to support such greater numbers of people.

But why the Carhuarazo Valley? Limited data from the Río Pampas valley do not indicate any major Wari occupation there, nor the thorough reorganization of that valley for agricultural production, even though it lies much closer to Wari. And good data from the Chicha/Soras valley show no such agricultural intensification, even though this valley lies the same distance from Wari as the Carhuarazo Valley. But, the Carhuarazo Valley differed from those other valleys by virtue of the fact that it had, already in place, a major Wari occupation. Perhaps it was more effective to elaborate the system already established there, and to produce agricultural produce for the direct support of Wari, rather than begin anew in some other region.

This suggestion must remain very tentative. It is clear that the Wari occupation of the Carhuarazo Valley changed, and that economic exploitation became very important. I suggest that the location of the valley, only six days from Wari, resulted in greater economic control than was normally the case. This level of economic control is seemingly rather rare in other regions of Wari occupation, except areas close to Wari.

The amount of labor required to build the Wari sites, maintain the roads, build the terraces, produce tens if not hundreds of thousands of pots, serve the foreign residents, and cultivate the old fields and new terraces probably far exceeded labor available locally. The number of villages was only about five, both before and during the Wari occupation, and none of these was very large. It is likely that one of the things imported to this valley was labor—people. There is no evidence of foreign villages in the valley, but there certainly was a tremendous amount of space available in Jincamocco, and in the smaller centers, to house such temporary residents.

All four Wari sites were abandoned at the end of the Willka phase, at the end of epoch 2 of the Middle Horizon. While superficially this would appear to be a rather sudden and abrupt event, excavation data from Jincamocco might suggest otherwise. At Jincamocco it is apparent that some patios were closed off, their doorways sealed. In one case, occupation of the patio may have continued on for some time after this. Not only were doorways closed up, but cross walls were built in corridors, perhaps further shutting off access to certain parts of the site. Eventually these areas served for the disposing of domestic trash of varying sorts; this probably occurred fairly late in the Willka phase, as earlier trash was deposited outside the site. So the abandonment of Jincamocco was not sudden, but rather, certain parts fell into disuse some time before the site was completely abandoned. While in archaeological terms this was an abrupt event, in human terms it was not. It may have taken several years or decades.

Finally, the settlement pattern data from the valley, and the artifacts collected from those sites, indicate something of the period just after the Wari collapse. In the Marke phase, not only were the Wari sites no longer occupied, but all but one of the local villages were also abandoned. New villages were established well within the kichwa zone. The number of villages dropped to four, perhaps indicating a slight depopulation. And two of the four villages were heavily fortified, a clear indication of a new turn of events. Through the ensuing Toqsa phase, this pattern continued. The number of villages increased, but all remained in the kichwa zone, and about half were fortified. It was not until the Toqsa phase that we see the emergence of local political centralization.

The Wari Strategy

The final point to be made is that the strategy employed by Wari was in many ways conditioned by local political organization, relative to the needs of Wari. For perhaps strategic reasons, Wari needed a base of control in this region. There was no extant political organization capable of carrying out its requirements, so a system of political control had to be created. In other words, the difference between Wari requirements and local conditions was so great that significant investment was made in the region. The local culture had no centralized political authority, and no hierarchy of control. So a major center was created at Jincamocco, and this center was the node that integrated the Carhuarazo Valley into a broader system of political control.

At some time after the initial conquest and the establishment of the Wari compound at Jincamocco, economic control took on greater importance, and Wari strategies changed slightly. Jincamocco was enlarged, three small sites built, and large tracts of the valley were terraced. The Carhuarazo Valley had become very important to Wari, in ways perhaps not anticipated at the time of its conquest. The great investment in, and the cost of, establishing economic control suggests some great need on the part of Wari. I have tentatively suggested that the need to expand the subsistence base of Wari itself may have occasioned the shift in policy in the Carhuarazo Valley.

Implications for Archaeological Investigations of Imperialism

The investigation of the Wari occupation of the Carhuarazo Valley has some general implications for the archaeological study and interpretation of the Wari expansion of the Middle Horizon, and for the study of political expansion in general.

First, a rather small point, the local styles of utilitarian pottery were hardly affected by the Wari occupation. There is no sharp break in the sequence, nor did they imitate Wari forms in preference to their own. As I said above, if we were to look only at utilitarian pottery, we would be hard pressed to detect evidence for any Wari occupation. On the other hand, local decorated styles did change somewhat. In part, the changes seen were probably normal developments in the local style, with continuity from earlier periods; but the changes may have been accelerated by the Wari presence, and particularly the great influx of painted pottery. But while the fancier styles do change somewhat, the utilitarian pottery does not. This has implications for the study of similar occupations, or suspected occupations. The lack of change in local utilitarian pottery is not necessarily to be expected during periods of foreign political control; and the lack of such change cannot be used reliably to argue against the existence of such control. Conversely, change in local prestige styles is to be expected, as new prestige styles and new symbols of power compete with older ones.

Second, it is clear that Wari established a system of direct control in this valley. The evidence is overwhelming: not only do we find a major Wari center, but a variety of other changes as well. Despite the relatively small size of Jincamocco, as compared with other Wari provincial sites, it was the focus of direct political control. In areas of more indirect forms of control we do not expect to find major administrative centers, or other facilities indicating great imperial investment in the local infrastructure of control. I have suggested generally, and specifically in the case of the Inka empire, that local structures may suffice for imperial purposes, and administration carried through collaboration with local elites.

The presence of a major Wari site is probably a reliable indication of direct political control of a region. This seems to be the case in the Inka example. And as we have also seen in the Inka example, many, if not most, regions did not have major administrative centers. Wari occupations so far are only clearly documented in regions in which major Wari administrative sites are located. These sites comprise Wari administrative architecture, a large rectangular enclosure subdivided into sectors, room blocks and characteristic patio groups. I suggest that these represent regions of direct control. And as a corollary, I would suggest that there are probably many areas that were only indirectly controlled by Wari; that is, they were entirely consolidated into the political and economic system but were ruled through alliance with local elites.

The third implication of the investigation of the Carhuarazo Valley is the fact that study of the provincial center alone does not yield a complete picture of the foreign occupation. While revealing certain activities or functions within a provincial site, it tells little of the effect of the foreign occupation on the local culture. In short, we have incomplete knowledge of the process of establishing political and economic control. By taking a regional approach, and also considering local sites, it was possible in the Carhuarazo Valley to see the change in settlement patterns and subsistence focus, and the establishment of economic forms of control by Wari; excavation of Jincamocco suggested none of this. Further, it was possible to reconstruct settlement patterns of the Kancha phase, and demonstrate that the region lacked any sort of political centralization prior to the Wari incursion. This lack of political organization probably conditioned the Wari strategy: it was necessary to build a new political organization. Again, none of this was visible in the data from just Jincamocco. And while in the present case I have not been able to intensively investigate any of the local villages, it was fortunate that there was a long earlier local occupation evident under the floors of Jincamocco. It has been possible to document some changes in local artifact inventory, and to distinguish between local and foreign styles. In a single component Wari site, this would have been impossible.

Finally, if we are interested in understanding the process by which one culture establishes new forms of control over another, investigations of the imperial capital city tell us very little of this process. While such investigations may serve to identify artifact styles and architecture associated with the center of power, they do not directly indicate any aspects of the expansion of control out of that center. And even the definition of the horizon styles may be problematic when based primarily on materials from the capital.

For example, in the case of the Middle Horizon the horizon styles have been defined by both comparison of Wari ceramics on distant sites, and ceramics encountered at Wari itself. The problem is that in the case of an expanding polity, the core of that polity should contain local utilitarian pottery and local decorated pottery, as well as pottery associated with the expansion—the horizon style. The styles defined for the Middle Horizon include many forms and decorations that are not found outside the Wari core. To separate the true horizon styles, those that are specifically associated with the spread of some sort of control, it is necessary to compare the styles of the capital with those found in the provinces. In this way it may be possible to separate out elements that are found widely distributed, and ones that are typical only of specific regions. And the provincial setting may again prove to be the more valuable; if local styles can be defined, they are likely to be very distinct from the foreign styles—as in the case of the Carhuarazo Valley—thus making those foreign horizon styles more easily definable. We are only at the point of beginning this process in the Middle Horizon.

To understand the process of imperial expansion, critical data come from the provinces. Only in the provinces can we see where the empire went, what it found, and how it modified its strategies of control in order to consolidate a region into the imperial administrative system. Only in the provinces can we see the effects of imperial occupation, and thereby understand some of the motivations behind the expansion.

EVIDENCE OF WARI IMPERIALISM

The evidence of the Carhuarazo Valley indicates the direct political control of the region by Wari. The Wari site at Jincamocco was the focus of this political power, the regional administrative center. I have argued that, even in the absence of other forms of data, the existence of one of these large building complexes in most cases can be taken as evidence of direct Wari control of a region. That is, most such sites were regional administrative centers, the foci of Wari political control over individual provinces.

The number of such Wari sites is limited. A present a maximum estimate is probably twelve administrative sites, outside the Wari heartland: Pikillaqta, Jincamocco, Wari Willka, Calpish, Yanahuanca, Wisajirca, Tocroc, Honco Pampa, Pariamarca, Ichabamba, Yamobamba, and El Palacio. Viracochapampa may have been planned and intended to be a major administrative, but it was never completed or occupied. Sites in and near the Wari core, such as Azángaro and Jargampata, were not political centers, but rather were probably specialized sites, providing economic support to Wari. And likewise, Willkaya, Anta, and Culluma were not political capitals, but small sites subsidiary to Jincamocco. But major centers certainly did exist out in the provinces, sometimes at great distance from Wari. And our sample of Wari sites is certainly incomplete.

If we can equate these complex architectural forms with direct political control, then what emerges is just a part of the Wari mosaic of control. What we can see is a series of sites, discrete pockets of direct control, stretching from Cuzco to Cajamarca. But what lies between and around these pockets? Typically, to identify the Wari presence, a Wari site is required. But as I have made clear in general terms, and in the specific case of the Inka, an imperial mosaic of control includes many other forms of control, forms that do not require the establishment of major administrative centers. The lack of a Wari site in a particular region cannot be taken alone to indicate the absence of any form of Wari control. We still lack evidence of indirect Wari control in those regions lacking clear Wari administrative centers.

We are, unfortunately, still at the level in most areas of approaching an empire from the perspective of imperial sites. What are lacking are regional data indicating other changes that might indicate foreign political control, especially changes in local political organization, and changes in local settlement patterns.

A characteristic of an empire, and one that sets it apart from other forms of political organization, is its diversity, which occurs along several lines. Empires include a diverse mix of ethnic groups. While Wari expanded from the Ayacucho Basin, characterized by Huarpa-style pottery, it moved into many different regions, each with its own ethnic identity. In archaeological terms we can equate regional artifact styles with interaction spheres, and in turn with particular ethnic groups. The Carhuarazo Valley was occupied by a distinct ethnic group; artifact styles in the valley likewise distinguish this valley from adjacent regions. It is not unlikely that Wari encountered a different ethnic group in each major valley or region. Extending from Cuzco to Cajamarca, it included a wide diversity of ethnic groups.

Empires control a diverse mix of ecological zones. Given the nature of the Andean environment, any expanding state must necessarily control a wide variety of environments. Wari sites are certainly found in ecologically diverse regions. Interestingly, however, the distribution of Wari sites is limited to the puna sierra; Wari did not extend north into the páramo sierra, or south into the altiplano/dry puna sierra.

Finally, the diversity of different levels of control is a critical variable in defining empires. Empires develop what I have called a mosaic of control. They use different strategies in different regions, depending in part on the needs of the empire, and in part on the level of extant political organization. In some areas direct control is imposed, and the imperial system created. In other areas, control is less direct, and may rely on local collaboration. Such areas are fully consolidated into the imperial administrative system, yet do not evidence intrusive facilities.

In the case of Wari, we see a wide distribution of Wari sites that probably represent pockets of direct control. Between these pockets we should expect to find other forms of control, from the very indirect, to the more direct. The lack of archaeological evidence of Wari administration in a particular region may have very little to do with the actual level of imperial control. So in the case of an empire, we should expect to find a good number of regions with direct imperial control, but many regions without direct control. This may be exactly what we are seeing in the Middle Horizon.

Wari evidences aspects of imperialism as well in the speed of its expansion and the duration of its existence. It would appear, on the basis of relative dating, that the expansion was quite rapid, taking place primarily in epoch 1B of the Middle Horizon—probably within two or three generations. Likewise, its duration was probably quite short, best estimated at about 150 years or so, again using the relative chronology developed in the Ica Valley.

In sum, available data are consistent with the interpretation that Wari was an imperialist state. It controlled a very large territory, from Cuzco to Cajamarca in the highlands, and possibly the coast as well. It was a territory that was ethnically and ecologically diverse. It expanded very rapidly, and lasted perhaps only 150 years. Above all, there is good evidence of direct Wari political control over a series of discrete regions; this gives us a glimpse of the most direct forms of Wari control, within the total mosaic of different forms of control.

The Wari Expansion

In Chapter 3, I summarized the evidence for the consolidation of the Wari core. The distribution of the Huarpa style of ceramics, dating to the Early Intermediate period, probably gives us the best approximation of the boundaries of the preexpansion Wari core region. While these boundaries are poorly defined to the north and west, they do include the eastern portions of the Cachi drainage, what is usually referred to as the Ayacucho Basin. Settlement pattern changes indicate that Wari grew into a major city, regional center, and capital of an empire in Middle Horizon 1. Once Wari developed into a regional state, it rapidly turned into an expanding empire; it is possible that state and empire emerged as part of a single process.

Beyond the Ayacucho Basin, a number of interesting things seem to have been happening elsewhere in the central Andean region. The Nasca civilization of the south coast underwent some major changes, perhaps several centuries prior to the Wari expansion. The Nasca center at Cahuachi had been abandoned at the end of Nasca 4, and during Nasca 5 there was a major shift in settlement patterns, and the construction of a system of aqueducts. By Nasca 7 times there is evidence of stylistic interaction between the south coast, the north coast, and the central highlands. Nasca 7 pottery began to share motifs with the Huarpa style, and even certain Moche designs—and Moche warriors—were depicted on Nasca pots. On the north coast, the Moche polity had reached its peak, its maximum spatial extent, in Moche IV times—immediately prior to the Middle Horizon. This, too, was about to change. Clearly the level of interregional interaction was more intensive than normal on the eve of the Wari expansion.

But why did Wari expand? While climatic and demographic factors might have set up certain conditions (Paulsen 1976), the human motivations behind the expansion remain elusive. Perhaps Wari went to war with and defeated their traditional enemies, some eighth century Chanka-like group, and just continued down the road of conquest. Perhaps they went out to confront some more distant rival, such as the remnants of Nasca or Moche. But we cannot know why the expansion began, relying as we must on only material cultural remains. We will never know the names of the Wari rulers, the conquering military leaders that led the Wari expansion.

The speed and the sequence of the Wari expansion are difficult to know, but we have some indications of some of the directions it took. The first line of evidence is the relative dating of Wari sites. Most of the Wari provincial sites, at least those that have been investigated up until now

The Middle Horizon and Andean Imperialism 269

(Pikillaqta, Cerro Baul, Jincamocco, Wari Willka, possibly Honco Pampa, and possibly Viracochapampa) seem to have been established in Middle Horizon 1B, given the presence of Chakipampa B–style ceramics at them. A few sites, such as Azángaro, appear to have been built in MH 2. So the great expansion would seem to have been mostly carried out in MH 1B, thought to be about 50 years long.

Radiocarbon dating, unfortunately, is of little help here. In the first place, to date the Wari expansion the best approach is to locate samples that indicate the construction date of each provincial site. Only in the case of Jincamocco are there dates that indicate construction; averaged and calibrated they suggest a date of construction at the end of the eighth century A.D. And as I have mentioned above, the precision of radiocarbon dating does not allow us to distinguish between events that took place within a single century or two. If the Wari empire lasted only 150 years, radiocarbon dates from its expansion, occupation, and demise will be virtually indistinguishable.

One line of evidence does perhaps suggest something about the sequence of the expansion. The distinctive Wari architectural style is not a style derived from any local Ayacucho tradition. Rather, Wari architecture most closely resembles the architecture of the northern part of the realm, the regions of Huamachuco and the Callejón de Huaylas. If Wari did adopt this style from the north, then it must have expanded to there prior to the construction of its other centers. This is not to say that Wari had not already expanded into other regions, but just that the sites it built in those regions postdate the Wari occupation of the north highlands.

Evidence for the Wari Mosaic of Control

I have already outlined in general terms the possible existence of a Wari mosaic of control, as evidenced by the existence of regional administrative centers and direct control throughout the highlands. Here let me discuss some of the sites and evidence, and suggest a few more aspects of this mosaic.

Wari Sites in the Sierra

The largest Wari provincial site, Pikillaqta, lies near the southern boundary of the distribution of the horizon style. No other sites with Wari architecture lie beyond it. Further, Gordon McEwan has suggested that a series of walls were built to restrict access to and from the south, and that there was a major Wari occupation in the region, apparent at several other sites in the region around Pikillaqta (McEwan 1979, 1985, 1987, 1989). There is little doubt that Wari directly controlled this region.

But why such an extreme occupation? The region is not particularly productive, nor is there indication of major population density. I suspect that the proximity of Pikillaqta to the border of Wari control may have had something to do with the extremely large size of the site. This boundary looks to have been fortified, given the presence of the walls, and the large size of the site, completed with a large sector of storehouses, might have provided quarters for military forces near the border. It is interesting to note that the only major political organization that existed beyond this boundary was Tiwanaku.

There is also data from two valleys in which Wari sites were not located. In the Chicha/Soras Valley, just to the east of the Carhuarazo Valley, no Wari site was found, although there was clear evidence of some sort of Wari influence. Unfortunately, the valley seems to have been unoccupied prior to the Middle Horizon, so no changes in settlement patterns can be measured to indicate a change in political or economic organization. Population was quite low in the Middle Horizon, and perhaps devoted to camelid herding for the empire (Meddens 1985, 1989).

And recent survey of the Chuquibamba Valley, in Arequipa, indicates a similar pattern. Occupation was sparse during the Middle Horizon, with no evidence of any Wari center; the valley had been unoccupied prior to this time (Sciscento 1989). These two valleys would suggest that perhaps population was increasing at a greater rate during the Middle Horizon, or that people were moving around and into new territories more than in earlier periods. But in both these valleys, although Wari sherds were located, no other evidence of Wari control was found. Either these valleys were ruled very indirectly, or, given their extremely low population and lack of any centralized organization, the empire simply did not pay much attention to them.

Finally, farthest to the south is the site of Cerro Baul, in Moquegua. This area lies outside the Wari sphere; it is within the distribution of Tiwanaku styles. This site was probably not any sort of administrative center, and there is no indication of any Wari control of the region. It is significant that this is the only Wari site in a clearly defensive location, and an extreme one at that. We have no way of knowing at this point exactly what Wari was doing in Tiwanaku territory, but it seems clear that local relations were not friendly (Feldman 1989).

To the north of Wari we find a whole string of sites along the spine of the Andes: Wari Willka (Flores 1959), Calpish (MacNeish, Patterson and Browman 1975), Yanahuanca, and Wisajirca (ibid.). Each of these sites is located in a region of probably relatively high population density, and likewise indicates direct Wari control of each region. In the Callejón de Huaylas, Wari political control is evidenced at three possible sites: Honco Pampa (Isbell 1989), Tocroc and Pariamarca (Williams and Pineda 1985).

The case of Viracochapampa is especially interesting, given that not only is it one of the largest Wari sites known, but that it was never finished (McCown 1945; J. Topic 1985; J. Topic and T. Topic 1985; T. Topic and J. Topic 1984). Here we have a situation in which, whatever was intended at the start, the strategy was altered. The construction of such a huge facility would suggest that Wari intended some sort of major occupation of the region, probably involving direct political control of this region. However, its extreme size would suggest that there was something particularly noteworthy about this region. This region was characterized by some of the most complex political organization encountered by Wari. The major site at Marca Huamachuco was the focus of local political power before and during the Middle Horizon.

The fact the site was never finished and never occupied indicates quite clearly that Wari changed its strategy at some point. Perhaps the change in Wari strategy was occasioned by a change in the strategy of the local polity—local elites at Marca Huamachuco decided to cooperate. Or, perhaps the Wari strategy changed, and political control of the region was no longer a priority, and only indirect relations were established. Whatever the explanation, Viracochapampa offers a cautionary situation: this large site was never the focus of any form of Wari control. This may be the case, as well, with any of the unexcavated sites that seem to have Wari-style architecture.

Beyond Viracochapampa, three sites have been located in and near the Cajamarca Basin that have tentatively been identified as Wari sites: Ichabamba (Williams and Pineda 1985), Yamobamba (Hyslop 1984), and El Palacio (Julien 1988). Again, this was probably a region of relatively high population density. These sites represent the end of the distribution of Wari sites, and therefore, probably the limits of any direct Wari political control. Wari Horizon-style artifacts do extend farther to the north, however, but these do not necessarily indicate any form of political control beyond Cajamarca.

The Wari Occupation of the Coast

The situation on the coast is quite different. No Wari sites, built in distinctive Wari architecture, are yet known from the coast of Peru. If Wari provincial sites indicate direct control, then the lack of such sites indicates either indirect control, or that the Wari empire did not control any of the coast. It is also possible that we just have not yet been able to define coastal forms of Wari administrative architecture. But regardless of these problems, it does seem that the Wari occupation of the coast was in some ways very different from that of the highlands.

The Nasca region had strong ties to Wari, given the presence of ceramic styles closely related to Wari: Nasca 9 in Middle Horizon 1, Atarco in MH 2. This has been interpreted to mean that Nasca was related to but independent of Wari. But the evidence of ceramic styles still requires other forms of supporting evidence. All of the ceramics known so far come from cemeteries, and the offering deposits.

Despite decades of research in Nasca and Ica, systematic regional surveys have only recently been undertaken. Thus, although it seems that the Nasca culture declined in Nasca 4, we do not know what sort of political centralization existed in the region at the time of the Wari incursion. Further, we do not have data to evaluate changes in settlement patterns that might have occurred commensurate with this event.

In sum, on the south coast, there is no evidence of any direct political control by Wari, nor do we have any data regarding local political organization at this time. However, the distinct Wari horizon styles so typical of this region do indicate some sort of Wari presence. It would appear that Wari control, if it existed at all, was toward the indirect end of the spectrum.

The central coast is somewhat different. There were large, dense populations occupying the central coast at such sites as Cajamarquilla, in the Rimac Valley. But again, no intrusive Wari sites have ever been located. The case of Pachacamac is especially important. This large ceremonial site—with perhaps a large resident population—was established in Middle Horizon 2. The ceramic style associated with site is very closely related to Wari styles of the highlands, but it differs in that it depicts one distinctive icon lacking in the Wari repertory. This stylistic independence of Pachacamac is interpreted to indicate its political independence from Wari as well. Again, supporting data are yet lacking, but it is clear that the distinctive Pachacamac style had a wide distribution on the coast, south to Ica and north to Supe, related to, but independent of, the Wari style. If Pachacamac operated in the Middle Horizon in some ways similar to its Late Horizon operation, then perhaps the spread of the local elite style was due to the influence of the oracle. And this might have operated perfectly well within the bounds of Wari political control, as was the case under the Inka empire.

In any case, the case of the central coast remains unresolved, as, outside of Pachacamac, the Wari occupation of the central coast would appear to be either indirect or nonexistent. However, the existence of a major and influential oracle within and under Wari political control is both reasonable, given the Inka-Pachacamac case, and consistent with extant data.

The Wari occupation of the north coast is a problem. Decades ago Kroeber (1930:111) reported the presence of Middle Horizon ceramics on the north coast, and suggested that these might represent an invasion from the sierra; Larco (1948) also made a similar argument, based on his own research in the north. Since then, some investigators have agreed with this position (Menzel 1964), while others have argued against it (Mackey 1982). The direct evidence of Wari is slight, but all investigators agree that major cultural changes occurred in the Middle Horizon. The Moche state had controlled a large portion of the north coast since at least Moche III times. Beginning with the development of the Moche core, in the Moche and Chicama valleys in Moche I and II, the Moche III styles of ceramics and architecture appear suddenly and intrusively in the next two valleys to the south: Virú and Santa. There is no doubt that these valleys were incorporated into the Moche polity at this time. In each valley a major center was established, with architecture following the tenets of the constructions at the Huaca del Sol and Huaca de la Luna. Additional sites form a hierarchy of secondary and tertiary sites, indicating a clear political hierarchy. In the following phase, the same things happens in the next valley, Nepeña, but the Moche occupation there is evidenced by fewer sites, and all these are clustered around the center at Pañamarca.

So the Moche polity, which was undoubtedly organized at the level of a state, controlled territory from Chicama to Nepeña, and as Moseley (1983) says, the state was so tightly integrated that it verged on being culturally homogeneous. But in Moche V something happened. The Moche capital was abandoned, as were all the centers in the valleys south of Moche. A new capital was established in the north, in the Lambayeque region, and the Moche valley became the southern frontier, rather than the center, of the newly reorganized polity. The site of Galindo is the only major site in the Moche Valley at this time, and may have functioned as a secondary site under direction from Pampa Grande (Bawden 1982).

There is no disagreement that Moche V corresponds to the beginning of the Middle Horizon, and that at that time the Moche state made a sudden move north. It seems an interesting coincidence that this should have occurred at about the time of the Wari expansion.

On the other hand, the direct evidence of any Wari presence on the north coast is scanty at best. There is no architectural evidence of any intrusive Wari sites. Wari ceramics do occur on the north coast, but in very low frequencies. However, the context of these ceramics does bear some examination. Four Wari-style keros were excavated from the Huaca del Sol itself (Mackey 1982: 325), all in mortuary contexts. In the survey of the Moche valley barely a dozen Wari sherds were located in surface collections; and only 14 Wari sherds were located in Virú (Mackey 1982: 325). Wilson's recent survey of the Santa Valley has turned up very few sherds that he identifies as Wari, but he does indicate (Wilson 1988: 489) that some pertain to a central coast style (by which he means Pachacamac).

Wilson has found such a notable presence of Black-White-Red ceramics in Santa in the Middle Horizon that he has suggested the existence of the "Black-White-Red State" that stretched at least from Santa to Casma. This would certainly explain the presence of similar sherds in the not-too-distant Moche valley. But it must be pointed out that such ceramics, which have geometric designs similar to fancy Wari styles (Mackey 1982: 325-326), are certainly Middle Horizon in date. And Black-White-Red ceramics with geometric designs are known on Wari sites, as in the case of Jincamocco. Certainly this style deserves careful analysis in order to define any regional differences between examples from the north coast, and those found on known Wari sites.

Prior to the Middle Horizon, Moche burials were extended. During the Middle Horizon a new pattern was introduced, and burials were interred seated and flexed from that period until the European invasion. Mackey suggests that this pattern was introduced from the central coast (probably via Pachacamac), and that this is the only possible evidence of Wari influence in the Moche region (1982:327). Wari burials are typically seated and flexed. What is important here is the fact that the Black-White-Red ceramics are associated with the seated flexed burials (ibid.:330), thus adding support to the interpretation that this style is associated with Wari, as well.

The data from the north coast, rather than casting doubt on the existence of the Wari empire, or its conquest of this region, actually provide the best case from the coast of Wari conquest and control. As I have argued in theoretical terms, and demonstrated in the case of the Inka, imperial control is not necessarily direct in all regions. Hence the archaeological evidence of imperial control can range from major reorganizations and huge administrative centers on the one hand, to minimal reorganization and few examples of imperial styles on the other. What are the data from the north coast? (1) There are Wari materials present on the north coast. (2) There is evidence of a major change in local political organization at the time that the Wari styles appear. (3) There is a major change in burial patterns, which is in turn associated with an intrusive style of pottery. (4) The greatest concentrations of Wari materials are associated with the former capital of the earlier polity. Given what we know of the Inka conquest of the Chimú state, these are exactly the sorts of evidence we should expect in the case of Wari conquest. In fact, it may be that the evidence for Wari conquest of the north coast is actually greater than that of the later Inka conquest.

Now, while the evidence from the north coast is consistent with the idea of Wari conquest, I only suggest this interpretation as a plausible alternative. Conversely, the Moche may have perceived the Wari threat (or some other threat; see, for example, Bawden 1982:320) and moved north by choice. There may have been no Wari conquest or control of the territory abandoned by Moche. Or the Moche move may have had nothing whatsoever to do with Wari. The presence of Wari styles could be a result of trade, or of the influence of the powerful religious cult emanating out of Pachacamac.

In any case, we do not have sufficient data to completely support any of these views. It is my view that the remains of the Wari occupation of the north coast are exactly what we should expect to find in the case of imperial takeover. In an area with a well-developed political organization, it is in the best interest of the empire to leave the system relatively intact. In the case of Moche, only part of the system was left to Wari, but we do see the greatest concentration of Wari remains associated with the former capital. As in the Inka conquest of the Chimú, the state may have been dismantled, and each valley ruled as a separate province.

In sum, current data from the coast of Peru are probably best interpreted as suggesting that coastal regions were only indirectly incorporated into the Wari empire. Perhaps the best evidence of Wari conquest comes from the north coast where the Moche polity fragmented at about the time of the Wari advance. Although we see no Wari sites on the north coast, changes in local culture, and the distribution of Wari remains are exactly what we might expect in the case of Wari conquest of a complex political organization. We know from the Inka example that the archaeological evidence of their conquest of the north coast is equally elusive; but the Middle Horizon data are perhaps even clearer than the later period. The central coast is not as well known, but the emergence of Pachacamac in Middle Horizon 2 may not have been independent of Wari political control. The south coast is the least well studied, but no clear Wari sites have yet been identified there. Again, control may have been relatively indirect. Thus, the lack of Wari sites, and lack of evidence of direct Wari control distinguish the coast from the highlands in the Middle Horizon.

THE WARI EMPIRE

Data currently available are entirely consistent with the notion that the Wari expansion was an imperial one and the Wari imperialism was responsible for the widespread distribution of the Wari horizon styles. Wari conquered much of the central Andes, and established political and economic control over its domain.

The Wari domain is quite large, extending from Cuzco to Cajamarca in the sierra, and possibly extending to the coast as well. While Wari began as a small local polity in the Ayacucho Basin, at its maximum extent its realm probably included dozens of equivalent regions. This was a realm of great ethnic and ecological diversity.

The relative chronology would indicate that the Wari expansion was extremely rapid, and that the empire did not last very long. Most Wari sites have ceramics of the Chakipampa B style, indicating that most of the expansion took place in Middle Horizon 1B. Each phase of the Middle Horizon, 1B, 2A and 2B, is estimated to have lasted only about 50 years, based on the Ica sequence. If this is accurate, the Wari empire lasted only about 150 years.

Absolute dating is, unfortunately, not of much use here. As I have pointed out, radiocarbon dating is too imprecise to distinguish between events that happened within a single century or two. At best we can say that the Wari empire rose and fell sometime in the second half of the first millennium. While we might suggest a rough date of the late eighth century for the initial expansion, we have no direct means of dating the collapse of Wari. But regardless of these problems, all lines of evidence suggest that the expansion was very rapid, and that the empire did not endure for very long.

Finally, the best evidence of the existence of the Wari empire is the distribution of pockets of direct control throughout the highlands. While the lack of Wari sites in many regions is certainly due to the fact that Wari sites did not exist everywhere, I also suspect that there are quite a few Wari provincial sites still out there that have not been identified. But more importantly, what we are lacking are regional studies of local sites and settlement patterns. If Wari were truly an empire we should expect to find a diversity of strategies of consolidation, a mosaic of control, not direct control in every valley. Sudden changes in local political organization, coupled with the presence of Wari artifacts—even in low numbers—may signal changes that were the result of the Wari expansion.

As we saw in the Inka case, the distribution of sites of different sizes indicates something about strategic locations, and regions lacking sufficient local centralization. But the sites do not fall into a hierarchical arrangement that directly documents the administrative hierarchy. This is likely true in the case of Wari as well. It is clear that Wari was the capital of the empire, but we cannot define sites in secondary and tertiary levels of the administrative hierarchy on the basis of their size.

So while our sample of Wari sites is probably very incomplete, and while most of the highlands still await investigations of the Middle Horizon, we still can make a good case to suggest that, in absolute terms, Wari was an empire.

Wari Ideology

As discussed in earlier chapters, empires typically develop ideologies that serve to promote and maintain the imperial systems of control. We can perhaps see elements of this in the iconography of the Wari Empire. Throughout the Wari domain are seen the ideological symbols, the iconography of power, left behind by the empire. Images of the Staff Deity, that supreme deity depicted in anthropomorphic form, were brought to all corners of the empire. Where the full depiction was not brought, at least the abbreviated form, the bodiless mythical front-face deity, was seen. More human symbols of power were also included in the expansion: the great face-neck jars, with realistically modeled and unique faces, possibly representing the actual Wari ruling elite. These were depicted in full regalia, complete with mythical creatures on their clothing, further legitimizing their authority.

Not only does the mythical content of Wari iconography indicate a strong focus on ideological power, so too does the context in which these artifacts are found. At Jincamocco, most of the vessels with mythical attributes were found together on the fine platform structure, suggesting some ceremonial activity within the site. While such a ceremony may have been largely political in content, the ideological symbols were there to reinforce the power of the actors.

The main context in which Wari iconography is known is, of course, the offering tradition. The intentional destruction and burial of the ideological symbols of power is seen in a variety of places and settings. These offerings have been interpreted as being the result of ceremonial behavior associated with the empire. This supports the notion of a strong ideological component to the establishment of Wari power.

An alternative interpretation of the offering deposits, one that likewise indicates the power symbolized by these icons, is that the destruction of the symbols of Wari power might have occurred at the time of the Wari collapse. In the case of Jincamocco, it is possible that the destruction of the fancy vessels was the result of vandalism at the time the site was abandoned. But might not the offerings have been the result of intentional destruction of the symbols of power, the symbols of imperialist oppression, by people suddenly freed from the imperial yoke? The fact that the offerings are usually found in unstructured pits indicates that not a great deal of care went into preparing a place to bury the offerings. A critical aspect of the offering seems to have been the destruction of the symbols—even with a blow to the face or the chest in some cases.

What We Don't Know about Wari

While we can just make out the outlines of the Wari empire, there are still important pieces missing. Most of all, we need more research both to find Wari sites, and to look for other changes that might be associated with the expansion of Wari control.

The lack of Wari sites in some regions may be due to the nature of the Wari occupation. Unless control was direct, no administrative center was built. So in areas of more indirect forms of control, intrusive Wari administrative sites do not exist. But there are several other reasons for the current paucity of Wari sites. The first problem is a pragmatic one: preservation. Wari sites are at least twelve centuries old, and have generally fallen into serious disrepair. In the Carhuarazo Valley, three of the four Wari sites have been intentionally dismantled; and the fourth was so poorly preserved that its exact plan could not be seen on the surface. Not only were Wari sites plundered in prehistoric times (a process that continues today), but they may be obscured under later sites. In particular, the Inka may have used the locations of Wari sites for some of their own facilities. In the case of the Carhuarazo Valley, two of the four Wari sites, Jincamocco and Culluma, have Inka remains on or immediately adjacent to them.

A second problem is the recognition of Wari sites. A Wari site is best recognized by the similarity of its architecture to the well-defined highland Wari style, and the presence of Wari horizon styles on its surface. There may exist other forms of Wari architecture that have not yet been defined. Even in the cases of sites that seem to have Wari architecture, it is a curious fact that these sites often have no diagnostic artifacts on the surface. Rowe, Collier, and Willey (1950) pointed out this problem when they tried to determine the cultural affiliation of Viracochapampa and Pikillaqta. As recently as 1988, Julien tentatively identified two sites as Wari sites, but noted that they have no artifacts of the surface that might confirm this identification. In the Carhuarazo Valley, no Wari sites had great quantities of surface material; and one of the Wari sites had no Wari ceramics on it, but did have local Middle Horizon sherds. It is very possible that a number of other Wari sites are known to archaeologists, but have not been defined as Wari sites owing to the lack of surface artifacts.

The third major problem in the identification of Wari highland sites is the lack of research in the sierra. Nearly all research has been devoted to the large urbanized valleys: Cuzco, Ayacucho, Junín, the Callejón de Huaylas. Very little research has been aimed at regions that today are marginal. Areas such as the Carhuarazo Valley, or Chuquibamba, or the Chicha/Soras Valley are difficult of access, and not particularly comfortable places in which to live and work. But the few that have been investigated have produced some interesting results.

WARI AND TIWANAKU

One of the biggest, and most important, areas in which we lack data and objective interpretation lies in the relationship between Wari and Tiwanaku. For over a century it has been clear that Wari and Tiwanaku artifact styles resemble each other very much. It is also clear that they are not the same, and that the two styles have complementary but discontinuous spatial distributions. Under normal circumstances we would not hesitate to say that these are distinctly different cultures. But the similarity in the iconography does present the possibility of some sort of close relationship between the two cultures.

The situation is compounded by the fact that Tiwanaku has been known for centuries, while Wari did not come to the attention of archaeologists until the 1930s. Further, Tiwanaku iconography is depicted on very impressive carved stones; this alone has led people to assume that Tiwanaku was the point of origin of the iconography.

The exact temporal relationship between Wari and Tiwanaku is impossible to know at present, except to say that they were probably roughly contemporaneous, both reaching their greatest development in the second half of the first millennium A.D. Relative dating depends on stylistic comparison; since the two styles differ in many ways, exact comparisons cannot be drawn. Absolute dating can indicate rough contemporaneity, but unless one culture is several centuries earlier than the other, radiocarbon dating is, unfortunately, not sufficiently precise to separate them.

There are other important similarities between the two cultures: they both produced horizon styles, and they both expanded over a fairly large region at roughly the same time. If we can support the interpretation that Wari was an empire, can the same be said about Tiwanaku?

It is not unlikely that two empires can exist near one another, but without overlap. Bipolar and multipolar political settings have been known in other places and at other times. Indications are that Tiwanaku was a major urban site that reorganized the economic exploitation of the altiplano (Kolata 1986). Further, other Tiwanaku sites are found throughout the altiplano, and south into Chile and Argentina (Mujica et al. 1983; Nuñez 1965; Rivera 1976, 1980). A system of roads in Bolivia may date to Tiwanaku times (Stothert 1967). Indications at present suggest that Tiwanaku may have been the capital of a large political empire (Browman 1978, 1980, 1985).

If two expanding polities existed side by side, and each expansion was limited by the presence of the other, relations between the two might not have been entirely friendly. And, indeed, this may be apparent in the case of Cerro Baul, a heavily fortified Wari site located in Tiwanaku territory

(Feldman 1989). Further, the large site at Pikillaqta and the fortified borders near that site might indicate that relations with the polity to the southeast were not amicable.

But there are some intriguing differences between Wari and Tiwanaku that suggest some differences between the two polities. First, the two polities are located in significantly different highland environments. While Wari extended through the length of the puna sierra, Tiwanaku was located in the dry puna/altiplano. The basic subsistence adaptation within the Wari realm is one of intensive exploitation of compressed vertical zones. In the Tiwanaku region, extensive systems involving the establishment of distant colonies—the archipelago system—was the norm, at least in late prehistoric times. So the basic economic adaptation of each polity was slightly different, and this might suggest that the resultant forms of political organization might also differ in some ways.

Even more interesting is the more subtle difference between the two polities in terms of their kind of iconography, and the layout of their sites. Tiwanaku iconography is depicted on immovable objects, very impressive ones to be sure, in the capital city. The ceremonial district in which the icons were located was designed to accommodate people, to bring people in. Wari iconography, on the other hand, was depicted on portable objects that could be taken out into the empire. And the great rectangular enclosures of Wari sites seem designed to restrict access and keep people out, than to invite them in.

In other words, the Tiwanaku system seems to be set up to bring people to the capital, rather than to bring the iconography to the people. In many ways this is typical of the Andean tradition of pilgrimage centers, such as Chavín or Pachacamac. But Tiwanaku was clearly much more than a pilgrimage center; it involved forms of extensive political and economic control as well. Wari, in sharp contrast, did not bring people to the icons, it took the icons to the people. Even Wari itself has no large open areas that might have served ceremonial purposes similar to those at Tiwanaku.

Thus, both Wari and Tiwanaku were probably roughly contemporary. Without more precise dating, it is not possible to demonstrate that one culture developed out of the other, or was subsidiary to the other. In part because Tiwanaku was so impressive and so well known from early research, "Coast Tiahuanaco" styles were seen to have had their ultimate origins at Tiwanaku. Even today, this old confusion colors interpretations of the Middle Horizon, and Wari is sometimes seen as having been later than and subsidiary to Tiwanaku. Based on present data, this does not appear to be the case.

Both Tiwanaku and Wari were large political organizations, and perhaps both were empires, occupying different kinds of highland environments. But there would seem to be a very basic and profound difference between Wari and Tiwanaku, in the manner in which they depicted their respective (but in many ways shared) ideological symbols, and in the manner in which the capital interacted with subject people.

There is still a very great deal that we do not know about the Middle Horizon.

WARI AND THE INKA

The Inka example has proved useful in discerning aspects of provincial control in an Andean setting, and variations in those strategies. In some ways the earlier Wari polity seems quite similar to the late Inka empire. But there are some interesting differences as well.

Both Wari and the Inka appear to have expanded rapidly out of a core area and established a mosaic of control over a huge territory. The Inka expansion was accomplished in two generations, as known from documents written at the time of the Spanish conquest. There are no data that directly indicate the speed of the Wari expansion, but the chronology developed on the south coast suggests that the expansion was rapid. Both polities were of short duration; the Wari lasted perhaps 150 years (again, based on the south coast chronology), and the Inka empire was cut off by the Spanish invasion after less than a century. Both empires probably used a variety of strategies of control ranging from very indirect to direct, resulting in what might be called discontinuous territoriality, or a "mosaic of control." This is clear in the case of the Inka, and strongly indicated in the Wari case by good evidence of pockets of direct control spread throughout its domain. In all these aspects, the Wari and Inka are similar to each other, and generally like other archaic empires.

While the motivations behind the Wari expansion are unknown, the Inka expansion began for largely political reasons: the defeat of their traditional enemies, the Chanka. And after the political restructuring of conquered territories, Inka attention turned to economic reorganization and the continuing acquisition of tribute, in that case, in the form of human labor. Wari, too, may have imposed political control initially, but quickly turned to economic concerns as well. In the case of the Carhuarazo Valley, the Wari conquest incurred the construction of a moderately sized facility, perhaps for political reasons: the strategic location of the valley with respect to the south coast. But it appears in this case that a great focus of Wari concern in this region was economic in nature, and that the Wari strategy changed through time toward even more economic exploitation of the region.

But there are some critical differences as well between the Wari and Inka polities. While both empires were very large, and ethnically and ecologically diverse, the Inka was much larger and more diverse than the Wari.

Whether measured in territorial extent, population, or resource zones controlled, the Inka empire was at least four times the size of the Wari empire. Simply by virtue of its larger size, it included more diversity of cultures and environments.

But, the Wari and Inka differ qualitatively in terms of ecological diversity. Wari did not expand beyond the limits of the puna sierra. The Inka not only controlled the puna sierra, but moved north through the páramo sierra, and south through the dry puna/altiplano regions and down to coastal valleys.

The Inka controlled a greater diversity of highland environments than did the Wari, and imposed more direct forms of rule in some areas, and more indirect forms in others. So far, in the case of Wari, no intrusive Wari centers have been found on the coast that might indicate direct control. Thus far, all evidence from the coast suggests only indirect control, and perhaps even autonomous but related polities, such as Pachacamac.

The archaeological evidence of the two cultures also differs in that Inka remains are more apparent in those areas controlled by both empires. Inka sites, or Inka artifacts, are frequently encountered, while Wari remains are much rarer. This is probably due in part to differential preservation. Inka remains are younger than Wari remains, by at least 600 years, and are simply more likely to be preserved. Inka facilities were described in ethnohistoric documents, so we often know where they are without having to locate them with archaeological surveys; and even if they are no longer preserved, we know that they once existed. Wari remains on the other hand are in a poorer state of preservation, and we have no documentary evidence to tell us of their existence where they are not apparent.

The relative lack of Wari remains may also be due in part to natural and cultural processes that produced the remains, making them difficult to identify as Wari sites. It is curious that Wari provincial sites often have no diagnostic artifacts on their surface, as discussed above. This is in marked contrast to village sites, even ones older than the Middle Horizon, that always have abundant sherds on the surface. Unlike village habitation sites, Wari sites were never reoccupied. It seems as though Wari sites were abandoned and buried, almost intentionally forgotten.

There appear to have been differences as well in certain aspects of Wari and Inka culture, relating to the imposition of control. Wari iconography includes a great many images of great men and mythical beings, the symbols of Wari power, depicted on pottery and textiles, on portable media. Inka portable art is typically nonrepresentational, and designs simple and geometric in form. Inka power, like that of Tiwanaku, was manifest in the imperial capital at Cuzco, and in the person of the Inka emperor himself. Inka Cuzco was in many ways a great ceremonial center (Rowe 1967), with sacred precincts, and golden images. Like Tiwanaku, the capital was designed to bring people in to see the symbols of power, of Inka divinity. In this aspect Inka Cuzco resembles Tiwanaku much more than it does Wari.

Finally, while the Inka may have used some aspects of the old Wari infrastructure, perhaps its roads or the locations of some of its sites, there is little direct historical connection between the Wari and the Inka. Although the area of the Inka capital, Cuzco, had once been part of the Wari domain, the territory dominated by Pikillaqta, Wari had disappeared long ago. Many centuries had elapsed since the collapse of Wari, centuries filled with local and interregional warfare. The Inka had to start the process all over again.

Bibliography

Adams, Robert McC.
1965   Land behind Baghdad: A History of Settlement on the Diyala Plains. Chicago: University of Chicago Press.

1981   Heartland of Cities. Chicago: University of Chicago Press.

Adams, Robert McC., and Hans J. Nissen
1972   The Uruk Countryside: The Natural Setting of Urban Societies. Chicago: University of Chicago Press.

Anders, Martha B.
1986   Dual Organization and Calendars Inferred from the Planned Site of Azangaro—Wari Administrative Strategies. Unpublished PhD dissertation, Cornell University.

1989   Evidence for the dual socio-political organization and administrative structure of the Wari state. In: The Nature of Wari: A Reappraisal of the Middle Horizon Period in Peru, edited by R.M. Czwarno, F.M. Meddens and A. Morgan, pp. 35-52. BAR International Series 525.

Bawden, Garth
1982   Galindo: a study in cultural transition during the Middle Horizon. In: Chan Chan: Andean Desert City, edited by Michael E. Moseley and Kent C. Day, pp. 285-320. Albuquerque: University of New Mexico Press.

Benavides, Mario
1971   Análisis de la cerámica Huarpa. Revista del Museo Nacional 37:63-88. Lima.

1976   Yacimientos arqueológicos en Ayacucho. Universidad Nacional de San Cristobal de Huamanga, Departamento Académico de Ciencias Histórico Sociales. Ayacucho, Peru.

1985   The Cheqo Wasi sector of Wari. Paper presented at the Huari Roundtable, Dumbarton Oaks, Washington, D.C.

Bennett, Wendell C.
1944   The north highlands of Peru. Anthropological Papers, American Museum of Natural History 39(1).

1946   The archaeology of the central Andes. In: Handbook of South American Indians, vol. 2, edited by Julian H. Steward. Bureau of American Ethnology, Bulletin 143. Washington, D.C.

1953   Excavations at Wari, Ayacucho, Peru. Yale University Publications in Anthropology 49. New Haven.

Betanzos, Juan de
1987   Suma y narración de los Incas [1551]. Transcripción, notas y prólogo por María del Carmen Martín Rubio. Ediciones Atlas, Madrid.

Betzig, Laura L.
1986   Despotism and Differential Reproduction: A Darwinian View of History. New York: Aldine.

Boone, James L., III
1986   Parental investment and elite family structure in preindustrial states: a case study of late Medieval-early modern Portuguese genealogies. American Anthropologist 88(4):859-78.

1987   Parental investment, social subordination, and population processes among the 15th and 16th century Portuguese nobility. In: Human Reproductive Behaviours: A Darwinian Perspective, edited by L.L. Betzig, M. Borgerhoff Mulder and P.W. Turke, pp. 201-219. Cambridge: Cambridge University Press.

Bragayrac, Enrique
1985   The Vegachayoq sector of Wari. Paper presented at the Huari Roundtable, Dumbarton Oaks, Washington, D.C.

Brewster-Wray, Christine C.
1983   Spatial patterning and the function of a Huari architectural compound. In: Investigations of the Andean Past, edited by Daniel H. Sandweiss, pp. 122-35. Ithaca: Cornell University Press.

1989   Excavations at Moraduchayoc, Huari. Unpublished Ph.D. dissertation, SUNY Binghamton.

Browman, David L.
1976   Demographic correlations of the Wari conquest of Junín. American Antiquity 41(4):465-77.

1978   Toward the development of the Tiahuanaco (Tiwanaku) state. In: Advances in Andean Archaeology, edited by David L. Browman, pp. 327-49. The Hague: Mouton.

1980   Tiwanaku expansion and altiplano economic patterns. Estudios Arqueológicos 5:107-20. Antofagasta.

1985   Cultural primacy of Tiwanaku in the development of later Peruvian states. Diálogo Andino 4:59-71.

Brush, Stephen B.
1977   Mountain, Field, and Family: The Economy and Human Ecology of an Andean Valley. Philadelphia: University of Pennsylvania Press.

Burger, Richard L., and Frank Asaro
1977   Análisis de rasgos significativos en la obsidiana de los Andes Centrales. Revista del Museo Nacional 43:281-325.

Buse, Hermann
1965   Introducción al Perú. Colegio Militar Leoncio Prado, Lima.

Carabajal, Pedro de
1881   Descripción fecha de la provincia de Vilcas Guaman por el illustre señor Don Pedro de Carabajal, corregidor y justicia mayor della, ante Xpistobal de Gamboa, escribano de su juzgado, en el año de 1586. Relaciones Geográficas de Indias— Perú, Tomo I, pp. 145-68. Congreso Internacional de Americanistas, Madrid.

Chávez, Karen L. Mohr
1982   The archaeology of Marcavalle, an Early Horizon Site in the Valley of Cuzco, Peru. Part I. Baessler-Archiv, n.F., Bd. 28, 1980, pp. 203-329. Berlin.

Cieza de León, Pedro de
1984   Crónica del Perú, primera parte (1553). Pontificia Universidad Católica del Perú, Lima.

Conrad, Geoffrey W.
1977   Chiquitoy Viejo: an Inca administrative center in the Chicama Valley, Peru. Journal of Field Archaeology 4:1-18.

1981   Cultural materialism, split inheritance, and the expansion of ancient Peruvian empires. American Antiquity 46(1):3-26.

Conrad, Geoffrey W., and Arthur A. Demarest
1984   Religion and Empire: The Dynamics of Aztec and Inca Expansionism. Cambridge: Cambridge University Press.

Cook, Anita G.
1979   The Iconography of Empire: Symbolic Communication in Seventh Century Peru. MA thesis, Department of Anthropology, SUNY Binghamton.

1985   Art and Time in the Evolution of Andean State Expansionism. Unpublished PhD dissertation, SUNY Binghamton.

Crosby, Alfred W.
1986   Ecological Imperialism: the Biological Expansion of Europe, 900-1900. Cambridge: Cambridge University Press.

Czwarno, R. Michael
1989   Social patterning and the investigation of political control: the case for the Moche/Chimu area. In: The Nature of Wari: A Reappraisal of the Middle Horizon Period in Peru, edited by R.M. Czwarno, F.M. Meddens and A. Morgan, pp. 115-45. BAR International Series 525.

D'Altroy, Terence N.
1981   Empire Growth and Consolidation: The Xauxa Region of Peru under the Incas. Unpublished PhD dissertation, University of California, Los Angeles.

1987   Transitions in power: centralization of Wanka political organization under Inka rule. Ethnohistory 34(1): 78-102. Special Issue: Inka Ethnohistory, edited by Terence N. D'Altroy.

D'Altroy, Terence N., and Timothy K. Earle
1985   Staple finance, wealth finance, and storage in the Inka political economy. Current Anthropology 26:187-206.

Day, Kent C.
1982   Ciudadelas: their form and function. In: Chan Chan: Andean Desert City, edited by Michael E. Moseley and Kent C. Day, pp. 55-66. School of American Research. Albuquerque: University of New Mexico Press.

de la Vera Cruz Chávez, Pablo
  1987   Cambio en los patrones de asentamiento y el uso y abandono de los andenes en Cabanaconde, Valle del Colca, Peru. In: Pre-Hispanic Agricultural Fields in the Andean Region, edited by W.M. Denevan, K. Mathewson, and G. Knapp. BAR International Series 389(1).

Demarest, Arthur A.
  1981   Viracocha: The Nature and Antiquity of the Andean High God. Peabody Museum Monographs 6. Harvard University, Cambridge.

Donkin, R. A.
  1979   Agricultural Terracing in the Aboriginal New World. Viking Fund Publications in Anthropology 56. Wenner-Gren Foundation for Anthropological Research, Inc. Tucson: University of Arizona Press.

Donnan, Christopher B.
  1968   An association of Middle Horizon epoch 2A specimens from the Chicama Valley, Peru. Ñawpa Pacha 6:15-18.

Doyle, Michael W.
  1986   Empires. Ithaca: Cornell University Press.

Dwyer, Edward B.
  1971   The Early Inca Occupation of the Valley of Cuzco, Peru. Unpublished doctoral dissertation, University of California, Berkeley.

Earle, Timothy K.
  1978   Economic and Social Organization of a Complex Chiefdom: The Halelea District, Kaua'i, Hawaii. Anthropological Papers, 63. University of Michigan Museum of Anthropology, Ann Arbor.

Earle, Timothy, Terence D'Altroy, Christine Hastorf, Catherine Scott, Cathy Costin, Glenn Russell, and Elsie Sandefur
  1987   Archaeological Field Research in the Upper Mantaro, Peru, 1982-1983: Investigations of Inka Expansion and Exchange. Monograph 28, Institute of Archaeology, University of California, Los Angeles.

Eisenstadt, S. N.
  1969   The Political Systems of Empires: The Rise and Fall of the Historical Bureaucratic Societies. New York: The Free Press.

Espinosa Soriano, Waldemar
  1973   Colonias de mitmas multiples en Abancay, siglos XV y XVI. Revista del Museo Nacional 39: 225-99. Lima.

Feldman, Robert A.
  1989   A speculative hypothesis of Wari southern expansion. In: The Nature of Wari: A Reappraisal of the Middle Horizon Period in Peru, edited by R.M. Czwarno, F.M. Meddens and A. Morgan, pp. 72-97. BAR International Series 525.

Flannery, Kent V.
  1972   The cultural evolution of civilization. Annual Review of Ecology and Systematics 3:399-426.

Flores Espinosa, Isabel
1959   El sitio arqueológico de Wari Willka, Huancayo. Actas y Trabajos del II Congreso Nacional de Historia del Perú 1:177-86. Lima.

Franquemont, Edward M
1986   The ancient pottery from Pucara, Peru. Ñawpa Pacha 24:1-30.

Grossman, Joel Warren
1983   Demographic change and economic transformation in the south-central highlands of pre-Huari Peru. Ñawpa Pacha 21:45-126.

Haas, Jonathan
1982   The Rise of the State. New York: Columbia University Press.

Hassig, Ross
1985   Trade, Tribute, and Transportation: The Sixteenth-Century Political Economy of the Valley of Mexico. Norman: University of Oklahoma Press.

Hastorf, Christine
1983   Prehistoric Agricultural Intensification and Political Development in the Jauja region of Peru. Unpublished PhD dissertation, University of California, Los Angeles.

Hodge, Mary G.
1984   Aztec City-States. Memoirs, 18. University of Michigan Museum of Anthropology, Ann Arbor.

Hyam, Ronald
1976   Britain's Imperial Century 1815-1914: A Study of Empire and Expansion. London: B.T. Batsford.

Hyslop, John
1984   The Inka Road System. New York: Academic Press.

INP-AG (Instituto Nacional de Planificación-Asesoria Geográfica)
1969   Atlas histórico geográfico y de paisajes peruanos. Lima, Peru.

Isbell, Billie Jean
1978   To Defend Ourselves: Ecology and Ritual in an Andean Village. Institute of Latin American Studies, University of Texas, Austin.

Isbell, William H.
1974   Ecología de la expansión de los Quechua-hablantes. Revista del Museo Nacional 40:139-55.

1977   The Rural Foundation for Urbanism: Economic and Stylistic Interaction between Rural and Urban Communities in Eighth-Century Peru. Urbana: University of Illinois Press.

1985   Conchopata, ideological innovator in Middle Horizon 1A. Ñawpa Pacha 22-23:91-126.

1987   State origins in the Ayacucho Valley, central highlands, Peru. In: The Origins and Development of the State in the Andes, edited by Jonathan Haas, Shelia Pozorski, and Thomas Pozorski, pp. 83-90. Cambridge: Cambridge University Press.

1988   City and state in Middle Horizon Wari. In: Peruvian Prehistory, edited by Richard W. Keatinge, pp. 164-89. Cambridge: Cambridge University Press.

1989   Honco Pampa: was it a Huari administrative centre? In: The Nature of Wari: A Reappraisal of the Middle Horizon Period in Peru, edited by R.M. Czwarno, F.M. Meddens and A. Morgan, pp. 98-114. BAR International Series 525.

Isbell, William H., Christine Brewster-Wray, and Lynda E. Spickard
1985   Huari and Moraduchayoq. Paper presented at the Huari Roundtable, Dumbarton Oaks, Washington, D.C.

Isbell, William H., and Katharina J. Schreiber
1978   Was Huari a state? American Antiquity 43(3): 372-89.

Julien, Daniel G.
1988   Ancient Cuismancu: Settlement and Cultural Dynamics in the Cajamarca Region of the North Highlands of Peru, 200 B.C.-A.D. 1532. Unpublished PhD dissertation, University of Texas at Austin.

Klein, Jeffrey, J.C. Lerman, P.E. Damon, and E.K. Ralph
1982   Calibration of radiocarbon dates. Radiocarbon 21(2):103-50.

Knobloch, Patricia J.
1976   A Study of the Huarpa Ceramic Style of the Andean Early Intermediate Period. Unpublished M.A. thesis, Department of Anthropology, SUNY Binghamton.

1983   A Study of Andean Huari Ceramics from the Early Intermediate Period to the Middle Horizon Epoch 1. Unpublished PhD dissertation, SUNY Binghamton.

Kolata, Alan L.
1983   The south Andes. In: Ancient South Americans, edited by Jesse D. Jennings, pp. 241-84. San Francisco: W H Freeman.

1986   The agricultural foundations of the Tiwanaku state: a view from the heartland. American Antiquity 51(4):748-62.

Kroeber, Alfred
1930   Archaeological Explorations in Peru: Part II, The Northern Coast. Field Museum of Natural History Memoirs 2(2). Chicago.

1944   Peruvian Archaeology in 1942. Viking Fund Publications in Anthropology 4. Wenner-Gren Foundation for Anthropological Research, New York.

LaLone, Mary B., and Darrell E. LaLone
1987   The Inka state in the southern highlands: state administrative and production enclaves. Ethnohistory 34(1):47-62. Special Issue: Inka Ethnohistory, edited by Terence N. D'Altroy.

Larco Hoyle, Rafael
1948   Cronología arqueológica del norte del Perú. Sociedad Geográfica Americana, Buenos Aires.

Bibliography 291

1966   Peru. Cleveland: The World Publishing Co.

Lattimore, Owen
1962   Studies in Frontier History: Collected Papers, 1928-1958. London: Oxford University Press.

Leach, Edmund R.
1954   Political Systems of Highland Burma. Boston: Beacon Press.

Lumbreras, Luis G.
1960   La cultura de Wari, Ayacucho. Etnología y Arqueología 1. Lima.

1974   The Peoples and Cultures of Ancient Peru. Translated by B. Meggers. Smithsonian Institution, Washington, D.C.

1975   Las Fundaciones de Huamanga. Lima: Editorial Nueva Educación.

1981   The stratigraphy of the open sites. In: Prehistory of the Ayacucho Basin, Peru, Vol. 2, Excavations and Chronology, edited by Richard S. MacNeish, et al., pp. 167-98. Ann Arbor: University of Michigan Press.

Luttwak, Edward N.
1976   The Grand Strategy of the Roman Empire, from the First Century A.D. to the Third. Baltimore: Johns Hopkins University Press.

Mackey, Carol J.
1982   The Middle Horizon as viewed from the Moche Valley. In: Chan Chan: Andean Desert City, edited by Michael E. Moseley and Kent C. Day, pp. 321-31. Albuquerque: University of New Mexico Press.

MacNeish, Richard S.
1981   Synthesis and conclusions. In: Prehistory of the Ayacucho Basin, Peru, Vol. 2, Excavations and Chronology, edited by Richard S. MacNeish, et al., pp. 199-257. Ann Arbor: University of Michigan Press.

MacNeish, Richard S., Thomas C. Patterson, and David L. Browman
1975   The Central Peruvian Prehistoric Interaction Sphere. Papers of the Robert S. Peabody Foundation for Archaeology, 7. Andover.

MacNeish, Richard S., Antoinette Nelken-Turner, and Angel García Cook
1981   Introduction. In: Prehistory of the Ayacucho Basin, Peru, Vol. 2, Excavations and Chronology, edited by Richard S. MacNeish, et al., pp. 1-18. Ann Arbor: University of Michigan Press.

McCown, Theodore D.
1945   Pre-Incaic Huamachuco: survey and excavations in the northern sierra of Peru. University of California Publications in American Archaeology and Ethnology 39(4):223-400.

McEwan, Gordon F.
1979   Principles of Wari Settlement Planning. Unpublished Master's thesis, Department of Anthropology, University of Texas at Austin.

1985   The Pikillacta site and its context. Paper presented at the Huari Roundtable, Dumbarton Oaks, Washington, D.C.

1987   The Middle Horizon in the Valley of Cuzco, Peru: The Impact of the Wari Occupation of the Lucre Basin. BAR International Series 372.

1989   The Wari empire in the southern Peruvian highlands: a view from the provinces. In: The Nature of Wari: A Reappraisal of the Middle Horizon Period in Peru, edited by R.M. Czwarno, F.M. Meddens and A. Morgan, pp. 53-71. BAR International Series 525.

Meddens, Frank M.
1985   The Chicha/Soras Valley during the Middle Horizon: Provincial Aspect of Huari. Unpublished PhD dissertation, Institute of Archaeology, University of London.

1989   Implications of camelid management and textile production for Huari. In: The Nature of Wari: A Reappraisal of the Middle Horizon Period in Peru, edited by R.M. Czwarno, F.M. Meddens and A. Morgan, pp. 146-66. BAR International Series 525.

Menzel, Dorothy
1959   The Inca occupation of the south coast of Peru. Southwestern Journal of Anthropology 15(2): 125-42.

1964   Style and time in the Middle Horizon. Ñawpa Pacha 2:1-105.

1968   New data on the Huari Empire in Middle Horizon epoch 2A. Ñawpa Pacha 6:47-114.

1977   The Archaeology of Ancient Peru and the Work of Max Uhle. Lowie Museum of Anthropology, University of California, Berkeley.

Menzel, Dorothy, and John H. Rowe
1967   The role of Chincha in late pre-Spanish Peru. Ñawpa Pacha 4:63-76.

Menzel, Dorothy, John H. Rowe and Lawrence E. Dawson
1964   The Paracas Pottery of Ica: A Study in Style and Time. University of California Publications in American Archaeology and Ethnology 50. Berkeley: University of California Press.

Molina de Cuzco, Cristóbal de
1942   Relación de las fábulas y ritos de los Incas. Las crónicas de los Molinas. Los Pequeños Grandes Libros de Historia Americana, serie 1, tomo 4, second paging. Lib. e Imp. D. Miranda, Lima

Monzón, Luis de
1881a   Descripción de la tierra del repartimiento de Atunsora, encomendado en Hernando Palomino, jurisdición de la ciudad de Guamanga. Año de 1586. Relaciones Geográficas de Indias—Perú, Tomo I, pp. 169-77. Congreso Internacional de Americanistas, Madrid.

1881b   Descripción de la tierra del repartimiento de los Rucanas Antamarcas de la corona real, jurisdición de la ciudad de Guamanga. Año de 1586. Relaciones Geográficas de Indias—Perú, Tomo I, pp. 197-215. Congreso Internacional de Americanistas, Madrid.

1881c Descripción de la tierra del repartimiento de San Francisco de Atunrucana y Laramati, encomendado en Don Pedro de Cordova, jurisdición de la ciudad de Guamanga. Año de 1586. Relaciones Geográficas de Indias—Perú, Tomo I, pp. 179-96. Congreso Internacional de Americanistas, Madrid.

Morris, Craig
1972 State settlements in Tawantinsuyu: a strategy of compulsory urbanism. In: Contemporary Archaeology, edited by Mark P. Leone, pp. 393-401. Carbondale: Southern Illinois University Press.

1982 The infrastructure of Inka control in the Peruvian central highlands. In: The Inca and Aztec States 1400-1800: Anthropology and History, edited by George A. Collier, Renato I. Rosaldo, and John D. Wirth, pp. 153-71. New York: Academic Press.

Morris, Craig, and Donald E. Thompson
1985 Huánuco Pampa: An Inca City and Its Hinterland. London: Thames and Hudson.

Moseley, Michael
1975a The Maritime Foundations of Andean Civilization. Menlo Park: Cummings.

1975b Prehistoric principles of labor organization in the Moche Valley, Peru. American Antiquity 40 (2, part 1):191-96.

1983 Central Andean civilization. In: Ancient South Americans, edited by Jesse D. Jennings, pp. 179-240. San Francisco: WH Freeman.

Moseley, Michael, Robert Feldman, and Paul Goldstein
1985 Cerro Baul and the Moquegua Valley. Paper presented at the Huari Roundtable, Dumbarton Oaks, Washington, D.C.

Mujica, Elias, M. A. Rivera and T.F. Lynch
1983 Proyecto de estudio sobre la complementaridad económica Tiwanaku en los valles occidentales del centro-sur andino. Chungara 11:85-109.

Murra, John V.
1972 El "control vertical" de un máximo de pisos ecológicos en la economía de las sociedades andinas. In: Visita de la Provincia de León de Huánuco (1582), Iñigo Ortiz de Zuñiga, visitador, Tomo II, pp. 429-76. Huánuco, Peru: Universidad Nacional Hermilio Valdizán.

1980 The economic organization of the Inka state. Research in Economic Anthropology, Supplement 1. Greenwich: JAI Press.

1982 The mit'a obligations of ethnic groups to the Inka state. In: The Inca and Aztec States 1400-1800: Anthropology and History, edited by George A. Collier, Renato I. Rosaldo, and John D. Wirth, pp. 237-62. New York: Academic Press.

1985 "El archipiélago vertical" revisited. In: Andean Ecology and Civilization, edited by Shozo Masuda, Izumi Shimada, and Craig Morris, pp. 3-13. University of Tokyo Press.

Murra, John V., and Nathan Wachtel
1986 Introduction. In: Anthropological History of Andean Polities, edited by John V. Murra, Nathan Wachtel, and Jacques Revel, pp. 1-8. Cambridge: Cambridge University Press.

Nials, Fred L., E. E. Deeds, M. E. Moseley, S. Pozorski, T. Pozorski, and R. Feldman
1979   El Niño: the catastrophic flooding of coastal Peru. Field Museum of Natural History Bulletin 50(7):4-14, 50(8):4-10.

Nuñez, L.
1965   Desarrollo cultural prehispánico en el norte de Chile. Estudios Arqueológicos 1:37-115.

Parsons, Jeffrey R.
1968   An estimate of size and population for Middle Horizon Tiahuanaco, Bolivia. American Antiquity 47:572-95.

Paulsen, Allison C.
1976   Environment and empire: climatic factors in prehistoric Andean culture change. World Archaeology 8:121-32.

1983   Huaca del Loro revisited: the Nasca-Huarpa connection. In: Investigations of the Andean Past, edited by D.H. Sandweiss, pp. 98-121. Cornell Latin American Studies Program, Ithaca.

Pease G.Y., Franklin
1982   The formation of Tawantinsuyu: mechanisms of colonization and relationship with ethnic groups. In: The Inca and Aztec States 1400-1800: Anthropology and History, edited by George A. Collier, Renato I. Rosaldo, and John D. Wirth, pp. 173-98. New York: Academic Press.

Ponce Sángines, Carlos
1969   La ciudad Tiwanaku. Arte y Arqueología 1:5-32.

1971   Tiwanaku: espacio tiempo y cultura. Pumapunku 3:29-44.

1972   Tiwanaku: espacio tiempo y cultura. Pumapunku 4: 7-24.

Posnansky, Arthur
1945   Tihuanaco: The Cradle of American Man, vol. 1 & 2. New York: J.J. Augustin.

Pozorski, Shelia
1987   Theocracy vs. militarism: the significance of the Casma Valley in understanding early state formation. In: The Origins and Development of the State in the Andes, edited by Jonathan Haas, Shelia Pozorski, and Thomas Pozorski, pp. 15-30. Cambridge: Cambridge University Press.

Pozorski, Shelia, and Thomas Pozorski
1987   Early Settlement and Subsistence in the Casma Valley, Peru. Iowa City: University of Iowa Press.

Pulgar Vidal, Javier
1987   Geografía del Perú: las ocho regiones naturales, la regionalización transversal, la microregionalización. Promoción Editorial Inca, Lima.

Ravines Sanchez, Rogger H.
1968   Un depósito de ofrendas del Horizonte Medio en la sierra central del Perú. Ñawpa Pacha 6:19-46.

1977   Excavaciones en Ayapata, Huancavelica, Peru. Ñawpa Pacha 15:49-100.

Raymond, J. Scott
1988   A view from the tropical forest. In: Peruvian Prehistory, edited by Richard W. Keatinge, pp. 279-300. Cambridge: Cambridge University Press.

Reichlen, Henry, and Paule Reichlen
1949   Recherches archéologiques dans des Andes du haut Utcubamba: deuxieme rapport de la Mission Ethnologique Francaise au Pérou Septentrional. Journal de la Société des Américanistes 39:219-46.

Reiss, Johann Wilhelm, and Moritz Alphons Stübel
1880-87 The Necropolis of Ancon in Peru: A Contribution to Our Knowledge of the Culture and Industries of the Empire of the Incas, Being the Results of Excavations Made on the Spot. Translated by A. H. Keane. Berlin: A. Asher and Co.

Renfrew, Colin
1986   Introduction: peer-polity interaction and socio-political change. In: Peer-Polity Interaction and Socio-Political Change, edited by Colin Renfrew and John F. Cherry, pp. 1-18. Cambridge: Cambridge University Press.

Rick, John W.
1980   Prehistoric Hunters of the High Andes. New York: Academic Press.

Rivera, Mario A.
1976   Nuevos aportes sobre el desarrollo altiplánico en los valles bajos del extremo norte de Chile, durante el periodo Intermedio Temprano. In: Universidad del Norte, homenaje al Dr. Gustano Le Paije, pp. 71-82. Santiago Alfabeta.

1980   Arqueología andina en al panorama de las investigaciones arqueológicas en Chile. In: Temas antropológicos del norte de Chile, Estudios Arqueológicos (número especial):71-103. Universidad del Norte, Antofagasta.

Robinson, Ronald
1972   Non-European foundations of European imperialism: sketch for a theory of collaboration. In: Studies in the Theory of Imperialism, edited by Roger Owen and Bob Sutcliffe, pp. 117-40. London: Longman.

Rowe, John H.
1944   An introduction to the archaeology of Cuzco. Papers of the Peabody Museum of American Archaeology and Ethnology 27:2.

1946   Inca culture at the time of the Spanish Conquest. In: Handbook of South American Indians, vol. 2, edited by Julien H. Steward, pp. 183-330. Bureau of American Ethnology, Bulletin 143. Washington, D.C.

1948   The kingdom of Chimor. Acta Americana 6(1,2):26-59.

1956   Archaeological explorations in southern Peru, 1954-1955. American Antiquity 22(2):135-51.

1963   Urban settlements in ancient Peru. Ñawpa Pacha 1:1-28.

1967   What kind of settlement was Inca Cuzco? Ñawpa Pacha 5:59-76.

1982   Inca policies and institutions relating to the cultural unification of the empire. In: The Inca and Aztec States 1400-1800: Anthropology and History, edited by George A. Collier, Renato I. Rosaldo, and John D. Wirth, pp. 93-118. New York: Academic Press.

Rowe, John H., and Catherine T. Brandel
1970   Pucara style pottery designs. Ñawpa Pacha 7-8:1-16.

Rowe, John H., Donald Collier and Gordon R. Willey
1950   Reconnaissance notes on the site of Huari, near Ayacucho, Peru. American Antiquity 16(2):120-37.

Salomon, Frank
1986   Native Lords of Quito in the Age of the Incas: The Political Economy of North Andean Chiefdoms. Cambridge: Cambridge University Press.

Sanders, William T.
1973   The Significance of Pikillakta in Andean Culture History. Occasional Papers in Anthropology, no. 8. Penn State University.

Sanders, William T., J. R. Parsons, and R. S. Santley
1979   The Basin of Mexico: Ecological Processes in the Evolution of a Civilization. New York: Academic Press.

Sarmiento de Gamboa, Pedro
1960   Historia de los Incas. Biblioteca de Autores Españoles 135: 194-279. Madrid: Ediciones Atlas.

Schaedel, Richard P.
1966   Incipient urbanization and secularization in Tiahuanacoid Peru. American Antiquity 31(3), part 1: 338-44.

Schiffer, Michael B.
1983   Toward the identification of formation processes. American Antiquity 48(4):675-706.

1987   Formation Processes of the Archaeological Record. Albuquerque: University of New Mexico Press.

Schreiber, Katharina J.
1978   Planned Architecture of Middle Horizon Peru: Implications for Social and Political Organization. PhD dissertation, SUNY Binghamton.

1984   Prehistoric roads in the Carahuarazo Valley, Peru. In: Current Archaeological Projects in the Central Andes: Some Approaches and Results, edited by Ann Kendall, pp. 75-94. British Archaeological Reports S 210. Oxford, England.

1987a   Conquest and consolidation: a comparison of the Wari and Inka occupations of a highland Peruvian valley. American Antiquity 52(2):266-84.

1987b   From state to empire: the expansion of Wari outside the Ayacucho Basin. In: The Origins and Development of the State in the Andes, edited by Jonathan Haas, Shelia Pozorski, and Thomas Pozorski, pp. 91-96. Cambridge: Cambridge University Press.

1989   On revisiting Huaca del Loro: a cautionary note. Andean Past 2:69-79.

Schreiber, Katharina J., and Josué Lancho Rojas
1988   Los puquios de Nasca: un sistema de galerías filtrantes. Boletín de Lima 10(59):51-62.

Sciscento, Margaret M.
1989   Inka and Wari Mastery of Chuquibamba. Unpublished PhD dissertation, University of California at Santa Barbara.

Service, Elman R.
1975   Origins of the State and Civilization: The Process of Cultural Evolution. New York: W.W. Norton.

Shady Solis, Ruth
1989   Cambios significativas ocurridos en el mundo andino. In: The Nature of Wari: A Reappraisal of the Middle Horizon Period in Peru, edited by R.M. Czwarno, F.M. Meddens and A. Morgan, pp. 1- 22. BAR International Series 525.

Shady, Ruth, and Arturo Ruiz
1979   Evidence for interregional relationships during the Middle Horizon on the north-central coast of Peru. American Antiquity 44(4):676-84.

Shepard, Anna O.
1954   Ceramics for the Archaeologist. Publication 609. Carnegie Institution of Washington, Washington D.C.

Shimada, Izumi
1985   Introduction. In: Andean Ecology and Civilization, edited by Shozo Masuda, Izumi Shimada, and Craig Morris, pp. xi-xxxii. University of Tokyo Press.

1987   Horizontal and vertical dimensions of prehistoric states in north Peru. In: The Origins and Development of the State in the Andes, edited by Jonathan Haas, Shelia Pozorski, and Thomas Pozorski, pp. 130-44. Cambridge: Cambridge University Press.

Silverman, Helaine
1986   Cahuachi: An Andean Ceremonial Center. Unpublished doctoral dissertation, University of Texas, Austin.

1988   Cahuachi: non-urban cultural complexity on the south coast of Peru. Journal of Field Archaeology 15(4):403-30.

Spickard, Lynda E.
1983   The development of Huari administrative architecture. In: Investigations of the Andean Past, edited by Daniel H. Sandweiss, pp. 136-60. Cornell University, Ithaca.

Squier, E. George
1877   Peru: Incidents of Travel and Exploration in the Land of the Incas. New York: Henry Holt and Co.

Stothert, S. Karen
1967   Pre-colonial highways of Bolivia. Publicación de la Academia Nacional de Ciencias de Bolivia 17. La Paz.

Strube Erdmann, León
1963   Vialidad imperial de los Incas. Universidad Nacional de Córdoba, Facultad de Filosofía y Humanidades, Instituto de Estudios Américanistas. Serie Histórica 33. Córdoba, Argentina.

Stübel, Moritz A., and Max Uhle
1892   Die ruinenstäette von Tiahuanaco in hochlande des Alten Peru: eine kulturgeschechtliche studie aufgrund selbstaindiger aufrahmen. Verlag von Karl W. Heirsermann, Leipzig.

Sun Tzu
1983   The Art of War. Edited by James Clavell. New York: Delacorte Press.

Tello, Julio C.
1942   Origen y desarollo de las civilizaciones prehistóricas andinas. 27th International Congress of Americanists, 1939, 1:589-723. Lima.

Terada, Kazuo, and Ryozo Matsumoto
1985   Sobre la cronología de la tradición Cajamarca. In: Historia de Cajamarca, I. Arqueología, edited by Fernando Silva Santisteban, Waldemar Espinoza Soriano and Rogger Ravines, pp. 67-89. Instituto Nacional de Cultura, Cajamarca and CORDE Cajamarca. Cajamarca, Peru.

Thatcher, John
1972   Continuity and Change in the Ceramics of Huamachuco, North Highlands, Peru. Unpublished PhD dissertation, University of Pennsylvania.

1975   Early Intermediate Period and Middle Horizon 1B ceramics assemblages of Huamachuco, north highlands, Peru. Ñawpa Pacha 10-12, 1972-1974:109-27. Berkeley.

1977   A Middle Horizon 1B cache from Huamachuco, north highlands, Peru. Ñawpa Pacha 15:101-10.

Thompson, Lonnie G., E. Moseley-Thompson, J. F. Bolzan, and B. R. Koci
1985   A 1500-year record of tropical precipitation in ice cores from the Quelccaya ice cap, Peru. Science 229:971-73.

Thompson, Lonnie G., E. Moseley-Thompson, and Benjamín Morales Arnao
1984   El Niño-Southern Oscillation events recorded in the stratigraphy of the tropical Quelccaya ice cap, Peru. Science 226:50-53.

Topic, John R.
1985   The Wari impact on Huamachuco. Paper presented at the Huari Roundtable, Dumbarton Oaks, Washington, D.C.

Topic, John R., and Theresa Lange Topic
1985   El horizonte medio en Huamachuco. Revista del Museo Nacional 47:13-52. Lima.

Topic, Teresa Lange, and John R. Topic
1984   Proyecto arqueológico Huamachuco: informe preliminar sobre la tercera temporada, junio-agosto 1983. Trent University Occasional Papers in Anthropology, no. 1. Peterborough.

Tosi, Joseph
1960   Zonas de vida natural en el Perú. Boletín Técnica No. 5. Instituto Inter-Americano de Ciencias Agrícolas de la OEA: Zona Andina, Lima.

Troll, Carl
1968   Geo-Ecology of the Mountainous Regions of the Tropical Americas. Proceedings of the UNESCO Mexico Symposium 1966. Ferd. Dummlers Verlag, Bonn.

Uhle, Max
1903   Pachacamac: Report of the William Pepper, M.D., LL.D., Peruvian Expedition of 1896. Philadelphia: University of Pennsylvania Press.

Willey, Gordon R.
1953   Prehistoric settlement patterns in the Virú Valley, Peru. Smithsonian Institution, Bureau of American Ethnology, Bulletin 155. Washington, D.C.

Williams León, Carlos and José Pineda
1985   Ayacucho-Cajamarca: formas arquitectónicas con filiación Wari, unidad del espacio andino. Boletín de Lima 7(40):55-61.

Wilson, David
1988   Prehistoric Settlement Patterns in the Lower Santa Valley. Washington, D.C.: Smithsonian Institution Press.

Wright, Henry T., and Gregory A. Johnson
1975   Population, exchange, and early state formation in southwestern Iran. American Anthropologist 77:267-89.

Appendix A. Survey Data

Key to ceramic categories:

RSW	red slipped ware
CPl	plainware
PPl	polished plainware
PKtac	pre-Kancha tactile designs
PKnec	pre-Kancha necked jar with serpentine design
Ktac	Kancha tactile designs
KWtac	Kancha/Willka tactile designs
KWib	Kancha/Willka incised bowls
KWnec	Kancha/Willka necked jar with serpentine design
Wpc	Willka fancy slip painted pottery
WPfsl	Willka and post-Willka fine slipped wares
WPles	Willka and post-Willka less fancy slip painted pottery
Ppnt	Post-Willka slip painted pottery

TABLE A.1.
Counts of Ceramic Categories, Village Sites

ceramics sites	17Q	17D	35Q	35D	5Q	5D	63Q	63D	67D	50D	41Q	41D
RSW	14	8	6	14	28	34	121	159	13	23	33	73
PL	32	34	153	142	611	134	350	96	10	22	217	127
PPL	103*	32*	14	10*	1	3	0	10	0	1	2	5
PKtac	0	1	0	4	0	0	0	0	0	0	0	0
PKnec	0	1	1	1	0	0	0	0	0	0	0	0
Ktac	0	0	1	1	0	7	0	0	0	0	0	0
KWtac	0	3	0	0	1	0	0	0	0	0	0	2
KWib	5	0	0	5	2	6	2	9	0	0	1	0
KWnec	0	0	2	1	1	15	1	1	0	0	0	0

Wpc	0	0	0	2	9	0	11	3	2	2	27
WPfsl	0	0	0	1	1	2	0	0	1	4	12
WPles	0	0	0	0	0	3	10	2	0	0	0
Ppnt	0	0	0	0	0	6	13	0	0	0	0
Pnk	0	0	0	0	0	0	1	0	0	0	0

*includes diagnostic pre-Kancha jar forms

TABLE A. 2.
Counts of Ceramic Categories, Small Wari Sites

ceramics sites	46D	51Q	51D	75D
RSW	134	33	32	14
Pl	65	530	98	13
PPl	8	1	0	1
PKtac	0	0	0	0
PKnec	0	0	0	0
Ktac	0	0	0	0
KWtac	5	0	1	0
KWib	1	1	3	1
KWnec	1	0	1	0
Wpc	5	1	*	0
WPfsl	6	0	0	1
WPles	6	0	1	2
Ppnt	0	0	0	0
Pnk	0	0	0	0

Appendix B. Jincamocco Data

TABLE B. 1.
Summary Counts of Ceramic Diagnostic Vessels from All Excavated Proveniences

Patio 1:

PROV	DATE	PLAIN WARE	LOCAL DECORATED STYLES:			RED-WARE	PAINTED	TOTAL
			IB	NJ	OTAC			
P1 -11-1	7	27	2	0	0	8	10	47
P1 -11-2	7	5	0	0	0	5	2	12
P1 -12-1	7	1	0	0	0	0	1	2
P1 -13-1	7	14	1	3	0	7	8	33
P1 -23-1	7	1	0	1	0	1	1	4
P1 -23-2	6	3	1	2	1	2	0	9
P1 -33-1	7	3	1	1	0	2	1	8
P1 -33-2	6	7	1	0	0	3	1	12
P1 -43-1	7	52	7	2	0	23	12	96
P1 -43-2	6	41	4	8	4	11	11	79

Patio 1, north bench:

PROV	DATE	PLAIN WARE	LOCAL DECORATED STYLES:			RED- WARE	PAINTED	
			IB	NJ	OTAC			
P1n-01-2	6	10	0	2	0	0	0	12
P1n-02-2	6	32	4	3	2	5	3	49
P1n-02-3	4	63	34	10	5	3	1	116
P1n-02-4	2	57	4	4	2	5	0	72
P1n-02-5	2	23	3	1	0	2	0	29
P1n-02-6	0	0	0	0	0	0	0	0
P1n-02-7	1	24	2	1	1	0	1	29
P1n-03-3	4	149	73	16	5	5	0	248
P1n-03-4	2	74	28	12	4	1	0	119
P1n-03-5	2	104	21	9	3	3	1	141
P1n-03-6	2	12	0	2	2	1	0	17
P1n-03-7	1	74	8	2	5	0	0	89
P1n-04-2	6	54	5	5	1	18	6	89
P1n-04-3	4	23	8	4	1	5	4	45
P1n-04-4	2	34	10	6	1	1	0	52
P1n-04-5	2	18	0	0	1	1	0	20
P1n-04-6	0	0	0	0	0	0	0	0
P1n-05-3	4	58	43	3	3	4	0	111
P1n-05-4	2	36	16	5	5	2	1	65
P1n-05-5	2	15	6	1	0	0	0	22
P1n-05-6	0	0	0	0	0	0	0	0

Patio 1, west bench:

PROV	DATE	PLAIN WARE	LOCAL DECORATED STYLES:			RED-WARE	PAINTED	
			IB	NJ	OTAC			
P1w-01-2	7	79	14	16	0	10	11	130
P1w-01-3	6	61	16	17	5	3	3	105
P1w-01-4	4	55	10	6	0	0	0	71
P1w-01-5	2	13	8	3	1	1	0	26
P1w-01-6	0	0	0	0	0	0	0	0
P1w-01-7	0	0	0	0	0	0	0	0
P1w-02-2	7	41	6	2	2	2	7	60
P1w-02-4	4	14	0	0	1	1	3	19
P1w-02-5	2	14	1	1	0	1	0	17
P1w-02-6	2	5	0	1	2	1	0	9
P1w-02-7	1	15	0	0	0	8	6	29
P1w-03-2	7	32	0	0	2	3	1	38
P1w-03-3	6	12	1	1	0	0	2	16
P1w-03-4	4	3	0	0	2	2	0	7
P1w-03-5	2	15	2	1	0	0	1	19
P1w-03-6	2	1	0	1	1	0	0	3
P1w-03-7	1	1	0	0	0	0	0	1
P1w-04-2	7	14	0	0	0	2	2	18
P1w-04-3	6	17	3	2	0	4	3	29
P1w-04-4	4	12	3	1	1	0	0	17
P1w-04-5	2	15	4	4	2	0	1	26
P1w-04-6	2	5	0	0	0	0	0	5
P1w-04-7	1	1	0	0	0	0	0	1
P1w-05-2	7	40	0	0	0	5	18	63
P1w-05-3	6	99	10	9	0	9	12	139
P1w-05-4	6	29	13	2	0	5	2	51
P1w-05-5	5	27	2	1	1	3	0	34

Patio 2:

PROV	DATE	PLAIN WARE	LOCAL DECORATED STYLES:			RED- WARE	PAINTED	
			IB	NJ	OTAC			
P2 -11-1	7	84	2	0	0	13	9	108
P2 -11-2	6	114	6	9	6	3	0	138
P2 -11-3	6	60	13	4	4	3	5	88
P2 -21-1	7	32	5	1	0	9	2	49
P2 -21-2	6	74	9	6	2	6	4	101
P2 -21-3	6	122	42	34	4	6	1	209
P2 -31-1	7	80	4	6	2	20	6	118
P2 -31-2	6	80	16	8	2	11	5	122
P2 -31-3	6	138	16	24	2	6	2	188
P2 -31-4	2	62	30	5	0	1	0	98
P2 -32-1	7	44	0	2	1	6	0	53
P2 -32-2	5	43	1	3	1	0	1	49
P2 -32-3	5	56	4	5	1	4	5	75
P2 -33-1	7	70	0	1	0	6	2	79
P2 -33-2	6	112	2	2	0	5	12	133
P2 -33-3	5	21	2	1	0	3	3	30
P2 -34-1	7	76	1	2	1	13	2	95
P2 -34-2	6	33	0	1	0	6	3	43
P2 -34-3	5	40	4	6	1	0	0	51

Patio 3:

PROV	DATE	PLAIN WARE	LOCAL DECORATED STYLES:			RED-WARE	PAINTED	
			IB	NJ	OTAC			
P3 -11-1	7	5	0	1	0	1	0	7
P3 -11-2	6	7	0	0	0	4	2	13
P3 -11-3	5	12	0	1	0	11	2	26
P3 -21-1	7	16	1	2	0	4	2	25
P3 -21-2	6	13	1	1	0	8	2	25
P3 -21-3	5	0	0	1	0	2	0	3
P3 -31-1	7	14	0	1	1	4	2	22
P3 -31-2	6	60	1	1	0	35	3	100
P3 -31-3	5	12	3	0	0	11	0	26
P3 -31-4	4	9	0	0	0	4	0	13
P3 -41-1	7	2	1	1	0	1	3	8
P3 -41-2	6	31	9	2	3	12	1	58
P3 -41-3	5	29	1	2	0	14	4	50
P3 -41-4	4	17	1	1	0	25	2	46
P3 -42-1	7	0	0	0	0	0	0	0
P3 -42-2	6	28	4	1	0	17	4	54
P3 -42-3	5	8	0	1	0	5	2	15
P3 -42-4	4	7	1	0	0	4	3	15
P3 -42-5	3	10	2	0	0	6	1	19
P3 -42-6	3	2	0	0	0	2	0	4
P3 -43-1	7	11	1	1	0	2	0	15
P3 -43-2	6	21	2	3	2	12	6	46
P3 -43-3	5	27	1	1	0	16	2	47

Gallery 1:

PROV	DATE	PLAIN WARE	LOCAL DECORATED STYLES: IB	NJ	OTAC	RED-WARE	PAINTED	
G1 -00-1	7	11	1	0	0	3	4	19
G1 -00-2	6	4	0	0	0	0	1	5
G1 -00-3	5	12	1	2	0	3	2	20
G1 -00-4	3	11	0	1	0	5	4	21
G1 -00-5	2	1	2	0	0	2	0	5

Corridor 1:

PROV	DATE	PLAIN WARE	LOCAL DECORATED STYLES: IB	NJ	OTAC	RED-WARE	PAINTED	
C1 -01-1	7	67	0	1	2	15	21	106
C1 -01-2	6	44	1	1	1	17	7	71
C1 -01-3	6	37	2	2´	0	29	9	79
C1 -01-4	5	30	3	7	0	11	7	58
C1 -02-1	7	138	4	1	1	27	34	205
C1 -02-2	6	79	0	0	2	15	23	119
C1 -02-3	6	67	5	1	1	15	17	106
C1 -02-4	5	15	3	2	0	12	3	35
C1 -02-5	2	11	6	2	1	3	1	24
C1 -02-6	2	35	13	11	3	3	0	65
C1 -02-7	2	5	9	5	1	3	0	23
C1 -02-8	1	4	11	0	1	0	0	16

Appendix B

Unit T1:

PROV	DATE	PLAIN WARE	LOCAL DECORATED STYLES: IB	NJ	OTAC	RED-WARE	PAINTED	
T1-00-1	7	4	0	0	1	0	0	5
T1-00-2	6	8	1	0	0	11	1	21
T1-00-3	6	5	1	1	1	13	3	24
T1-00-4	5	4	2	1	0	15	4	26
T1-00-5	3	9	1	1	0	4	2	17
T1-00-6	2	1	7	4	1	1	0	14
T1-00-7	2	9	13	3	0	2	0	27
T1-00-8	2	2	3	2	0	0	0	7
T1-00-9	2	3	1	0	0	0	0	4

Unit T2/3:

PROV	DATE	PLAIN WARE	LOCAL DECORATED STYLES: IB	NJ	OTAC	RED-WARE	PAINTED	
T2-00-1	7	0	0	0	0	0	0	0
T2-00-2	6	0	0	0	0	1	10	11
T3-00-1	7	0	0	0	0	0	0	0
T3-00-2	6	0	0	0	0	0	1	1

Other coded diagnostics:

		4	0	0	0	1	7	12

TABLE B. 2.
Lithics from All Excavated Proveniences, by Raw Material and Artifact Type

PROV	DATE	J1	J2	J3	JU	JB	JK	JD	O1	O2	O3	OU	OB	OP	OK	B1	S2	B3	BU	BB	BP	Q1	Q2	Q3	QU	QB	QK	S1	S2	S3	SU	X1	X2	X3

Patio 1

PROV	DATE	J1	J2	J3	JU	JB	JK	JD	O1	O2	O3	OU	OB	OP	OK	B1	S2	B3	BU	BB	BP	Q1	Q2	Q3	QU	QB	QK	S1	S2	S3	SU	X1	X2	X3
P1 -11-1	7	0	2	7	.	.	.	.	0	0	9	.	.	.	.	0	1	0	.	1	.	0	0	0	.	.	.	0	0	1	.	0	0	0
P1 -11-2	7	0	0	1	.	.	.	.	0	0	0	.	1	.	.	0	0	0	.	.	.	0	0	1	.	.	.	0	0	0	.	0	0	0
P1 -12-1	7	.	.	.	.	.	.	.	.	.	.	.	.	.	.	.	.	.	.	.	.	.	.	.	.	.	.	.	.	.	.	.	.	.
P1 -13-1	7	0	1	3	.	.	.	.	0	0	3	.	1	1	.	1	1	1	.	.	.	0	0	0	.	.	.	0	0	0	.	0	0	0
P1 -23-1	7	0	0	2	.	.	.	.	0	0	2	.	.	.	.	0	0	0	.	.	.	0	0	0	.	.	.	0	0	0	.	0	0	0
P1 -23-2	6	.	.	.	.	.	.	.	.	.	.	.	.	.	.	.	.	.	.	.	.	.	.	.	.	.	.	.	.	.	.	.	.	.
P1 -33-1	7	.	.	.	.	.	.	.	.	.	.	.	.	.	.	.	.	.	.	.	.	.	.	.	.	.	.	.	.	.	.	.	.	.
P1 -33-2	6	.	.	.	.	.	.	.	.	.	.	.	.	.	.	.	.	.	.	.	.	.	.	.	.	.	.	.	.	.	.	.	.	.
P1 -43-1	7	2	4	5	.	.	.	.	0	1	4	.	.	.	2	.	0	0	0	.	.	.	0	0	0	.	.	.	0	0	0	.	0	0	0
P1 -43-2	6	8	12	12	.	.	.	.	0	0	5	.	1	1	.	0	1	1	.	.	.	0	0	0	.	.	.	0	1	1	.	0	1	0

Patio 1, north bench

PROV	DATE	J1	J2	J3	JU	JB	JK	JD	O1	O2	O3	OU	OB	OP	OK	B1	S2	B3	BU	BB	BP	Q1	Q2	Q3	QU	QB	QK	S1	S2	S3	SU	X1	X2	X3
P1n-01-2	6	0	0	2	.	.	.	.	0	0	0	.	.	.	.	0	0	0	.	.	.	0	0	0	.	.	.	0	0	0	.	0	0	0
P1n-02-2	6	1	6	16	.	.	.	.	0	0	2	.	.	.	.	0	0	0	.	.	.	0	1	3	.	.	.	0	1	0	.	0	0	1
P1n-02-3	4	26	74	73	.	.	.	.	0	0	4	.	.	3	.	0	6	2	.	.	.	1	1	2	.	.	.	3	11	4	.	0	0	1
P1n-02-4	2	30	22	49	.	.	.	.	0	0	1	.	.	.	.	0	0	3	.	.	.	0	0	1	.	.	.	2	7	5	.	0	0	1
P1n-02-5	2	9	19	16	1	.	.	.	0	0	0	.	.	.	.	0	0	0	.	.	.	0	0	0	.	.	.	0	0	3	.	0	1	1
P1n-02-6	2	.	.	.	.	.	.	.	.	.	.	.	.	.	.	.	.	.	.	.	.	.	.	.	.	.	.	.	.	.	.	.	.	.
P1n-02-7	1	14	22	22	.	.	.	.	0	2	1	.	.	3	.	0	0	0	.	.	.	0	0	0	.	.	.	1	2	6	.	0	0	0
P1n-03-3	4	36	55	92	.	.	.	.	2	0	8	.	.	.	.	0	3	6	.	.	.	1	0	2	3	.	.	4	3	6	.	0	0	2
P1n-03-4	2	15	38	26	.	.	.	.	0	0	2	.	.	.	.	0	2	1	.	.	.	0	0	0	.	.	.	1	5	5	.	0	2	0
P1n-03-5	2	41	104	54	1	.	.	.	0	0	3	.	.	3	1	0	1	1	.	1	.	0	0	0	.	.	.	1	3	2	.	0	0	0
P1n-03-6	2	6	10	12	.	.	.	.	0	0	0	.	.	.	.	0	0	0	.	.	.	0	0	0	.	.	.	1	2	2	.	0	0	0
P1n-03-7	1	43	68	64	.	.	.	.	2	1	4	.	.	2	.	0	1	1	.	.	.	0	0	0	.	.	.	1	3	5	.	0	1	0
P1n-04-2	6	3	4	16	.	.	.	.	0	0	5	.	1	3	.	0	0	0	.	.	.	0	1	0	.	.	.	2	2	3	.	0	1	0

Appendix B

```
P1n-04-3   4  11  10 11  . . . . 0 0 0 . . . . 0 2 1 . . . 0 0 1 . . . 0 1 1 . 0 0 0
P1n-04-4   2  16  34 23  . . . . 0 0 1 . . 1 . 1 0 2 . . 1 0 0 0 . . . 0 0 2 . 0 0 0
P1n-04-5   2   8  15 11  . . . . 0 0 1 . . . . 0 0 0 . . . 0 3 1 1 . . 1 1 5 . 0 0 0
P1n-04-6   2   0   0  2  . . . . 0 0 0 . . 1 . 0 0 0 . . . 0 0 0 . . . 0 0 0 . 0 0 0
P1n-05-3   4  20  44 45  . . . . 0 0 1 . . 2 . 0 0 1 . . . 0 0 1 . . . 2 2 4 . 0 0 0
P1n-05-4   2  21  35 18  . . . . 0 0 0 . . . . 0 0 0 . . . 0 0 1 . . . 0 5 2 . 0 1 0
P1n-05-5   2   6  23 17  . . . . 0 0 0 . . 1 . 0 0 0 . . . 0 0 0 . . . 3 3 2 . 0 0 2
```

Patio 1, west bench

```
P1w-01-2   7   6   3 11  . . . 1 1 2 4 . . 1 . 1 1 2 1 . . 0 0 3 . . . 4 2 2 . 1 2 6
P1w-01-3   6   1   4  5  . . . . 0 1 0 . . . . 0 0 0 . . . 0 0 1 . . . 0 0 2 . 0 0 0
P1w-01-4   4   1   2  3  . . . . 0 0 2 . . . . 0 0 0 1 . 0 0 0 1 . . 0 0 2 . 0 0 0
P1w-01-5   2   1   1  7  . . . . 0 0 0 . . 2 . 0 0 0 . . . 0 0 1 . . . 0 1 0 . 0 0 0
P1w-02-2   7   1   1  3  . . . . 0 0 1 . . . . 0 0 0 . . . 0 0 0 . . . 0 1 0 . 0 0 0
P1w-02-4   4   0   0  0  . . . . 0 0 0 . . . . 0 0 0 . . . 0 0 1 . . . 0 0 0 . 0 0 0
P1w-02-5   2   0   1  8  . . . . 0 0 0 . . . . 0 0 0 . . . 0 0 0 . . . 0 0 0 . 0 0 0
P1w-02-6   2   2   0  2  . . . . 0 0 1 . . 2 . 0 0 2 . . . 0 0 0 . . . 0 0 0 . 0 0 0
P1w-02-7   1   1   1  4  . . . . 0 0 0 . . . . 0 1 0 . . . 0 1 0 . . . 1 0 0 . 0 0 0
P1w-03-2   7   1   0  1  . . . . 0 0 0 . . . . 0 0 0 1 . 0 0 0 . . . 0 0 1 . 0 0 0
P1w-03-3   6   .   .  .  . . . . . . . . . . . . . . . . . . . . . . . . . . . . . .
P1w-03-4   4   0   0  0  . . . . 0 0 0 . . . . 0 0 0 . . . 0 0 0 . . . 0 0 1 . 0 0 0
P1w-03-5   2   2   1  2  . . . . 0 0 0 . . . . 0 0 0 . . . 0 0 0 . . . 0 0 1 . 0 0 0
P1w-03-6   2   .   .  .  . . . . . . . . . . . . . . . . . . . . . . . . . . . . . .
P1w-03-7   1   .   .  .  . . . . . . . . . . . . . . . . . . . . . . . . . . . . . .
P1w-04-2   7   .   .  .  . . . . . . . . . . . . . . . . . . . . . . . . . . . . . .
P1w-04-3   6   0   0  1  . . . . 0 0 0 . . . . 0 0 0 . . . 0 0 0 . . . 0 0 0 . 0 0 0
P1w-04-4   4   0   1  0  . . . . 0 0 0 . . . . 0 0 0 . . . 0 0 0 . . . 0 0 0 . 0 0 0
P1w-04-5   2   0   0  3  . . . . 0 1 0 . . . . 0 0 0 . . . 0 0 0 . . . 2 0 0 . 0 0 0
P1w-04-6   2   0   1  0  . . . . 0 0 0 . . . . 0 0 0 . . . 0 0 0 . . . 0 0 0 . 0 0 0
P1w-04-7   1   .   .  .  . . . . . . . . . . . . . . . . . . . . . . . . . . . . . .
P1w-05-2   7   2   1  2  . . . . 0 3 4 1 . . . 0 0 0 . . . 0 0 0 . . . 0 0 0 . 0 4 0
```

```
P1W-05-3   6   3   4 15    . . . . 0  1  0 . . . 2 . 0  0  1 . . . 0  0  0 . . . 0  1  1 . 0  0  0
P1W-05-4   6   4  10 19    . . . . 0  0  3 . . . . . 0  0  2 . . . 0  0  1 . . . 1  2  3 . 1  0  0  0
P1W-05-5   5   9  13 22    . . . . 0  0  2  1  1 . . 0  0  0 . . . 0  0  1 . . . 0  0  1 . 0  1  0
```

Patio 2

```
P2 -11-0   6  10 21 14    . . . . 0  5  9 . . . 1 . 2  2  3 . . . 0  2  3 . . . 1  2  2 . 0  0  0
P2 -11-1   7   4 12  7    . . . . 0  2  3 . . . 1 . 0  0  3 . . . 0  0  1 . . . 0  1  2 . 0  0  0
P2 -11-2   6  30 25 20    . . . . 0  1  2 . . . . . 0  0  0 . . . 0  3  4  1 . . 1  0  5 . 0  2  1
P2 -11-3   6   7 17 17    . . . . 0  2  4 . . . . . 0  1  3 . . . 0  1  3 . . . 1  1  1 . 1  3  1
P2 -21-1   7   3  9  8    . . . . 0  0  2 . . . . . 0  0  1 . . . 0  0  1 . . . 0  2  2 . 0  0  0
P2 -21-2   6  12 23 35    . . . . 0  2  4  1  1 . 0  0  1 . . . 0  1  1 . . . 0  2  5 . 0  0  0
P2 -21-3   6  25 54 46    . . . . 2  2  3 . . . 3 . 0  1  2 . . . 2  3  8 . . . 0  1  3 . 0  2  0
P2 -31-1   7   5 10 13    . . . . 0  2  2 . . . . . 0  0  2 . . . 1  4  0 . . . 1  1  3 . 0  0  1
P2 -31-2   6   5 18 20    . . . . 0  3  5 . 1 . . . 0  3  2 . . . 0  1  0 . . . 2  0  2 . 2  2  1
P2 -31-3   6  25 40 46    . . . . 0  0  6 . . . 2 . 2  4  1 . . . 1  3  5 . 1 . 0  2  2  1  0  0  1
P2 -31-4   2  14 20 26    . . . . 0  1  5 . . . 1 . 0  0  2 . . . 0  2  1 . . . 0  1  1 . 0  0  1
P2 -32-1   7   9  6  5    . . . . 0  0  1 . . . . . 0  0  1 . . . 0  0  0 . . . 0  1  2 . 0  0  0
P2 -32-2   5   0  8 13    . . . . 0  0  3 . . . 1 . 1  0  0 . . . 0  1  1 . . . 0  1  6 . 0  3  3
P2 -32-3   5  12 12 15    . . . . 0  0  3 . . . . . 0  0  0 . . . 0  0  0 . . . 1  1  1 . 0  0  0
P2 -33-1   7   2  4  7    . . . . 0  0  1 . . . . . 0  0  1 . . . 0  0  0 . . . 0  1  1 . 0  0  0
P2 -33-2   6   0  8  8    . . . . 0  0  1 . . . . . 0  1  0 . . . 0  0  0 . . . 1  0  1 . 0  0  0
P2 -33-3   5   0  3  6    . . . . 0  1  0 . . . . . 0  0  0 . . . 0  0  1 . . . 0  1  0 . 0  1  0
P2 -34-1   7   1  2  4    . . . . 0  0  1 . . . . . 0  0  1 . . . 0  0  1 . . . 0  0  1 . 0  0  0
P2 -34-2   6   1  3  5    . . . . 0  0  0 . . . . . 0  0  0 . . . 0  0  0 . . . 0  1  0 . 0  0  0
P2 -34-3   5   3  9 10    . . . . 0  0  1 . . . 1 . 0  0  0 . . . 0  0  1 . . . 0  2  3 . 0  0  1
```

Patio 3

```
P3 -11-1   7   .  .  .     . . . . .  .  . . . . . . .  .  . . . . .  .  . . . . .  .  . . .  .  .
P3 -11-2   6   0  0  1    . . . . 0  0  0 . . . . . 0  0  0 . . . 0  0  0 . . . 0  0  0 . 0  0  0
P3 -11-3   5   1  1  3    . . . . 0  0  0 . . . . . 0  0  0 . . . 0  0  0 . . . 1  0  0 . 0  0  0
```

Appendix B 315

```
P3 -21-1  7  2 1  0 . . . . 0 1 1 . . . . 0 0 0 . . . 0 0 0 . . . 0 0 1 . 0 0 0
P3 -21-2  6  0 0  2 . . . . 0 1 0 . . . . 0 0 0 . . . 0 0 1 . . . 0 0 0 . 0 0 0
P3 -21-3  5  0 0  2 . . . . 0 0 0 . . . . 0 0 0 . . . 0 0 0 . . . 0 0 1 . 0 0 0
P3 -31-1  7  1 0  2 . . . . 0 1 1 1 . . . 0 0 1 . . . 0 0 0 . . . 0 0 0 . 0 1 0
P3 -31-2  6  6 2  8 . . . . 0 0 1 1 1 . . 0 0 1 1 . . 0 0 0 . . . 0 0 0 . 1 1 0
P3 -31-3  5  0 0  0 . . . . 0 0 1 . . . . 0 0 0 . . . 0 0 0 . . . 0 0 1 . 0 0 0
P3 -31-4  4  3 4  2 . . . . 2 0 2 . . . . 0 0 0 . . . 0 0 0 . . . 0 0 0 . 0 0 0
P3 -41-1  7  . .  . . . . . . . . . . . . . . . . . . . . . . . . . . . . . .
P3 -41-2  6  2 9 11 . . . . 0 3 8 . . 1 . 0 1 1 . . . 0 0 0 . . . 0 0 1 . 0 0 0
P3 -41-3  5  0 0  2 . . . . 0 0 4 . . 1 . 0 0 0 . . . 0 0 1 . . . 0 0 1 . 0 0 0
P3 -41-4  4  0 4  2 . . . . 0 1 4 . 3 1 . 0 0 0 . . . 0 0 0 . . . 0 0 0 . 0 0 0
P3 -42-1  7  . .  . . . . . . . . . . . . . . . . . . . . . . . . . . . . . .
P3 -42-2  6  1 8 13 . . . . 0 2 1 2 . 1 1 0 0 0 . . . 0 0 0 . . . 0 2 2 . 0 0 0
P3 -42-3  5  1 6  7 . . . . 0 1 2 . 1 . . 0 0 0 . . . 0 0 0 . . . 0 1 0 . 0 1 0
P3 -42-4  4  0 1  1 . . . . 0 0 3 . . . . 0 0 0 . . . 0 0 0 . . . 0 1 0 . 0 0 0
P3 -42-5  3  0 2  3 . . . . 0 3 0 . . . . 0 0 0 . . . 0 0 0 . . . 0 1 1 . 0 0 0
P3 -42-6  3  . .  . . . . . . . . . . . . . . . . . . . . . . . . . . . . . .
P3 -43-1  7  3 3  3 . . . . 0 1 1 . . . . 0 0 0 . . . 0 0 0 . . . 0 2 1 . 0 0 0
P3 -43-2  6  1 6  3 . . . . 0 0 1 . 2 1 . 0 0 0 . . . 0 0 0 . . . 0 1 0 . 0 0 0
P3 -43-3  5  0 3  1 . . . . 0 0 0 1 . . . 0 0 0 . . . 0 0 0 . . . 0 0 2 . 0 0 0
```

Gallery 1

```
G1 -00-1  7  . .  . . . . . . . . . . . . . . . . . . . . . . . . . . . . . .
G1 -00-2  6  0 0  1 . . . . 0 1 0 . . . . 0 0 0 . . . 0 0 0 . . . 0 0 0 . 0 0 0
G1 -00-3  5  3 2  2 . . . . 0 7 1 . . . . 0 0 0 . . . 0 0 1 . . . 2 0 0 . 0 0 0
G1 -00-4  3  2 5  6 . . . . 0 5 2 . . . . 1 0 1 . . . 0 0 0 . . . 0 0 0 . 0 0 1
G1 -00-5  2  0 0  0 . . . . 0 1 2 . . . . 0 0 0 . . . 0 0 0 . . . 1 0 0 . 0 0 0
```

Corridor 1

```
C1 -01-1  7  1 1  4 . . . . 0 0 2 . . . . 0 0 0 . . . 0 0 2 . . . 1 0 1 . 0 0 1
```

```
C1 -01-2   6   0    2   2  .  .  .  .  0   3   4  .  .  .  .  0   0   1  .  .  .  0   1   2  .  .  1   0   1   2  .  0   1   0
C1 -01-3   6   1    3   2  .  .  .  .  1   1   4  .  .  .  .  1   1   0  .  .  .  0   0   0   1  .  .  0   0   4  .  0   0   0
C1 -01-4   5   1    8   8  .  .  .  .  0   0   5  .  1   1  .  0   0   3  .  .  .  0   1   1  .  .  .  0   0   2  .  1   1   1
C1 -02-1   7   2    2   3  .  .  .  .  0   0   1  .  .  .  .  0   0   0  .  .  .  0   1   3  .  .  .  0   0   2  .  0   0   0
C1 -02-2   6   0    0   2  .  .  .  .  0   1   3  .  .  .  .  0   0   0  .  .  .  0   0   1  .  .  .  0   0   0  .  0   0   0
C1 -02-3   6   2    4   6  .  .  .  .  0   1   3  .  .  .  .  0   0   0  .  .  .  0   0   1  .  .  .  0   0   1  .  0   0   0
C1 -02-4   5   3    8  16  .  .  1  .  0   1   9  .  1  .  .  0   1   1  .  .  .  0   1   2  .  .  .  0   0   5  .  0   0   1
C1 -02-5   2   2    2  14  .  .  .  .  0   0   5  .  3  .  .  0   0   3  .  .  .  0   0   0   1  .  .  0   0   2  .  0   0   0
C1 -02-6   2  16   20  41  .  .  .  .  0   0   4  .  .  .  .  0   0   0  .  .  .  0   0   4  .  .  .  5   2   1   1  0   1   1
C1 -02-7   2   3    2   9  .  .  .  .  0   0   0  .  .  .  .  0   0   0  .  .  .  0   0   0  .  .  .  1   0   0  .  0   0   0
C1 -02-8   1   1    6  17  .  1  .  .  0   0   1  .  .  1  .  0   1   1  .  .  .  0   0   0  .  .  .  0   0   2  .  0   0   0

Unit T1

T1 -00-1   7   2    3   3  .  .  1  .  0   2   1  .  .  .  .  0   1   1  .  .  .  0   2   1  .  .  .  0   3   2  .  0   0   2
T1 -00-2   6   5    6   7  .  .  .  .  0   2   2  .  .  .  .  0   1   0  .  .  .  0   1   1  .  .  .  0   1   0  .  0   4   1
T1 -00-3   6   6   10   5  .  .  .  .  1   4   3  .  .  .  .  1   0   1  .  .  .  0   1   0  .  .  .  3   0   0  .  0   2   1
T1 -00-4   5   4   19   7  .  .  .  .  0   2   0  .  .  .  .  0   0   0  .  .  .  0   0   3  .  .  .  0   4   2  .  0   3   2
T1 -00-5   3   5    8   9  .  .  .  .  0   3   0  .  .  .  .  0   0   0  .  .  .  0   1   1  .  .  .  0   0   0  .  0   1   3
T1 -00-6   2   0    8   4  .  .  .  .  0   1   0  .  .  .  .  0   0   0  .  .  .  0   1   0  .  .  .  0   0   0  .  0   0   0
T1 -00-7   2   5    7   8  .  .  .  .  0   0   0  .  .  1  .  0   0   0  .  .  .  0   1   1  .  .  .  0   0   0  .  0   0   0
T1 -00-8   2   2    3   2  .  .  .  .  0   0   0  .  .  .  .  0   0   0  .  .  .  0   0   0  .  .  .  0   0   0  .  0   0   1
T1 -00-9   2   0    3   1  .  .  .  .  0   0   0  .  .  .  .  0   0   0  .  .  .  0   0   0  .  .  .  0   0   0  .  0   0   0

Unit T2/3

T2 -00-1   7   0    0   0  .  .  .  .  0   0   1  .  .  .  .  0   0   0  .  .  .  0   0   0  .  .  .  0   0   0  .  0   0   0
T2 -00-2   6   1    2   0  .  .  .  .  0   1   1  .  .  .  .  0   0   0  .  .  .  0   0   0  .  .  .  0   1   1  .  0   0   0
T3 -00-1   7   0    1   1  .  .  .  .  1   0   0  .  .  .  .  0   0   0  .  .  .  0   0   0  .  .  .  0   0   0  .  0   0   0
T3 -00-2   6   0    1   1  .  .  .  .  0   0   1  .  .  .  .  0   0   0  .  .  .  0   0   0  .  .  ., 0   0   0  .  0   0   0
```

Appendix B

Key:

Raw materials:

J=red jasper
O=obsidian
B=basalt
Q=quartzite
S=other silicate
X=other, unidentified

Artifact types:

1=core
2=unutilized flake
3=utilized flake
U=uniface
B=biface
P=projectile point
K=blade
D=drill

TABLE B. 3.
Summary Counts of Artifact Types and Artifact Densities from All Excavated Proveniences

PROV	DATE	VOLUME	CERAMIC	CDENSE	LITHICS	LDENSE	BONE	BDENSE	WHORLS	SPECIAL
Patio 1:										
P1 -11-1	7	24.3100	671	27.60	21	0.86	0	0.00	0	0
P1 -11-2	7	18.7000	83	4.44	0	0.00	100	5.35	0	0
P1 -12-1	7	9.3500	49	5.24	0	0.00	0	0.00	0	0
P1 -13-1	7	9.3500	350	37.43	12	1.28	690	73.80	0	b
P1 -23-1	7	14.9600	57	3.81	4	0.27	0	0.00	0	0
P1 -23-2	6	13.7750	50	3.63	0	0.00	0	0.00	0	0
P1 -33-1	7	18.7000	78	4.17	0	0.00	45	2.41	0	0
P1 -33-2	6	13.7750	86	6.24	0	0.00	22	1.60	1	0
P1 -43-1	7	37.4000	837	22.38	18	0.48	115	3.07	0	0
P1 -43-2	6	13.7750	829	60.18	44	3.19	1515	109.98	1	f

Appendix B

PROV	DATE	VOLUME	CERAMIC	CDENSE	LITHICS	LDENSE	BONE	BDENSE	WHORLS	SPECIAL
Patio 1, north bench:										
P1n-01-2	6	1.000	120	120.00	2	2.00	125	125.00	0	0
P1n-02-2	6	4.800	397	82.71	31	6.46	260	54.17	1	0
P1n-02-3	4	0.750	889	1185.33	211	281.33	987	1316.00	3	0
P1n-02-4	2	0.750	440	586.67	121	161.33	2080	2773.33	1	0
P1n-02-5	2	0.750	249	332.00	50	66.67	1095	1460.00	2	0
P1n-02-6	0	0.750	0	0.00	0	0.00	0	0.00	0	b
P1n-02-7	1	0.750	226	301.33	73	97.33	2065	2753.33	1	0
P1n-03-3	4	1.400	1820	1300.00	223	159.29	4080	2914.29	7	0
P1n-03-4	2	1.400	1037	740.71	97	69.29	4655	3325.00	2	0
P1n-03-5	2	1.400	1188	848.57	216	154.29	5644	4031.43	6	b
P1n-03-6	2	1.400	125	89.29	33	23.57	900	642.86	1	0
P1n-03-7	1	0.560	782	1396.43	196	350.00	6632	11842.86	5	0
P1n-04-2	6	5.550	882	158.92	41	7.39	170	30.63	1	0
P1n-04-3	4	0.975	412	422.56	38	38.97	330	338.46	2	b
P1n-04-4	2	0.975	441	452.31	81	83.08	1300	1333.33	1	0
P1n-04-5	2	0.975	172	176.41	47	48.21	1900	1948.72	1	0
P1n-04-6	2	0.975	6	6.15	3	3.08	745	764.10	0	0
P1n-05-3	4	1.800	853	473.89	122	67.78	2330	1294.44	1	0
P1n-05-4	2	1.800	400	222.22	83	46.11	2530	1405.56	1	b
P1n-05-5	2	1.800	257	142.78	57	31.67	5082	2823.33	2	b
P1n-05-6	2	0.720	4	5.56	0	0.00	277	384.72	0	0

PROV	DATE	VOLUME	CERAMIC	CDENSE	LITHICS	LDENSE	BONE	BDENSE	WHORLS	SPECIAL
Patio 1, west bench:										
P1w-01-2	7	4.400	907	206.14	51	11.59	5	1.14	0	0
P1w-01-3	6	2.200	1068	485.45	13	5.91	0	0.00	3	g
P1w-01-4	4	2.200	1346	611.82	12	5.46	0	0.00	0	0
P1w-01-5	2	2.200	258	117.27	13	5.91	0	0.00	0	c
P1w-01-6	0	2.200	0	0.00	0	0.00	0	0.00	0	0
P1w-01-7	0	2.200	0	0.00	0	0.00	0	0.00	0	0
P1w-02-2	7	4.400	489	111.14	7	1.59	152	34.55	2	0
P1w-02-4	4	2.200	158	71.82	1	0.46	70	31.82	1	0
P1w-02-5	2	2.200	138	62.73	9	4.09	230	104.55	0	0
P1w-02-6	2	2.200	69	31.36	9	4.09	295	134.09	1	0
P1w-02-7	1	2.200	501	227.73	9	4.09	660	300.00	1	0
P1w-03-2	7	4.400	318	72.27	4	0.91	14	3.18	3	0
P1w-03-3	6	2.200	135	61.36	0	0.00	0	0.00	0	0
P1w-03-4	4	2.200	95	43.18	1	0.46	0	0.00	3	0
P1w-03-5	2	2.200	154	70.00	6	2.73	70	31.82	0	0
P1w-03-6	2	2.200	47	21.36	0	0.00	0	0.00	0	0
P1w-03-7	1	2.200	48	21.82	0	0.00	0	0.00	0	0
P1w-04-2	7	3.740	97	25.94	0	0.00	0	0.00	1	s
P1w-04-3	6	1.870	199	106.42	1	0.54	0	0.00	0	0
P1w-04-4	4	1.870	162	86.63	1	0.54	0	0.00	0	0
P1w-04-5	2	1.870	351	187.70	6	3.21	15	8.02	0	0
P1w-04-6	2	1.870	98	52.41	1	0.54	0	0.00	0	0
P1w-04-7	1	1.870	17	9.09	0	0.00	0	0.00	0	0
P1w-05-2	7	4.840	416	85.95	14	2.89	135	27.89	2	0
P1w-05-3	6	2.420	1102	455.37	27	11.16	370	152.89	3	0
P1w-05-4	6	2.420	464	191.74	46	19.01	382	157.85	6	0
P1w-05-5	5	2.420	264	109.09	51	21.07	1404	580.17	5	0

Appendix B

PROV	DATE	VOLUME	CERAMIC	CDENSE	LITHICS	LDENSE	BONE	BDENSE	WHORLS	SPECIAL
Patio 2:										
P2 -11-1	7	5.3400	958	179.40	113	21.16	345	64.61	1	0
P2 -11-2	6	1.6688	1116	668.76	95	56.93	1215	728.09	2	0
P2 -11-3	6	1.6688	667	399.70	63	37.75	810	485.39	1	0
P2 -21-1	7	6.3412	439	69.23	28	4.42	160	25.23	1	0
P2 -21-2	6	1.6688	1074	643.60	89	53.33	520	311.61	3	0
P2 -21-3	6	1.6688	1851	1109.21	157	94.08	1450	868.91	3	0
P2 -31-1	7	6.0075	722	120.18	45	7.49	130	21.64	1	0
P2 -31-2	6	1.6688	1167	699.33	67	40.15	1160	695.13	0	0
P2 -31-3	6	1.6688	1617	968.99	142	85.09	1890	1132.58	4	0
P2 -31-4	2	1.6688	662	396.70	75	44.94	2060	1234.46	2	0
P2 -32-1	7	5.3400	377	70.60	25	4.68	22	4.12	0	0
P2 -32-2	5	1.6688	567	339.78	41	24.57	570	341.57	2	0
P2 -32-3	5	1.6688	506	303.22	45	26.97	535	320.60	1	0
P2 -33-1	7	5.3400	588	110.11	17	3.18	55	10.30	1	0
P2 -33-2	6	1.6688	1156	692.73	20	11.99	1725	1033.71	2	0
P2 -33-3	5	1.6688	342	204.94	13	7.79	750	449.44	3	0
P2 -34-1	7	5.3400	666	124.72	11	2.06	110	20.60	0	0
P2 -34-2	6	1.6688	375	224.72	10	5.99	372	222.92	2	0
P2 -34-3	5	1.6688	538	322.40	31	18.58	445	266.67	0	0

PROV	DATE	VOLUME	CERAMIC	CDENSE	LITHICS	LDENSE	BONE	BDENSE	WHORLS	SPECIAL
Patio 3:										
P3 -11-1	7	5.1840	140	27.01	0	0.00	0	0.00	0	0
P3 -11-2	6	2.1600	78	36.11	1	0.46	17	7.87	0	0
P3 -11-3	5	2.1600	226	104.63	6	2.78	100	46.30	1	0
P3 -21-1	7	4.3200	454	105.09	6	1.39	25	5.79	0	0
P3 -21-2	6	2.1600	250	115.74	4	1.85	75	34.72	3	0
P3 -21-3	5	2.1600	87	40.28	3	1.39	80	37.04	2	0
P3 -31-1	7	4.3200	264	61.11	8	1.85	27	6.25	0	0
P3 -31-2	6	2.1600	803	371.76	23	10.65	1370	634.26	1	0
P3 -31-3	5	2.1600	156	72.22	2	0.93	495	229.17	0	0
P3 -31-4	4	2.1600	96	44.44	13	6.02	72	33.33	0	0
P3 -41-1	7	4.7520	103	21.68	0	0.00	117	24.62	0	0
P3 -41-2	6	2.1600	719	332.87	37	17.13	334	154.63	1	0
P3 -41-3	5	2.1600	486	225.00	9	4.17	825	381.94	1	0
P3 -41-4	4	2.1600	484	224.07	15	6.94	935	432.87	2	0
P3 -42-1	7	4.3200	19	4.40	0	0.00	0	0.00	0	0
P3 -42-2	6	2.1600	731	338.43	33	15.28	200	92.59	0	0
P3 -42-3	5	2.1600	349	161.57	20	9.26	50	23.15	2	0
P3 -42-4	4	2.1600	295	136.57	6	2.78	270	125.00	0	0
P3 -42-5	3	2.5920	330	127.31	10	3.86	720	277.78	3	0
P3 -42-6	3	2.5920	36	13.89	0	0.00	53	20.45	0	0
P3 -43-1	7	4.3200	184	42.59	14	3.24	70	16.20	0	c
P3 -43-2	6	2.1600	396	183.33	15	6.94	320	148.15	0	0
P3 -43-3	5	2.16000	488	225.926	7	3.24	170	78.70	1	0

Appendix B 323

PROV	DATE	VOLUME	CERAMIC	CDENSE	LITHICS	LDENSE	BONE	BDENSE	WHORLS	SPECIAL
Gallery 1:										
G1 -00-1	7	8.88487	810	91.166	0	0.00	200	22.51	0	0
G1 -00-2	6	2.33812	96	41.059	2	0.86	20	8.55	0	0
G1 -00-3	5	2.33812	205	87.677	18	7.70	182	77.84	0	0
G1 -00-4	3	2.33812	274	117.188	23	9.84	375	160.38	1	0
G1 -00-5	2	2.33812	21	8.982	4	1.71	110	47.05	0	0

PROV	DATE	VOLUME	CERAMIC	CDENSE	LITHICS	LDENSE	BONE	BDENSE	WHORLS	SPECIAL
Corridor 1:										
C1 -01-1	7	4.840	891	184.09	13	2.69	380	78.51	0	0
C1 -01-2	6	2.420	822	339.67	20	8.26	1965	811.98	0	0
C1 -01-3	6	2.420	821	339.26	19	7.85	2422	1000.83	4	0
C1 -01-4	5	3.872	719	185.69	34	8.78	440	113.64	5	0
C1 -02-1	7	10.560	745	70.55	14	1.33	635	60.13	3	0
C1 -02-2	6	3.300	1295	392.42	7	2.12	3595	1089.39	0	b
C1 -02-3	6	3.300	912	276.36	18	5.46	1755	531.82	1	c
C1 -02-4	5	3.300	411	124.55	50	15.15	575	174.24	1	0
C1 -02-5	2	3.300	330	100.00	32	9.70	280	84.85	2	0
C1 -02-6	2	3.300	1126	341.21	96	29.09	270	81.82	2	0
C1 -02-7	2	3.300	246	74.55	15	4.55	175	53.03	0	0
C1 -02-8	1	3.300	242	73.33	31	9.39	270	81.82	1	0

PROV	DATE	VOLUME	DIAGCER*	CDENSE	LITHICS	LDENSE	BONE	BDENSE	WHORLS	SPECIAL
Unit T1:										
T1 -00-1	7	0.50000	10	.	24	48.00	22	44.00	0	0
T1 -00-2	6	0.50000	40	.	31	62.00	665	1330.00	0	0
T1 -00-3	6	0.50000	45	.	38	76.00	1320	2640.00	0	0
T1 -00-4	5	0.50000	42	.	46	92.00	545	1090.00	1	0
T1 -00-5	3	0.50000	24	.	31	62.00	305	610.00	0	0
T1 -00-6	2	0.50000	16	.	14	28.00	50	100.00	0	0
T1 -00-7	2	0.50000	41	.	23	46.00	370	740.00	0	0
T1 -00-8	2	0.50000	13	.	8	16.00	30	60.00	0	0
T1 -00-9	2	0.50000	4	.	4	8.00	105	210.00	0	0

* in unit T1 only ceramic diagnostics were counted, so ceramic densities were not calculated.

PROV	DATE	VOLUME	CERAMIC	CDENSE	LITHICS	LDENSE	BONE	BDENSE	WHORLS	SPECIAL
Unit T2/3:										
T2 -00-1	7	2.80000	99	35.357	1	0.36	5	1.79	0	0
T2 -00-2	6	2.00000	85	42.500	7	3.50	17	8.50	1	0
T3 -00-1	7	2.00000	54	27.000	3	1.50	0	0.00	0	0
T3 -00-2	6	2.00000	85	42.500	3	1.50	2	1.00	0	0

Appendix B

Notes:

PROV = Provenience: architecture unit - excavation unit - level.

DATE = Temporal designatiow of level; 6 indicates unmixed Willka Phase deposit; 2 indicates unmixed Kancha Phase deposit.

VOLUME = Total volume of unit excavated, expressed in cubic meters.

DIAG = Counts of diagnostic ceramics.

NDIAG = Counts of non-diagnostic ceramics.

CERAMIC = Total of diagnostic and non-diagnostic ceramics.

CDENSE = Density of ceramics, sherds per cubic meter.

LITHICS = Counts of chipped stone artifacts.

LDENSE = Density of lithics, artifacts per cubic meter.

BONE = Weight, in grams, of butchered animal bone.

BDENSE = Density of animal bone, grams per cubic meter.

WHORLS = Counts of worked sherds and spindle whorls.

SPECIAL = Exotic artifacts: b=worked bone tool; c=copper artifact; f=ceramic figurine; g=gold artifact; s=shell artifact.

Appendix C. Ceramic Diagnostic Coding System for Jincamocco

PROVENIENCE
1-5 architectural unit

6-7 excavation unit

8 level

9-11 artifact number

CONSTRUCTION TECHNOLOGY
12 paste color
   1 red/pink
   2 buff
   3 orange
   4 brown
   5 black

13 temper
   1 fine
   2 medium
   3 coarse
   4 boulder

14-15 surface finish (interior-exterior)
   0 eroded (no surface)
   1 rough
   2 smoothed
   3 polished (with marks)
   4 fine polish

16-17 surface treatment (interior-exterior)
   0 not visible
   1 none
   2 fully slipped
   3 partially slipped—rim/neck only
   4 partially slipped—other
   5 multiple colors fully slipped—rim
   6 multiple colors fully slipped—other
   7 multiple colors partially slipped

18-19 principal slip/surface color (interior-exterior)
   1 none
   2 cream/white
   3 orange

4 red-orange
5 red
6 brown
7 dark brown
8 black
9 Ocros orange

DECORATION
(three digit code: 2-decoration, 1-location)

1 incision
   1 band
   2 band with painted insides
   3 all over
   4 base
   5 post-fire (potter's/owner's mark?)
   6 necklace
   7 vertical band
   8 large gouges
   9 other

2 appliqué
   1 necklace
   2 nubbin
   3 bump
   4 raised ridge
   9 other

3 modeling
   1 face
   2 ear
   3 nose
   9 other

4 painted design
   1 single color
   2 polychrome
   3 fine polychrome
   4 red line

5 punctation
   1 necklace
   2 raised band
   3 circles

6 hole
   0 purpose unclear
   1 mending
   2 decorative

Location
   1 rim
   2 band below rim
   3 neck
   4 base
   5 body
   6 whole

Appendix C   329

        7 over rim and down
        8 handle
        9 neck-body juncture

20-22 primary interior decoration

23-25 secondary interior decoration

26-28 primary exterior decoration

29-31 secondary exterior decoration

VESSEL FORM
32-43 vessel form
        1 bowl
            1 incurving profile
            2 vertical profile
            3 open profile
                1 concave sides
                2 straight sides
                3 convex sides

        2 jar
            1 necked
            2 neckless

        3 lyre cup

        4 tumbler

        5 spoon

        6 bottle

ATTRIBUTES OF RIM
35-36 rim diameter (cm)

37-39 vessel angle at rim

   40 vessel profile at rim (exterior)
           1 incurve   concave
           2   straight
           3   convex
           4 vertical   concave
           5   straight
           6   convex
           7 open   concave
           8   straight
           9   convex

   41 rim profile at mouth (exterior)
        (as above)

42-44 curvature of rim with respect to vessel (exterior)
   1-3 curves in (concave, straight, convex)
   4-6 follows line of vessel (ditto)
   7-9 curves out (ditto)
      1 slightly
      2 45
      3 90
      4 >90
         1 without sharp angle
         2 with sharp angle interior
         3 with sharp angle exterior
         4 with sharp angle both sides

45-48 profile of rim/lip (with respect to vessel walls)
   1 thinner
   2 tapered
   3 same thickness
   4 bulges in
   5 bulges out
   6 bulges both sides
   7 small added coil
   8 medium added coil
   9 large added coil
      1 pointed end
      2 round
      3 flat end
         1 without angle
         2 with angle interior
         3 with angle exterior
         4 with angle both sides
            1 lip to interior
            2 lip symmetrical
            3 lip to exterior

ATTRIBUTES OF NECK
49-50 neck diameter (cm) (exterior of neck-body juncture)

51-52 height (cm) (neck juncture to rim, vertical)

53 angle of neck with body
   1 acute
   2 right angle
   3 obtuse

54 neck form
   1 conical
   2 cylindrical
   3 flaring
   4 wide flaring

ATTRIBUTES OF BASE
55-56 base diameter (cm)

57-59 angle of body with respect to base

Appendix C 331

60 vessel profile at base
   1 incurve   concave
   2   straight
   3   convex
   4 vertical   concave
   5   straight
   6   convex
   7 open   concave
   8   straight
   9   convex

61-62 base form
   1 concave
   2 flat
      1 sharp angle
      2 rounded angle
   3 convex
      2 round
      3 pointed
      4 very pointed
   4 ring

ATTRIBUTES OF HANDLE
   63 form
      1 vertical strap
      2 horizontal
      3 strap (can't tell direction)
      4 vertical vestigial strap
      5 horizontal vestigial strap
      6 flat arch
      7 vestigial flat arch
      8 braided strap (vertical)
      9 pan handle

   64 location
      1 rim—rim
      2 rim—neck
      3 rim—body
      4 neck—neck
      5 neck—body
      6 body—body
      7 rim—?
      8 neck—?
      9 body—?

ATTRIBUTES OF APPENDAGE
   65 form
      1 spout
      2 tripod leg
      3 tongue
      4 paw
      5 scalloped ridge

66 location
   1 rim
   2 neck
   3 body
   4 base
   5 body-base juncture

OTHER ATTRIBUTES
67-68 wall thickness (mm)

69-70 vessel height (cm)

71-72 maximum vessel diameter

72-74 number of sherds comprising vessel

78 visuals
   0 none
   1 drawn
   2 photographed
   3 both

80 type
   1 Black Decorated
   2 Ocros
   3 incised bowl
   4 serpentine jar
   5 other tactile
   6 plainware
   7 polychrome
   8 redware

www.ingramcontent.com/pod-product-compliance
Lightning Source LLC
Jackson TN
JSHW070313120426
100741JS00007B/36